Patents, Invention, and Economic Change

DATA AND SELECTED ESSAYS

BY JACOB SCHMOOKLER

Edited by Zvi Griliches and Leonid Hurwicz

Harvard University Press
Cambridge, Massachusetts   1972

Contents

Jacob Schmookler

Foreword

by Simon Kuznets

Jacob Schmookler's life, like that of many devoted scholars, was uneventful — on the surface. Born in 1918 in a small town in New Jersey, he received his university education in Philadelphia: first at Temple University, and then, after a delay due to World War II, at the graduate school of the University of Pennsylvania, which awarded him the Ph.D. in economics in 1951. From 1946 to the end of his life, he taught — as instructor, assistant professor, full professor — at the University of Pennsylvania, Michigan State University, and, for the longest term, at the University of Minnesota. He enjoyed the usual academic fellowships, including a Guggenheim award and a Ford Faculty Research Fellowship. After several years of recurrent and painful illness, his life was cut all too short in 1967, when Jack was barely 49 years old.

His scholarly life, for all its apparent calm, was filled with intellectual adventure, continuous struggle with difficult problems, frequent frustrations, and significant success. From the very beginning of his research, in his doctoral dissertation, Jack took hold of a major intellectual task, a research problem of overshadowing magnitude, with which he stayed to the end of his life — and the wider ramifications of which he was still exploring at the time of his death. The challenging task he selected was to attain better understanding of man's inventive activity in its effects on economic growth and change — and to do so not by imaginative leaps based on a few cases and resulting in essentially untestable conjectures, but by the use of quantitative evidence both on the rate and direction of inventive activity and on those loci within the economy to which the effects could be traced. Considering the variety of types of invention, the difficulty of establishing comparable units for the product of this distinctively human activity, and the paucity of previous quantitative work in the field, it took great courage and persistence for a young scholar to struggle with the ambiguous statistics on patents, to attempt to wrest from them results of sufficient relevance to demonstrate the effects of invention on the economy and of the economy on invention. All of this was begun in the late 1940s, well before the emphasis on technology and knowledge became fashionable.

Given the recalcitrance of the data, it is hardly surprising that acceptable, and publishable, findings were difficult to come by. A list of his publications shows a series of journal articles, beginning in 1950 and continuing to recent years, at the rate of barely one a year. It was only after more than fifteen years of work in the field that Jack decided to put most of his results in a single monograph, which finally appeared in 1966. Yet the apparent meagerness of the record is deceptive. His publications served to illuminate a number of far-reaching aspects of technological change in its relation to economic growth and structure. These papers and the monograph introduced into the field of economic study a hitherto little-used body of data; and they pioneered the expansion of economic analysis to include a major source of long-term changes in level and structure of economic production.

A mere listing of the major topics of Jack's publications reveals the broad field that he covered. First, and expectedly, there was his careful probing into the coverage of patent statistics, and their meaningfulness as an index of inventive activity, with respect to both volume and locus. This was followed by papers that dealt with the characteristics of the inventors, the patentors, with a related finding that cast justifiable doubt on the claim that "bigness" made for a higher level of inventive activity. Then there were articles that traced the relation between patents, capital formation, and growth — the earliest of which, in 1952 (reprinted in this volume), was the first study of efficiency, of the "residual" after subtraction of the combined inputs of labor and capital. And there were studies of the distribution of inventions by the industry of probable use, which led to the hypothesis that such inventive activity and the changes they generated were responses largely to demand — rather than reflections of changes in the supply of new knowledge, the latter perhaps exogenous in character. Finally, there were papers bearing on the relation between the progress of science, basic research, and invention. Toward the end of his life, Jack was exploring the broader question of the relevance of demand-linked inventive activity (in turn affecting efficiency and the capacity to grow) to the established corpus of economic theory. And he was considering the relation between demand-induced inventions and those empirical findings (on the "law of industrial growth") that stress the limited life cycle of any single industry or of any circumscribed component of a country's production structure.

Many of these papers were absorbed into his 1966 monograph,

Invention and Economic Growth (published by Harvard University Press), which is the best single source for a reader interested in Jack's work on inventions and their economic linkages. Since the book did not include all of Jack's papers, the most significant of the remaining articles have been collected in the present volume. Of even greater value to scholars will be the detailed tables also included herein: these classify patents by year, type, and industry of probable use, and give circumstantial notes on the criteria of classification. All of these provide the foundation upon which much of the analysis in the 1966 monograph was based, but which could not be included there for technical reasons. In addition to supplying other analysts in the field with valuable raw materials not otherwise available, these tables and notes reveal clearly the magnitude of the task Jack faced and carried out in transforming what were records of administrative action into quantitative measures relevant to economic analysis.

Innovative research represents a significant beginning, an opening up of something new. But being research, that is, testable exploration, it continues to be incomplete until its results are absorbed into a revised and tested analytical framework — a drawn-out process. The process is particularly long in economic and social fields, where the data are not under the control of the scholar and where creative changes continuously shift the magnitudes and structures under observation. Jacob Schmookler's work could not be completed, and would not have been completed even had the fates been kinder and granted him the usual span of working life. In 1965, in addition to working on the later papers, he was exploring the possibility of organizing in several European countries detailed studies of the patent data to parallel his own studies of the U.S. data. But apparently nothing tangible has developed. It will take decades before further research will build sufficiently on Jack's pioneering exploration for the field to be relatively fully covered, for his work to be "completed" by being absorbed into an even wider analytical framework that will encompass not only technological change but other sources of economic and social growth and transformation as well. One can only hope that such sustained research and development will occur, and that it will not be delayed unduly by shifts in the winds of intellectual fashion in response to current social crises.

In concluding these few notes of appreciation on the lifework of a student and friend, I cannot refrain from commenting on Jack's optimistic courage. All scholars in economics must be optimists, for how otherwise could they bear the burden of recognized ignorance, of lack of tested knowledge on some of the major economic problems where knowledge is of such great value? And they must possess the courage of optimism, rather than of despair, for without it they could hardly face, or have the incentive for, research that is so often frustrating. Jacob Schmookler possessed this kind of optimistic courage to an unusual degree. It sustained him through years of difficult research, and it helped him through the last years of his life – so that he could continue working despite his knowledge that the end was near.

Editors' Introduction

Jacob Schmookler died in 1967, at the age of 49, in the midst of a productive scholarly career. He left behind a major unpublished body of work: over four hundred time series on patents granted, classified by industry of use, together with a detailed description of the methods used in collecting and constructing these series. Only a small number of aggregate series were used and reproduced in his magnum opus, *Invention and Economic Growth*. It was Schmookler's intent to bring out these series as a separate publication. Even though incomplete in industrial coverage, they form a useful and fascinating record of inventive activity in the United States during the last hundred years.

These time series, together with an introduction describing their construction and a detailed description of the connection between the Patent Office product classification and Schmookler's rearrangement of them by industrial use, constitute the second part of this volume. In the first part we bring together a number of his published writings which had not been incorporated in his book and one unpublished and unfinished paper.

The first paper is his 1952 article on "The Changing Efficiency of the American Economy." This is a seminal article, one of the first to compute a "total factor productivity" or "residual" index. Written years before the topic of total factor productivity had become popular, it has been unjustly neglected and shows that Schmookler was well aware of most of the problems that were to be debated in this field in subsequent years.

The second paper, "The Size of Firm and the Growth of Knowledge," is reclaimed from the records of a 1965 congressional hearing. It deals with a topic of peripheral but continuous interest to Schmookler: the relation of inventive activity to industrial organization and market structure. He had dealt with this topic earlier in his chapter in the 1959 Mason volume, *The Corporation in Modern Society* (see the bibliography of Schmookler's writings for a complete citation) and in his debate with Henry Villard in the *Journal of Political Economy*, but the paper reproduced here is the most recent and complete statement of his views on this subject.

The last three papers were written after the completion of his major research effort, *Invention and Economic Growth*, and show him pursuing the implications of his findings into the fields of history of science, economic theory, and economic history.

The article called "Catastrophe and Utilitarianism in the Development of Basic Science" provides a demand-induced explanation for scientific activity similar to that advanced by him for inventive activity.

The paper on "Technological Change and Economic Theory" urges economists to stop treating technological change as something that affects the economic system but comes from outside. On this Schmookler has been heeded; much of the recent work on endogenous theories of technological change and the sources of economic growth can be ascribed to the influence of his work and example.

The last paper in the first part of this volume, "Technological Change and the Law of Industrial Growth," was found among his manuscripts in the form of a number of fragments. In it, after summarizing the major findings of his book, he moves on to consider their implication for the explanation of patterns of industrial growth. From the various fragments we have endeavored to reconstruct a version, incomplete but suggestive of the main lines of his argument, which we hope will inspire further research on this topic.

We are grateful to Simon Kuznets for providing a foreword to this volume and for the advice and encouragement he extended to us in assembling it. The "Bibliography of Work in the Schmookler Tradition: 1966 to 1970," which follows immediately after the bibliography of Schmookler's own writings and complements the extensive bibliography in *Invention and Economic Growth*, was prepared by Professor F. M. Scherer of the University of Michigan. We are grateful to him for performing this task. We wish to thank the Ohio State University Press and the American Economic Association for their permission to reprint two of Schmookler's articles. We are also indebted to the Inter-University Research Program on the Micro-Economics of Technological Change and Economic Growth (supported by the Ford Foundation), of which Schmookler was a member for many years, and to the University of Minnesota for financial support that made the publication of this volume possible.

Z. G. and L. H.

Bibliography of Jacob Schmookler's Writings

BOOK

Invention and Economic Growth (Cambridge, Mass.: Harvard University Press, 1966).

ARTICLES

"The Interpretation of Patent Statistics," *Journal of the Patent Office Society,* February 1950, 123-146.

"The Changing Efficiency of the American Economy, 1869-1938," *Review of Economics and Statistics,* August 1952, 214-231.

"The Utility of Patent Statistics," *Journal of the Patent Office Society,* June 1953, 407-412.

"Patent Application Statistics as an Index of Inventive Activity," *Journal of the Patent Office Society,* August 1953, 539-550.

"The Bituminous Coal Industry," in Walter Adams, ed., *Structure of American Industry* (New York: Macmillan, 1954), 76-113.

"Invention, Innovation, and Competition," *Southern Economic Journal,* April 1954, 380-385.

"The Level of Inventive Activity," *Review of Economics and Statistics,* May 1954, 183-190.

Prices, Business Firms, and Economic Welfare (Michigan State University Press, 1955), mimeo., 67pp.

"The Age of Inventors," *Journal of the Patent Office Society,* April 1956, 223-232.

"Inventors Past and Present," *Review of Economics and Statistics,* August 1957, 321-333.

"Bigness, Fewness, and Research," *Journal of Political Economy,* December 1959, 628-632.

"Michigan State Experiment in Micro-Economics," in Kenyon A. Knopf and James H. Stauss, eds., *The Teaching of Elementary Economics* (New York: Holt, Rinehart, and Winston, 1960), 181-190.

"Technological Progress and the Modern American Corporation," in Edward S. Mason, ed., *The Corporation in Modern Society* (Cambridge, Mass.: Harvard University Press, 1959), 141-165.

"An Economist Takes Issue," *Technology and Culture,* summer 1960, 214-220.

"Repartition des inventions dans l'industrie," *Economie appliquée,* February 1961, 335-344.

"Comments" on papers by Simon Kuznets, Fritz Machlup, and B. S. Sanders, in Richard R. Nelson, ed., *The Rate and Direction of Inventive Activity: Economic and Social Factors* (Princeton, N.J.: Princeton University Press, 1962), 43-51, 78-83, 167-169.

"Changes in Industry and in the State of Knowledge as Determinants of Industrial Invention," in Richard R. Nelson, *ibid.,* 195-232.

"Invention, Innovation, and Business Cycles," in *Variability of Private Investment in Plant and Equipment, Part II, Some Elements Shaping Investment Decisions,* materials submitted to the Joint Economic Committee of the Congress of the United States, 87th Congress, 1962 (Washington, D.C.: Government Printing Office), 45-55.

"Economic Sources of Inventive Activity," *Journal of Economic History*, March 1962, 1-20.

"Determinants of Inventive Activity," with O. H. Brownlee, *American Economic Review,* May 1962, 165-185.

"Patents, Research, and the Public Interest," in National Academy of Sciences, *The Role of Patents in Research*, pt. 2, proceedings of a symposium, 1963, 18-32.

"Inventing and Maximizing," with Zvi Griliches, *American Economic Review,* September 1963, 725-729.

"Catastrophe and Utilitarianism in the Development of Basic Science," in Richard A. Tybout, ed., *Economics of Research and Development* (Columbus: Ohio State University Press, 1965), 19-33.

"Technological Change and Economic Theory," *American Economic Review*, May 1965, 333-341.

"The Size of Firm and the Growth of Knowledge," in *Concentration, Invention, and Innovation*, hearings, pt. 3, Subcommittee on Antitrust and Monopoly of the Committee on the Judiciary of the U.S. Senate, 89th Congress, May 18-June 17, 1965 (Washington, D.C.: Government Printing Office), 1257-1269.

"Technological Change and the Law of Industrial Growth," this volume.

Bibliography of Work in the Schmookler Tradition: 1966 to 1970

Legend for Classification of Subject Matter:

(A) Economic characteristics of technological innovation; demand-pull and science-push influences
(B) Firm size, market structure, and incentives to innovate
(C) The contributions of technological change to economic growth
(D) Economic returns to inventive activity
(E) The methodology of patent statistics
(F) The economics of the patent system
* Directly influenced by Schmookler's work

Adams, William James, "Firm Size and Research Activity: France and the United States," *Quarterly Journal of Economics*, August 1970, 386-409 (B).

Baldwin, W. L., and G. L. Childs, "The Fast Second and Rivalry in Research and Development," *Southern Economic Journal*, July 1969, 18-24 (B).

Barr, James L., and Kenneth E. Knight, "Technological Change and Learning in the Computer Industry," *Management Science*, July 1968, 661-681 (C).

Barzel, Yoram, "Patents and Economic Activity," University of Washington, Institute for Economic Research Discussion Paper 109, 1969 (*, A).

Baxter, Nevins D., and Henry G. Grabowski, "Imitation, Uncertainty, and the Research and Development Decision," paper presented at a conference of the Institute of Management Sciences, April 1967 (A, B).

Branch, Ben S., "Research and Development, Profits, and Sales Growth," Ph.D. dissertation, University of Michigan, 1970 (B, D, E).

Brown, Murray, *On the Theory and Measurement of Technical Change* (Cambridge: Cambridge University Press, 1966) (C).

Castro, Barry, "The Scientific Opportunities Foregone Because of More Readily Available Federal Support for Research in Experimental than Theoretical Physics," *Journal of Political Economy*, July/August 1968, 601-614 (A).

Comanor, William S., "Market Structure, Product Differentiation, and Industrial Research," *Quarterly Journal of Economics*, November 1967, 639-657 (B).

———and F. M. Scherer, "Patent Statistics as a Measure of Technical Change," *Journal of Political Economy*, May/June 1969, 392-398 (*, E).

Denison, Edward F., *Why Growth Rates Differ* (Washington, D.C.: Brookings Institution, 1967) (C).

Encel, S., and A. Inglis, "Patents, Inventions, and Economic Progress," *Economic Record*, December 1966, 572-588 (*, E).

Evenson, Robert, "The Contribution of Agricultural Research to Production," *Journal of Farm Economics*, December 1967, 1415-1425 (C).

Fellner, William, "Technological Progress and Recent Growth Theories," *American Economic Review*, December 1967, 1073-1098 (C).

——— "Trends in the Activities Generating Technological Progress," *American Economic Review*, March 1970, 1-29 (C).

Grabowski, Henry G., "The Determinants of Industrial Research and Development," *Journal of Political Economy*, March/April 1968, 292-306 (B).

Griliches, Zvi, and Dale Jorgenson, "The Explanation of Productivity Change," *Review of Economic Studies*, July 1967, 249-283 (C).

Gruber, William, Dileep Mehta, and Raymond Vernon, "The R&D Factor in International Trade and International Investment of United States Industries," *Journal of Political Economy*, February 1967, 20-37 (A, B).

Hohenberg, Paul M., *Chemicals in Western Europe: 1850-1914* (Chicago, Ill.: Rand McNally, 1967) (A).

Hufbauer, Gary C., *Synthetic Materials and the Theory of International Trade* (London: Duckworth, 1966) (A).

Isenson, Raymond S., "Project Hindsight," in William Gruber and D. G. Marquis, eds., *Factors in the Transfer of Technology* (Cambridge, Mass.: MIT Press, 1969) (A).

Johnston, R. E., "Technical Progress and Innovation," *Oxford Economic Papers*, July 1966, 158-176 (*, A, B).

Kamien, Morton I., and Nancy L. Schwartz, "Optimal 'Induced' Technical Change," *Econometrica*, January 1968, 1-17 (A).

———"Effects of Market Structure and Rivals' Response upon the Firm's Rate of Technical Advance," Carnegie-Mellon University Graduate School of Industrial Administration Research Memorandum, October 1968 (B).

———"Timing of Innovations under Rivalry," forthcoming in *Econometrica* (B).

Kaufer, Erich, *Patente, Wettbewerb und technischer Fortschritt* (Bad Homburg: Athenäum, 1970) (*, A, B).

Keesing, Donald B., "The Impact of Research and Development on United States Trade," *Journal of Political Economy*, February 1967, 38-48 (A, B).

Kelly, Thomas M., "The Influences of Size and Market Structure on the Research Efforts of Large Multiple-Product Firms," Ph.D. dissertation, Oklahoma State University, 1969 (B).

Lorant, J. H., "Technological Change in American Manufacturing during the 1920s," *Journal of Economic History*, June 1967, 243-246 (C).

McGee, John S., "Patent Exploitation: Some Economic and Legal Problems," *Journal of Law and Economics*, October 1966, 135-162 (F).

Mansfield, Edwin, *Industrial Research and Technological Innovation: An Econometric Analysis* (New York: Norton, 1968) (A, B, D).

———*The Economics of Technological Change* (New York: Norton, 1968) (A, B, C, D).

———"Industrial Research and Development: Characteristics, Costs, and Diffusion of Results," *American Economic Review*, May 1969, 65-71 (A).

Marschak, Thomas, Thomas K. Glennan, Jr., and Robert Summers, *Strategy for R&D: Studies in the Microeconomics of Development* (New York: Springer, 1967) (A).

Mathias, P., "Who Unbound Prometheus? Science and Technical Change, 1600-1800," *Yorkshire Bulletin of Economic and Social Research*, May 1969, 1-14 (A).

Mueller, Dennis C., "The Firm Decision Process: An Econometric Investigation," *Quarterly Journal of Economics*, February 1967, 58-87 (A, B).

———"Patents, Research and Development, and the Measurement of Inventive Activity," *Journal of Industrial Economics*, November 1966, 26-37 (*, E).

Nelson, Richard R., M. J. Peck, and E. D. Kalachek, *Technology, Economic Growth, and Public Policy* (Washington, D.C.: Brookings Institution, 1967) (A, B).

Nevel, R. O., "Technological Change in Agriculture," *Agricultural Economics Research*, January 1969, 13-18 (C).

Nordhaus, William D., *Invention, Growth, and Welfare: A Theoretical Treatment of Technological Change* (Cambridge, Mass.: MIT Press, 1969) (*, A, F).

———"An Economic Theory of Technological Change," *American Economic Review*, May 1969, 18-28 (*, A).

Phillips, Almarin, "Patents, Potential Competition, and Technical Progress," *American Economic Review*, May 1966, 301-310 (B).

Phlips, Louis, "Concentration, dimension et recherche dans l'industrie manufacturière belge," *Recherches économiques de Louvain*, February 1969, 15-35 (B).

Sandor, Richard L., "A Note on the Commercial Value of Patented Inventions," University of California at Berkeley, mimeograph, 1970 (*, D).

Scherer, F. M., "Market Structure and the Employment of Scientists and Engineers," *American Economic Review*, June 1967, pp. 524-531 (B).

———"Research and Development Resource Allocation under Rivalry," *Quarterly Journal of Economics* August 1967, 359-394 (B).

———*Industrial Market Structure and Economic Performance* (Chicago, Ill.: Rand McNally, 1970), chaps. 15 and 16 (*, A, B, F).

———"Nordhaus' Theory of Optimal Patent Life: A Geometric Reinterpretation," University of Michigan, mimeograph, 1970 (F).

Smyth, D. J., J. M. Samuels, and J. Tzoennos, "Patents, Profitability, Liquidity, and Firm Size," State University of New York at Buffalo, Economics Research Group Discussion Paper No. 131, November 1970 (B).

Tilton, John E., Jr., *International Diffusion of Innovation* (Washington, D.C.: Brookings Institution, forthcoming in 1971) (A, B, E).

Verma, P., "Patents in British Industry: A Note," *Yorkshire Bulletin of Economic and Social Research*, November 1969, 114-118 (E).

Part I   Selected Essays

The Changing Efficiency of the

American Economy, 1869 to 1938[1]

Reprinted from the *Review of Economics and Statistics*, August 1952.

The index of output per unit of total input that is discussed in this article is intended to describe the pattern and magnitude of technical change for the United States as a whole from 1869 to 1938.

Based on national output and input, the index possesses the following attributes:

(*1*) Output equals gross national product in 1929 prices (the Kuznets series).

(*2*) Input equals the sum of labor, land, capital, and enterprise inputs in 1929 prices.

(*a*) Labor input, involving separate weighting of agricultural and nonagricultural labor by 1929 wage rates, is presented in two variants — one measuring labor in man-hours, the other in man-years. Two alternate total input measures result.

(*b*) Other than capital consumption, property input (including enterprise) is determined by weighting the given period's combined value of land and reproducible producers' wealth in 1929 prices by the 1929 rate of return on property.

(*c*) Changes in the amount of farm acreage dominate the land component. The land valuation weight, however, reflects the 1929 value per acre of both urban and farm land.

(*d*) Reproducible producers' wealth in 1929 prices is derived from one of Kuznets' series.

(*e*) Capital consumed in 1929 prices is included in nonlabor input.

(*3*) Input and output are presented in overlapping decade averages.

We may now note the leading merits and shortcomings of the indexes. Formally our statistics measure output and input for the period in 1929 prices. Our objective is, however, to measure them as

[1] The author gratefully acknowledges that he has benefited from valuable suggestions by Simon Kuznets, Victor E. Smith, and Robert L. Bishop in the preparation of this paper.

though valued by base-period buyers. Since relative quantities of different products and resources varied over the period, we can assume that base-period buyers would have valued each ingredient otherwise than in the base period. Because of these variations, the precise relation of our indexes to the "true" valuation of aggregate inputs and outputs is indemonstrable. This flows from the permanent and insoluble defect of index numbers.

For the index exactly to fulfill its intended purpose, the measurement of technical change, linearity should pervade transformation relations between goods, substitution relations between factors, consumer indifference relations between goods, and production relations between factors and goods (including constant returns to scale). Though these requirements are not met, so long as the defects are not destructive of all significance of results, a defective tool is preferable to none at all. For shorter-period comparisons, an index number can give fairly valid results. For longer-term comparisons, the uncertainties mount, but the need for at least a rough approximation remains.

Linked by common language, government, and monetary system, America's economy with all its manifold diversity has been a fairly coherent whole. Averages of attributes of its parts are not only computationally possible: the averages themselves in a real sense significantly influence the parts. For this reason aggregative measures, conceptual flaws notwithstanding, are indispensable. That the secular and cyclical position of the economy exerts great force upon the corresponding characteristics of its components cannot be gainsaid. In this paper adumbrations of one more such influence will appear. As we shall also see, our indexes describe patterns of technical change corroborated by independent evidence.

We shall discuss first the components of the indexes, and then compare the aggregative efficiency index with similar indexes for major industrial segments.

THE MEANING OF OUTPUT

Output may be defined as the national income, that is, as "the net value of all economic goods produced by the nation."[2] More specifically, the national income for a given year is the sum of the values of the consumer goods and services produced plus capital

[2] Simon Kuznets, *National Income and Its Composition, 1919-1938* (New York: National Bureau of Economic Research, 1941), vol. 1, p. 3.

formation (net or gross capital formation, depending on whether net or gross national income is sought).

Granted that the purpose of economic activity is the production of want-satisfying goods and services, and that activity undergone for their production is simply a means, national output in constant prices attempts to measure the want-satisfying capacity of the goods and services produced as though given-period consumers had base-period tastes. National input, in turn, tries to measure the output which given-period resources could have produced in the base period. The movements in the output-input ratio thus reflect the changing relation between benefits received and benefits attainable with base-period technique. These movements consequently measure a basic economic phenomenon, the changing efficiency of the transformation of economic means into economic ends.

Ideally, any innovation would affect the ratio by changing output, input, or both. Innovations either originate new consumer products or improve methods of producing old ones, the latter category including new capital goods. Qualitative changes in existing consumer goods would come under the former. New consumer goods would usually raise the numerator of the output-input ratio, since presumably they either yield greater satisfaction than the goods directly displaced, or release purchasing power for expenditure on other consumer goods, which amounts to the same thing. If a new consumer good failed to increase output because of increased leisure or technological unemployment, input would fall, and output per unit of input would rise nonetheless.

Our index of output is therefore an index, albeit a crude one, of the want-satisfying capacity of the goods produced by the business and public sectors of the economy. It is a subjective evaluation which tries to reflect the judgment of the composite base-year consumer, a judgment levied in the light of a particular quantity combination, a specific set of living conditions, and a given pattern of social values. (Since we shall use the Kuznets series, the base year is 1929.)

MEANING AND MEASUREMENT OF INPUT

Our input index must be analogous, although little conceptual groundwork exists in economic literature in this instance.[3] *Input may*

---

[3] See, however, M. A. Copeland and E. M. Martin, "The Correction of Wealth and Income Estimates for Price Changes," and the ensuing discussion by R. T. Bye, Solomon Fabricant, and

be defined as the net value of the services of all economic resources whose products appear in the national income. By net we mean that only the services of individuals or their property to persons or firms are included. Interfirm transactions, reflecting contributions of individuals already counted, are excluded. By value we mean the market appraisal of the services of the resources involved, for example, the wage rate for a given grade of labor. By services is meant the use by entrepreneurs of resources, including resources contributed by entrepreneurs. By economic resources we mean the traditional land, labor, and capital. No method of measuring enterprise separately has been developed that would be both materially effective and logically defensible. As will be seen, enterprise is actually made a function of the amount of capital and land. Managerial labor is "included" in labor input, and entrepreneurial capital in capital input. The input for a given year in current prices therefore is the sum of payments to owners for services of resources used in production.

A series for input in constant prices implies sufficient homogeneity over time in the various resources to permit construction of a continuous index. If the inputs of 1900 were entirely different from those employed in 1929, we should not be able to compare the magnitudes of the inputs of the two years. (In other problems, comparisons could be made in terms of the productivities of the two annual inputs if outputs were comparable. This procedure would be useless here since defining input in terms of productivity precludes measurement of productivity.) Probably the greatest changes of all have occurred in the physical composition of capital goods. This difficulty is mitigated somewhat since our capital data are corrected essentially by material and labor price indexes. Thus our capital measure in constant prices reflects what base-year entrepreneurs would have bought with the same inputs of the more fundamental resources, land and labor, utilized in the production of the given-year capital instruments.

Resources have probably altered less than products. If we exclude, as we should, changes in labor that merely embody technological progress, such as the fact that today's farmer can operate and perhaps repair a tractor, while the farmer of a hundred years ago could not, human labor of most grades and occupations has probably not changed so

Milton Friedman, with replies by Copeland and Martin, in Conference on Research in National Income and Wealth, *Studies in Income and Wealth* (New York: National Bureau of Economic Research, 1938), vol. 2.

much as to make impossible direct comparison of the same grade and occupation between years a few decades apart. Natural resources have changed in character mainly through depletion and erosion. Thus the principal difficulty, a difficulty both for input and output, is the changing composition of capital, and this problem has been reduced in the manner indicated above.

We discuss next details of individual input measurement, after which we return to larger aspects of the procedure.

Labor input. The derivation of an index of labor input raises interesting questions. Indexes of output per labor unit usually weight different grades of labor equally. An increase in the quantity of that labor which produces more highly valued products could therefore increase product without increasing total labor input and cause an increase in the efficiency of resource use to appear.

The correctness of such a procedure depends upon our definition of a resource, which in turn depends upon the inferences we wish to elicit from the results. Since we seek to isolate effects of changing technique, treatment of labor as homogeneous would imply that changes in labor-force composition are caused by technical change. The latter unquestionably significantly affects the occupational distribution, but in devious ways, and in any case is not the sole force at work. The reduction in the relative importance of agricultural labor, for example, is attributable to the income elasticity of demand for food, public education, urban social standards, tariff policy, development of agricultural areas in other parts of the world, and so on, as well as to improvements in the technique of production in agricultural and nonagricultural industries.

Caution dictates imputing to "other" forces changes in the occupational distribution, and accordingly defining a resource in terms of its valuable physical characteristics at the time of employment rather than characteristics it might have acquired if nurtured in the fashion and milieu of base-period resources. This definition is intended to facilitate isolation of the effects of changing technique, although obviously only the direct effects will be uncovered. Our index of output per unit of input will therefore try to measure the actual product turned out against the product which could have been turned out had the same resources been similarly employed but combined with base-period efficiency.

Available data greatly limit the elegance the index can display. While a tolerable index of skilled workers might be constructed back to 1870, total labor input would not be appreciably affected. In the respective decennial censuses from 1910 to 1940, for example, skilled workers and foremen comprised 11.7, 13.5, 12.9, and 11.7 percent of the total.[4] These are hardly changes on a grand scale.

Though a labor input index weighted according to occupation did not seem practicable within the scope of this paper, differentiation according to industry was possible. Presumably there are qualitative differences in the labor employed by different industries, since rather persistent interindustry wage differentials seem to exist. Preliminary investigation revealed, however, that differentiation of the nonagricultural labor force by industry would not appreciably affect the aggregate labor input index. On the other hand, the considerable agricultural and nonagricultural wage differential and the revolutionary transformation in the proportions of the two segments of the labor force over the period made desirable a division of the labor input into these two components, each weighted by the appropriate base wage rate.[5]

Another difficulty is the selection of the labor unit, given the classification scheme. Should it be the man-year, man-hour, or some unattainable ideal unit? The substantial reduction in the workweek over the period means that our labor component will be greatly affected by the unit chosen.

One argument on behalf of the man-year is that the intensity of work may have risen, more or less compensating for the reduction in hours. Another argument in favor of the man-year is that the decline in child labor and the rise in the level of education have meant a corresponding improvement in labor quality. Consequently, one could contend that failure to take account of the decline in the workweek compensates for our inability to adjust for the improvement in the quality or intensity of labor itself. Moreover, estimates of average hours worked per week are extremely crude.

These questions can only be enumerated here. Lacking substantial reasons for deciding the issue either way, we have calculated two alternative sets of labor input statistics, one based on man-years, the

[4] Bureau of the Census, *Comparative Occupation Statistics for the United States, 1870 to 1940* (Washington, D.C.: Government Printing Office, 1943), Table 27, p. 187.

[5] Inspection of various series presented in *Historical Statistics* reveals that the relative prices of agricultural and nonagricultural labor have not changed substantially for nearly a hundred years.

other on man-hours. The resulting period-to-period, but not long-run, movements of the two resulting efficiency indexes are fairly similar. Agricultural labor input is shown in Tables 1 and 2; nonagricultural labor input, in Table 3.

For 1869 to 1918 the data underlying both farm and nonfarm labor input indexes are statistics of gainfully occupied workers. The basic problem of the agricultural group is the persistent condition of seasonality and part-time work in agriculture, which makes it misleading to weight the number of gainfully occupied by the base-year wages of a full-time employee. Yet to weight them by the base-period wage per gainfully occupied seems equally erroneous, since the ratio of farmers (who probably approach the position of full-time workers) to the total fluctuated. Statistics of farmers were therefore used to break the data on gainfully occupied into farmers and employees. Farmers are treated as full-time employees and their labor weighted at full-time rates. Employees, however, are weighted by the average wage paid hired hands (full- and part-time) in 1929. This treatment avoids to a degree the twin dangers of long-run overstatement of agricultural labor input and short-run insensitivity to fluctuations in the utilization of the agricultural labor force. Beginning with 1914, however, statistics are for full-time equivalents only.

Adjustment for part-time workers was impossible for nonagricultural industries for the earlier period, but from 1870 to 1920 rough estimates of unemployment were made. It was assumed that a change in the nonfarm workweek occurred from 1929 to 1930 in deriving the nonagricultural wage rate per hour per year. In the case of agriculture, this adjustment was not made, in the belief that changes in the agricultural workweek are secular, not cyclical.

Land valuation. The measurement of land input over time is perplexing conceptually and practically. What criteria should be applied in distinguishing one kind of land input from another? Should a given acre be valued the same before and after a highway is built near it? When it is pasture land and when it becomes residential? If valued the same before and after, the shift in use is treated implicitly as an increase in efficiency. If valued sufficiently more afterward, the shift, treated as an increase in input, leaves efficiency unchanged. Presumably, we should value the acre the same when the shift results from technical change and differently when from other causes. Construction of a land

Table 1. Agricultural Labor Input, Man-Hour and Man-Year Bases, 1929 Prices, 1869 to 1918 (men in thousands, dollars and man-hours in millions)

	Agricultural labor force			Hours per full workweek			Agricultural labor input					
							Man-hours unit			Man-years unit		
Decade	Total	Farmers	Employees (1) – (2)	Weekly hours	Farmers (2) × (4)	Employees (3) × (4)	Farmers (5) × $11.04	Employees (6) × $7.29	Total (7) + (8)	Farmers (2) × $651.45	Employees (3) × $430.29	Total (10) + (11)
	(1)	(2)	(3)	(4)	(5)	(6)	(7)	(8)	(9)	(10)	(11)	(12)
1869–78	7,374	3,132	4,242	71.0	222.4	301.2	$2,455.3	$2,195.7	$4,651.0	$2,040.3	$1,825.3	$3,865.6
1874–83	8,294	3,807	4,487	71.0	270.2	318.6	2,984.1	2,322.6	5,306.7	2,480.1	1,930.7	4,410.8
1879–88	9,130	4,204	4,926	70.7	297.2	348.3	3,281.1	2,539.1	5,820.2	2,738.7	2,119.6	4,858.3
1884–93	9,930	4,482	5,448	70.0	313.7	381.4	3,463.2	2,780.4	6,243.6	2,919.8	2,344.2	5,264.0
1889–98	10,443	4,975	5,468	69.7	346.8	381.1	3,828.7	2,778.2	6,606.9	3,241.0	2,352.8	5,593.8
1894–03	10,833	5,561	5,272	69.0	383.7	363.8	4,236.0	2,652.1	6,888.1	3,622.7	2,268.5	5,891.2
1899–08	11,090	5,956	5,134	68.7	409.2	352.7	4,517.6	2,571.2	7,088.8	3,880.0	2,209.1	6,089.1
1904–13	11,410	6,269	5,141	68.0	426.3	349.6	4,706.4	2,548.6	7,255.0	4,083.9	2,212.1	6,296.0
1909–18	11,115	6,471	4,644	66.0	427.1	306.5	4,715.2	2,234.4	6,949.6	4,215.5	1,998.3	6,213.8

Source:

Column 1: Interpolated on a straight-line basis from *Historical Statistics*, D48.

Column 2: Interpolated from *Historical Statistics* E1 for 1869 to 1913. Before 1910 the data are at decade intervals. Interpolation uields 1.2 percent error in 1909–18, when annual figures, used here, become available.

Column 4: From J. F. Dewhurst et al., *America's Needs and Resources*. Twentieth Century Fund, 1947, App. 1 and 3, interpolated on a straight-line basis.

Columns 7 and 10: Wage-rate weight is wage estimated for full-time equivalent employees in agriculture in 1929, based on Simon Kuznets, *National Income and Its Composition, 1919–1938*, vol. 1, Tables 50 and 51. Wage weight for column 10 is the annual wage. That for column 7 is the result of dividing the annual wage by hours worked per week in 1930. It represents the amount paid in 1929 to a full-time employee for working an hour a week for the working year. This approach avoids estimating either the weeks worked per year or the hourly pay. It assumes the number of weeks worked per year was constant throughout the period.

Columns 8 and 11: The hours per week per year multiplier of column 8 is calculated by dividing the annual wage multiplier of column 11 by hours worked per week in 1930, the annual multiplier being obtained by dividing the number of hired workers in 1929, 2,984,000, into the year's total employee compensation given by Kuznets, *ibid*., yielding $430.29 per year per employee. The number of hired workers is from *Agricultural Statistics for 1948*, p. 547.

Table 2. Agricultural Labor Input, Man-Hour and Man-Year Bases, 1929 Prices, 1914 to 1938 (men in thousands, dollars in millions)

| Decade | Agricultural labor force | | | | | Agricultural labor input | |
	Farmers	Equivalent full-time employees	Full-time labor force (1) ÷ (2)	Weekly hours	Man-hours (3) X (4)	Man-hours unit (5) X $11.04	Man-years unit (3) X $651.45
	(1)	(2)	(3)	(4)	(5)	(6)	(7)
1914–23	6,495	2,175	8,670	63.8	553.1	$6,106.2	$5,648.1
1919–28	6,392	2,015	8,407	61.6	517.9	5,717.6	5,476.7
1924–33	6,381	1,865	8,246	59.6	491.5	5,426.2	5,371.9
1929–38	6,522	1,695	8,217	56.7	465.9	5,143.5	5,353.0

Source:

Column 1: Same as Table 1, column 2.
Column 2: 1919 and after, from Simon Kuznets, *National Income and Its Composition, 1919–1938*, vol. 1, Table 51. 1914–18 estimated at 48.84% of all agricultural employees, the 1919–23 relationship. The number of employees in agriculture is obtained by subtracting the underlying data of column 1 from NICB statistics on employment in agriculture, *Historical Statistics*, D66.
Column 4: Same as Table 1, column 4.
Column 6: Wage weight same as Table 1, column 7.
Column 7: Wage weight same as Table 1, column 10.

Table 3. Nonagricultural Labor Input, Man-Hour and Man-Year bases, 1929 Prices, 1869 to 1938 (men in thousands, dollars in millions)

	Nonagricultural labor force			Hours worked per week	Weekly man-hours (3) × (4) (millions)	Nonagricultural labor input	
Decade	Total	Annual unemployed	Employed (1) − (2)			Man-hours unit (5) × $33.32	Man-years unit (3) × $1,539.23
	(1)	(2)	(3)	(4)	(5)	(6)	(7)
1869–78	7,111	600	6,511	60.6	394.6	$13,148.1	$10,021.9
1874–83	8,425	600	7,825	60.0	469.5	15,643.7	12,044.5
1879–88	10,476	500	9,976	58.8	586.6	19,545.5	15,355.4
1884–93	12,840	500	12,340	57.4	708.3	23,600.6	18,994.1
1889–98	15,150	1,364	13,786	56.0	772.0	25,723.0	21,219.8
1894–03	17,434	1,556	15,878	55.3	878.1	29,258.3	24,439.9
1899–08	20,658	833	19,825	54.1	1,072.5	35,735.7	30,515.2
1904–13	24,282	962	23,320	52.9	1,233.6	41,103.6	35,894.8
1909–18	27,316	1,431	25,885	51.7	1,338.3	44,592.2	39,843.0
1914–23			29,938*	49.8	1,490.9	49,676.8	46,081.5
1919–28			32,275	48.3	1,558.9	51,942.5	49,678.6
1924–33			32,776	44.5	1,458.5	48,597.2	50,449.8
1929–38			32,148	40.6	1,305.2	43,489.3	49,483.2

*1914–23 obtained by averaging NICB estimate of nonagricultural employment for 1914–18 (*Historical Statistics*, series D64 minus D66) with Simon Kuznets' estimates of full-time equivalent workers and entrepreneurs in *National Income and Its Composition, 1919–1938*, vol. 1, Tables 51 and 53. Subsequent figures from latter.

Source:

Column 1: 1869–1918 interpolated on straight-line basis from *Historical Statistics*, D48.

Column 2: Estimates for 1889–1918 based on decade geometric averages calculated from Paul H. Douglas, *Real Wages in the United States, 1890–1926* (Cambridge, Mass., 1930), Table 164, which gives annual percentage estimates of unemployment in manufacturing and transportation. Estimated unemployed is then obtained by multiplying these percentages by column 1. Estimates for 1869–93 are based upon inspection of Persons' index of physical production and NBER business annals, business conditions in these decades being compared with those for which unemployment estimates were already available. Beginning with 1869–78, the percentage unemployed are estimated at 8, 7, 5, and 4, the latter for 1884–93. The results were further rounded off in column 2.

Column 4: Prior to 1889 derived by interpolation from the series for standard or customary hours in nonagricultural industries presented by J. F. Dewhurst et al., *America's Needs and Resources*, Twentieth Century Fund, 1947, App. 3, column 8, the result reduced by 2.0 hours, on the assumption that this was the difference between the actual and the standard or customary workweek. Beginning 1889 to

1928, we use the Douglas series from *Real Wages in the United States, 1890–1926*, Table 75. The resulting annual averages from this series were in turn reduced by 2.0 hours. For 1889–98 we use the average for 1890–98; for 1919–28, the average for 1919–26.

Averages for decades beginning with 1924 are estimated on the assumption that the ratio of average weekly hours of manufacturing production workers for the given decade to their workweek in 1930 corresponds to the ratio for nonagricultural industry as a whole. This assumption permits estimates for the period beginning in 1924 based on Dewhurst's figures, *ibid*. Manufacturing production workers averaged 42.6 hours a week in 1924–33, and 38.8 in 1929–38, including time allowed for vacation. In 1930, this group worked 42.1 hours. Thus, the 1924–33 annual average was 101.19 percent of the 1930 figure, and the 1929–38, 92.16 percent. The necessary estimates for our decades are obtained by applying these percentages to Dewhurst's figure for all nonagricultural industries in 1930, 44.0 hours per week actually worked.

Columns 6 and 7: Wage weights derived as follows:

1929 nonagricultural full-time equivalent employees (000)	33,088
1929 nonagricultural full-time equivalent employees compensation (000,000)	$50,930

Weight for column 7:

Compensation per full-time equivalent employee per year	$1,539.23
Estimated hours worked per week, 1930	44.0
(See column 4)	
Adjustment to 1929 level, 44.0 X 5%	2.2
Estimated hours worked per week, 1929	46.2

Weight for column 6:

Compensation per employee for working one hour a week per working year in 1929. $1,539.23/46.2	$33.32

The 5 percent adjustment of 1930 hours to 1929 basis was by the percentage differential of 1929 workweek in manufacturing over that for 1930. See *Statistical Abstract* for 1946, p. 210.

input index based on such considerations is a monumental undertaking beyond the scope of the present effort.

The land input index is based on the land utilization statistics of the Bureau of Agricultural Economics used in Table 4. The acreage included consists of (*a*) farm land (column 1) and (*b*) nonfarm private land other than grazing or forest, that is, urban, industrial, mineral, and so forth (column 5). The value of their combined acreage is taken throughout to be the same per acre as in 1929 (column 9). Column 9 of the table can be compared with column 7 which shows the results of valuing the two kinds of land separately by their respective 1929 prices. Since the values yielded by both methods do not differ markedly, especially after the subsequent reduction to an interest charge, column 9 is used in preference to column 7 because of the crudity of the acreage estimates of nonfarm private land in column 5, which estimates underlie the divergences between the alternate total land values.

We deal first with the two kinds of land included in the index, then with those excluded. Treatment of farm acreage as homogeneous over the period, while undesirable, is apparently not a serious defect, the percentage of total farm land in cropland having been rather stable from 1870 to 1945. Other than nonfarm grazing and forest land, the balance of the nation's acreage consisted of residential, industrial, mineral, and public land, the latter including streets, roads, parks, beaches, deserts, and other barren land. Analysis of land into these parts was impossible for want of refinement in the data. Estimates of wasteland acreage are available only for 1945, but its elimination for the whole period is especially desired. This objective was crudely accomplished by assuming that wasteland was publicly owned and constituted a stable percentage of public land other than forest or grazing. On this basis deduction of this public acreage (column 4) from total nonfarm acreage other than forest or grazing (column 3) leaves us with an index of nonfarm land in use other than grazing or forest (column 5). Since the valuation weight of $2,472.26 per acre represents the division of the 1930 acreage of this kind into the total estimated 1929 value of all nonfarm land, public land included, column 6 represents an index of nonfarm land in 1929 prices. Because the pre-1920 values in this column rest on unreliable estimates in column 4, column 6 is not used in our aggregate input index. Instead, we use column 9, the magnitude of which depends on the movement of farm and nonfarm private acreage other than forest or grazing, weighted by the 1929 value per acre of both combined.

Table 4. Value of Farm and Nonfarm Land in 1929 Prices, 1870 to 1940 (area in millions of acres, value in millions of dollars)

Year	Land in farms	Value of farm land (1) X $35.71	Nonfarm land other than grazing or forest	Public land except crop, pasture, grazing, or forest	Nonfarm private land other than grazing or forest (3) – (4)*	Value of nonfarm private land (5) X $2,472.26*	Total land value (2) + (6)	Total acreage used (1) + (5)	Alternate total land value (8) X $126.03
	(1)	(2)	(3)	(4)	(5)	(6)	(7)	(8)	(9)
1870	407.7	$14,559			22	$ 54,390	$ 68,949	430	$ 54,193
1880	536.1	19,144	116	92	24	59,334	78,478	560	70,577
1890	623.2	22,255	118	92	26	64,279	86,534	649	81,793
1900	838.6	29,946	121	92	29	71,696	101,642	868	109,394
1910	878.8	31,382	123	92	31	76,640	108,022	910	114,687
1920	955.9	34,135	126	92	34	84,057	118,192	990	124,770
1925	924.3	33,007	130	92	38	93,946	126,953	962	121,241
1930	986.8	35,239	130	92	38	93,946	129,185	1,025	129,185
1935	1,054.5	37,656	131	92.5	38.5	95,182	132,838	1,093	137,751
1940	1,060.9	37,885	137	93	44	108,779	146,664	1,105	139,263

*Figure for 1870 derived by the method described in the column footnote.

Source:

Column 1: *Agricultural Statistics for 1948*, Department of Agriculture, 1949, Table 606. Figures for earlier years are probably understated. See *Historical Statistics*, p.115.

Column 2: Value of farm land reported for April 1, 1930 was $34,930 million (*Fifteenth Census of the United States, 1930, Agriculture*, vol. 2, pt. 3, U.S. Table 1), or $35.40 per acre. This figure was in turn adjusted to 100.87 percent of its value to compensate for a decline in value per acre of farm real estate from 1929 to 1930. *The Farm Real Estate Situation, 1939–40, 1940–41, and 1941–42*, U.S. Department of Agriculture, Circular No. 662, p. 4.

Column 3: Same as column 1, Table 605.

Column 4: 1920, 1930, 1940, from *Historical Statistics*, F46. Includes publicly owned parks, roads, military lands, sand dunes, open swamp, rock, and desert. Figures for other years estimated on the assumption that no great changes in this type of land occurred over the period.

Column 5: Figure for 1870, used in calculating column 8 but not for column 6, derived by extrapolating the percentage rate of change from 1880 to 1890.

Column 6: The figure for 1870 was obtained by extrapolating from 1880 on the basis of the percentage rate of change from 1880 to 1890. The derivation of our estimate of the value per acre of the nonagricultural land may be summarized by stating that it is based on the following steps:

1. The relative distribution between land and improvements in assessed property values in New York City from 1922–29 (Edwin H. Spengler, *Land Values in New York in Relation to Transit Facilities*, New York, 1930, p. 142) was assumed to have characterized the increase in assessed property values in all cities of over 30,000 population for the same period. On the basis of this assumption it was found that the value of the 1922 acreage if these cities increased by 36.3 percent from 1922 to 1929. *Financial Statistics of Cities Having a Population of over 30,000, 1922 and 1929.*

2. The value given by Simon Kuznets (*National Product since 1869*, Tables IV–1 and IV–2) whether at book or market valuation, for all nonagricultural land for 1922 was then inflated by 36.3 percent, yielding a value for this land in 1929 of $93.946 million. (Book value constituted about 35 percent of the 1922 value of nonagricultural land given by Kuznets. Its conversion to market value was not feasible. Consequently, to the degree that 1922 book values in the aggregate failed to reflect the preceding inflation, our nonagricultural land will be undervalued in 1929 prices.)

3. For both 1925 and 1930, the estimated amount of privately owned nonagricultural land other than grazing or forest was 38 million acres. Dividing this into $93.946 million, the estimated value of all nonagricultural land in 1929, yields our estimated value per acre of $2,472.26 as of 1929.

Column 9: Multiplier for value per acre for 1930 divided into the total value for 1930, given in column 7.

The acreage in column 8 includes neither nonfarm grazing nor nonfarm forest land. Column 9 therefore does not reflect changes in utilization of either of these kinds of land. Whereas the approximate constancy of the ratio of farm to private nonfarm acreage other than forest or grazing justifies the use of a single price to value their combined acreage (columns 8 and 9), nonfarm forest and grazing land did not exhibit any such stable relation to the others. These omissions, necessary because suitable individual base values could not be assigned, are fortunately of little moment. Primitive calculations suggest that the annual services of the 883 million acres of nonfarm grazing land in 1880 (the highest figure recorded) would have been worth about $19 million, compared with a minimum labor input of $17 billion for that year. Grazing land can therefore certainly be ignored. Neglect of nonfarm forest land input, although its value was considerable, is also not serious because of the relative stability of its acreage over the period: the maximum acreage (1880) was only 20 percent greater than the minimum (1910). Hence, including or excluding the item would only slightly affect the comparative efficiencies of different periods.

Capital valuation. The underlying statistics for the value of capital are derived from Kuznets' statistics on reproducible producers' wealth, intangibles excluded, in the fashion described in Table 5. The omission of intangibles for the purpose at hand seems desirable, since these constitute either ordinary monopolistic advantages or superior technical knowledge. Increments in either of these ought obviously to be excluded.

Input of land, capital, and enterprise. Having valued land and capital by the methods discussed, we must next measure their annual services. As with labor and product, so here we endeavor to use 1929 prices. None of the interest rates in existence in 1929 can be applied with justice to the aggregate value of capital and land, since different kinds of capital and land entail differences in risk and liquidity,[6] and it is impractical to attempt to differentiate the wealth items according to such criteria. The alternative chosen was cruder but also more

---

[6] If only a "pure" interest charge were desired, a single interest rate would be applicable. Since extraneous elements necessarily appear in most interest payments, and these, like pure interest, are part of the costs of the use of property, there is no reason to eliminate them from our index.

Table 5. Value of Capital and Land, and Value of Capital, Land, and Entrepreneurial Inputs, 1929 Prices, 1869 to 1938 (millions of dollars)

Decade	Total producers' reproducible wealth	Land value	Total capital and land	Property input	
				Interest charge (3) X 5.2372%	Capital consumption
	(1)	(2)	(3)	(4)	(5)
1869–78	$ 15,962	$ 59,927	$ 75,889	$ 3,974.5	$ 994
1874–83	25,122	68,119	93,241	4,883.2	1,240
1879–88	35,482	74,503	109,985	5,760.1	1,587
1884–93	51,272	80,111	131,383	6,880.8	2,101
1889–98	69,302	91,453	160,755	8,419.1	2,577
1894–03	90,492	105,254	195,746	10,251.6	3,178
1899–08	113,252	111,247	224,499	11,757.5	3,873
1904–13	141,082	113,893	254,975	13,353.6	4,855
1909–18	172,032	118,216	290,248	15,200.9	5,966
1914–23	206,982	123,258	330,240	17,295.3	7,274
1919–28	237,532	122,300	359,832	18,845.1	8,744
1924–33	277,142	126,802	403,944	21,155.4	9,555
1929–38	281,182	135,181	416,363	21,805.8	9,699

Source:

   Column 1: To obtain estimates for the midpoints of our decades, we successively subtract ten times the annual average net capital formation given by Simon Kuznets in Table II-15, *National Product since 1869*, from the total on hand at the start of 1939 or the estimated amount for January 1, 1934, *ibid.*, Table IV-10, depending on the date. This procedure was preferred to use of Kuznets' estimates of the actual reproducible wealth for the specific dates back to 1879, because the capital consumption charges used in obtaining net capital formation include depletion of nonreproducible wealth. *Ibid.*, pp. 196–7. Unable to reflect depletion in our land values, we accomplish the purpose here.
   Column 2: By straight-line interpolation from column 9, Table 4.
   Column 4: See Table 6 for derivation of interest rate.
   Column 5: Kuznets, *ibid.*, Tables II-16 and I-16. For the later years, total capital consumption including war is taken.

defensible than a mean of published interest rates, since these omit the rate of return to owners of most unincorporated enterprises.

The alternative, shown in Table 6, was to estimate 1929 property income and calculate the rate of return to producers' wealth which this income constituted. Since property returns in available data include profits, the method actually ties entrepreneurial input to the amount of producers' wealth. Because entrepreneurial risk is largely proportional to the amount of wealth entrepreneurs administer, this linkage, though entirely a necessity, is also partly a virtue.

The linkage of entrepreneurial and property inputs through our interest rate also compensates for any constant proportional error in

Table 6. Calculation of 1929 Rate of Return on Property (millions of dollars)

Estimated Producers' Wealth, June 30, 1929	
1. Reproducible wealth, January 1, 1939 (Simon Kuznets, *National Product since 1869*, Table IV-10)	$287,582
2. Less (net capital formation 1930–37 + ½ 1929 net capital formation) (*ibid.*, Table I-19)	5,150
3. Estimated reproducible wealth, June 30, 1929	$282,432
4. Estimated land value, 1929 (interpolated from Table 4)	127,596
5. Estimated total producers' wealth	$410,028

Estimated Return on Property		
6. Total property income including rent but excluding that of entrepreneurs		$ 16,822
Estimate of farmers' property income:		
7. Total withdrawals	$5,899	
8. Net savings	77	
9. Total farmer income	$5,976	
10. Less estimated service income:		
No. of farmers times wages of full-time equivalent farm worker = 6,234,000 times $651.45 =	4,061	
11. Estimated farmers' property income	$1,915	
12. Percent of farmers' income from property	32.045%	
13. Total entrepreneurial income, including savings	$14,516	
14. Estimated entrepreneurial income from property (line 12 times line 13)		4,652
15. Total property income (line 6 and line 14)		$ 21,474
16. Rate of return on property (line 15 divided by line 5 times 100)		5.2372%

the valuation of capital and land combined. The correctness of either the interest rate or the property valuations is irrelevant to the accuracy of the input index. If the *absolute* value of property income in 1929 and the *relative* values of land and capital combined for the various periods are correct, then the value of the services of capital and land for any period is necessarily correct.

We come now to the final component of capital input, capital consumption. Since interest pays for the use of capital on the assumption that the principal is returned intact, depreciation is distinguishable from other costs. Reduction of depreciation is a significant form of technical progress. Hence inclusion of capital consumption in input seemed logical.

Yet the inclusion is largely ceremonial. In the first place, the capital consumption estimates are necessarily crude, involving the assumption of a constant life for major capital instruments, construction, and producers' durable equipment,[7] an assumption which conceals any alteration in their durability. Secondly, inclusion of capital consumption in input requires incorporation of capital replacement in output. We use gross and not net national income to measure output. We thus add the same figure to the numerator and the denominator of our output-input ratio. While this procedure conceivably can alter the relative standing of two periods, such a result is unlikely since the other components dominate both parts of the index. Indeed the index presented differs little from an index which excludes capital consumption and replacement.

COMPARISON OF TOTAL INPUT AND TOTAL OUTPUT

We may now inquire whether our two input series conform to such criteria of reasonableness as it is possible to erect. Unfortunately, no alternative input series of comparable scope and method exists. We can, however, expect that: (*a*) total input should evince a slower rate of growth than does total output; (*b*) the fluctuations of input and output about their respective trends should be in broad agreement; and (*c*) the expansion of output per unit of input should be greatest for those periods when general knowledge leads us to anticipate the existence of periods of unusually rapid technical change.

That the first requirement, necessary if the expected technical progress is to be found at all, will be met by each of our input series is a foregone conclusion. However, the respective rates of growth are of interest. Requirement (*b*) rests on the assumption that the rate of technical progress is sufficiently equable as to result in some positive association of input and output. Yet this cannot be too rigid a requirement since marked fluctuation in the rate of technical change must cause disparate movements of input and output, as anticipated by requirement (*c*). The latter criterion will be more readily considered together with the output per unit index itself.

Secular movements and deviations. Second-degree potential curves to the logs provided rather close-fitting trend lines for each series. A

[7] Simon Kuznets, *National Product since 1869* (New York: National Bureau of Economic Research, 1946), p. 80. Any error in this assumption also reduces the accuracy of our capital value estimates.

Gompertz curve fitted to gross national product failed to bisect the long swings as well as the second-degree potential to the logs, which was therefore retained. The trend values are plotted against the original data, both in log form, in Figures 1, 2, and 3. The underlying data are presented in Table 7.

Table 8 presents the more important trend measures of the series. As expected, GNP rose considerably more rapidly than either input series, nearly 19 percent per quinquennium as contrasted with 12 percent for total cost A and over 14 percent for total cost B. The more rapid growth of total cost B as compared to total cost A is attributable, of course, to the adjustment of the latter for the decline in the workweek. It is difficult to suggest any reason for the practical identity in the rates of retardation for total cost A and GNP. The greater retardation of total cost A relative to total cost B is explained by the greater absolute decline of the workweek in the last half of the period.

Over the period, GNP increased approximately eight times; total cost A, three and a half times; and total cost B, four and a half times. On this reckoning, of the historic increase in GNP, about half represented the effect of increased resources and half, the effect of increased efficiency of resource use.

The greater relative deviations from trend in GNP shown in column 3 of Table 8 compared to those in both total cost series, the greater relative deviations in total cost A compared to those of total cost B, and the broad similarities in the timing and direction of the deviations to be discussed shortly all combine to suggest an interesting possibility regarding the long swings in production. The higher peaks and lower troughs in output suggest that efficiency improvements are introduced most extensively during long "cycle" prosperity and least extensively during depression. This suggestion is reinforced by the probability that the quality of input deteriorates at peaks of employment and improves at troughs, a factor which by itself would tend to produce smaller variations in output than input, results opposite to those observed.[8] That the average deviation in total cost A exceeds that of total cost B suggests that the pressure to exceed or fall below trend is released

---

[8] Even the deviations from trend of man-hour labor input alone average only 0.01578 (in logs), demonstrating that the greater stability in input is not entirely due to inclusion of a fraction of land and capital. The greater stability in the more volatile of the labor series is apparent even though the trend line in this case (second-degree potential to the logs) does not fit, in terms of bisection of the long cycles, as well as in the other series. The trend for this series is not reproduced here.

Table 7. Second-Degree Potentials to Logs, Gross National Product, and Total Inputs, A and B, 1929 Prices, United States, 1869 to 1938

Decade	Gross national product			Total input estimate A			Total input estimate B		
	Log of GNP $ billions (log Yp)	Trend (logs) (log Ypc)	Deviations from trend (logs) (1) – (2)	Log of total input A $00 millions (log Ya)	Trend (logs) (log Yac)	Deviations from trend (logs) (4) – (5)	Log of total input B $00 millions (log Yb)	Trend (logs) (log Ybc)	Deviations from trend (logs) (7) – (8)
	(1)	(2)	(3)	(4)	(5)	(6)	(7)	(8)	(9)
1869–78	0.01410	0.03544	−0.02134	2.35736	2.34340	+0.01396	2.27554	2.26475	+0.01079
1874–83	0.17143	0.15105	+0.02038	2.43249	2.43283	−0.00034	2.35372	2.35622	−0.00250
1879–88	0.28914	0.25933	+0.02981	2.51468	2.51493	−0.00025	2.44028	2.44060	−0.00032
1884–93	0.36436	0.36027	+0.00409	2.58917	2.58970	−0.00053	2.52166	2.51947	+0.00219
1889–98	0.42732	0.45387	−0.02655	2.63679	2.65716	−0.02037	2.57761	2.59232	−0.01471
1894–03	0.51759	0.54013	−0.02254	2.69531	2.71730	−0.02199	2.64108	2.65912	−0.01804
1899–08	0.61490	0.61906	−0.00416	2.76686	2.77011	−0.00325	2.71800	2.71991	−0.00191
1904–13	0.69767	0.69065	+0.00702	2.82328	2.81560	+0.00768	2.78104	2.77466	+0.00638
1909–18	0.75228	0.75491	−0.00263	2.86159	2.85378	+0.00781	2.82750	2.82338	+0.00412
1914–23	0.80983	0.81183	−0.00200	2.90499	2.88462	+0.02037	2.88252	2.86607	+0.01645
1919–28	0.89092	0.86141	+0.02951	2.93069	2.90815	+0.02254	2.91772	2.90272	+0.01500
1924–33	0.91814	0.90367	+0.01447	2.92804	2.92435	+0.00369	2.93717	2.93282	+0.00435
1929–38	0.91249	0.93858	−0.02609	2.90385	2.93324	−0.02939	2.93621	2.95795	−0.02174
Totals	7.38017		−0.00003	35.34510		−0.00007	34.81005		+0.00006

X units 5 years, origin 1903–04.
Log Ypc = 0.619059 + 0.075261X − 0.003668X^2.
Log Yac = 2.77011 + 0.0491525X − 0.0036609X^2.
Log Ybc = 2.71991 + 0.057766X − 0.0030156X^2.

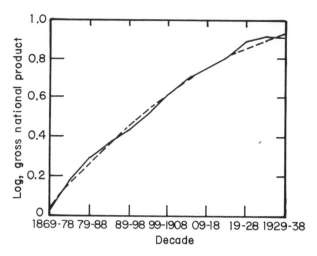

Figure 1. Gross National Product, Second-Degree
Potential Curve Fitted to Logarithms of the
Data, 1869 to 1938. *Source:* Table 7.

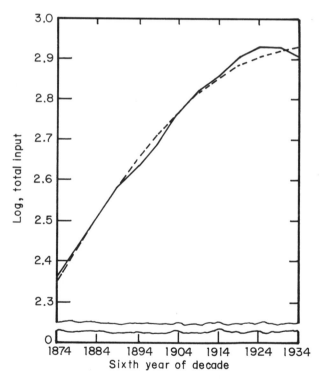

Figure 2. Total Cost, Estimate *A*, Second-Degree
Potential Curve Fitted to Logarithms of the
Data, 1869 to 1938. *Source:* Table 7.

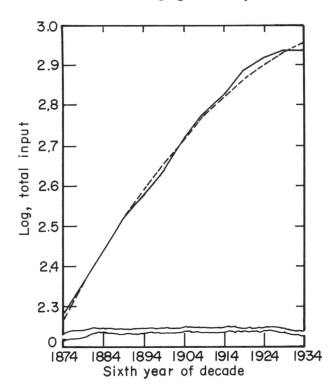

Figure 3. Total Cost, Estimate *B*, Second-Degree
Potential Curve Fitted to Logarithms of the
Data, 1869 to 1938. *Source:* Table 7.

Table 8. Rates of Change and Retardation in Gross National Product and Total
Inputs, Based on Second-Degree Potential Curves Fitted to Logs of Decade
Averages, 1869 to 1938

Series	Rate of change per quinquennium (%)	Rate of change in quinquennial rate of change (%)	Average deviation (logs)
	(1)	(2)	(3)
Gross national product	18.922	−1.675	0.01620
Total cost *A*	11.983	−1.672	0.01171
Total cost *B*	14.226	−1.379	0.00912

partly through varying the workweek rather than the number of workers. Much more evidence is necessary, however, before the inference suggested concerning technical change can be seriously entertained, since an alternative explanation for the results might be that maximum efficiency of plant is attained in periods of peak (long-cycle) employment. Similarly, the relatively greater output drops might be attributed to decreased efficiency at below-capacity operation levels.

Figure 4 shows deviations from trend in logs for each series. We expect that each total cost series should vary with GNP, except during periods of great technical change. Beginning with 1884-93 in Table 1, the anticipated covariation is observable on a broad scale with minor differences only. For the twenty years 1869 to 1888, however,

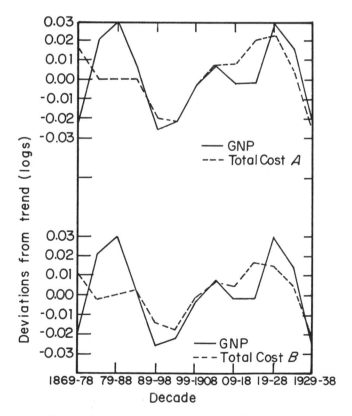

Figure 4. Logarithms of Deviations from Trend, Total Input, and GNP. *Source:* Table 7.

there is no apparent relationship. At this juncture, we can say that there is considerable but not complete conformity between the deviations. The divergences between the series including the greater upswing in output in 1919-28, we shall see, are approximately those one might have anticipated.

Output per unit of input. Table 9 and Figure 5 present our two output-per-unit series. Estimate *A* measures labor in man-hours, estimate *B*, in man-years. In columns 6 and 7 of Table 9 are the estimates of change in output per unit. These estimates controvert the time-honored belief in a continuous increase in the rate of technical progress.

From 1869-78 to 1929-38, output per unit increased 122 percent, or at a compound rate of 1.36 percent per year according to estimate *A*; 75 percent, or at a rate of 0.92 percent per year according to estimate *B*. Both per annum rates are lower than those based on output per labor unit, the inclusion of capital input which grew more rapidly than labor depressing our estimates below the other estimates of productivity growth. Because of the decrease in working hours, the growth demonstrated in estimate *B* is less than that in estimate *A*.

According to columns 6 and 7, major peaks in growth of output per unit occurred at the start of the series and in 1919-28, and secondary peaks in 1894-1903 and 1904-13 in estimate *A*, and in 1894-1903 in estimate *B*. No improvement came in the decade 1884-93.

What caused great increases in productivity in the second and third periods of our series? Why did no increase occur in 1884-93? That the fluctuations are due to business conditions not reflected in the statistics seems unlikely. The NBER business annals show the second decade, 1874-83, to have been almost as bad as 1869-78, and 1879-88 to have been better than 1874-83. Yet 1874-83 shows greater improvement over the preceding decade than does 1879-88 over its predecessor; and 1884-93, which was subject to somewhat similar durations of the various cycle phases, shows no improvement.

Perhaps the start of our series reveals the tail of a long innovation cycle terminating in 1879-88. That our economy grew relatively more during the decades immediately preceding 1890 than ever before or after is well known. Railroad mileage doubled from 1865 to 1873, and doubled again from 1878 to 1893. After the Civil War the Great Plains area was settled, and exploitation of the West's mineral resources began

Table 9. Two Estimates of Output per Unit of Input, 1929 Prices (millions of dollars)

Decade	Total input		GNP	Output per unit of input		Increase in output per unit of input over preceding overlapping decade	
	Estimate A	Estimate B		Estimate A (3) ÷ (1)	Estimate B (3) ÷ (2)	Estimate A	Estimate B
	(1)	(2)	(3)	(4)	(5)	(6)	(7)
1869–78	$22768	$18857	$10334	$0.454	$0.548	—	—
1874–83	27073	22578	14842	0.548	0.657	$0.094	$0.109
1879–88	32713	27561	19462	0.595	0.706	0.047	0.049
1884–93	38826	33240	23143	0.596	0.696	0.001	-0.010
1889–98	43326	37810	26747	0.617	0.707	0.021	0.011
1894–03	49576	43761	32929	0.664	0.752	0.047	0.045
1899–08	58456	52235	41197	0.705	0.789	0.041	0.037
1904–13	66568	60400	49847	0.749	0.825	0.044	0.036
1909–18	72709	67224	56526	0.777	0.841	0.028	0.016
1914–23	80352	76299	64543	0.803	0.846	0.026	0.005
1919–28	85249	82744	77791	0.913	0.940	0.110	0.094
1924–33	84733	86532	82820	0.977	0.957	0.064	0.017
1929–38	80138	86341	81745	1.020	0.947	0.043	-0.010

Source:

Column 1: Comprised of Property Input, which is the sum of capital consumption (Table 5, column 4); plus Manhour Labor Input, the sum of agricultural labor (Table 1, column 9, or Table 2, column 6, column 5) and an interest charge (Table 5, column 6).

Column 2: Same as column 1, except that Labor Input is in man-years, the data for which also appear in Tables 1, 2, and 3, columns 12, 7, and 7 respectively.

Column 3: Simon Kuznets, *National Product since 1869*, Table II-16.

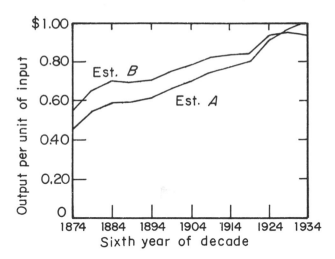

Figure 5. Two Estimates of Gross National Product per Unit of Total Input, 1869 to 1938, 1929 Prices. *Source:* Table 9.

on a grand scale. Steel refining was revolutionized, and conversion to mechanical power in manufacturing generally accelerated tremendously.

Hence the large increments in output per unit for the second and third overlapping decades of our series seem genuine, not flukes emerging from unreliable data. Even the apparent absence of improvement in 1884-93 over 1879-88 corresponds to the behavior of per capita income at the time. Per capita income grew by 29.3 percent from 1869-78 to 1874-83, and by 17.3 percent from 1874-83 to 1879-88. Yet from 1879-88 to 1884-93, the growth was only 5.5 percent, [9] which is small enough to result only from growth in resources per capita, including, in this context, a transfer of labor from agricultural to nonagricultural industries. Even so, the total absence of improvement in efficiency in the decade involved is hard to believe, and perhaps the better part of wisdom is to accept the evidence as indicating small improvement in efficiency, rather than none at all.

The great rise in output per unit in 1919-28 likewise is supported by external evidence. Per capita income rose over the preceding overlapping decade by 12.1 percent,[10] an increase higher than any other

[9] Simon Kuznets, *National Income, A Summary of Findings* (New York: National Bureau of Economic Research, 1946), Table 10.
[10] *Ibid.*

after 1899-1908. Stigler's index of output per man for agriculture, manufacturing, mining, gas and electric utilities, and steam railroads combined, leads to the same expectation. With 1899 as base 100, his index[11] moved from 127 in 1919 to 189 in 1929, a greater increase than in any other decade from 1899 to 1939. Since these industries employed two-thirds of the labor force in 1899 and nearly half in 1939, their behavior and that of the economy as a whole would be closely allied.

Conclusion. In sum, the overall behavior of our output-per-unit series corresponds generally to external evidence but not to the myth that technical progress necessarily accelerates with time. The estimates of efficiency improvement are lower than those based on labor input alone. The general pattern of the long swings about trend in total input parallel those in total output, except in periods of unusually rapid technical progress. While insistence on the precision of either of the indexes would be absurd in the face of the numerous estimates which underlie them, the broad trends shown in columns 6 and 7 of Table 9 are too sharp to be erased by any reasonable refinements and corrections. These trends are the decline of the increment in output per unit from the start to a low in 1884-93, its generally diminishing size after 1894-1903 to a low in 1914-23, and the subsequent peak in 1919-28.

COMPARISON WITH EFFICIENCY IN INDIVIDUAL INDUSTRIES

Do individual segments of the economy move with the economy as a whole with respect to the rate of technical progress, or do they go their own separate ways? A thorough comparison along the lines suggested by the question is an undertaking of considerable magnitude. We can only foreshadow here some results which might be yielded by finer tools.

Nature of the individual industry measures. From Kuznets' estimates for successive decades from 1869 to 1928 of the percentage of net national income in constant prices produced by agriculture, mining, and manufacturing, indexes of output per unit of input were constructed.

[11]George J. Stigler, *Trends in Output and Employment* (New York: National Bureau of Economic Research, 1947), p. 3.

Labor inputs for manufacturing and mining are in man-year units, derived from the same source as our aggregative data (gainfully occupied), unadjusted for changes in employment or hours of work. The great amplitude of the long cycles in construction made the use of such data inadvisable in this industry, and it was therefore excluded. In mining and manufacturing, the error through failure to adjust for unemployment is probably not serious for the period involved. For agriculture, the man-year labor input series developed for our aggregative index was employed. The numbers of mining and manufacturing workers in each period were weighted by each industry's 1929 full-time equivalent wage rate.

Mining and manufacturing property inputs were obtained by applying an interest rate to real estate improvement and equipment estimates, omitting any weight for capital consumption (or depletion), land, inventory changes, and changes in claims against foreign countries or other industries. The resulting measures, although covering the major part of input, are thus incomplete. Agricultural property input includes the land estimate previously calculated, but otherwise omits the same elements as the other two.

Since the industry output indexes assume a constant ratio of each industry's gross physical output to national income, they likewise suffer from imperfections, the difficulty in this case being the transfer of functions from one industry to another over the period. It seems reasonable to assume that our indexes overstate the growth of agricultural product in particular, although none of the specific values established can be accepted as accurate. Nonetheless, that the data reveal in a general way the broad movements, and the direction and order of magnitude of the period-to-period changes for both input and output, seems reasonable.[12]

---

[12]Our agricultural efficiency index may be compared with one somewhat similar in conception described by J. W. Kendrick and C. E. Jones in "Gross National Farm Product in Constant Dollars, 1910-1950," *Survey of Current Business,* September 1951, 13-19. The Commerce Department index is a significant improvement over ours in three respects: it measures farm output net of purchases from other industries, covers nonlabor inputs more completely, and is in annual form. On the other hand, it values inputs and outputs in prices of different years; and while its product measure is gross of capital consumed, its input measure is net of same.

The Commerce index shows a growth in farm efficiency of composite factor input of 0.9 percent per year from 1910 to 1950, while our index shows an annual increase of 1.1 percent from 1869 to 1928. That these differences are not explained entirely by the different periods covered may be inferred from the great improvement in efficiency in 1919-28 over 1909-18 according to our index, in contrast to the negligible improvement shown by the Commerce

Table 10 presents output per unit and the underlying data for the three commodity industries individually and combined. Lines 1 to 16 of Table 11 show the industrial output per unit of input indexes and estimate B for the economy. The latter, being also based on the man-year, is used here.

Line 7 of Table 11 reveals that the productivity growth in the commodity industries exceeded that for the whole economy. Whereas the economy's efficiency increased 1.09 percent per annum (for the period 1869 to 1928, according to estimate B), these three industries increased their efficiency 1.23 percent per year. This difference is probably not hard to explain. Except for construction, transportation, and public utilities, the rest of the economy exhibited severely limited possibilities for technical improvement. Trade, service, government, finance, and real estate, which comprise the remainder of the economy, were unable to mechanize many operations during the period.

Line 7 of Table 11 shows also that the annual rate of efficiency improvement in mining, 2.5 percent, exceeded those in the other two industries, agriculture being last with 1.1 percent despite the presump-

---

index (which is presented only graphically). Part of the discrepancy lies in the increase in the ratio of purchased inputs to farm output over the period covered by the Commerce index. In this respect, our long-term estimate of 1.1 percent per annum increase in efficiency is an obvious overstatement, as anticipated.

However, part of the disagreement results from the different measures of labor input used. Our farm labor input is determined mainly by census data on the number of farms and by the ratio of total farm labor payments to wage rates. These show a significantly declining trend from 1909 through 1929. The Commerce index, however, employs the estimates of farm labor requirements presented by Hecht and Barton, which show no secular change from 1910 to 1930 (R. W. Hecht and G. T. Barton, *Gains in Productivity of Farm Labor*, [Washington, D.C.: U.S.D.A., Technical Bulletin 1020, December 1950], Table 55). The Hecht-Barton estimates were in turn based upon the W.P.A. National Research Project series on changing techniques in agriculture, the data for which were obtained largely from an N.R.P. farm survey conducted in 1936 (unpublished).

In the 1936 N.R.P. farm survey, farmers were asked questions on farm labor, plantings, yields, and the like, in 1909, 1919, and 1929. "Based on the memory of farmers interviewed," and in the light of other scattered information of varying degrees of reliability, the N.R.P. estimates for farm labor requirements for crops by regions were constructed. While such estimates may be useful for individual crops, their aggregation is a dubious improvement over the data used here. On the contrary, since these data show a constant labor input from 1910 through 1930, when the number of persons gainfully occupied in farming was declining, and since their use yields the conclusion that farm efficiency did not rise perceptibly in the 1920s, although farm mechanization is know to have been considerable, we have good reason to prefer the farm labor estimates used here, crude as they are. (Hecht and Barton justify their index of farm labor requirements on the basis of its resemblance to the Shaw-Hopkins series on farm employment. See their *Gains in Productivity of Farm Labor*, pp. 50 et seq.). It is my understanding that the latter series has been seriously outmoded by subsequent revisions of the census estimates and is defective in other respects as well. See H. Barger and H. H. Landsberg, *American Agriculture, 1899-1939* (New York: National Bureau of Economic Research, 1942), pp. 239–244.

tive upward bias in the agricultural output estimates. Indeed, the rate for agriculture is approximately the same as for the whole economy. The annual growth rate for manufacturing, 1.4 percent, is considerably greater than that for the economy, but not nearly so great as that for mining. These results agree with Stigler's analysis of labor per unit of output for these industries,[13] although his investigation commences with 1899 rather than 1869.

Comparing the percentage increases in output per unit from one decade to the next in estimate *B* for the economy with those of the three commodity industries combined, shown in lines 8 to 12 of the table, we find that in every decade except 1879-88 the industries expanded more than the economy did. This pattern might have been anticipated from the more rapid overall growth in efficiency for the commodity-producing industries. The single exception, 1879-88, is rather puzzling and may reflect deficiencies in the data.

We may now compare the individual movements in the aggregate index with those of the individual industries. The comparison is facilitated if we assign, as in lines 13 to 16, a plus sign to each industry when its percentage change in efficiency moves similarly to that of the whole economy, a minus sign when it moves in the opposite direction, and a zero when no change in its percentage rate occurs. In all, there are thirteen instances of positive conformity, one of negative conformity, and two when the percentage rates of change for the individual series were unaltered in the face of changes in estimate *B*. This general picture of conformity between series suggests that while differences in amplitude exist, innovations occur in waves affecting the major commodity sectors of the economy more or less simultaneously, as hypothesized by Schumpeter.[14]

[13] Stigler, note 11, Table C.

[14] Equally interesting in its suggestiveness is the comparative behavior of efficiency improvement in the three industries in 1919-28. Agriculture expanded output per unit by 21 percent over the previous decade, mining by 26 percent, and manufacturing by only 9 percent. Since the demand for agricultural products is inelastic both price- and income-wise, and since the demand for the products of mining is largely derived (and hence presumably likewise inelastic), one wonders whether the failure of manufacturing to improve correspondingly in the decade, coupled with its internal rigidities, was in any way responsible for the debacle of the 1930s. Perhaps, if manufacturing had kept pace, despite its internal rigidities, employment opportunities would have been created for workers displaced by drastic technical change in industries with inelastic demands. Of course, whether parallel productivity growth in manufacturing would have mitigated or intensified the problem would have depended upon the nature of any innovations with respect to their effect upon manufacturing's demand for labor. As it was, from 1919 to 1928, there were small decreases in employment within all three industries as measured by full-time equivalent employees and entrepreneurs.

Table 10. Output per Unit of Input, Agriculture, Manufacturing, and Mining, 1929 Prices, 1869 to 1928 (output and input in millions of dollars)

Decade	Producers' wealth	Partial property input (1) × 5.2372%	Labor input	Total input (2) + (3)	Output	Output per unit of input	Increase in output per unit over previous decade
	(1)	(2)	(3)	(4)	(5)	(6)	(7)
Agriculture							
1869–78	$19,632	$1,028	$ 3,866	$ 4,894	$ 2,569	$0.525	—
1879–88	26,465	1,386	4,858	6,244	3,644	0.587	$0.062
1889–98	33,324	1,745	5,594	7,339	4,447	0.606	0.019
1899–08	42,088	2,204	6,089	8,293	5,748	0.693	0.087
1909–18	48,042	2,516	6,214	8,730	6,573	0.753	0.060
1919–28	47,327	2,479	5,477	7,956	7,250	0.911	0.158
Manufacturing							
1869–78	1,146	60	3,782	3,842	1,597	0.416	—
1879–88	2,970	156	5,586	5,742	2,914	0.507	0.091
1889–98	6,429	337	7,828	8,165	4,544	0.557	0.050
1899–08	11,727	614	10,481	11,095	7,241	0.653	0.096
1909–18	19,816	1,038	13,834	14,872	11,376	0.765	0.112
1919–28	30,442	1,594	16,475	18,069	15,121	0.837	0.072
Mining							
1869–78	264	14	350	364	93	0.255	—
1879–88	569	30	552	582	215	0.369	0.114
1889–98	1,118	59	841	900	411	0.457	0.088
1899–08	2,070	108	1,272	1,380	784	0.568	0.111
1909–18	3,248	170	1,659	1,829	1,264	0.691	0.123
1919–28	3,822	200	1,780	1,980	1,726	0.872	0.181
Agriculture, Manufacturing, and Mining Combined							
1869–78	21,042	1,102	7,998	9,100	4,259	0.468	—
1879–88	30,004	1,571	10,996	12,567	6,793	0.541	0.073
1889–98	40,871	2,140	14,263	16,403	9,402	0.573	0.032
1899–08	55,885	2,927	17,842	20,769	13,773	0.663	0.090

1909–18	71,106	3,724	21,707	25,431	19,213	0.755	0.092
1919–28	81,591	4,273	23,732	28,005	24,097	0.860	0.105

Source:

Column 1: Consists only of real-estate improvements and equipment in the case of manufacturing and mining. Agricultural producers' wealth also includes land, derived by straight-line interpolation from Table 4, column 2. The value of real-estate improvements and equipment for each industry in 1869–78 was obtained by assuming that the same ratio of the industry's real-estate improvements and equipment to the total governed on Jan. 1, 1874 as in 1880 (Simon Kuznets, *National Product since 1869*, various tables). All subsequent values, except for 1919–28, were derived by straight-line interpolation from *ibid.*, Table IV-12. The values for 1919–28 were obtained by adding to the value for 1922 the amount of entrepreneurial net savings in this industry for 1923, given by Kuznets, *National Income and Its Composition*, 1919–1938, vol 1, Table 46, p. 312.

Column 2: 5.2372% is the 1929 rate of return on property including profits derived in Table 6.

Column 3: For agriculture, from Table 1, column 12, and Table 2, column 7. For the others, Fabricant's series of gainfully occupied in *Historical Statistics* for decennial years were interpolated and multiplied by the 1929 annual wage rates derived from Kuznets, *National Income and Its Composition*, 1919–1938, vol. 1, Tables 51 and 52.

Column 5: Derived by applying percentage estimates given by Kuznets, *National Income, A Summary of Findings*, Table 13, to net national income for the given decades. See text.

Table 11. Output per Unit of Input, Estimate B, and Preliminary Estimates for Commodity-Producing Industries, 1869 to 1928

		Decade	Estimate B (whole economy) (1)	Three commodity-producing industries (2)	Agriculture (3)	Manufacturing (4)	Mining (5)
Output per unit of input (1929 prices)	1	1869–78	$0.548	$0.468	$0.525	$0.416	$0.255
	2	1879–88	0.706	0.541	0.587	0.507	0.369
	3	1889–98	0.707	0.573	0.606	0.557	0.457
	4	1899–08	0.789	0.663	0.693	0.653	0.568
	5	1909–18	0.841	0.755	0.753	0.765	0.691
	6	1919–28	0.940	0.860	0.911	0.837	0.872
Annual rate of increase (%)	7	–	1.09	1.23	1.11	1.41	2.49
Percent increase over previous decade	8	1879–88	28.8	15.6	11.8	21.9	44.7
	9	1889–98	0.1	5.9	3.2	9.9	23.8
	10	1899–08	11.6	15.7	14.4	17.2	24.3
	11	1909–18	6.6	13.9	8.7	17.2	21.7
	12	1919–28	11.8	13.9	21.0	9.4	26.2
Conformity to estimate B in direction of movement in percentage increase	13	1889–98		+	+	+	+
	14	1899–08		+	+	+	+
	15	1909–18		o	+	o	+
	16	1919–28		o	+	–	+

Source: Tables 9 and 10.

This conformity of major sectors to our aggregative index also strengthens the assumption that the latter is a useful measure of the economy-wide rate of technical change.

SUMMARY

Imperfect in conception and execution, the aggregate efficiency index described here nonetheless throws useful new light on the pattern of the nation's economic development. Its general validity is attested by the broad correspondence of the deviations of aggregate input to those of aggregate output, of the efficiency index itself to general historical evidence, to per capita income, to output per unit of labor, and to similar efficiency indexes for major industries.

Substantively, the index reveals that the increase in gross national product over the period reflected in roughly equal parts an increase in resources and an increase in resource efficiency. The efficiency increases were unevenly distributed, the maximum technical change transpiring in 1874-88 and 1919-33. Little or no evidence was found to support the common belief that technical progress grows at an ever-increasing rate. The decade-to-decade changes of pace in the aggregate rate of technical progress were largely duplicated in the commodity industries as a group, and in agriculture and mining individually, but not in manufacturing. This conformity suggests the possibility of innovation waves which penetrate diverse quarters of the economy.

These results suggest that further research may profitably concern itself with explaining the following: the relation between the growth of inputs and efficiency, and between each of these and other variables; interregional and interindustry differentials in the growth of efficiency and resources; and short-period variations in the rate of technical change. Finally, while our efficiency indexes seem superior to output-per-unit-of-labor indexes as measures of the economic effects of technical change, they are not entirely free of the kinds of deficiencies which beset the latter. Accordingly, the development of estimates of the significance of differential rates of growth between inputs, of economies of scale, of changes in consumer (and producer) preferences must also have a high place on the agenda for future research. When we can bring these phenomena and their interrelations into sharper focus, our comprehension of the nation's pattern of economic growth will be immeasurably enhanced.

The Size of Firm and the

Growth of Knowledge

Testimony of Jacob Schmookler before the Subcommittee on Antitrust and Monopoly of the Committee on the Judiciary, United States Senate, May 26, 1965.

The effect of the size of firm and market structure on economic progress has been a source of controversy for centuries. Much has been said but very little has been proved on both sides. If public policy is to reflect wisdom on this score, we shall have to replace plausible conjecture with hard fact.

This we are just beginning to do, but in my judgment many new facts will have to be put in evidence before abandonment of our antitrust laws can be justified. Quite the contrary, unless the evidence examined below can be explained away, it suggests that a more vigorous antitrust policy than our present one may be appropriate. Such an interpretation may indeed prove correct in the end. However, while I believe the evidence damages the case for bigness, it hardly seems solid enough to prove the case for smallness.

I shall confine my discussion to the effect of size of firm on the production of technological knowledge, because I know more about it. Of course, a balanced view of the relation of antitrust to economic progress would also need to take into account the effect of size of firm on the *use* of knowledge, and of market structure on both the production and use of technological knowledge, as well as other matters.

As soon as we ask, how does an increase in the size of firm affect the rate at which it produces new technological knowledge, a very embarrassing problem arises to cast a pall over the whole proceedings: how do you measure new technological knowledge? Theoretically it could be measured, at least for the purposes of the present problem, by the increase in output per unit of composite input that it makes possible. We have no such measure now, and until we do, any inferences based on other data must necessarily be provisional.

There are, however, two other kinds of indexes of output of knowledge available that are at least worth looking at: statistics of all patented inventions, and statistics of important inventions. While both kinds of data leave much to be desired, they point to identical conclusions with respect to the question at hand. For this reason if for no other, they merit serious attention.

Considered jointly, these two kinds of evidence suggest that beyond a certain not very large size, as a firm gets bigger it has to spend more to get an invention, the probability that it will use the inventions it makes declines, and so does the probability that its inventions will be significant.

Before discussing the implications of these conclusions, let me present the evidence on which they are based.

Table 1 shows the research and development expenditures per patent pending for firms in six different industries by size of firm. The data relate to 1953, because unfortunately the National Science Foundation Office of Special Studies stopped collecting data on patents in its subsequent surveys. Only firms having R & D programs are included.

Inspection of Table 1 reveals that in every industry, firms with 5,000 or more employees spent more on R&D per patent pending than did firms with less than 1,000 employees. Moreover, in every industry except chemicals, firms with 5,000 or more employees spent more on

Table 1. Research and Development Outlays per Patent Pending, 1953 (thousands of dollars)

Industry	Size of firm			Industry average (unweighted)
	Under 1,000 employees	1,000–4,999 employees	5,000 or more employees	
Machinery	$ 8.5	$14.2	$24.2	$15.6
Chemicals	11.2	24.4	23.6	19.7
Electrical equipment	15.7	12.6	25.6	18.0
Petroleum products and extraction	10.0	8.4	15.6	11.3
Instruments	15.8	14.4	37.5	22.6
All other industries	15.4	7.1	27.8	16.8
Average, all industries (unweighted)	$12.8	$13.4	$25.6	

Source:
National Science Foundation, *Science and Engineering in American Industry: Final Report on a 1953–54 Survey*, NSF 56–16, Appendix Tables A-34 and A-35.

R&D per patent pending than did firms in the next smaller size class. As shown by the last line in the table, for all industries combined, firms in the largest size class spent about twice as much as did firms in the two smaller size classes.

The greater R&D outlays per patent of large firms has several possible explanations. One is simply that large firms patent relatively less. This is probably true. However, well over three-fourths of the large firms participating in the N.S.F. survey reported in interviews that they patented "everything that is patentable or worthwhile".[1] In any case the difference in outlays per patent between large and small firms seems too great to be accounted for in this way.

Another possible explanation is that (*a*) the patents pending per firm reflect the efforts of both R&D and other technical and supervisory personnel, and (*b*) the inventive output of non-R&D personnel declines as the size of firm increases. The result is that small firms have a smaller R&D outlay per patent, because some of the relevant costs of inventing are borne by operating departments. I believe that a significant part of the result is to be explained this way, and I shall return to this point in another context later in the paper.

Still another possibility is that the inventions made differ according to size of firm, with big firms producing bigger, better, and more expensive inventions. Undoubtedly the inventions of big firms differ from those of small ones. They certainly seem to be more expensive. That they are, on the average, better in some significant sense seems very doubtful, however. Professor Edwin Mansfield found that holding R&D outlays constant, the number of significant inventions made by large firms in the chemical, petroleum, and steel industries declined as the size of firm increased. In Mansfield's words, "Thus, contrary to popular belief, the inventive output per dollar of R&D expenditure in most of these cases seems to be lower in the largest firms than in large and medium-sized firms."[2] Since the inventions made by large firms are more likely to receive publicity than those by small firms, and therefore were more likely to be included in Mansfield's study, I regard this result as especially significant since it emerges despite the presumptive bias in the opposite direction.

[1] National Science Foundation, *Science and Engineering in American Industry: Final Report on a 1953-54 Survey*, NSF 56-16, p. 37.

[2] Edwin Mansfield, "Industrial Research and Development Expenditures: Determinants, Prospects, and Relation to Size of Firm and Inventive Output," *Journal of Political Economy*, August 1964, 336.

The assumption that the inventions of large firms tend to be inferior to those of small ones receives support from another direction. Two independent studies indicate that small firms use commercially a larger proportion of their patented inventions than do big firms. A very extensive survey, based on a 2-percent random sample of inventions patented in 1938, 1948, and 1952, conducted by the Patent Foundation of George Washington University, found that large firms used only 51 percent of their inventions commercially compared to 71 percent for small firms. "Large" firms were defined as those holding over 100 patents, or with some patents and over $100 million in assets. The group also included some firms with between 75 and 100 patents. "Small" firms consisted simply of those not defined as large.[3] The use rate for patents held by large firms, indeed, was not significantly larger than the 49-percent use rate for inventions made by independent inventors.[4] This fact is indeed striking, since independents often have to go into business for themselves before they can use their ideas.

An entirely different study, conducted at the Harvard Business School, of very large firms exclusively, and covering all patents held by the firms surveyed, found that firms with 1956 sales exceeding $500 million used only 51 percent of their patented inventions, compared to 56 percent for firms with sales of less than $500 million.[5]

In brief, existing comprehensive indexes of output of new technological knowledge suggest that beyond a certain not very large size, the bigger the firm the less efficient its knowledge-producing activities are likely to be. Evidently, as the size of firm increases, there is a decrease per dollar of R&D in (a) the number of patented inventions, (b) the percentage of patented inventions used commercially, and (c) the number of significant inventions.

These apparent disadvantages of bigness could be offset if R&D expenditures per firm rise as fast as R&D efficiency declines. While there is some tendency for this to happen, the tendency does not persist among the largest firms — the size group that is the natural focus of antitrust questions. It is true that the proportion of firms doing research and development increases as the size of firm increases. For

[3] Barkev S. Sanders, "Patterns of Commercial Exploitation of Patented Inventions by Large and Small Companies," *Patent, Copyright, and Trademark Journal*, spring 1964, Tables 1 and 3.
[4] *Patent, Copyright, and Trademark Journal*, conference supplement, 1958, Appendix Table 11.
[5] Frederic M. Scherer *et al., Patents and the Corporation*, a report on industrial technology under changing public policy compiled by nine graduate students at Harvard Business School during the 1957-58 academic year, p. 112.

example, in 1958, about nine out of ten manufacturing firms with 5,000 or more employees had their own R&D programs, compared to only about six out of ten manufacturing firms with between 1,000 and 5,000 employees, and a much smaller fraction for firms with less than 1,000 employees. And it is also the case that in 1960, among manufacturing firms with R&D programs, firms with 5,000 or more employees spent 2.0 percent of the sales dollar on R&D compared to 1.4 percent for firms with 1,000 to 5,000 employees.[6]

However, impressions derived from such gross size classifications of firms are not fine enough for the present issue. No one today regards a firm with even 10,000 employees as big enough ordinarily to pose a potential antitrust problem. The real question is whether the very biggest firms in each industry engage in proportionally more research and development than firms somewhat smaller, thereby offsetting their presumptive R&D inefficiency. The answer is that, on the whole, they do not. Mansfield found that in petroleum, drugs, glass, and steel, over the period 1945 to 1959 the largest firms spent less on R&D as a percentage of sales than did somewhat smaller firms. Only in chemicals did the largest firms spend more on R&D per dollar of sales.[7]

This kind of result, together with the tendency for the number of significant inventions produced per dollar of R&D to fall as the size of firm increases, led Mansfield (in another article) to advance the very tentative estimate that the sixth largest firms in petroleum and coal mining, and an even smaller firm in steel, would have been of optimal size from the standpoint of maximizing the rate of innovation.[8] Because I believe that technological progress comes more from many small inventions that from a few large ones, and that smaller inventions are more likely to come from small firms than big firms, I am inclined to the view that the optimal size from this standpoint is even smaller than he estimated.

The impression derived from the evidence sketched above that, on the whole, very large firms contribute less to the advancement of technology in proportion to their size than do firms somewhat smaller

[6] National Science Foundation, *Research and Development in Industry, 1960: Final Report on a Survey of R&D Funds and R&D Scientists and Engineers*, NSF 63-7, Table 17, p. 41.

[7] Mansfield, note 2, 334. D. Hamberg reports substantially similar results in his article, "Size of Firm, Oligopoly and Research: The Evidence," *Canadian Journal of Economics and Political Science,* February 1964, 70-74.

[8] Edwin Mansfield, "Size of Firm, Market Structure, and Innovation," *Journal of Political Economy*, December 1963, 556-576.

is, of course, at variance with much contemporary opinion on the subject. To a considerable extent, the contrary view that the larger the firm, the greater its relative contribution to the progress of technological knowledge, rests on deductive logic. I do not wish to enter into that debate here. However, I should like to point out that deductive logic can contribute to our knowledge on the subject only to the extent that it begins from premises that approximate the salient facts. I submit that we do not yet know or understand all the salient facts, and that the logical briefs on behalf of the progressiveness of big firms ignore aspects of the problem which may be crucial.

On the factual side, the case for bigness appears to rest on two kinds of evidence: (a) the apparent progressiveness of a few big firms, and (b) the greater participation of large firms than small firms in formal R&D. Let me simply note, with respect to the first point, that the case for bigness has to be proved in terms of the record of big firms generally against that of small firms generally, because the performance of individual firms is far too variable for individual cases to prove anything.

The use of R&D data in the debate has been misleading on two counts. A study I did over a decade ago of inventions patented in 1953, when private industry was spending about $4 billion of its own money on R&D and the government was spending a good deal of its own, indicated that R&D men contributed about 40 percent of the inventions patented in that year, while supervisors, engineers, and scientists in the operating end of industry contributed about 20 percent, and independents contributed about as many patents as did the R&D men — roughly 40 percent.[9]

There is, of course, much that we would like to know, and do not, about the relative quality of the inventions involved. However, as indicated above, the inventions of independents are evidently commercialized about as frequently as are those of R&D men in big firms. Moreover, indirect evidence suggests that the inventions of operating personnel may be more often used than those of R&D men.[10]

[9] See my article, "Inventors Past and Present," *Review of Economics and Statistics,* August 1957, 321-333.
[10] Barkev S. Sanders, Joseph Rossman, and L. James Harris, in "Patent Acquisition by Corporations," *Patent, Trademark, and Copyright Journal*, fall 1959, Table 15, indicate that the corporately owned patents on inventions made by employees not under contract to assign patent rights are used commercially with greater frequency than are those on inventions by employees contractually obligated to assign patent rights.

Undoubtedly, the substantial growth of corporate research and development since the period covered by my study has increased its relative importance. Yet there is no question that the contributions of the hundreds of thousands of engineers, scientists, and supervisors in the operating end of business and of independents still remains very substantial.

What is more, even on their own terms and disregarding the serious questions of accuracy that can be raised about them, the R&D data relate entirely to expenditures and employment in R&D. They are thus measures of input alone. They tell us nothing whatever about output. There is no reason to suppose that input and output are perfectly correlated, and many reasons to suppose that they are not. Both indexes of output cited here — statistics of all patented inventions, and statistics of the number of important inventions — present a picture of the effect of bigness on the production of knowledge that differs radically from that derived from data on R&D inputs.

Indeed, if we tentatively accept the proposition that on the average a big firm has to spend more than a small firm to get an invention, or an invention it can use, or an important invention — as the evidence indicated above suggests — then the greater participation of big firms in the R&D process is explained not by the advantages of bigness but by its disadvantages: big firms have to run faster to stay in the same place. Actually, such an explanation is probably too simple. There are advantages as well as disadvantages of bigness, and what we observe (and that very inadequately) is the net effect of both. Hopefully, as research on the problem proceeds, the nature of the problem will become clearer.

In the balance of this paper I should like to focus on some aspects of the production of technological knowledge which seem to me to help explain the apparent disadvantages of excessive bigness suggested by the facts presented above. Producing a useful addition to technological knowledge requires many things. Among these are (a) an understanding of the problem to be solved, (b) a knowledge of whatever technological lore, science, or engineering bears on the problem, (c) access to the facilities needed to try out solutions, and (d) time.

With greater resources, big firms are better able than small ones to hire those knowledge specialists who can solve problems that others have indentified — when the solutions require formal training in science and engineering. They can give these men more time and better laboratory facilities. Yet, despite these clear advantages, the production of technological knowledge seems less efficient, on the average, in large than in small firms. Why? To answer this question it is helpful to consider the efforts of R&D personnel and operating personnel separately.

Professor Arnold C. Cooper of the Graduate School of Industrial Administration at Purdue University suggests several tentative conclusions based on a study of the problem which accord with my own impressions. After reporting that most R&D managers in both large and small firms agreed in interviews that a large company typically spends far more on R&D to develop a given product than does a small firm, Cooper suggested that the main reasons for this were that (a) "the average capabilities of technical people are higher in small firms than in large ones;" (b) R&D people in small companies "are more often concerned over how much a project costs than are their counterparts in larger companies;" and (c) "the problems of communication and coordination tend to be less acute in the smaller organizations."[1]

The suggestion that the technical people in small firms are likely to be, on the average, more competent than those in large firms may come as a shock to some, and possibly Cooper's finding is biased since his sample was drawn from the New England area – which is, after all, famous for the technological complex that radiates out from Cambridge. Nonetheless, the reasons he advances for his finding are cogent and bear reflection. Small, research-based firms, he argues, attract men who want to have a substantial effect on their environment and who want that effect recognized and appreciated; and such firms hire men of proven creativity rather than green graduates. By contrast, he argues, big firms tend to provide a haven for the mediocre in search of anonymity.

That the R&D men in small companies should be more sensitive to costs, and have smaller problems of communication and coordination, is obvious and I shall not pursue these points here, important though they are in explaining the phenomenon under discussion.

Instead, let me turn from R&D to the comparative contribution to knowledge of operating personnel in small and large firms. The big advantage of an operating man – whether he is a production engineer, a production supervisor, or a sales engineer – over an R&D man is that he

[1] Arnold C. Cooper, "R&D Is More Efficient in Small Companies," *Harvard Business Review*, May-June 1964, 78-81.

bumps up against technical problems and opportunities daily. He is therefore often in the best position to identify what needs bettering. However, I would suggest that there is a marked difference in both opportunity and incentive between an operating man in a small firm and one in a large firm. Even if this is not intuitively obvious, the fact was very apparent in the sample of inventions covered in my study cited above, for virtually all the inventions made by operating men in my sample were employees of small and medium-sized firms.

From the logic of the situation and from discussions with scientists, engineers, and executives in firms of all sizes, I would suggest several possible reasons why operating men in small firms are likely to contribute more new ideas than are those of large firms.

(a) A simple increase in size of the enterprise tends to make the productive process less comprehensible to the men who engage in it, simply because each man sees less of it.

(b) Big firms tend to be more than mere scaled-up versions of small ones: they cut the work up finer and narrow each man's responsibility, thereby further reducing his range of vision. Understanding less of what is going on, each man is less able to contribute to its improvement. Adam Smith was probably correct for his time when he suggested that inventiveness increases as the division of labor progresses, because the shops of the eighteenth century were tiny by our standards. However, the small factories of today would have been giants then. There seems little doubt that many of today's firms have subdivided labor so much that operating employees no longer understand the relation of their work to the rest of the enterprise well enough to make significant improvements, even when they have the native ability to do so.[12]

(c) The growth in the size of enterprise militates against invention by operating personnel in another way. The extreme division of labor and the larger numbers of individuals involved create a greater need for coordination and control by management, and of one tier of managers by another above it. Each man's influence is watered down, and his suggestions have less chance of acceptance. There are more managers, and therefore more potential vetoers. The channels of communication tend to become clogged if only because they are so long. Creative men in operating departments tend to find themselves frustrated by red tape and bureaucracy.

[12] This does not imply that such extreme division of labor is unjustified from the standpoint of current operating costs.

(*d*) As the organization becomes more formal, engineering and research men who are supposed to do the thinking tend to resent and discount suggestions by production and sales men who are supposed to do the doing. Whether warranted or not I do not know, but old-timers in the production line in any large-scale enterprise tell of good ideas that engineers blocked because they couldn't claim credit for them.

(*e*) Finally, there is the additional fact that independent inventors tend to steer clear of fields dominated by big firms. Indeed, even big firms in one industry tend to avoid fields dominated by established big firms. The reason in both cases is simply that outsiders are discouraged from entering such fields as producers, and generally are at a bargaining disadvantage if they try to sell their ideas to large potential customers for them. Hence, independently of any adverse effects of bigness on the *internal* rate of production of ideas, there is also an adverse effect on the rate at which ideas are produced outside the industry.

Let me now try to summarize my position. While we have much still to learn about what affects the rate of production of new technological knowledge, existing evidence suggests that there are significant adverse effects of bigness. On the average, very large firms seem to have to spend more than small ones to produce a patentable invention, to produce a useful invention, or to produce an important invention. These disadvantages are to some extent offset by the greater participation of large firms in the R&D process. However, very large firms generally do not participate in that process relatively more than do firms somewhat smaller.

The superior efficiency of smaller firms in the R&D process apparently reflects the superior quality of their technical personnel, greater cost consciousness, and better understanding of the problem to be solved resulting from closer contact with the firm's operations and better communications.

To the advantages of the small firm in R&D are added its more hospitable atmosphere for creative contributions by operating personnel, in consequence of the lesser division of labor and greater influence of individuals in such enterprises. There is the further fact that industries characterized by small firms provide a greater inducement for invention by outsiders.

By contrast, the case for bigness, while not wholly without merit, appears to rest on incomplete assumptions and misinterpreted evidence. The assumptions fail to take into account the effect of size of enterprise on individual incentives and opportunities to generate new ideas, while the evidence commonly adduced in support of bigness — statistics of R&D input or cost — presuppose a correspondence between input and output which apparently does not exist. While part of the greater participation of big firms in R&D — to the extent that it is indeed greater — probably does reflect some advantages of big firms, it also probably reflects the effort of large firms to compensate for their comparative inefficiency in the R&D process.

In the light of these considerations I conclude that it would be very imprudent to relax the antitrust laws in the hope of inducing thereby a more rapid rate of growth of the nation's technological knowledge.

Catastrophe and Utilitarianism in

the Development of Basic Science

Reprinted from Richard A. Tybout, ed., *Economics of Research and Development*, Ohio State University Press, 1965.

Recent findings lead to the conclusion that inventors respond far more to demand conditions than had customarily been assumed.[1] This result raises once again the question of whether a more or less similar relation exists between demand and the development of basic science. The present paper represents a preliminary approach to some aspects of the question.

Since the origins of basic science have been the subject of lengthy debate among historians and sociologists of science, it would appear that an economist dabbling in the area must be guilty of hunting without a license. There are, however, extenuating circumstances. On the one hand, economists share with other social scientists a concern about the nature of the interconnections between economic development and other aspects of social change such as the growth of science. On the other hand, the tools of the economist's trade may enable us to come more effectively into contact with some phases of this question in which several disciplines share an interest. In any case, if the advance of science is man's noblest enterprise, it is nonetheless a part of the seamless web of history. It is therefore proper for an economist to examine some of its economic aspects.

Before coming to the body of my paper, I should like to make a few, perhaps unnecessary, parenthetical remarks about motives. In the first place, let me record the impression I have that some previous

---

[1] See the author's "Changes in Industry and in the State of Knowledge as Determinants of Industrial Invention," in Richard R. Nelson, ed., *The Rate and Direction of Inventive Activity* (Princeton, N. J.: Princeton University Press, 1962), 195-232; "Economic Sources of Inventive Activity," *Journal of Economic History* (March 1962), 1-20; "Invention, Innovation, and Business Cycles," in Joint Economic Committee, *Variability of Private Investment in Plant Equipment* (Washington, D. C.: 1962), pt. 2; and, with O. H. Brownlee, "Determinants of Inventive Activity," *American Economic Review* (May 1962), 165-185.

discussions of the subject are either naïve or out of focus. Labor economists and sociologists have long known that the supply of labor in any market is influenced by many factors, only some of which are economic. This is no less true of scientists. Any given scientist may pursue a particular project mainly to make a living, to please his dean, to spite a colleague, to build a research empire, or to isolate himself from or stand out above his peers. Such more or less conscious motivations may themselves reflect deeper and darker reaches of the human spirit, which are the special province of psychology. Viewed in this perspective, the common dichotomy drawn between "the disinterested pursuit of truth" and research devoted to the advancement of the general welfare obviously does not exhaust the range of influences to which scientists are subject. What sets these two objectives in a class by themselves is that, for a scientist, other more personal motives can be reached only through them. The reason for this is simply that the rewards to scientists in terms of income, prestige, position, honors, and the like are rationed by his colleagues and the outside world only on grounds of these two criteria. These, the "public goals" of scientific endeavor, have constituted the exclusive focus of earlier discussions of our subject. I propose here to continue the precedent.

Furthermore, I believe considerable controversy can be eliminated by recognizing two things. First, a scientist may pursue a project because of its prospective contribution to knowledge, and his colleagues may applaud his results for the same reason, at the same time that his financiers, private or public, expect and perhaps receive "useful" knowledge. This suggests that whatever the motives of academic scientists were during the last century or two, the external support of science may have had a primarily utilitarian animus, with great consequences for the growth of science. Secondly, research without a *specific* utilitarian objective may nonetheless be broadly utilitarian in intent. By this I do not wish to suggest, as some Marxist writers have, that scientists who thought they sought knowledge only for its own sake were in fact responding to broad socioeconomic forces.[2] Rather, I am suggesting the much more obvious point that society has become increasingly appreciative both of the cornucopia that is science and of the unpredictable character of its results. In consequence, over the generations society has become increasingly willing to provide support

[2] This, of course, is possible, although it behooves those who suggest the existence of such a mechanism to demonstrate its modus operandi in each instance.

for general non-mission-oriented research for reasons as utilitarian as those which largely motivated the spread of popular education or, before that, of geographic exploration.

This paper is concerned primarily, then, with the question of whether science has been *supported* during the past century or two primarily for humanistic or for utilitarian reasons. To a lesser extent, it is concerned with the motives of the scientists themselves. Since our focus is on basic science, this means that, as a matter of course, we are concerned primarily with academic science, for it is mainly in the institutions of higher learning that the leading scientific discoveries of the modern age have been made.

We may take as our paradigm the course of support of basic research in the United States in the last two decades, and inquire whether or not the pattern so clearly etched there is exceptional or typical of the growth of basic research in the last century or two. Both government and industry in America have greatly expanded their support of basic research since the close of World War II. The lessons the war taught about the military, medical, and industrial potentialities of science were well learned. As the National Science Foundation recently expressed it, "Science supplies not only the information needed to solve specific problems but, more importantly, it opens up new opportunities which usually cannot be foreseen until the new knowledge is obtained. To insure such new opportunities, research support is required for the acquisition of new fundamental knowledge."[3] The strong influence of military considerations in the promotion of basic research is reflected both in the extensive postwar support given it by the Office of Naval Research before the establishment of the National Science Foundation and by the marked increase in basic research funds following the launching of the Russian Sputnik. Many spokesmen for the scientific community have lamented the heavy weight accorded instrumental considerations in the nation's scientific program and have yearned for a condition in which science would be supported for its own sake. I strongly share these sentiments, but it is worth asking whether American experience has been indeed as different from European in this regard as has often been assumed. A hasty survey of the progress of science since the seventeenth century suggests that it has not.

[3] National Science Foundation, *Eleventh Annual Report, 1961*, NSF 62-1, p. 3.

If I read the record correctly, to some extent from the beginning of modern science and certainly in the last two centuries, basic research was financed by European governments primarily to implement the traditional purposes of state policy – to promote the health and welfare of the citizenry and the military power of the state. Even the great private foundations which financed most of the basic research in America until recently were similarly motivated. The second lesson writ large by the history of modern science is that substantial changes in the level of external support are usually attributable to some specific, extrascientific, dramatic event or circumstance. In brief, I suggest that *the great propulsive force exerted by the Soviet satellite successes on American research and education is typical of the events which promoted the growth of modern science.*

Before any justification of these statements, it seems in order to recall that in earlier ages, particularly in classical Greece[4] and in post-Renaissance Europe,[5] a love of learning for its own sake played a greater role than now. Perhaps it even dominated the scientific enterprise. Let me simply note in this connection that (*a*) the capacity of science to serve utilitarian ends varies directly with its level of development, so that if science was to be pursued at all in an earlier age, it had to be pursued largely for its own sake – it was less likely than now to yield a valuable by-product; and (*b*) man's constant desire to know the design of the cosmos and the place of the earth and of man in it meant that an unusually high premium would be paid for new knowledge for its own sake when traditional beliefs were shattered in the early days of classical Greece and in Renaissance and post-Renaissance Europe.

The broad humanistic animus behind early modern science is indicated by the backgrounds of a few of the leading scientists of the time: Copernicus was a protege of his uncle, the sovereign Bishop of Ermland, who arranged a canonry for his nephew to enjoy in absentia; Kepler was a mathematician to Rudolph II of Bohemia, a post previously occupied by Tycho Brahe, himself an aristocrat; Galileo's patron was a Medici, the Grand Duke of Tuscany; and Newton was professor of mathematics at Cambridge.

[4] Benjamin Farrington, *Greek Science*, vols. 1 and 2 (London: Penguin Books, 1944 and 1949).
[5] Alfred Rupert Hall, *The Scientific Revolution, 1500-1800: The Formation of the Modern Scientific Attitude* (London: Longmans, Green, 1954), chap. 7.

Nonetheless, utilitarian considerations provided a powerful stimulus to the activities of scientists themselves almost from the beginning of the scientific revolution. Francis Bacon's vision, foreshadowing that of eighteenth-century Enlightenment, of a world from which science had banished want was widely shared, at least from the beginning of the seventeenth century on, by the doctors, philosophers, mathematicians, craftsmen, artistocrats, and dilettantes who cultivated science then. Thus Butterfield writes of this period:

The passion to extend the scientific method to every branch of thought was at least equalled by the passion to make science serve the cause of industry and agriculture, and it was accompanied by a sort of technological fervor; . . . it is difficult, even in the early history of the Royal Society, to separate the interest shown in the cause of pure scientific truth from the curiosity in respect of useful inventions. . . . It has become a debatable question how far the direction of scientific interest was itself affected by technical needs or preoccupations in regard to shipbuilding and other industries; but the Royal Society followed Galileo in concerning itself, for example, with the important question of the mode of discovering longitude at sea.[6]

Gillispie comments in a similar vein:

Baconism has always held a special appeal as the way of science in societies which develop a vocation for the betterment of man's estate and which confide not in aristocracies, whether of birth or brains, but in a wisdom to be elicited from common pursuits – in seventeenth-century England, in eighteenth-century France, in nineteenth-century America, among Marxists of all countries. . . . *His [Bacon's] was the philosophy that inspired science as an activity, a movement carried on in public and of concern to the public. This aspect of science scarcely existed before the seventeenth century. Since then it has accompanied and at times enveloped intellectual effort.*[7]

Hall concurs, saying: "The ideal of social progress was . . . a commonplace among seventeenth-century scientists, and with varying degrees of assurance the attainment of this ideal was linked with the application of scientific knowledge to technology."[8] Indeed, the progress of technology and science inevitably raised among educated men generally the humanitarian hope that through the development of

[6] H. Butterfield, *The Origins of Modern Science, 1300-1800,* rev. ed. (New York: Macmillan, 1959), p. 185. (Italics supplied.)
[7] Charles Coulston Gillispie, *The Edge of Objectivity, An Essay in the History of Scientific Ideas* (Princeton, N. J.: Princeton University Press, 1960), p. 75. (Italics supplied.)
[8] Alfred Rupert Hall, *The Scientific Revolution, 1500-1800: The Formation of the Modern Scientific Attitude,* paperback ed. (Boston: Beacon Press, 1956), p. 218.

science the prosperity of the period could somehow be spread to include all classes of society.

This hope runs like a thread through the intellectual history of the eighteenth century and, of course, formed an important and integral element in the ideology of the American and French Revolutions. Diderot's influential *Encyclopédie* was perhaps the most full-bodied expression of these aspirations.

Even in England, where the support of science with public funds was negligible, the utilitarian orientation of early scientists and the influence of the geographic and commercial revolutions on the direction of inquiry are plainly evident. Christopher Wren, professor of astronomy at Gresham College, said in 1657 in his inaugural address that "there was hardly anything more glorious to be aimed at in art than the knowledge of longitude." The solution to this problem lay in improved theory and construction of clocks; and English scientists, including Robert Hooke, the first curator of the Royal Society, devoted considerable time to these matters. Members of the society also enlarged navigational technology by astronomical observations, geographic exploration, and meteorological studies. Similarly, an interest in solving the problems of agriculture, medicine, and industry (particularly textiles) motivated many of the chemical pursuits of the members.[9]

If the prospect of applications seriously affected the unsupported efforts of scientists, the support of science by monarchs and aristocrats hardly expressed an unalloyed love of knowledge. On the Continent the state promoted science and scientific education as an instrument of policy. In an age when the nations of modern Europe were emerging and struggling with one another for survival, science was seized upon and cultivated to accomplish military or economic ends otherwise unattainable, or attainable only at great cost under the prevailing state of the technical arts. It was the mercantilist Colbert who established the French Académie Royale des Sciences in 1666 and who "suggested problems to it in accordance with political interests."[10] A generation later the members of the Académie were engaged in developing cascades and fountains for the palace at Versailles. This may signify that science was still too immature for its cultivation to have been profitable, but it

---

[9] The Royal Society Tercentenary (London: 1961), compiled from a special supplement to the London *Times*, July 1960.

[10] Hall, note 5, p. 195.

also indicates to what extent the early Académie was a creature of the state. The first scientific academy in Berlin, founded in 1700 by Frederick I under the guidance of the scientist-philosopher-statesman Leibniz, was likewise a mercantilist creation, "aimed at furthering the interests of the German nation and raising its technological standards."[11]

The quest for national power, apparently more than any other influence, accounted for the growth of science and interest in scientific matters in France during the eighteenth century, an era dominated by France's struggle to displace England as the premier power in the world. The monarchy's utilitarian orientation is illustrated by the kinds of scientific institutions which it established: the Royal Academy of Surgery in 1731; the Veterinary School in 1766; the School of Bridges and Roads (founded by the physiocratic economist Turgot) in 1775; and the Royal School of Mines in 1783.[12]

While the scientific institutions of the old regime were destroyed by the Jacobins during the Terror "in a fit of vulgar, sentimental petulance against the hauteur of abstract science, the personal tyranny of mathematics, the superiority of science over the artisan," Gillispie writes:

Upon the *tabula rasa* left by the Jacobins, the Directory erected a new set of scientific institutions: the first *Ecole Normale*, the *Ecole Polytechnique*, new medical faculties in Paris, Strasbourg, and Montpellier, the *Conservatoire des Arts et Métiers*. Only the *Museum d'Histoire Naturelle* emerged flourishing from the Terror, favored by the romantic enthusiasm for Botany and Rousseau's Nature. Other schools were revived, the *Ecole des Mines*, the *Ecole des Ponts et Chaussées,* the *Collège de France*. Finally at the summit was created the *Institut de France*. Thus, France was endowed at one stroke with her scientific institutions, and the first generation who taught and studied in them assured the restoration of her scientific leadership and its enlargement in the early nineteenth century.

It was a remarkable effort, animated by a consistent philosophy, which was nothing less than to unify the sciences through a common conception of scientific

---

[11] *Ibid., p. 201.*

[12] John T. Merz, *A History of European Thought in the Nineteenth Century* (London: Blackwood, 1907), vol. 1, 107n. Merz comments on pp. 106-107, "For the growth and diffusion of the scientific spirit itself, the great schools in Paris were even of greater value than the popular writings of Voltaire and Buffon. Most of the academicians were trained in these schools, and many of them taught there for many years." In addition to these establishments founded by the Crown, independent provincial academies of science, chartered by the King, were affiliated with the Académie des Sciences. Suggestive of the link between science and social reform is that the provincial academies numbered among their members Rousseau, Robespierre, Marat, Danton, and Bonaparte.

method, and in so doing to link them both institutionally and philosophically to realizing the idea of progress. So for a time, science was organized as a function of its educational mission. *Polytechnique* assembled the first scientific faculty, as distinguished a faculty, man for man, as has ever existed. For the first time, students were offered systematic technical instruction, directed toward engineering to be sure, but under the foremost men. Students, able and eager, chosen by competition, were immensely exhilarated by the sense of being conducted at once to the very forefront of scientific conquest, and at being told that the future of the Republic, which was to say mankind, depended on how they acquitted themselves in so exposed a situation.[13]

This crucial role of state support, with its essentially utilitarian animus, in the growth of French science to pre-eminence in the eighteenth and early nineteenth centuries is repeated later in Germany and England. It is noteworthy that when Napoleon conquered Prussia, he closed the University of Halle, where *Wissenschaft*, the critical, empirical approach to knowledge, was flourishing. It is equally significant that the creation of the University of Berlin, established in 1809 to replace that at Halle, was part of an effort of the Prussian rulers "to modernize their country in order to avoid a recurrence of another military catastrophe."[14]

Wilhelm von Humboldt, scholar and statesman, was responsible for the reorganization of Prussian education generally and the establishment of the University of Berlin in particular. A memorial of his published in 1810 brilliantly developed the political benefits of academic freedom and the unfettered pursuit of science:

On the whole the State should not look to the Universities at all for anything that directly concerns its own interests, but should rather cherish a conviction that, *in fulfilling their real destination, they will not only serve its own purposes, but serve them on an infinitely higher plane, commanding a much wider field of operation, and affording room to set in motion much more efficient springs and forces than are at the disposal of the State itself.*[15]

At the University of Berlin, the emphasis was on professional training, rather than on the classical, humanist tradition. In this as in

[13] Gillispie, note 7, p. 176.
[14] John Joseph Beer, *The Emergence of the German Dye Industry* (Urbana, Ill.: University of Illinois Press, 1959), p. 58; see also Sir Eric Ashby, *Technology and the Academics* (London: Macmillan, 1959), pp. 20-27, and Friedrich Paulsen, *The German Universities and University Study*, trans F. Thilly and W. W. Elwang (New York: Scribners, 1906), pp. 50-55.
[15] Cited in Friedrich Paulsen, *German Education, Past and Present*, trans. T. Lorenz (London: Scribners, 1908), pp. 185-187. (Italics supplied.)

other respects the university set the pattern not only for other German universities – Breslau (1811), Bonn (1818), Munich (1826)[16] – but also for universities throughout the world. By the 1820s, because the continuing drive of the German states to develop their economies pressed upon existing manpower, while the older universities displayed a characteristic reluctance to develop vocationally oriented curricula, *Technische Hochschulen* were established on the pattern of the *Ecole Polytechnique* to relieve the shortage of military, civil, and mechanical engineers. At the University of Giessen, the great German chemist, Justus von Liebig, himself educated at the Polytechnique, instituted the teaching laboratory and laid the foundations for German chemical supremacy. For a considerable time, however, Germany was a net exporter of chemists, for it was not until a native textile industry had developed, under the auspices of government and foreign private investment, that a market for chemists developed in the coal-tar dye industry in the 1860s and 1870s in Germany.[17]

With the rise of the chemical industry in Germany, private enterprise moved into position beside the state itself as a source of support for German academic science. It provided such support directly by hiring its graduates, but it also provided considerable indirect support.

Beer writes:

The chemical industrialist got the chemical students interested in dye research and, as is often the case, once these young men started certain lines of investigation, many spent the rest of their lives going in the same direction. When these boys graduated, they were frequently offered positions by the dye companies to continue their lines of investigation. Furthermore, if, in the course of their academic researches, they had come up with compounds or processes that seemed of practical value, those firms that donated the original chemicals or had perhaps cooperated with the research in other ways, were usually able to get first option on the use of these discoveries.

The older chemists engaged in industry used their company's money and their personal influence with the heads of the university laboratories as means of advancing the search for new colors and color intermediates. . . .

Cooperation with university chemists was so actively sought by the various German companies that a veritable competitive struggle arose between them over the "control" of the most important academic laboratories; and in time each company managed to establish strong ties with certain schools to the exclusion of all other rivals. . .

[16]*Ibid.*, pp. 184-197.
[17]Beer, note 14, chap. 6.

The means by which the competing dye firms tried to outdo each other for the favor of the professors is shrouded in mystery. It required a certain amount of circumspection to secure such cooperation without offending academic dignity and propriety; . . . some of the ways generally used in rewarding professional cooperation are perfectly well known and were considered proper. First, there was the payment of royalties; second, there was the promise of expert technical and legal assistance to bring the discovery under the protection of an effective patent that would safeguard it from legal attack, infringement, or circumvention; third, there were consulting fees that were usually extremely handsome, considering the time and effort involved; and fourth, the dye firm could offer scientific cooperation which not only involved the already mentioned donation of rare and expensive chemicals, and the use of the company's laboratories and staff for tedious confirmatory and analytical tests, but went so far occasionally as to furnish the professor with one or more company chemists who would work in his laboratory on specific projects that were of special interest to the company.[18]

The indifference toward science exhibited by the British government until the middle of the last century stands in instructive contrast to the active concern and support provided by the governments of France and Germany. It is probably not much of an oversimplification to suggest that England's economic and military supremacy during the period explains the contrast. To us it seems ludicrous that the reward which the Crown saw fit to bestow on Newton for his monumental work was to take him from Cambridge and make him Warden of the Mint. It is no less strange that the state's only other major gesture toward science in the same century was even more economical: where the continental monarchies financed their academies, the British allowed its counterpart to *call* itself the Royal Society. Not until the middle of the nineteenth century, when the German-born Prince Albert threw his weight into the scales, did His Majesty's government, initially by establishing the Royal College of Chemistry in 1845 under August Hofmann (a student of Liebig), begin to press for the creation of institutions of higher scientific and technological education.

The scale of these early British efforts, however, was modest. Only when the Great Exhibition of 1851 and, even more dramatically, the Paris Exhibition of 1867 revealed that French, German, and Swiss industry gravely threatened England's economic hegemony did state support of science and science education become appreciable in Britain. In the decade between 1871 and 1880, seven new colleges of higher education and the Cavendish Laboratory at Cambridge and Clarendon

[18] *Ibid.*, pp. 64-65.

at Oxford were established.[19] That Britain's response in important respects proved in the long run inadequate to the challenge is interesting, but the instrumental character of that response is as apparent in her case as in the others.

The history of basic science in America repeats the story with differences only in the details. The promotion of science as an instrument of human betterment greatly appealed to the founding fathers, who numbered among their ranks the educated elites of Virginia and New England. The hope which many of them later shared of founding a national university vanished, however, with the rise of Jacksonian democracy, although the states' rights doctrine had never permitted it to burn brightly. The establishment of the land-grant colleges and universities after mid-century did little to promote fundamental research, partly because of Americans' concern with matters of immediate utility,[20] and partly because a local educational institution is a suboptimal location for basic research since its utilitarian benefits are diffused and uncertain. The transplantation to American shores of the German university model in the form of Johns Hopkins University in 1877 marked the serious beginning of basic research in this country, but, according to I. Bernard Cohen, President Gilman's inaugural address and the university's early course offerings make its utilitarian orientation abundantly clear. Similarly, as noted earlier, the substantial research undertakings supported by the Rockefeller, Carnegie, and Ford Foundations in this century have been motivated, not by a desire merely to advance our understanding of the world, but by a desire to change it, by advancing health and welfare.

In short, the recent spectacular involvement of the American government in basic science is not one of the new things under the sun. What is new in America is the combination of a sense of national peril and a recognition by the governing authorities that basic science can help to meet it and yield other benefits as well; but as we have seen, this combination has appeared elsewhere before. There is undoubtedly some merit in Tocqueville's contention that America neglected basic science because democracy promotes an interest in immediate material results, while Europe pursued it because aristocracies "facilitate the

[19] Ashby, note 14, chaps. 2 and 3.
[20] Alexis de Tocqueville, *Democracy in America* (New York: Vintage Books, 1959), vol. 2, pp. 45-46.

natural impulse of the mind to the highest reaches of thought, and they naturally prepare it to conceive a sublime, almost a divine love of truth."[21]

One may grant, and not only for the sake of the argument, Tocqueville's premise, but at the same time question whether its weight is great enough to explain the great observed international differences in state support of science. A complacent English aristocracy ignored fundamental science when revolutionary French democracy energetically pursued it, while a later and more democratic English government initiated a much more active policy toward science. Undoubtedly the governing classes of Western nations were characterized by marked differences in their regard for science, both for its own sake and for its capacity to assist in the accomplishment of state purposes. Yet such differences apparently affected the level of state support less than did their different locations in the international constellation of power. Over the last two centuries or so, when states supported science, they did so primarily for utilitarian, not humanistic, reasons, as a way of accomplishing, by intellectual means, objectives beyond the reach of their material resources. A major reason that England ignored science in the eighteenth century and most of the nineteenth, while first France and then Germany vigorously fostered it, was that England was the pre-eminent power in the world and the others aspired to that position.

Marked increases in the level of state support of science seem generally to have been the by-product of large-scale changes in national posture arising from threatened or realized catastrophe, as we have seen in the case of post-Jena Germany, post-Paris Exposition England, and post-Sputnik America. It has apparently been a difference not so much in the value placed on science for its own sake, or in the abstract appreciation of the utility of science, as in the problems confronted, the urgency with which these problems were felt, and the effectiveness of the state in commandeering resources that accounts for the main international differences in the support of science.

Thus it would appear that the question with which this paper opened can be tentatively answered in the affirmative, at least with respect to the level of support for basic research. Just as inventive activity has been distributed among industries in accordance with the demand for

[21] *Ibid.*, p. 46. See also Richard H. Shryock, "American Indifference to Basic Science during the Nineteenth Century," *Archives internationales d'histoire des sciences*, no. 5 (1948).

inventions, so support of basic research has apparently tended to be distributed among nations in accordance with the demand for more general science. It may be conjectured that, as science became more useful, within each nation basic research tended also to become distributed among fields roughly in accordance with demand; but I can only guess that this is so and hope that others better qualified will examine the possibility.

There are, of course, many differences between science and invention. From a utilitarian standpoint, scientific knowledge tends to be more of a general-purpose tool than invention. Moreover, the former represents an expression in the indicative, the latter, in the imperative. For both these reasons, invention is usually more immediately useful and therefore, in all likelihood, more immediately bound up with utilitarian considerations and more immediately responsive to urgent problems which are often dramatized by real or threatened catastrophes. Finally, unlike scientific discovery, invention is nothing if it is not useful. For these and other reasons, it seems plausible to believe that scientific discovery, in the small as well as in the large, has been — and should continue to be — less affected by want-satisfying objectives than has invention. On the other hand, that, in a general way, such objectives have played a substantial role seems undeniable.

Technological Change and

Economic Theory

Reprinted from the *American Economic Review*, May 1965.

During the last dozen years or so economists have shown that the production, diffusion, and use of new knowledge are more important for the growth of output per capita than is the accumulation of physical capital. It seems safe to say that this discovery occasioned more surprise among economists than among educated men generally. The differential surprise is an instructive example of how damaging to the understanding professional knowledge can sometimes be.

Surely what distinguishes the twentieth from the eighteenth century is less its physical plant than the knowledge embodied or used in that plant. It seems, for example, utterly obvious that the technological knowledge possessed by its people played a bigger role in Germany's post-World War II recovery than did the devastated and rundown plant which survived the war.

If it is true that most educated men knew a vital truth about economics that many economists did not, the reasons for this would seem to be of interest. In this paper I propose to explore these reasons and their implications.

We can bring the problem into focus if we recognize at the outset that the recent evidence in itself would have caused little stir among our intellectual forebears, even though it was they who, for the sake of analysis, put the accumulation of capital at the center of attention, and even though they knew at most only the agricultural and industrial revolutions rather than the seemingly permanent technological revolution of our time. Adam Smith, Karl Marx, and John Stuart Mill, to cite just a few outstanding examples, discussed at length the contribution of the knowledge and skills of a nation's labor force to its aggregate output, and perforce assigned to new inventions and discoveries and to the more widespread dissemination of old knowledge a vital role in development. Likewise, much of List's infant-industry argument on behalf of protection was based on the time needed for investment in labor to take place.

Among more modern economists Alfred Marshall, Frank W. Taussig, and Irving Fisher come to mind as having been likewise appreciative of these matters.[1] The point is not that the great men of the profession understood, but that the troops in the line did too, partly because of their professional education but also simply because they were generally well educated.

And of course, I am not trying to say that a decade ago the leading members of the profession did not equally understand. The basic point is that the generality of contemporary economists were surprised by the evidence, and the question is, why? The answer, I think lies essentially in an inadequate strategy for the advancement of knowledge in our field. It lies not in what we have done but in what we have not done. We declined in understanding because we grew without balance.

Teaching aside, the activities of the overwhelming majority of the profession have been directed toward two entirely proper objectives: (a) the further refinement and, more recently, the empirical testing of received principles, and (b) the solution of pressing social problems. The pursuit of the first of these goals led inevitably to a considerable growth of the formal apparatus of our science. This was precisely what was desired and indeed needed. However, since we needed more time to learn and teach it, we had less time than before to learn and teach other knowledge, however vital such other knowledge might be to an understanding of those economic phenomena that the formal theory failed to deal with.

And so we were forced to rediscover with a worm's-eye view what the birds of earlier generations knew as a familiar feature of the landscape. Lacking time to learn the history of economic thought, we were doomed to repeat it.

Obviously there is more to it than that. For the evolution of the formal apparatus might have brought technological change to the fore instead of pushing it into the background. That the theoretical apparatus grew as it did, however, was predestined by the very nature of the underlying principles on which that growth fed. On the one hand, the law of variable proportions presupposes a given state of the

---

[1] Obviously, the writers listed are only those in the orthodox tradition. Heterodox economists like Veblen, Schumpeter, and Kuznets usually put technological or technical change at the heart of their analysis.

technical arts. On the other, the law of diminishing marginal utility (or its more modern form, the law of diminishing marginal rate of substitution) presupposes a given set of preferences. To a large extent, the theoretical apparatus which has evolved consists of the precise formulation of these principles and their application under various assumed conditions. Constructing this theory has preoccupied most of the best minds of the profession for generations. The most convenient setting for this purpose was, of course, a static framework. While the results derived were readily transferable to comparative statics, and then, not quite so readily, to dynamics, in both the latter changes in technology, tastes, and so forth are assumed, not explained. They are, in short, exogenous variables of the theory.

These developments in theory and the mathematical and econometric techniques which evolved with them were, and will prove in the future to be, enormously valuable. On the other hand, a perhaps inevitable by-product was a distinct tendency to forget that the knowledge gained in the process was merely a knowledge of the assumptions and their consequences, and that the precise relation of such knowledge to phenomena remained to be discovered. Earlier economists studied the world and knew it was round. Only their maps were flat. Too many later economists studied the maps and mistook them for the world.

Probably the outstanding example of this misplaced "concreteness" is technological change itself, by which I mean in this context the production of new knowledge useful in production. With few exceptions generations of economists regarded technological change analytically as an exogenous variable. Not knowing its precise linkages, they could not make it a dependent variable in their analysis. With the passage of time, however, economists came to believe that it really was primarily a noneconomic phenomenon; that is, that its causes lay in other domains of human behavior and therefore should in principle be treated in the same way as earthquakes. Now, there undoubtedly is some exogenous component in technological change, but there is also an endogenous one (a fact which was recognized, to cite just a few examples, by Smith, Marx, Mill, Marshall, and Hicks). What is more, recent evidence indicates that the endogenous component is usually dominant, at least in modern economies.[2]

[2] See my forthcoming book on invention to be published by Harvard University Press [*Invention and Economic Growth*, 1966]; also my note with Zvi Griliches, "Inventing and Maximizing," *American Economic Review*, September 1963, 725-729, and references cited therein.

When this fact also becomes more widely known, we will again be surprised. Yet if we had really thought about it, we would not be. Economic activity is concerned with the satisfaction of human wants. Technological progress permits those wants to be satisfied better than pre-existing knowledge did. While some inventions are made by accident, most of them are made on purpose. Since making them is neither easy nor costless, that inventive resources tend to be allocated among alternative projects in accordance with anticipated profits is only to be expected. In short, in the main the production of new technology is itself an economic activity. It represents in essence the mobilization of society's creative energies to relieve the scarcities which existing resources and products cannot. Far from being an exogenous variable, it is one of the most interesting endogenous variables of them all.

Be that as it may, the necessarily heavy emphasis in recent decades on the increasingly complex analytical framework conditioned our minds to the view that technological change was exogenous, not only from the standpoint of our theoretical models, but also from that of the economic system. And of course, out of sight, out of mind. When once again our attention turned to economic growth, too many of us found it natural to suggest as its chief cause capital formation – the main variable internal to our models which could make output per capita rise.

That it was our renewed interest in economic growth that led to the rediscovery of the importance of technological progress is significant, because that renewal of interest primarily reflected developments not internal but external to our science. On the whole, neither our interest in growth nor our interest in technological change derives from a steady scientific evolution and a clear scientific vision. Rather our current interest in both phenomena exemplifies the other principal reason for our diminished awareness, until recently, of the significance of technological progress. The second reason is our concern, in itself admirable, with pressing current social problems. More specifically, our attention has been turned to technological progress and investment in human capital, primarily because governments and people generally today place economic growth and military power high on the agenda and toward that end make large public and private outlays on research and education. The profession's interest in these matters has followed, not led, informed opinion.

One can confidently assert that, if the pressing economic problems of the interwar years had been not monetary policy, tariffs, labor, and business cycles but the problems of today, then most of what we are just beginning to learn about technological progress would have been known long ago. Thus, once again we find ourselves, as we have so many times in the past, running from behind to catch up to the events of the day. In the meantime, the world pays, as it did in the big depression, a heavy price for our ignorance.

In brief, most of us have been preoccupied either with problems of immediate public concern, or with the elucidation of received principles which do not illuminate economic phenomena of major significance. These endeavors were noble and necessary, but our inability to cope first with the big depression and now with the problems of economic growth suggests that they were not enough.

What has been lacking is that respect for the facts which characterizes the natural sciences.[3] We are presumably interested in explaining events which we call economic – events having to do with the social aspects of the satisfaction of wants. We develop a few powerful principles and then allocate virtually our entire fundamental research effort to evolving, refining, and, more recently, testing them. Other than that, with a few notable exceptions, we spend our time putting out fires – fires which too often reach inferno dimensions because our fire-fighting apparatus is so inadequate.

Such a research strategy would be entirely appropriate if the theory thus developed dealt substantially with the whole range of phenomena to be explained. That it does not is perfectly plain. To get something empirical out of a theory, you have to put something empirical in. While more theoretically-oriented empirical work is being done by the profession now than ever before, not nearly enough is being done in those areas where such knowledge is needed if we are to enlarge the range of economic phenomena that our science explains. A theory which can tell us what will happen if technology, preferences, resources, and institutions change can be at best but a stage in the

---

[3] To an extent, econometricians are exempt from the charge, since their avowed mission is the empirical testing of theory. But only to an extent, for the number of untested econometric models still exceeds the number of tested ones. In many respects the rise of econometrics is the most heartening recent development in economics, since it represents a clear professional recognition of the necessity for empirically testing hypotheses. Nonetheless, for the reasons given below, this will not be enough, if our hypotheses continue to be confined to only a narrow range of phenomena.

growth of our science, not its terminus. We also need theories about how these change.[4]

Even if these variables were in fact exogenous to the economic system as is commonly assumed, we would still need adequate theories of them. Without such theories we will be unable either to explain or control major economic phenomena. What transpires when the state of the arts, for instance, is unchanged or changes in an assumed way is hardly coterminous with the range of phenomena to be explained. In particular, since economic growth is caused to a large extent by changes in variables with respect to which our existing theory is silent, that theory cannot be expected to yield an adequate theory of growth without substantial emendation. What we shall probably need in the end, to repeat, is a theory which explains what our existing theory takes as given.

There are two further points which need to be made in this connection. The first is that to assert with confidence that a given variable is exogenous to the economic system may require that we know what does influence it. Thus the grandmothers' tales sometimes found in economic treatises to justify treating technological change as exogenous reflect not our knowledge but our ignorance. That this assumption should have gone unchallenged for so long reflects that inadequate interest in the facts to which I referred above.

The second point is that to the degree that such variables as technological change, tastes, and resources prove on examination to be

---

[4] Paul A. Samuelson, on p. 316 of *Foundations of Economic Analysis* (Cambridge, Mass.: Harvard University Press, 1947), says: "However, there is nothing sacred about the conventional boundaries of economics; if the cycle were meteorological in origin, economists would branch out in that direction, just as in our day a political theory of fiscal policy is necessary if one is to understand empirical economic phenomena." See also James Tobin, quoted on p. 209 of T. C. Koopmans, *Three Essays on the State of Economic Science* (New York: John Wiley, 1957) "What is wrong with economics is not so much the putting together of the pieces. . . .What is wrong is the poor quality of the pieces that we put together in such models." And Koopmans himself, "The test of suitability of a tool of reasoning is whether it gives the most logical and economical expression to the basic assumptions *appropriate to the field in question*, and to the reasoning that establishes their implications. *The difficulty in economic dynamics has been that the tools have suggested the assumptions rather than the other way around. Until we succeed in specifying fruitful assumptions . . ., we shall continue to be groping for the proper tools of reasoning."* (*Ibid.,* pp. 182-83. Italics supplied.) Tobin's and Koopmans' complaints relate entirely to the inadequacy of our information about behavior, especially with respect to decision making. However, as the quotation from Samuelson suggests, we may also need better information about the state of nature; for example, in the present context, the production function for new technology.

endogenous, existing economic theory is inaccurate even with respect to the phenomena with which it purports to deal. For example, if recent evidence is to be credited, the rate of technolgical progress tends to be higher in industries with higher rates of investment. If this is correct, then an industry in long-run equilibrium in the neoclassical sense will not be in equilibrium at all – not because of external but because of internal conditions. The so-called "long-run" supply curve of the industry will shift, and, other things being equal, the proportional shift will be greater, the greater the initial size of the industry. Whether this is indeed so will require further empirical research to determine. No amount of postulating alternative possibilities will tell us which possibility nature elects.

There are other even more interesting problems awaiting investigation. The old adage, "Necessity is the mother of invention," emphasizes the induced element of invention and suggests that demand tends to create its own supply; in other words, a reversal of Say's Law. The general pattern of development of new consumer goods suggests indeed that to a large extent new goods are invented in response to changes in income and preferences. Similarly, the evidence alluded to previously suggests an allocation of inventive effort among existing production processes in accord with the prevailing rate of investment in them. If anything like such forces is operative, then our present dynamic models are seriously incomplete. To improve them we have no recourse but to develop solid knowledge about relations of the sort suggested and incorporate them into our theory.

A common objection, not to be taken lightly, to undertakings of the sort proposed is that we lack the tools to perform them. The answer to this is twofold. First, whether we shall need concepts and research techniques beyond those already at our disposal will not become apparent until we begin to work on the site. So far work in the field of technological change has progressed appreciably with only modest modification of pre-existing tools. The main problems have been to ask the right questions and get the right data. Second, if we need new tools, we can get them in the same way that we got the old tools: by making them, or borrowing them from some neighboring discipline. No doubt there will be failures, and in any case the work will not be easy. In some instances ingenuity rivaling that displayed on occasion by natural scientists will be required. But if we do not do it, nobody will, and our science will remain but a fragment, dealing with only some and by no means the most important economic phenomena.

A second but related objection is the judgment that we shall make more progress if we advance outward from our present well-established base rather than, so to speak, dropping troops by air deep in enemy territory. The more conservative strategy has the advantage of preserving lines of communication more effectively, and the disadvantage that what is communicated is less interesting.

Finally, the more conservative strategy seems rather shortsighted in any case. Sooner or later, if the past is any guide, we shall have to advance anyway in the directions indicated. If we do not proceed now with deliberate speed, we shall find ourselves doing so with desperate haste as members of an emergency government task force of one sort or other, seeking instant wisdom to palliate some pressing social problem, just as we now find our advice sought on the economics of growth, automation, the patent system, the space program, military research, education, manpower retraining, and so forth. One cannot say with certainty that our advice would now be much better on these matters if our predecessors had possessed a more scientific attitude toward our subject. To make such a statement would require that we guess what, if anything, that we now know that is also relevant would have gone undiscovered. It is obvious from what has been said above what my guess on this question is.

Like the other policy sciences, for example medicine and engineering, economics tends to attract into it men with a strong interest in immediately useful results. Even without a strong predisposition in this direction, we would be less than human not to feel an obligation to assist in the solution of those social problems which may be supposed to lie within our professional competence. Moreover, the bracing effect of reality to which economists are subjected when they try to solve practical problems is especially valuable when the conceptual framework of the science is narrow and the scientific interest in widening it is weak.

Nonetheless, a strong orientation toward immediate social problems presents two obstacles to the development of any science. In the first place, the problems tend to abate before their scientific aspects are adequately explored. The patient gets well, or well enough, before the cure is discovered. When the disease recurs, as it usually does, the profession has to start over again, often almost from scratch. Scientific activity thus tends to be repetitive instead of cumulative, because we do not stay long enough with a single topic to break through to new ground.

Aspects of this seem evident, for example, in the case of the Keynesian revolution. Two key ingredients for the multiplier – the distinction between savers and investors and the association of saving with income – appear often in the "business cycle" literature of the nineteenth century, as well as in Keynes's own *Treatise on Money*. Yet it was more the depth and duration of the big depression than the work of earlier economists which led Keynes to the doctrines of the *General Theory*. It is perhaps not too much to suggest that had the profession exhibited a greater interest in economic phenomena for their own sake rather than in terms of their obvious relevance to pressing social problems or their compatibility with received theory, then the multiplier would probably have emerged before it did.

Be that as it may, it is obvious that only chance could assure that the period of public concern with a problem would be at least as long as the gestation period for scientific discovery. Hence, when public concern governs the duration of scientific work, the scientific yield tends to be smaller than would otherwise be the case. In addition, of course, the pressure for immediate results often necessitates the use of "quick and dirty" methods, which further deteriorates the scientific value of the work. Granting that many economists must be deployed in applied work, the scientific residue left by their efforts would be increased if, after the emergency has passed, they undertook as a matter of routine to develop the more general aspects of their work.

The second impediment to scientific progress posed by a preoccupation with applied problems is the lack of any necessary identity between socially urgent problems and scientifically promising ones. Any given phenomenon which gives society trouble is usually a member of a larger class, the other members of which do not. A study of one of the latter may be scientifically more illuminating, and in the end may permit a more effective assult on the troublesome member than would a frontal assault upon it.

Unfortunately, when time seems of the essence, a frontal assault which yields a rough but useful answer is always preferred by policy-makers. In some cases, such preferences are legitimate; that is, when the quick solutions we give are indeed useful, and the problems they ameliorate are indeed serious.

Even in such cases, however, let alone when these criteria are not satisfied, there is a cost, both to our science and to society at large. The cost to our science is obviously slower progress than would have prevailed had the same resources been allocated to scientifically more promising work. The social cost, which follows from the scientific, is our reduced ability to solve future social problems; for to the extent that our future understanding is diminished by past concentration on social problems, our ability to cope with future social problems is likely to be impaired.

In recent decades medical researchers and their sponsors have begun to awaken to this truth, partly no doubt because such major problem areas as cancer have proved too refractory thus far to yield to the half-blind empiricism which characterized so much earlier research. The earlier approach yielded, tardily to be sure, thousands of specifics for individual diseases and eased and prolonged life. Yet perhaps more often than not the reasons why they work or fail are not known. Because the necessary fundamental knowledge was not developed, each disease entity was *sui generis*. The more recent strategy, which emphasizes the development of fundamental knowledge, is, from the standpoint of treatment, a roundabout method of production, but like other roundabout methods it is calculated to enhance the ultimate yield. Because of the greater understanding to which fundamental research leads, the future lag between the commencement of research on a disease and the discovery of a cure should be reduced.

This lesson, which medical scientists have begun to learn, is also one which experience has driven home recently to American engineers who generally had to draw on Europe in the past for advances in engineering theory. We economists, who are just beginning to study the formation of intellectual capital, should not be among the last to recognize that the economies of more roundabout methods of production apply to the production of knowledge as well as to the production of other goods.

As suggested above, however, for that roundabout process to be as productive as possible, it seems essential that the boundaries of the terrain explored reflect not only those established by received theory but also those set by nature, for the gap between these two remains large.

Technological Change and the

Law of Industrial Growth[1]

Not previously published.

While neoclassical economic theory has many important applications, it is poorly related to what really happens in the long run. It suffers from this deficiency mainly because it makes no provision for changes in technological knowledge. Such changes obviously can be taken into account by shifts of the supply curve. Indeed, this is a major use of comparative statics. Yet this is precisely the trouble – technological change has to be introduced into the analysis from the outside. It is assumed, not explained. Thus what is certainly one of the most important determinants of price and output in the long run is entirely outside the range of the theory.

Of course, it can be argued that whether or not economists should account for technological change itself, as distinct from its economic effects, depends on whether technological change is itself substantially influenced by economic variables. To take an analogous case, in order to explain the price of wheat we may need to know the amount of rainfall. Yet under present circumstances one may defensibly contend that it is not an economist's business to *explain* the amount of rainfall. We simply take it as given. This position is logical and often necessary in the short run, but it is seldom satisfactory in the long run. It may be necessary in the short run because economists are not meteorologists. It may be unsatisfactory in the long run because an inability to predict rainfall may subject our predictions of the price of wheat to

[1] The author's research mentioned in this paper is described more extensively in his "Changes in Industry and in the State of Knowledge as Determinants of Industrial Invention," in Richard R. Nelson, ed., *The Rate and Direction of Inventive Activity: Economic and Social Factors* (Princeton, N. J.: Princeton University Press, 1962), 195-232; "Economic Sources of Inventive Activity," *Journal of Economic History*, March 1962, 1-20; his joint paper with O. H. Brownlee, "Determinants of Inventive Activity," *American Economic Review*, May 1962, 165-185; and his joint communication with Zvi Griliches, "Inventing and Maximizing," *American Economic Review*, September 1963, 725-729.

unacceptable ranges of error. Hence, if the matter is sufficiently pressing, the best way to advance the science of economics in the long run may be to advance the science of meteorology.

Whether this means that meteorology should be advanced by economists or by others is an open question. It is relevant, however, to record that the recent notable advances in understanding of biological phenomena have come from physics, and have led to the development of a whole new and exciting field — moelcular biology. The history of science is replete with comparable instances of fusion, although fission seems more common. In general, while the domain of any science seems to be dominated in the short run by its inherited techniques, intellectual and physical, in the long run it seems to be dominated by its underlying subject matter. It is a fair guess that future biologists will be better trained in physics than are their present-day counterparts. And it would not be surprising if agricultural economists learned more than the rest of us about meteorology, even if they make no contributions to it.

What really complicates the issue is not the question of proper strategy in drawing useful boundaries for the economics profession. The real problem will arise when rainfall is converted from an act of nature into an industry. Once that happens, the price of wheat may be one of the indexes used in deciding how much rain we want. If that day comes, regardless of their range of error, pre-existing predictive models for the price of wheat will no longer be satisfactory, for the price of wheat will then help determine rainfall, which will as before help determine supply, which helps determine the price of wheat. What was an exogenous variable determined outside the model will become a partially endogenous one determined partly inside it. Willy-nilly economists will become predictors of the output of rain without becoming meteorologists, as they are predictors of farmers' planting intentions without being agronomists.

Now the question I should like to consider is whether technological change defined as additions to the social stock of industrially useful knowledge is in the same class of phenomena as the weather up to now, influencing economic activity but not influenced by it. Or whether it is like the weather of the hypothetical future just described, both influencing and influenced by economic activity. I am concerned, in short, with the question of whether in the large view of things, technological change is an exogenous variable or an endogenous one.

The answer to this question cannot be all black or all white. Some technological change is accidental, and some of it clearly originates from the efforts of pure scientists — men whose only goal is understanding, but who produce useful knowledge as an unsought by-product. To the extent that it reflects such factors, technological change is clearly exogenous for most purposes. Moreover, it is entirely possible, if not indeed likely, that the relative importance of exogenous technological change has changed over time. Hence, to be more precise, I am concerned with the question of whether technological change has been *primarily* one or the other over the last century or two.

There is an even deeper aspect of this question to which I must at least allude here. A given phenomenon may be exogenous in some of its dimensions and endogenous in others. Hence let me further limit my topic by saying that, because of concentration of my own research in this field, my immediate concern is with the allocation of the amount of inventing among different end-uses — for instance, the distribution of inventive activity at a given point in time among capital goods for different industries — and with variations over time in the amount of inventive activity devoted to a given end-use. Later in the course of my paper I will broaden the topic somewhat.

Much light on these questions is shed by two bodies of data. One consists of over a fifth of all the United States patents ever issued, reclassified on the basis of industry of use. These data cover the period 1837 to 1957 on an annual basis. For the period 1874 to 1950, the patents are counted as of the date of application; for other years, as of the date of grant. The patent data have undoubted defects — those resulting from my own deficiencies as well as those which are inherent in them. But they are the most comprehensive available; the items which comprise them have all passed a rather rigorous examination for novelty administered in accord with what would appear to be a rather stable set of criteria, and they yield interesting results.

The second class of data consists of descriptions of over nine hundred important inventions made anywhere in the world since 1800 in paper making, petroleum refining, farming, and railroading. While these inventions were painstakingly selected from an enormous literature by competent researchers, temporal variations in the proportion of important inventions included are almost certainly considerable.

The behavior of these two classes of data throws much light on the issue of whether inventive activity, and by implication, technological change are or are not independent of economic activity. One theme in modern thought that recurs so often, that is built into the phraseology of the language and indeed is one of the great organizing principles of social thought, is the idea that inventions – at least modern inventions – spring from scientific discovery. This conception of events is reflected, for example, in the very expression, "research and development," and it is embedded in the common belief that the course of modern history has somehow been shaped by scientific discoveries.

With this hypothesis in mind we were interested in ascertaining the events or conditions that stimulated inventors to create the nine hundred and more important inventions in the four industries mentioned above. The literature unfortunately was silent in most cases, but on several hundred cases the record was clear. Sometimes the initiating stimulus was an accident. Usually, however, it was an event or condition conceived by the inventor in economic terms – a felt deficiency in the product or process of one sort or other. In only two or three cases did there seem a bona fide possibility that a scientific discovery provided the immediate stimulus to the making of the invention. The most probable of these was V. N. Ipatieff's work on hydrogenation of petroleum, which came a few years after Paul A. Sabatier's Nobel Prize-winning work on hydrogenation.

Of course, many of these important inventions were *possible* only because certain scientific discoveries preceded them. (Many others, however, owed to science at most a spirit of inquiry and an empirical attitude toward phenomena.) But it seems probable from our analysis – and I think the same conclusion applies to the major twentieth-century inventions turned up by Jewkes, Sawers, and Stillerman – that major inventions are made normally because particular economic problems have become more pressing or economic opportunities have become more inviting, and not because some scientific finding suddenly pushed them over the horizon.

We also tried to check the commonly held related idea that inventive activity in a field generally flows as major inventions create new possibilities, and ebbs when major inventions decline. Again, the question is not whether these major inventions are necessary for the minor ones which imitate, modify, adapt, and supplement them. That this is so goes without saying. What we were interested in rather is the validity of the proposition that inventive activity in a field is primarily a routine, direct response to the major inventions in the field. Let me first note that inventive activity in any pair of competing fields — say metal buildings and wooden buildings, or leather nailing and leather sewing — tends to be synchronized over the short run. This short-run synchronization of competitive fields obviously suggests that common external forces dominate their course.

Secondly, it is noteworthy that major inventions, on the whole, fluctuate with inventive activity in their fields. This being so, they can hardly be classed as prime determinants of invention in their fields. There are some interesting qualifications to this conclusion, the most important being that the major inventions which create a field seem to be a relatively larger component of total inventive activity in that field at the outset. Even this may be an optical illusion resulting from the natural bias of the chroniclers of the growth of an industry's technology toward recording industry-establishing inventions while ignoring inventions of equal economic magnitude which came later.

I am not trying to say that scientific discovery is without influence on inventive activity. Certainly for well-educated inventors (it is surprising how many are not) received science sets the conceptual framework in one dimension, and such men undoubtedly file news of interesting discoveries for future reference. Moreover, whole fields, like chemistry and electricity, owe their start to scientific discoveries. However, it is important to recognize that fields such as these, unlike food, clothing, and shelter, are essentially not consumer-goods fields — although they occasionally produce substitutes for older consumer products. Chemistry, electricity, and analogous fields are largely intermediate goods in the realm of knowledge classified economically, and I suspect that the intensity with which they are cultivated at any given time is proportional to their prospective contributions, insofar as these can be anticipated, toward the satisfaction of private and public wants.

The foregoing brings me to the positive side of our findings. Broadly speaking, our results indicate that inventive activity in a field tends very much to fluctuate with economic activity in that field.

Originally it appeared that total inventive activity in the United States varied directly with economy-wide employment of labor and capital combined. This result supported the hypothesis that the potential saving in total cost constituted the source of prospective profit from inventing, that such potential saving would tend to be proportional to total cost of production, and that therefore inventive activity would tend to vary with the total cost, that is, the volume of resources employed.[2] This chain of reasoning later proved mistaken. Measures of the two were indeed highly correlated but they were equally correlated with a third variable — gross investment — and this now appears to have been the critical factor.

This error was revealed once the statistics of patents classified by industry were available and patents in the railroad field were compared with an index of total output in the railroad industry. No similarity such as that which had appeared earlier in the case of aggregate inventive activity and total national output emerged.[3] Instead we found that railroad investment and railroad patents were very similar in their long-run and shorter-run movements. The main difference between them, and a very suggestive difference it was, was that the patent statistics lagged slightly behind those of investment.

Not unexpectedly, a similar moving average of railroad stock prices adjusted for changes in the general level of wholesale prices was also substantially synchronized with investment and invention, with stock prices tending to lead the other two. These general relationships definitely hold in the long run, with railroad stock prices and railroad patents rising to all-time peaks in 1908 and investment in 1911. The relations hold with comparable clarity over Kuznets cycles — cycles of about fifteen to twenty years in duration. On a year-to-year basis they are not so evident.

Since this initial discovery we have checked for the existence of a similar relation between investment and invention in capital-goods fields in a wide variety of industries. Wherever the economic data existed to compare with the capital-goods patent series, that relation has been found. That is, the ebb and flow of investment, or something associated with it, seems to induce a corresponding ebb and flow of inventive activity directed toward improving the capital goods.

[2] See also Schmookler's "The Level of Inventive Activity," *Review of Economics and Statistics*, May 1954, 183-190.

[3] The first draft of Schmookler's paper had the following passage at this point: "Since the project had cost me about two years of work and my sponsors several thousands of dollars, I was, to say the least, disconcerted. A few weeks later I chanced upon a graph of a five-year moving average of *railroad investment* in an NBER Occasional Paper by Melville J. Ulmer. The shock of recognition was an experience which comes only infrequently in the life of a social scientist. I knew I had seen that graph before, but under a different name. The graph reminded me very much of a seven-year moving average of railroad patents that I had plotted several weeks before. Actual comparison proved my memory had not tricked me."

Moreover, when we shifted from intertemporal comparisons within an industry to cross-section comparisons involving several industries at the same time, the same relation was observed. Just as more inventive activity is devoted to improving an industry's equipment when more of that equipment is being produced, so more inventive activity is devoted toward improving capital goods in those industries which are buying more equipment. For example, when 1939 investment per worker is correlated with capital-goods patents per worker in 1940 to 1942, the simple coefficient of determination, r^2, is about 0.6.

Finally, it was possible to compare the course of output of railroad freight cars, passenger cars, locomotives, and rails with patents in each of those fields from about 1860 or 1870 to about 1950. In every case the respective long-term patterns and major cycles were similar, and in some instances even the year-to-year movements were remarkably alike.

I think it is fair to say that these results are the complete reverse of a priori expectations, for most of us would have expected investment to follow inventive activity, not lead it. These common expectations are traceable to a long, honored, and active tradition going back even beyond Schumpeter's *Theory of Economic Development* and forward even more recently than Salter's *Productivity and Technical Change*. The most recent development along this line consists of correlations between rates of industrial growth and R&D expenditures as a percent of sales, with the obvious and, I think, erroneous inference commonly drawn that the observed high positive correlation between the two variables implies that some industries grow faster than others because they do relatively more R&D. The fundamental interpretation of such correlations, I think, is simply that R&D is more profitable in industries with a greater growth potential, and that the ranking of industries with respect to growth rates over the last few decades would not have been much different if there had been no technological progress whatever – although the growth rates of some would have been lower and others higher.

In other words, while invention does affect investment and the rate of growth of an industry, and may affect them deeply, such effects are not the only important feature of the connection between invention on the one hand and investment and growth on the other. This must be true, given the timing relations among the variables disclosed in the research I have summarized above.

The significant question is what is implied by the fact that inventive activity in a capital-goods field tends to vary directly with the output of the capital goods concerned. I think the best guess is that invention in a field is likely to be more profitable when the class of goods it pertains to is selling, or is expected to sell well; and that when invention is more profitable, more of it is done. The implication of this for the underlying question of this paper is obvious. Whatever it may legitimately be in the framework of some other discipline, from the standpoint of economics invention is mainly an economic activity. As in other economic activities, resources tend to be allocated among its branches, and probably between it and other classes of economic activity, in accord with profit expectations of net return.

Probably there are also other factors, likewise economic in nature, that contribute to the empirical results observed. Specifically, the funds available for support of inventive activity in a given field, the manpower available to carry it out, and the amount of attention focused on the field are all likely to be positively associated with the amount of economic activity in the field itself. But the dominant influence on the amount of inventing in a field seems to be the income expected from it.

Against this background let us turn next to the Law of Industrial Growth. The law is essentially a generalization, based on observation, which holds that the trend curve of output of any industry, when plotted on an arithmetic scale, tends to describe an S-shaped pattern. The percentage rate of growth generally declines with time. I should like to examine the adequacy of the dominant current explanation for this characteristic pattern — in particular, the role which technological change [plays in it].

[Editors' note: The manuscript in our hands breaks off at this point. What follows are two fragments that seem to be related to what should have been the conclusion of this paper. The first dates from a later period (1967) and seems to be related to an attempt to work further on this topic, already staked out in Chapter 5 and page 204 of *Invention and Economic Growth*, where the decline in the price elasticity of demand was to be the principal explanatory force of the S-shaped pattern of industrial growth. The second fragment appears to be a draft of the conclusion to the above, or a similar, paper.]

Over three decades ago Professor Kuznets published the classic analysis of the Law of Industrial Growth — the tendency for the output of any given good to describe an S-shaped course over time, with the percentage rate of growth generally declining throughout.[4] The pattern, he concluded, was primarily a reflection of retardation in the rate of technical progress in the industry as revealed by the downward sweep at a declining rate of the product's price over time. The retardation in the rate of technical progress in turn was explained by the gradual exhaustion of the industry's inventive potential, or stating the matter in other terms, the approach to perfection of the industry's technique.

More recently, W. E. G. Salter has re-presented substantially the same thesis.[5]

The evidence referred to above suggests that these analyses largely reversed cause and effect: the rate of growth of an industry has probably a greater effect on the rate of growth of the technology associated with it than the other way round. (At least this is so unless further research reveals an exceedingly perverse variation in the economic quality of the inventions made in an industry at different times.) For what Kuznets took to be evidence that an industry's inventive potential was being played out – the decline in the number of inventions made in it – now distinctly appears to be a consequence of a decline in the market for inventions, which is a corollary of declining investment in the field. This interpretation seems indisputable in the face of the marked tendency for investment to lead invention on capital goods in any given industry.

If this is correct, then we need a new explanation in place of the old. In the next few paragraphs, I should like to sketch some of the problems and possibilities presented by this situation. The facts to be explained appear to be approximately as follows: (a) output of a given good increases over time at a declining percentage rate; (b) accompanying the changing level of output is a path of product price which falls and then rises when measured in terms of the general level of commodity prices; (c) the value of the total product first rises and then falls; and (d) the effort expended in improving the industry's technology first increases and then decreases.

Kuznets and Salter assumed that (d) essentially reflected the richness of technological potential of the industry at the beginning when the field first opened up, and its subsequent gradual exhaustion as it was

[4] Simon Kuznets, *Secular Movements in Production and Prices* (Boston and New York: Houghton Mifflin, 1930).

[5] W. E. G. Salter, *Productivity and Technical Change*, University of Cambridge, Department of Applied Economics, Monograph No. 6 (Cambridge, England: University Press, 1960).

worked. The initial rise in technological effort they interpret, at least by implication, as the inflow of lesser creative talent induced by the basic discoveries and inventions which opened up the area, for the number of major inventions in a field tends to decline virtually from the start. The subsequent diminution in technological effort they interpreted mainly as a response to the hypothesized field's approach to perfection, or, what amounts to the same thing, the gradual exhaustion of its technological potential.[6]

The general line of causality implied by Kuznets-Salter is that the product's relative price declines when its technique improves at an above-average rate but later rises when it improves at a below-average rate. Then, for example, if the price elasticity of demand is [declining] and we ignore the effects of changes in income, relative prices, and population, the declining magnitude of relative price changes will result in a declining rate of increase in output. By the same token, if at a moment of time the price elasticity of demand for different products is the same, then young industries with rapid rates of technological and therefore technical progress and therefore greater percentage price cuts occurring in them will have faster rates of growth in output than will older industries.

The fact that the amount of invention on capital goods tends to be distributed among the capital goods of different industries in proportion to the amount of investment going on in each, and the related fact that the temporal variations in the amount of invention on the capital goods of a given industry tends to vary directly with but lag slightly behind the amount of investment in the industry, cast an entirely new light on the problem. If we assume, as seems reasonable, that some form of the acceleration principle governs the rate of investment in an industry, then the line of causality seems to run from the industry's rate of growth to its rate of investment to its rate of technological progress to price changes and back to rate of growth of output.

This in itself does not vitiate the Kuznets-Salter hypothesis, since it could still be true that the field's technological potential declines as it

---

[6] The first draft of Schmookler's paper had the following passage at this point: "Perhaps a field's potential does become exhausted. Certainly, to prove it does not require one to disprove a negative, that is, to prove that while more inventions were not made in a field in a given period, more could have been; such a proof would be extremely difficult to provide. (But not necessarily impossible: one would have to show that later inventions were intellectually feasible earlier.) The question is whether this assumption is necessary, or whether a more plausible explanation can be developed."

is cultivated. What is more, Kuznets and Salter are entirely in the right in imputing the shifts in supply primarily to technical changes which permit production to proceed at lower and lower costs. What our evidence suggests, however, is that the shifts in the supply curves are largely induced by those in the demand curves.

The law, of course, has by now an ancient lineage since it was first enunciated in the early twenties. It received its most sophisticated exposition by Kuznets in his classic *Secular Movements in Production and Prices*. The central part of the explanation for the observed pattern proferred by Kuznets was that once an industry was established, the opportunities for improving the product and the method of producing it became exhausted as more improvements were made. The consequence was continuous retardation in the long-run percentage rate of growth, a consequence perhaps hastened by tendencies for demand to become inelastic, for resource increments to press ever more strongly against alternative resource uses, for the development of rival products, and perhaps for resources to become depleted. While the advent of the industry itself was unexplained, its subsequent rate of growth was thus assumed to be dominated by the extent to which the industry's inventive potential was depleted by earlier inventions.

Stating the traditional view in other terms, if the root idea of the industry's technology is interpreted as a fixed factor, successive doses of inventive effort are subject to the law of diminishing marginal returns, returns being measured, say, in terms of percentage cuts in production cost per unit of output. The occurrence of the root idea was ostensibly an extraeconomic event, determining the appearance of the industry, while the rate at which diminishing returns to inventive effort set in determined the industry's rate of growth.

This conception of social processes obviously had an enormous appeal, as did Schumpeter's *Theory of Economic Development* and his *Business Cycles*, which were written in the same spirit. These works may be accurately characterized for the present purpose as postulating the appearance of new industries and deducing the putative economic consequences thereof. The appeal of these works arose more from their consistency with prevailing modes of thinking about economic phenomena than from any demonstrated explanatory power. Schumpeter suggested how the continual appearance of new industries might affect the state of business at large, while Kuznets described how an industry's own rate of growth would decline as its inventive potential became exhausted. Both had in common the salient feature that technological change was a cause of economic phenomena, not a result. In this both men followed the neoclassical tradition of regarding technological change — that is, the growth of technical knowledge — as exogenous, something for economists to assume, not explain.

The result was that in seeking to explain the Law of Industrial Growth in neoclassical terms, they would merely postulate the creation of the industry at some point in time (if one followed Schumpeter, the point would be an equilibrium neighborhood following recovery) and then a series of successively shorter shifts (in percentage terms) of the static long-run supply curve. While one might add the twist that demand likewise increased as consumers' understanding of the product improved and their income rose, this was clearly a response to innovation, not a cause of it. Thus, precisely in the style of neoclassical economics which they sought to counterpoise, these great heterodox economists made technological change an exogenous variable — a variable which explained economic events but was unexplained by them.

Now our research demonstrates beyond a shadow of doubt, although common knowledge of the contemporary world of corporate R & D should make such a demonstration unnecessary, that the *effort* applied to advance technology in an established industry is economically determined. We have not shown that this is equally true of the amount of *the advance actually achieved*, nor have we shown that it is true of the appearance of entirely new technologies. Certainly, at a minimum, both of these variables are affected by seemingly noneconomic influences — discoveries in pure science particularly, and both are subject to a larger random element than is the amount of inventive effort itself. Still, as Mansfield has shown, there is probably a substantial correlation between the effort expended and the results achieved, and the volume of general scientific research in modern times is demonstrably related to the expected value of anticipated results.[7] Moreover, most new industrial technologies are found because they are sought.[8] They almost never emerge full-blown as by-products of some purely scientific undertaking.

[7] Edwin Mansfield, "Rates of Return from Industrial Research and Development," *American Economic Review*, May 1965, 310-322.

[8] See Schmookler's previous paper in this volume.

If these assumptions be granted, we can leap from the evidence that inventive activity in investment goods is economically determined to the conjecture that the amount of technological advance in any direction is economically determined in more or less the same way that the output of any good is determined.

Loosely speaking, this implies that new consumer goods and cost-cutting methods tend to be invented when inventing them promises to be profitable. Moreover, while the accumulation of new knowledge often makes it possible to satisfy at one point in time wants long unmet, the marked tendency noted above of inventive activity to follow demand suggests that within the limits set by the state of knowledge, wants tend to be satisfied one way or another to some extent when they arise, and to be satisfied better when they become more intense.

In other words, I am suggesting that technological knowledge grows primarily in directions determined by man's wants. From the standpoint of analytical significance, the key event behind the appearance of a new product therefore may often be not the invention of the product itself but the growth of the potential demand for it. The most important characteristic of the S-shaped growth curve in such cases is the time when the asymptote which the curve of sales tends to approach rises above the level at which a critical mass of inventive effort begins to seem economically worthwhile. It is, in short, in these cases not the technical possibility of an industry which accounts for its appearance but the growth of the market potential.

This changed market potential, in the case of consumer goods, may take its provenance from any event or condition which changes men's tastes – a rising level of income, a more urban character of life, a change in the constellation of goods consumed, a shift in age, sex, geographic or occupational distribution, a change in morals or in our apprehension of our relation to nature or our duties, or whatnot. The recognition of this potential demand by one or more perceptive and inventive men is the next requirement, a requirement which may or may not be fulfilled. If it is and if the state of knowledge is adequate, the product will probably be invented and the industry created. The industry will then grow toward its market potential. As a first approximation, one may say that once the foundations are laid the industry's rate of growth to maturity tends to be proportional to the difference between its existing level and the market potential; for following Fechner's law, the response is proportional to the stimulus – in this case, prospective profits – and the latter tend to be proportional to the difference between the actual and potential level.

Now the crucial difference between this view of industrial growth and the traditional one is in the active role assigned to demand. In the traditional view, the demand for the product plays no explicit role whatever. One is free to imagine either that the demand was always there, waiting to be awakened by the inventor, or that it was created miraculously when the invention was made. In any case, once the product has been invented, according to this view, it is, in terms of product improvement and cost reduction, the product's own inventive potential which establishes the upper limit to the industry's growth. Thus the market potential presumably is created by the product. It reflects the effects on demand of changed availability and prices of goods, with tastes unchanged.

While there are undoubtedly cases, some very important, in which the potential demand existed long before the product, they are relatively infrequent. Economists have never systematically studied tastes, but it is hard to believe they do not change. Such changes, once felt, trigger inventive activity on the part of those who are especially perceptive and more gifted than others in sensing these changes.

Outside the traditional economic [sphere], these patterns are obvious. The history of medical research is a history of successive shifts of attention from one set of diseases to another, with the primary focus of attention generally on diseases which are nonfatal or otherwise of pressing interest. As any given disease is eliminated or at least [alleviated], another necessarily takes its place as a principal cause of death or sickness and research activity tends to shift accordingly. Of course, it is the felt significance of the diseases involved that is important, not their objective measurements (though those are generally well correlated). Thus Franklin Roosevelt's affliction dramatized polio, while the Kennedy family's interest dramatized mental retardation. Likewise, some diseases to which moral opprobrium attaches, venereal diseases, as an example, for a long time received less attention than otherwise would have been the case. In any event, the significant point for our purposes is the inevitability of the succession of foci of research – an inevitability which flows from man's mortality.

Similarly, in the military field, the perpetual battle between defense and offense continually shapes the direction of research in ways too well known to warrant elaboration.

These disparate examples drawn from the medical and military arts illustrate what would appear to be a fundamental trait of man, or at least man in Western civilization. We seek solutions to problems only to find that the solution itself creates new problems. Economists recognized this obliquely by postulating the inexhaustibility of human wants, but I think this postulate is plausible only if we recognize that men create new wants as old ones are satisfied. The Buddhists recognized the phenomenon more truly, I feel, when they held that no amount of material resources would yield true contentment and urged instead a renunciation of desire as the only road to what one might call a stationary state of bliss.

These deep philosophical notions aside, what we confront, I think, is a serious possibility that the prevailing view of the role of scientific and technological progress in social and economic development is wrong. That view holds that scientific and technological progress is the primary determinant of social and economic change. From a narrow and therefore incorrect standpoint, the view has merit. In any case, it provides a useful point of departure for the analysis of certain important classes of problems. From an analytical standpoint the difficulty with it is its [ad hoc] nature: it may leave scientific and technological progress unexplained, which is unsatisfactory; alternatively, it explains scientific and technological progress as self generated, which is dreadfully wrong. Such a view is wrong both scientifically and morally. It is wrong scientifically because, as argued above, it is simply not true. It is wrong morally not only because it is false, but also because it deprives men generally of any sense of responsibility for the course of social and economic development. For if the changing character of man's wants tends to govern the growth of knowledge, then all men must accept some measure of responsibility for what happens next.

Part II   Patent Statistics

Editors' Note on Sources

and Methods

The remainder of this volume contains the time series of patent statistics assembled by Jacob Schmookler, together with the industrial groupings of the Patent Office classes and subclasses underlying these time series.

The basic entry in the tables is the number of patents in a given year within a specified industrial commodity grouping. Below we reproduce a section of Schmookler's previous book *Invention and Economic Growth* (1966), which is particularly valuable in describing the origin and content of these series. Because of the importance of various details, we also provide very explicit explanations of the sources of these data and of the principles of their classification.

These explanations are based on several sources: our own reading of the passage from *Invention* and of the appendix to Schmookler's 1962 paper "Changes in Industry and in the State of Knowledge as Determinants of Industrial Invention"; Schmookler's correspondence (in particular his letter of October 24, 1966 to Professor Robert Baldwin, University of Wisconsin); and our communications with his former collaborators.

For a major part of the period covered, 1874 to 1950, the patents are counted as of the date of application. However, the tables give also for the overlapping periods 1837 to 1876 and 1947 to 1957 data on a when-issued basis. (This is stated in the above-cited letter to Baldwin. The comments in *Invention* are consistent with the above except for silence with regard to the 1951 to 1957 series.)

According to Schmookler's letter to Baldwin, "For the period 1837 to 1957 as a whole, the statistics cover about 20% of all patents issued, with coverage amounting to about 35% in the 19th century and about 15% in the 20th." Schmookler adds: "I sought the maximum number of industries given the number of patents I could afford to cover."

THE DATA

The following is a reproduction of Section 2, Chapter 2, pages 20 to 23 of Schmookler's *Invention and Economic Growth,* entitled there "The Data for the Present Study."

Statistics of patents classified into about two dozen industries, some of them since 1837, constitute the prime data to be used. They were prepared from Patent Office records with the advice of the appropriate Principal Examiner of the Office. Industries were included for which coverage promised to be reasonably comprehensive and cheap, and for which comparable economic data existed.

Inventions create new capital goods, materials, or consumer goods, or methods of making them that are not embodied in new goods. Their analysis may focus either on the industry expected to make or the industry expected to use them. Reasonably comprehensive statistics could be prepared only on capital goods inventions classified according to the industry expected to use them, and these data yielded our most important results. . . .

The basic procedure was to assign Patent Office subclasses to individual industries as defined in the *Standard Industrial Classification Manual.*[3] The subclass is the elementary unit of the Patent Office's system of classification. Designed to expedite the search of the prior art, this system is based primarily on technological-functional rather than on industrial principles.[4] Hence, converting from the Patent Office classification to the industrial classification for use in this study required a year of work in the search room of the Patent Office.

Using the subclass made the undertaking manageable. There were, at the time, only about fifty thousand subclasses, allocated to about three hundred main classes, compared to nearly three million patents. To have used the individual patent as the initial unit of investigation would have required far more resources than were available. The average subclass in 1957, when the initial work was done, had slightly more than fifty patents in it. When the subclass definition clearly indicated that nearly all the inventions in it would be made or used (if at all) by a single industry, the entire subclass was assigned to that industry. When, as was usually the case, the definition alone left the matter unsettled, the patents in the subclass were sampled directly. If the sampling indicated that at least two-thirds of the patents belonged to a given industry, the whole subclass was assigned to it.

Within industries subclasses were grouped into economically meaningful categories, sometimes with technological subcategories. Since each patent number is associated with a given date of issue, the Patent Office was able to count by machine the number of patents granted annually from 1836 to 1957 in each

---

[3] Vol. I, Part I (November 1945) and Vol. II (May 1949), Executive Office of the President, Bureau of the Budget.

[4] Some insight into the distinction between an industrial and a technological-functional classification of inventions may be gained from two examples: Within a main class which deals with dispensing liquids is a subclass containing, among other things, a patent for a holy water dispenser. Another patent in the same subclass is for a water pistol. Again, in a subclass within a main class covering the dispensing of solids, one patent was on a manure spreader; another, on a toothpaste tube.

category and industry. Preliminary analysis of these time series, however, indicated that important substantive issues would remain unclarified, because significant intertemporal and interindustry variations exist in the interval between the filing of an application and the granting of a patent. Accordingly, the data were converted from a *when-granted* to a *when-applied-for* basis beginning with 1874, by finding the date of application for each patent as given in the *Patent Office Gazette*,[5] and producing time series on the new basis. In consequence of this transformation, all the data used here — except those for glass, tobacco products, and shoe-making[6] — beginning with 1874 are for patents counted when the application was filed. (Prior to 1874 the average interval between application and grant was only about six months. Hence splicing the pre- and the post-1874 data creates no serious problems.)

The substance underlying the data will be more readily understood if we bear in mind the fact that, in most cases, the inventive activity reflected by a patent application *began* about a year or two before the application was filed. This estimate is based on several considerations. For independent inventors the mean duration from conception of the original invention to reduction to patentable form is about twenty months; for captive inventors, about nine months.[7] Because the distribution is skewed, the median and modal values are lower. On the other hand, patent attorneys customarily need a few months to have a search of the literature made to determine the advisability of filing and to prepare the application, and the inventions of captive inventors are frequently tested commercially prior to filing.

One deficiency of the data is that an undetermined number of the patents relating to the industries are omitted. This deficiency arises partly from the use of the subclass rather than the individual patent in finding the items to be included. Such omissions probably were not appreciable for any industry, though there may be significant interindustry and intertemporal differences in their proportion. Another form of the same general deficiency arose from the fact that I could not assign many inventions to a single industry. In part this resulted from my own ignorance, but often it reflected the interindustry character of technology. Thus, a given improvement in the diesel engine may be used in generating electricity or driving a locomotive, a given bearing may be used in a shoemaking machine or a lawn mower, and a given knife may be used in harvesting or in kitchens. In consequence, the patent statistics used below generally do not include power plant inventions, electric motors, bearings, or other instruments or materials whose industry of use or origin was either multiple or simply not evident. Unfortunately, this means that the railroad data do not include inventions in the field of the steam or diesel engines, and that neither the farm nor the construction data include inventions on tractors.

---

[5] When more than one application date was given, the earliest date was chosen.

[6] The data for the three excepted industries were prepared before the main project, and it was not feasible to convert them from a when-granted basis. When patent statistics for these three industries are used below, numbers are shifted back in time to the years when the patents were presumably applied for.

[7] Barkev S. Sanders, "Some Difficulties in Measuring Inventive Activity," in R. R. Nelson, ed., *The Rate and Direction of Inventive Activity*, p. 71.

On the other hand, despite the fact that subclasses were included so long as at least two-thirds of the patents pertained to the industry, probably 95 percent of the inventions actually included in the series belong to the industries to which they are assigned. Thus, while the series are in some measure incomplete, they are relatively pure.

GROUPING CRITERIA

The principles of classification underlying Schmookler's patent statistics time series are discussed in the above-quoted passage and also in the appendix to his "Changes in Industry and in the State of Knowledge as Determinants of Industrial Invention" (1962). To provide time series meaningful for his purposes, Schmookler had to group these patents according to industries. Since, as he said in his article, "one industry may inspire the invention, another manufacture it, and a third use it," there arises the problem of choosing the criteria for assigning a given invention to a particular industry. In the 1962 study, Schmookler stated that inventions were to be assigned to the current main producing or using industry. Where both the producing and using industries were included in the study, the invention was assigned to both. Inventions with significant multiple-industry applications, such as bearings, motors, and engines were excluded.

As for *Invention and Economic Growth* (as well as the statistics in the present volume), the prospective *use* seems to have been the chief criterion. Thus, on page 20 we read: "Reasonably comprehensive statistics could be prepared only on capital goods inventions classified according to the industry expected to use them, and these data yielded our most important results." This is corroborated by the following excerpt from Schmookler's 1966 letter to Professor Baldwin: "Generally speaking, inventions are classified according to the using rather than the making industry, but there are exceptions that are obvious on the face (and a few that aren't but that are minor)." Silos constitute one such exception; they are listed both under agriculture (series 19) and under construction (series 94).

Ideally, Schmookler would have examined each of the nearly three million patents and allocated each to an appropriate prospective user (and/or producer) industry group. This, of course, was impossible. On the other hand, the Patent Office classification was based, as he put it, on technological-functional rather than on industrial principles and was therefore unsuitable for Schmookler's purposes. A compromise solution was to adopt as the basic unit of classification a *subclass* of the Patent Office classification (containing about fifty patents on the average) and to allocate the subclass to prospective user industries. The decision as to user industry to which to allocate a given subclass was made in one of two ways: on the basis of the definition of the subclass, or – if the definition was inconclusive – on the basis of direct sampling of patents in the subclass.

The subclass definition was used as the basis for allocation when it indicated that nearly all the inventions in it pertained to a single industry. Actually, Schmookler says: "When the subclass definition clearly indicated that nearly all the inventions in it would be made or used (if at all) by a single industry, the entire subclass was assigned to that industry." In the light of the earlier comments, it would seem that use (rather than production) would be more typically the criterion.

When the subclass definition was inconclusive, the patents in the subclass were sampled directly and "if the sampling indicated that at least two-thirds of the patents belonged to a given industry, the whole subclass was assigned to it." Presumably, the term "sampling" is to be taken literally, that is, Schmookler examined a randomly selected subset of patents in a subclass, checked whether in that sample at least two-thirds of the patents qualified for a given industry, and allocated the whole subclass on the basis of the evidence from the sample.

The difficulties of decision-making in allocating subclasses, or even individual patents, to industries are stressed by Schmookler in his letter to Baldwin: "Conceivably, you might yourself want to work up a sample of the original data. In that event you will quickly discover that many inventions are usable by several industries, each invention in its own peculiar proportions with its own peculiar industry mix. What is worse, the relevant industries are seldom obvious on the face. Possibly correspondence with the patentee, providing him with the list of industries you are interested in, might be a reasonable way of solving the classification problem."

INDUSTRY GROUPINGS

The industrial categories used by Schmookler in grouping the subclasses were the individual industries defined by the Standard Industrial Classification Manual, as published in 1945 and 1949. The inventions dealt with involve primarily capital goods relevant to the prospective user industries. Listed further on are the major industrial categories subdivided into activity types and their corresponding series numbers.

The *industrial categories* for which time series are constructed are:

> Agriculture
> Construction
> ....

However, the time series are given for groupings that are much finer than the broad industrial categories. For instance, the industry category Agriculture is subdivided according to what one may call *activity types,* such as:

> Earth Preparation and Planting
> Harvesting
> Livestock and Miscellaneous Agriculture
>
> ....

In turn, the time series themselves constitute *commodity groups*[1] within these activity types. Thus, activity type Earth Preparation and Planting contains the following time series:

> 1. Harrows and Diggers
> 2. Plows
> 3. Planting
> 4. Manure Spreaders
> 5. Total Earth Preparation and Planting
>   (the sum of time series 1 through 4)
> 6. Fruit Harvesters and Orchard Plows

(It will be noted that the heading for time series 5 is the same as for the activity type which includes time series 1 to 6. However, the total in 5 does not include commodity group 6, probably because 6 partly qualifies under Harvesting. Other such "semi-inclusive" totals appear elsewhere in the series.)

Schmookler does not formally group according to industrial categories, although he refers to them in a general way. For example, in

---

[1] The names of these commodity groups are not given in the listing, although the corresponding numbers are given. The full commodity group names are to be found in the Industrial Classification of Patent Office Subclasses.

the quote from *Invention,* he says that patent statistics are "classified into about two dozen industries." His major headings correspond to a combination of what we have called industrial categories and activity types and are given by him as follows:

> Agriculture – Earth Preparation and Planting
> Agriculture – Harvesting
> Agriculture – Livestock and Miscellaneous Agriculture
>
> . . . .
> Construction – General
> Construction – General: Masonry and Concrete Structures
>
> . . . .

The only numbering provided by Schmookler is for what we have called *commodity groups,* such as Harrows and Diggers; Plows; Planting. These commodity groups (and hence the time series themselves) are numbered consecutively with a single numbering system for all industrial categories and activity types. Thus, the first product group under Agriculture – Harvesting, which is Harvesters – Cutting, has the order number 7, because it comes after the six commodity groups under Agriculture – Earth Preparation and Planting. The total number of time series (commodity groups) is 458, the last of which is the product group labeled: "458. Glass Container Related: Bottle and Jar Caps and Other Closures," grouped by Schmookler under the industry-activity heading "Special Series – Glass."

INDUSTRIAL CLASSIFICATION

The relation between the Patent Office subclasses and Schmookler's commodity group (time series) number is shown in the Industrial Classification of Patent Office Subclasses which follows the time series. In column 1 is given the commodity group (time series) number and title, for example, 2. Plows (under the major heading Agriculture – Earth Preparation and Planting). Columns 2 and 3 indicate the composition of these commodity groups in terms of Patent Office subclasses. Since the Patent Office groups subclasses according to its classes, the classification specifies both the Patent Office class title (column 2) and Patent Office subclass (column 3). Thus, Schmookler's commodity group (time series) "2. Plows" is drawn from the following Patent Office categories:

> Class 22 (Metal Founding): subclasses 175 and 176 (plow chills and plow vent chills)
> Class 29 (Metal Working): subclass 14 (making plow and cultivator irons)
>
> . . . .
>
> Class 97 (Plows): subclasses 1-10,24-47,91, . . . , 233-245 (plows, cultivators, . . . , control and adjustment devices, . . . , sharpeners, etc. Excluded are cotton chopper type plows and orchard cultivators.)

. . . .

It will be noted that verbal descriptions, as well as class and subclass titles and numbers, are given.

The Industrial Classification was prepared by Schmookler with the help of James Rosse, then a graduate student at the University of Minnesota, now on the faculty of Stanford University. We have printed it from what appears to be the most up-to-date typed version found among Schmookler's papers. The few minor corrections made are based on correspondence between Schmookler and Rosse. (A mimeograph stencil, referred to in Schmookler's correspondence, has not been found.)

Major Industrial Categories

Covered in Time Series[1]

	Time Series No.
Agriculture	
Earth preparation and planting	1–6
Harvesting	7–19
Livestock and miscellaneous agriculture	20–30
Animal power	31–44
Animal trapping and destroying (insecticides and related)	45–49
Fences and gates	50–59
Greenhouses, nursery equipment, gardening	60–61
Cotton Ginning and Compressing	62–63
Veterinary Medicine	64
Hunting and Trapping	65–69
Construction	
Excavating	70–75
Masonry and concrete structures	76–82
Other general	83–86
Building	87–105
Highway and street	106–112
Hydraulic and earth engineering	113–119
Sewage	120
Heating systems	121
Wood buildings and other wood products	123
Total	122
Railroads	
Rolling stock	124–150
Track	151–155
Switches and signals	156–165
Other and total	166–170

[1] The industry names are given here in somewhat abbreviated and edited form. For a complete description see the Industrial Classification of Patent Office Subclasses.

Time Series of Patents Classified by

Industry, United States, 1837 to 1957

The data contained herein were compiled in connection with research supported by the National Science Foundation, the John Simon Guggenheim Foundation, the University of Minnesota, and Michigan State University.

The first time series, from 1837 to 1876, and the last, from 1947 to 1957, count patents granted as of the year of issuance. The second series, from 1874 to 1950, counts patents granted as of the year of application. Each time series continues from right- to left-hand page, with column numbers repeated on the right-hand page for ease of reference.

Patent Office subclasses covered by each series are indicated in the next section of the book.

Agriculture: Earth Preparation and Planting

Year	Harrows & Diggers (1)	Plows (2)	Planting (3)	Manure Spreaders (4)	Total 1–4 (5)	Fruit Harvesters & Orchard Plows (6)
1837	–	8	–	–	8	–
1838	–	11	3	–	14	–
1839	1	9	4	–	14	–
1840	–	6	7	–	13	–
1841	–	6	5	–	11	–
1842	–	17	1	–	18	–
1843	–	15	2	–	17	–
1844	2	13	4	–	19	1
1845	–	13	2	–	15	–
1846	–	14	2	–	16	1
1847	1	11	1	–	13	1
1848	1	18	5	–	24	–
1849	–	27	12	–	39	–
1850	1	20	14	–	35	–
1851	–	8	7	–	15	–
1852	1	17	12	–	30	–
1853	3	17	14	1	35	–
1854	5	26	17	–	48	1
1855	5	26	28	–	59	–
1856	2	30	24	–	56	–
1857	5	74	56	–	135	2
1858	7	80	64	–	151	–
1859	9	106	79	–	194	–
1860	17	189	95	–	301	2
1861	10	116	47	–	173	4
1862	13	76	24	–	113	3
1863	6	77	31	–	114	1
1864	6	94	38	–	138	1
1865	13	166	50	1	230	5
1866	29	256	82	–	367	16
1867	42	378	137	1	558	18
1868	54	363	122	–	539	17
1869	83	425	156	–	664	8
1870	48	321	140	1	510	2
1871	51	267	102	–	420	5
1872	43	242	63	1	349	10
1873	38	236	78	–	352	4
1874	51	242	78	2	373	6
1875	63	229	74	1	367	8
1876	64	319	111	2	496	6
1874	54	242	74	2	372	5
1875	68	234	91	1	394	7
1876	69	317	109	2	497	8
1877	82	281	123	1	487	10
1878	65	308	112	–	485	12
1879	71	250	111	–	432	6
1880	76	265	109	1	451	8
1881	73	278	123	3	477	6
1882	119	341	168	3	631	6
1883	95	337	172	4	608	10
1884	121	352	178	3	654	10
1885	109	331	160	1	601	11
1886	126	308	141	3	578	16
1887	100	298	147	4	549	8
1888	100	272	107	1	480	10
1889	85	293	120	1	499	24
1890	92	271	141	4	509	15
1891	84	317	110	–	511	17
1892	94	277	109	2	482	14
1893	60	207	109	–	376	13
1894	60	216	89	3	368	13

Year	(1)	(2)	(3)	(4)	(5)	(6)
1895	32	219	87	–	338	5
1896	42	191	81	–	314	17
1897	66	226	98	1	391	15
1898	75	193	89	2	359	8
1899	89	235	101	4	429	11
1900	59	266	123	3	451	16
1901	68	251	93	6	418	8
1902	67	259	116	9	451	14
1903	70	284	108	18	480	14
1904	69	248	91	28	436	19
1905	80	314	106	18	518	11
1906	105	345	104	19	573	16
1907	86	305	108	29	528	13
1908	96	347	113	25	581	16
1909	101	368	100	26	595	12
1910	106	332	112	21	571	16
1911	91	394	124	22	631	24
1912	135	403	115	22	675	28
1913	93	353	103	21	570	25
1914	112	349	74	16	551	23
1915	89	363	75	14	541	13
1916	82	319	90	10	501	17
1917	65	310	58	15	448	18
1918	61	282	50	11	404	24
1919	89	341	57	10	497	11
1920	90	308	33	3	434	19
1921	57	233	35	4	329	17
1922	46	266	35	5	352	15
1923	46	231	20	3	300	11
1924	51	201	27	5	284	10
1925	54	236	39	4	333	9
1926	44	255	36	7	342	7
1927	68	242	45	2	357	7
1928	69	179	37	9	294	4
1929	58	188	54	3	303	7
1930	50	185	64	4	303	6
1931	30	146	51	4	231	2
1932	21	124	39	–	184	4
1933	13	96	33	1	143	–
1934	22	79	35	1	137	2
1935	21	140	41	3	205	1
1936	25	140	47	–	212	2
1937	34	144	44	1	223	5
1938	29	129	43	4	205	4
1939	30	161	36	2	229	2
1940	53	167	52	5	277	1
1941	25	146	38	6	215	1
1942	27	90	32	5	154	1
1943	13	82	16	1	112	7
1944	25	139	17	2	183	5
1945	27	129	26	4	186	8
1946	28	163	35	3	229	8
1947	41	128	29	2	200	5
1948	48	151	33	1	233	13
1949	35	178	35	3	251	7
1950	30	161	33	7	231	5
1947	8	64	11	1	84	2
1948	7	52	13	–	72	4
1949	12	68	11	3	94	5
1950	19	115	28	5	167	15
1951	48	155	37	2	242	9
1952	66	200	47	4	317	7
1953	42	211	34	4	291	7
1954	36	150	33	4	223	16
1955	34	156	34	10	234	6
1956	42	247	42	4	335	12
1957	25	139	26	4	194	19

Year	Harvesters–Cutting (7)	Cutting, Conveying, & Binding (8)	Harvester Motors (exc. corn & cotton) (9)	Shockers (10)	Tedders & Rakes (11)	Corn Harvesting, Threshing, Cutting (12)
1837	–	2	–	–	–	1
1838	–	1	–	–	–	4
1839	–	1	–	–	–	5
1840	1	–	–	–	–	2
1841	–	1	–	–	–	5
1842	–	–	–	–	–	2
1843	–	–	–	–	–	4
1844	2	1	–	–	–	2
1845	1	1	–	–	–	2
1846	1	3	–	–	–	7
1847	3	1	–	–	–	1
1848	–	3	–	–	–	5
1849	3	4	–	–	–	6
1850	4	3	–	–	–	6
1851	1	7	–	–	–	1
1852	4	10	–	–	–	4
1853	11	4	–	–	–	8
1854	13	8	–	–	–	9
1855	35	11	–	–	2	8
1856	64	26	–	–	–	29
1857	50	31	–	–	–	37
1858	59	32	–	–	–	42
1859	47	35	–	–	3	34
1860	43	26	–	–	–	26
1861	44	21	–	–	1	16
1862	38	19	–	–	1	18
1863	28	23	–	–	–	9
1864	45	31	–	–	–	11
1865	52	26	–	1	5	16
1866	42	49	–	1	3	34
1867	51	60	–	–	8	51
1868	91	78	1	–	12	62
1869	70	58	–	–	35	53
1870	54	68	–	–	17	46
1871	51	53	–	1	14	43
1872	49	37	1	–	5	43
1873	42	43	–	2	5	33
1874	40	64	–	–	5	24
1875	36	59	–	1	1	30
1876	42	77	–	1	4	20
1874	43	69	–	–	5	24
1875	41	77	–	1	2	24
1876	26	61	–	1	3	29
1877	35	24	–	1	5	22
1878	27	29	–	–	5	29
1879	33	35	–	–	3	21
1880	22	46	–	1	7	33
1881	38	50	–	4	8	41
1882	45	57	1	1	3	31
1883	40	68	–	2	11	52
1884	35	59	2	2	25	48
1885	45	54	–	–	14	33
1886	52	38	–	–	12	27
1887	48	37	–	–	10	45
1888	35	26	–	4	4	44
1889	44	16	–	2	4	60
1890	60	18	–	1	6	72
1891	37	21	–	5	4	66
1892	32	17	–	2	4	60
1893	24	19	–	2	3	49
1894	29	10	–	3	4	49

Year	(7)	(8)	(9)	(10)	(11)	(12)
1895	25	16	—	4	3	80
1896	40	9	2	3	2	59
1897	38	9	—	2	1	54
1898	32	6	—	2	2	33
1899	48	15	—	4	1	37
1900	61	17	2	9	2	52
1901	46	19	3	10	2	73
1902	61	17	9	15	4	77
1903	67	18	2	15	7	73
1904	48	16	4	10	5	82
1905	41	14	2	7	5	74
1906	36	9	3	14	2	79
1907	38	15	6	14	5	66
1908	34	7	8	10	4	71
1909	45	8	13	17	12	67
1910	40	8	11	13	6	64
1911	28	10	13	11	6	60
1912	25	11	7	23	1	52
1913	44	10	13	37	2	67
1914	31	6	11	23	2	63
1915	26	12	15	16	1	55
1916	42	13	31	20	2	55
1917	36	10	11	21	2	40
1918	19	10	20	25	5	38
1919	31	8	23	19	—	52
1920	30	8	27	22	2	38
1921	32	3	18	18	—	41
1922	12	5	16	15	2	35
1923	19	6	10	15	2	42
1924	25	6	10	12	—	57
1925	22	5	13	7	1	36
1926	19	2	25	9	1	51
1927	20	5	16	7	3	43
1928	28	10	28	5	1	41
1929	23	4	30	8	—	36
1930	27	5	26	2	1	30
1931	20	4	27	2	1	31
1932	12	1	13	1	2	24
1933	27	2	18	2	—	18
1934	25	4	18	2	1	11
1935	18	3	18	1	—	9
1936	21	2	28	2	1	21
1937	21	2	22	4	2	15
1938	23	3	46	1	—	32
1939	15	6	42	1	—	31
1940	21	5	48	4	1	31
1941	10	4	30	—	2	33
1942	8	9	17	—	—	23
1943	9	4	22	—	1	24
1944	16	7	20	—	2	30
1945	14	4	41	—	—	23
1946	13	10	61	—	3	21
1947	24	4	69	—	—	27
1948	21	12	66	1	3	23
1949	19	6	42	1	4	33
1950	15	5	40	—	—	19
1947	9	3	4	—	—	15
1948	5	2	10	—	—	12
1949	20	11	65	1	1	23
1950	31	19	108	—	4	46
1951	24	6	46	1	2	26
1952	14	3	50	—	1	24
1953	19	3	46	—	3	30
1954	22	10	55	—	5	24
1955	23	5	72	—	1	21
1956	20	3	50	—	4	26
1957	38	8	99	—	6	38

Year	Hay Handling (13)	Cotton Harvesting, Picking & Chopping Plows (14)	Grain Harvesting, Threshing, Cutting (15)	Misc. Harvesting (16)	Unearthing Plants (17)	Total 7-17 (18)	Bins and Granaries (19)
1837	–	–	7	2	–	12	–
1838	1	–	13	2	1	22	–
1839	–	–	4	4	–	14	–
1840	–	–	7	–	–	10	–
1841	–	–	2	–	–	8	–
1842	–	–	3	1	–	6	–
1843	–	–	9	2	–	15	–
1844	–	–	7	–	1	13	–
1845	–	–	3	1	–	8	–
1846	–	–	9	5	1	26	–
1847	–	2	3	5	1	16	–
1848	–	–	10	2	–	20	–
1849	–	–	7	7	–	27	–
1850	–	1	11	5	–	30	–
1851	–	–	3	1	1	14	–
1852	–	–	8	3	3	32	–
1853	–	–	8	3	3	37	–
1854	1	2	11	2	4	50	–
1855	–	2	5	5	2	70	–
1856	–	2	9	18	4	152	–
1857	–	4	8	19	7	156	–
1858	2	1	21	29	6	192	–
1859	–	7	18	31	10	185	2
1860	2	15	14	32	8	166	1
1861	2	4	29	30	3	150	–
1862	7	–	25	25	8	141	3
1863	13	–	15	27	9	124	–
1864	23	1	17	42	7	177	–
1865	21	–	20	60	12	213	–
1866	52	9	17	77	22	306	1
1867	62	14	25	110	43	424	–
1868	97	7	35	116	45	544	3
1869	68	9	50	115	49	507	9
1870	30	15	46	93	35	404	3
1871	17	18	47	67	26	337	2
1872	12	8	34	53	25	267	3
1873	10	14	37	43	18	247	–
1874	11	14	20	80	19	277	1
1875	11	10	21	72	21	262	1
1876	12	9	36	114	24	339	2
1874	8	13	21	82	18	283	1
1875	13	6	30	102	25	321	2
1876	12	11	36	112	16	307	2
1877	11	13	54	101	17	283	–
1878	11	13	39	100	14	267	1
1879	13	19	40	90	7	261	1
1880	6	18	50	90	17	290	1
1881	18	28	62	91	12	352	2
1882	20	27	77	124	13	399	3
1883	16	27	62	129	22	429	1
1884	29	35	77	107	28	447	2
1885	18	43	78	139	34	458	5
1886	19	40	58	99	26	371	2
1887	14	38	40	101	26	359	–
1888	14	17	29	82	21	276	2
1889	15	32	71	71	29	344	1
1890	11	31	51	87	30	367	2
1891	19	47	64	77	26	366	1
1892	17	27	55	73	32	319	4
1893	10	16	72	70	23	288	2
1894	7	12	64	56	23	257	3

Year	(13)	(14)	(15)	(16)	(17)	(18)	(19)
1895	11	12	66	62	21	300	1
1896	6	21	40	43	30	255	1
1897	7	15	39	46	16	227	6
1898	13	8	36	45	20	197	2
1899	18	24	52	46	28	273	6
1900	14	16	72	62	27	334	10
1901	18	31	81	73	30	386	23
1902	23	29	82	81	25	423	19
1903	15	32	64	98	29	420	11
1904	32	64	63	69	33	426	17
1905	30	49	73	84	21	400	8
1906	33	63	52	97	45	433	11
1907	39	69	36	84	47	419	5
1908	27	82	47	99	55	444	14
1909	29	63	44	86	57	441	14
1910	36	70	30	65	40	383	18
1911	21	60	43	87	32	371	40
1912	20	54	38	93	43	367	51
1913	22	42	34	83	49	403	51
1914	25	43	44	89	47	384	62
1915	24	29	30	89	61	358	53
1916	22	25	33	110	49	402	47
1917	19	41	26	81	67	354	18
1918	18	24	25	69	56	309	29
1919	17	36	25	74	47	332	26
1920	15	52	36	61	48	339	23
1921	14	22	23	73	44	288	25
1922	6	14	33	67	32	237	15
1923	13	19	19	63	27	235	14
1924	14	27	25	67	29	272	8
1925	8	30	22	56	18	218	10
1926	7	30	22	67	21	254	11
1927	7	42	21	81	25	270	10
1928	10	35	28	61	25	272	13
1929	8	29	20	87	28	273	10
1930	6	41	19	69	21	247	10
1931	4	15	10	62	27	203	14
1932	4	17	5	50	12	141	7
1933	6	6	6	44	11	140	6
1934	2	9	13	43	10	138	–
1935	5	6	17	45	12	134	5
1936	5	5	15	45	20	165	4
1937	6	13	24	35	14	158	5
1938	5	7	12	41	7	177	7
1939	11	11	22	42	15	196	2
1940	6	5	25	38	17	201	5
1941	8	6	16	35	18	162	7
1942	4	7	12	51	11	142	7
1943	–	11	10	30	20	131	3
1944	2	21	7	38	27	170	–
1945	5	23	6	39	31	186	2
1946	5	21	8	62	17	221	2
1947	11	20	5	48	21	229	4
1948	6	22	4	62	23	243	1
1949	6	28	13	54	18	224	6
1950	6	32	7	56	15	195	8
1947	2	3	3	20	14	73	–
1948	2	8	7	21	10	77	–
1949	2	19	4	58	16	220	1
1950	7	41	7	73	29	365	5
1951	15	22	6	41	34	223	3
1952	5	18	8	61	15	199	1
1953	2	41	13	73	27	257	7
1954	6	63	9	53	17	264	2
1955	7	40	8	57	15	249	7
1956	8	30	10	67	20	238	7
1957	13	60	21	107	22	412	6

103

Year	Bee Culture (20)	Milkers (21)	Misc. Dairy Farm Eqpt. (22)	Poultry Husbandry Eqpt. (23)	Animal Housing & Confining (24)	Animal Feeding (25)
1837	–	–	–	–	–	–
1838	1	–	–	–	–	–
1839	3	–	–	–	–	–
1840	2	–	–	–	–	–
1841	4	–	–	–	–	–
1842	13	–	3	–	–	–
1843	9	–	–	1	–	–
1844	6	–	–	–	–	–
1845	11	–	–	–	–	–
1846	4	–	–	–	–	–
1847	1	–	–	2	–	–
1848	1	–	–	–	–	–
1849	4	1	2	–	–	–
1850	3	–	–	–	–	–
1851	2	–	2	–	–	–
1852	2	–	–	–	–	1
1853	3	–	2	1	–	–
1854	3	–	2	–	–	1
1855	–	–	1	–	1	–
1856	4	1	–	–	2	–
1857	5	–	2	–	–	3
1858	10	–	6	–	–	1
1859	15	2	7	–	–	2
1860	18	2	9	–	2	2
1861	29	2	7	–	3	1
1862	13	–	2	–	3	6
1863	25	1	5	1	2	4
1864	20	3	4	1	1	12
1865	15	1	2	–	1	11
1866	26	1	10	2	3	29
1867	48	3	12	2	3	22
1868	73	5	13	2	7	14
1869	62	1	19	1	13	8
1870	40	2	5	1	8	7
1871	64	2	12	2	16	7
1872	49	–	9	–	11	7
1873	33	–	11	–	12	9
1874	25	4	8	2	21	10
1875	23	2	15	4	19	7
1876	27	1	11	3	25	12
1874	24	5	14	1	21	6
1875	22	1	11	3	20	9
1876	31	2	10	5	25	11
1877	45	1	14	7	16	12
1878	35	6	11	4	13	8
1879	28	2	9	6	11	6
1880	9	–	9	7	10	11
1881	8	–	12	3	14	10
1882	16	1	10	10	12	11
1883	18	2	11	10	12	15
1884	16	1	5	13	15	23
1885	18	4	9	16	15	18
1886	12	2	6	15	12	24
1887	10	5	5	17	7	27
1888	11	1	6	6	12	27
1889	9	4	17	8	13	31
1890	8	4	15	9	20	17
1891	22	6	8	11	13	38
1892	9	4	13	17	8	25
1893	7	9	5	19	18	13
1894	5	7	7	8	10	10

Year	(20)	(21)	(22)	(23)	(24)	(25)
1895	9	9	5	7	15	18
1896	6	7	7	19	14	14
1897	7	3	11	16	6	18
1898	6	5	3	12	12	8
1899	4	9	11	28	7	13
1900	6	2	9	30	9	17
1901	6	6	8	27	19	14
1902	3	7	3	29	17	28
1903	8	9	8	39	20	29
1904	8	15	6	38	16	31
1905	6	11	9	59	19	18
1906	11	16	10	63	24	45
1907	12	31	13	59	21	43
1908	16	29	6	51	27	56
1909	8	30	12	45	31	35
1910	11	30	15	45	30	39
1911	12	25	18	58	37	70
1912	11	23	9	61	41	51
1913	19	21	19	59	22	33
1914	14	40	14	52	38	61
1915	12	47	7	76	38	35
1916	8	32	9	58	50	65
1917	8	38	8	52	28	39
1918	10	27	2	27	18	35
1919	12	31	5	44	21	73
1920	18	27	5	45	30	41
1921	14	27	2	32	24	28
1922	20	20	6	64	47	41
1923	7	13	5	53	28	38
1924	13	7	4	63	47	34
1925	6	11	9	39	29	24
1926	8	13	6	44	41	36
1927	13	12	11	69	47	36
1928	13	8	6	41	39	29
1929	7	11	8	49	33	33
1930	7	5	3	37	44	29
1931	6	14	3	27	31	27
1932	10	10	2	25	24	10
1933	7	6	2	6	19	7
1934	3	4	9	8	23	9
1935	6	4	8	18	15	5
1936	2	12	8	26	11	10
1937	7	8	3	9	11	18
1938	6	5	6	11	21	20
1939	7	5	4	23	22	12
1940	8	14	4	17	22	14
1941	10	3	4	6	14	12
1942	2	8	1	5	7	12
1943	4	7	2	9	7	18
1944	8	10	–	6	8	14
1945	4	12	2	4	8	24
1946	8	6	1	9	20	26
1947	17	18	1	11	15	17
1948	5	12	–	8	16	19
1949	9	19	2	16	16	22
1950	9	17	2	6	17	34
1947	–	5	2	1	6	9
1948	8	3	1	7	6	12
1949	4	16	–	2	11	16
1950	11	19	1	11	22	34
1951	10	17	2	10	16	28
1952	16	19	2	17	22	29
1953	8	10	1	9	22	33
1954	3	21	1	12	19	23
1955	3	15	–	7	19	27
1956	–	19	–	12	18	29
1957	5	17	2	15	35	64

105

Agriculture: Livestock and Miscellaneous Agriculture

Year	Animal Watering (26)	Animal Grooming (27)	Animal Controlling (28)	Misc. Animal Husbandry (28a)	Total 21–28a Livestock (exc. bee culture) (29)	Total 5,6, 18–20,29 "Pure" Agriculture (30)
1837	–	–	–	–	–	20
1838	–	2	–	–	2	39
1839	–	–	–	–	–	31
1840	–	–	–	–	–	25
1841	–	–	–	–	–	23
1842	–	–	–	–	3	40
1843	–	–	–	–	1	42
1844	–	1	–	–	1	40
1845	–	–	–	–	–	34
1846	–	1	–	–	1	48
1847	–	1	–	–	3	34
1848	–	–	1	–	1	46
1849	–	2	–	–	5	75
1850	–	–	1	1	2	70
1851	–	–	–	–	2	33
1852	–	–	–	–	1	65
1853	–	1	–	–	4	79
1854	–	–	1	–	4	106
1855	–	–	1	–	3	132
1856	–	2	1	–	6	218
1857	–	1	1	–	7	305
1858	–	2	4	–	13	366
1859	–	2	–	–	13	409
1860	–	–	4	–	19	507
1861	–	3	6	–	22	378
1862	–	1	5	–	17	290
1863	–	3	6	–	22	286
1864	–	4	5	–	30	366
1865	–	1	8	–	24	487
1866	2	3	18	–	68	784
1867	2	3	47	–	94	1142
1868	–	9	30	–	80	1256
1869	–	6	17	–	65	1315
1870	–	2	22	–	47	1006
1871	1	4	24	–	68	896
1872	–	6	26	2	61	739
1873	–	3	15	1	51	687
1874	4	12	28	1	90	772
1875	1	18	33	3	102	763
1876	2	25	40	2	12	991
1874	5	16	31	2	99	786
1875	–	20	28	3	92	841
1876	3	23	39	1	118	964
1877	3	10	36	1	99	925
1878	4	10	27	3	83	886
1879	7	6	35	1	82	811
1880	4	6	32	2	79	840
1881	4	9	37	–	89	934
1882	5	6	42	3	97	1155
1883	4	6	29	2	89	1157
1884	11	7	31	2	106	1237
1885	7	13	36	6	118	1217
1886	7	11	56	3	133	1115
1887	8	11	55	5	135	1066
1888	4	12	50	2	118	899
1889	8	11	49	3	141	1021
1890	13	17	44	4	139	1044
1891	11	6	41	3	134	1054
1892	7	12	42	7	128	963
1893	8	5	33	6	110	802
1894	7	7	24	2	80	728

Year	(26)	(27)	(28)	(28a)	(29)	(30)
1895	6	7	30	5	97	755
1896	12	8	31	3	112	708
1897	9	10	40	5	113	764
1898	14	4	36	3	94	669
1899	16	10	50	9	144	876
1900	18	12	49	5	146	968
1901	10	12	62	5	158	1004
1902	11	5	60	11	156	1077
1903	9	6	56	8	180	1121
1904	8	7	47	9	168	1083
1905	21	7	56	12	200	1155
1906	27	5	67	6	257	1307
1907	20	8	79	21	274	1272
1908	24	9	62	10	264	1345
1909	18	6	63	8	240	1318
1910	25	9	61	8	254	1261
1911	30	16	43	13	297	1388
1912	31	8	58	12	282	1426
1913	23	11	65	14	253	1335
1914	27	10	76	17	318	1369
1915	22	5	62	35	292	1304
1916	27	10	83	42	334	1351
1917	35	5	81	20	286	1152
1918	25	3	49	14	186	976
1919	56	5	59	15	294	1187
1920	28	—	58	7	234	1074
1921	15	3	59	9	190	872
1922	30	—	62	10	270	919
1923	27	2	47	10	213	790
1924	26	2	32	21	215	823
1925	30	1	30	11	173	760
1926	23	—	40	9	203	834
1927	30	3	34	8	242	907
1928	19	4	26	13	172	781
1929	27	—	22	7	183	790
1930	20	1	26	3	165	741
1931	13	1	27	4	143	603
1932	6	1	14	2	92	440
1933	8	—	14	5	62	363
1934	1	1	12	6	67	353
1935	9	—	15	6	74	431
1936	8	—	14	5	89	479
1937	5	1	19	8	74	480
1938	3	2	16	8	84	491
1939	6	—	9	5	81	522
1940	10	—	20	8	101	601
1941	6	—	15	4	60	459
1942	5	—	9	3	47	356
1943	10	—	10	4	63	324
1944	6	—	15	10	59	435
1945	7	2	17	6	76	468
1946	18	3	27	9	110	587
1947	13	—	19	10	94	559
1948	12	1	20	11	88	594
1949	13	1	19	8	108	613
1950	12	1	24	13	113	574
1947	1	1	4	—	29	188
1948	7	1	13	—	50	211
1949	14	—	19	—	78	402
1950	24	4	34	—	149	712
1951	9	1	30	—	113	600
1952	13	—	26	—	128	668
1953	12	1	20	—	108	678
1954	12	1	16	—	105	613
1955	12	2	25	—	107	606
1956	7	1	22	—	108	700
1957	4	2	42	—	181	817

107

Agriculture Mixed with Other Fields: Animal Power

| Year | Animal Draft Appliances | | Animal-Powered Motors | Harness | | | Total 34–36 |
| | I | II | | Bridles & Harness | Buckles | Misc. | |
	(31)	(32)	(33)	(34)	(35)	(36)	(37)
1837	–	–	2	–	1	2	3
1838	–	1	2	–	–	–	–
1839	–	2	–	1	–	1	2
1840	1	1	2	–	–	1	1
1841	–	–	3	1	–	1	2
1842	2	–	–	1	–	1	2
1843	1	–	–	–	1	2	3
1844	2	–	1	2	3	1	6
1845	1	1	2	–	3	1	4
1846	2	3	3	1	–	4	5
1847	1	3	1	–	2	2	4
1848	1	1	2	2	2	–	4
1849	–	1	–	1	2	4	7
1850	3	3	1	3	2	3	8
1851	–	–	1	–	–	3	3
1852	3	2	1	2	–	4	6
1853	–	2	–	–	1	4	5
1854	3	8	1	2	2	4	8
1855	6	6	1	2	–	6	8
1856	3	16	–	1	1	10	12
1857	3	9	3	4	2	5	11
1858	1	4	6	5	4	8	17
1859	6	15	4	7	1	10	18
1860	9	21	6	10	–	21	31
1861	4	14	4	4	1	7	12
1862	6	9	6	6	7	7	20
1863	6	9	2	7	6	12	25
1864	7	13	4	8	11	16	35
1865	12	22	5	7	20	29	56
1866	15	40	5	20	16	34	70
1867	24	93	8	41	31	83	155
1868	34	106	14	48	32	103	183
1869	29	78	20	29	32	95	156
1870	21	57	19	29	24	78	131
1871	22	64	21	17	26	62	105
1872	30	76	20	30	25	69	124
1873	29	49	14	19	20	56	95
1874	40	67	14	33	13	58	104
1875	33	86	17	47	24	57	128
1876	45	82	9	36	22	83	141
1874	44	72	14	34	13	58	105
1875	34	90	17	45	21	65	131
1876	47	74	6	38	29	73	140
1877	40	100	12	33	25	90	148
1878	38	90	16	37	19	86	142
1879	46	83	14	43	37	107	187
1880	47	96	16	63	36	93	192
1881	37	92	11	44	30	108	182
1882	43	99	15	65	50	139	254
1883	56	142	8	92	59	151	302
1884	53	135	11	83	47	184	314
1885	43	159	6	91	36	185	312
1886	63	143	4	67	40	152	259
1887	87	179	9	70	30	161	261
1888	57	148	6	54	31	150	235
1889	86	189	7	78	32	188	298
1890	59	182	2	66	22	202	290
1891	69	161	8	72	21	151	244
1892	58	154	7	59	25	130	214
1893	58	113	4	55	22	106	183
1894	34	99	4	33	12	111	156

Year	(31)	(32)	(33)	(34)	(35)	(36)	(37)
1895	43	107	5	48	22	120	190
1896	35	110	2	34	13	112	159
1897	58	129	4	27	16	78	121
1898	37	118	5	25	16	73	114
1899	59	133	—	34	16	68	118
1900	71	128	—	45	16	76	137
1901	58	122	3	32	25	92	149
1902	70	114	3	34	38	107	179
1903	79	105	1	41	36	108	185
1904	94	96	3	43	16	115	174
1905	92	107	2	51	34	125	210
1906	71	118	1	35	44	82	161
1907	78	119	3	39	33	124	196
1908	87	93	2	48	28	125	201
1909	80	105	3	29	25	111	165
1910	67	64	2	42	19	107	168
1911	53	65	2	26	21	77	124
1912	63	69	2	22	16	108	146
1913	48	65	3	35	16	67	118
1914	35	68	3	31	13	70	114
1915	17	46	2	25	10	43	78
1916	30	42	1	17	16	43	76
1917	18	32	—	11	10	44	65
1918	14	22	1	11	12	20	43
1919	19	29	—	11	25	26	62
1920	9	19	—	5	8	21	34
1921	12	16	—	10	6	17	33
1922	11	16	—	5	11	20	36
1923	6	14	—	3	11	33	47
1924	7	6	—	15	6	22	43
1925	9	6	1	8	7	24	39
1926	14	6	1	6	9	19	34
1927	6	5	—	5	2	27	34
1928	4	5	1	2	9	14	25
1929	4	6	—	3	7	19	29
1930	2	3	1	5	8	5	18
1931	1	2	—	2	7	7	16
1932	—	—	—	—	7	4	11
1933	—	1	—	4	2	7	13
1934	—	2	—	3	4	3	10
1935	1	4	—	1	4	11	16
1936	—	2	—	2	6	9	17
1937	2	2	—	—	8	9	17
1938	—	1	—	2	9	4	15
1939	—	1	—	4	5	3	12
1940	—	—	—	1	2	7	10
1941	—	1	—	2	7	2	11
1942	—	—	—	—	7	—	7
1943	—	—	—	1	5	1	7
1944	—	1	—	1	2	1	4
1945	—	1	—	4	7	3	14
1946	—	3	—	8	6	6	20
1947	—	3	—	2	10	12	24
1948	—	—	—	2	2	8	12
1949	1	—	—	3	8	4	15
1950	—	—	—	5	12	5	22
1947	—	1	—	4	2	4	10
1948	—	1	—	1	—	6	7
1949	—	5	—	6	5	12	23
1950	1	1	—	5	13	8	26
1951	—	—	—	2	7	3	12
1952	—	—	—	3	11	3	17
1953	—	—	—	3	12	3	18
1954	—	—	—	2	5	3	10
1955	—	—	—	—	2	2	4
1956	—	—	—	2	6	3	11
1957	—	—	—	2	6	2	10

Agriculture Mixed with Other Fields: Animal Power

Year	Farriery Shoes (38)	Calks (39)	Making Shoes (40)	Misc. (41)	Total 38–41 (42)	Whips & Whip Apparatus (43)	Total 31–33,37,42, 43 Animal Power Related (44)
1837	–	–	1	–	1	–	6
1838	–	–	–	–	–	–	3
1839	–	–	–	–	–	–	4
1840	–	–	–	–	–	–	5
1841	–	–	–	–	–	–	5
1842	1	–	–	–	1	1	6
1843	–	–	3	–	3	–	7
1844	–	–	–	–	–	–	9
1845	–	–	–	–	–	–	8
1846	–	–	–	–	–	1	14
1847	–	–	1	–	1	–	10
1848	–	–	–	–	–	–	8
1849	–	–	1	–	1	–	9
1850	–	–	1	1	2	3	20
1851	–	–	1	–	1	–	5
1852	1	–	1	–	2	1	15
1853	2	–	–	–	2	–	9
1854	1	–	1	1	3	–	23
1855	–	–	–	–	–	–	21
1856	3	–	–	1	4	–	35
1857	–	1	1	3	5	2	33
1858	3	–	7	1	11	–	39
1859	1	1	4	3	9	–	52
1860	2	2	6	2	12	–	79
1861	2	1	7	–	10	1	45
1862	–	1	6	1	8	–	49
1863	1	1	7	1	10	–	52
1864	12	2	5	–	19	–	78
1865	13	5	3	1	22	–	117
1866	23	10	11	5	49	1	180
1867	17	9	13	9	48	3	331
1868	17	16	14	10	57	10	404
1869	8	12	17	9	46	6	335
1870	9	4	14	4	31	12	271
1871	4	3	12	3	22	4	238
1872	11	4	3	6	24	8	282
1873	8	5	8	6	27	3	217
1874	14	5	15	5	39	8	272
1875	21	9	31	8	69	4	337
1876	12	11	26	14	63	5	345
1874	16	5	20	4	45	9	289
1875	21	8	31	6	66	3	341
1876	15	11	23	12	61	4	332
1877	24	10	12	9	55	10	365
1878	27	8	16	13	64	4	354
1879	25	11	23	10	69	6	405
1880	15	4	5	7	31	6	388
1881	29	10	4	12	55	11	388
1882	17	10	12	7	46	13	470
1883	31	18	2	13	64	5	577
1884	21	14	25	6	66	8	587
1885	15	22	14	11	62	8	590
1886	17	18	10	14	59	16	544
1887	17	4	13	7	41	16	593
1888	11	10	10	11	42	7	495
1889	31	7	10	10	58	8	646
1890	31	3	17	15	66	9	608
1891	24	16	13	6	59	9	550
1892	36	8	7	8	59	2	494
1893	42	14	7	9	72	4	434
1894	26	7	9	6	48	–	341

Year	(38)	(39)	(40)	(41)	(42)	(43)	(44)
1895	30	14	6	9	59	2	406
1896	27	24	5	13	69	2	377
1897	36	22	4	17	79	1	392
1898	35	15	9	13	72	2	348
1899	44	15	4	20	83	5	398
1900	32	9	6	12	59	–	395
1901	34	18	6	22	80	5	417
1902	40	25	7	26	98	7	471
1903	36	23	11	23	93	11	474
1904	29	30	9	16	84	4	455
1905	28	39	6	21	94	4	509
1906	37	34	6	14	91	5	447
1907	29	27	8	12	76	1	473
1908	24	33	8	14	79	4	466
1909	22	38	9	23	92	3	448
1910	12	31	8	21	72	1	374
1911	18	38	11	18	85	2	331
1912	23	56	8	16	103	1	384
1913	15	46	3	15	79	3	316
1914	28	32	5	8	73	2	295
1915	29	40	8	13	90	8	241
1916	17	27	1	11	56	1	206
1917	16	11	4	6	37	–	152
1918	11	7	4	6	28	–	108
1919	12	7	2	10	31	–	141
1920	10	10	2	3	25	–	87
1921	11	9	2	5	27	1	89
1922	8	6	4	4	22	–	85
1923	7	3	1	2	13	–	80
1924	3	4	2	3	12	–	68
1925	2	2	2	–	6	–	61
1926	3	5	–	–	8	–	63
1927	5	–	–	–	5	1	51
1928	4	–	1	–	5	1	41
1929	4	3	–	2	9	–	48
1930	5	1	–	–	6	–	30
1931	4	2	–	1	7	1	27
1932	5	3	1	–	9	–	20
1933	5	1	–	–	6	–	20
1934	1	5	2	–	8	–	20
1935	7	–	1	2	10	–	31
1936	3	2	–	1	6	–	25
1937	3	–	–	–	3	1	25
1938	–	–	–	1	1	2	19
1939	1	–	–	–	1	4	18
1940	–	–	–	1	1	–	11
1941	1	–	–	1	2	–	14
1942	–	–	–	–	–	–	7
1943	–	1	–	–	1	–	8
1944	–	–	–	–	–	–	5
1945	–	1	–	–	1	–	16
1946	–	–	1	–	1	1	25
1947	1	–	–	–	1	1	29
1948	–	–	–	1	1	2	15
1949	–	–	–	–	–	–	16
1950	3	–	–	–	3	1	26
1947	–	–	–	–	–	–	11
1948	–	–	–	–	–	1	9
1949	–	1	–	–	1	2	31
1950	1	–	–	2	3	–	31
1951	–	–	1	–	1	1	14
1952	1	–	–	–	1	–	18
1953	–	1	–	–	1	–	19
1954	1	–	–	–	1	1	12
1955	2	–	–	–	2	–	6
1956	3	–	–	–	3	1	15
1957	1	–	–	–	1	–	11

111

Year	Insect & Vermin Destroying (45)	Insecticides, Fungicides, Germicides & Disinfectants		Misc. Poisons (48)	Total 45–48 (49)
		Inorganic (46)	Organic (47)		
1837	–	–	–	–	–
1838	–	–	–	–	–
1839	–	–	–	–	–
1840	–	–	–	–	–
1841	–	–	–	–	–
1842	–	–	–	–	–
1843	–	–	–	–	–
1844	–	–	–	–	–
1845	–	–	–	–	–
1846	1	–	–	–	1
1847	–	–	–	1	1
1848	1	–	–	–	1
1849	–	–	–	–	–
1850	1	–	–	–	1
1851	1	–	–	–	1
1852	–	–	–	–	–
1853	–	–	–	–	–
1854	2	–	–	–	2
1855	–	–	–	–	–
1856	6	–	–	1	7
1857	–	–	–	–	–
1858	3	–	–	–	3
1859	7	1	–	–	8
1860	6	–	–	–	6
1861	–	1	1	–	2
1862	–	–	–	–	–
1863	1	2	–	–	3
1864	4	2	1	–	7
1865	1	4	–	2	7
1866	7	4	3	1	15
1867	12	4	3	4	23
1868	6	9	3	4	22
1869	12	5	5	4	26
1870	8	5	2	1	16
1871	13	10	2	5	30
1872	20	2	3	5	30
1873	18	6	3	4	31
1874	11	5	3	3	22
1875	16	6	–	4	26
1876	12	10	2	4	28
1874	12	6	2	4	24
1875	18	10	–	4	32
1876	16	8	5	3	32
1877	22	5	1	3	31
1878	12	3	1	6	22
1879	11	8	1	3	23
1880	7	2	1	5	15
1881	10	7	–	9	26
1882	11	4	3	5	23
1883	8	8	4	3	23
1884	10	7	1	4	22
1885	8	7	1	6	22
1886	10	7	–	3	20
1887	15	10	4	6	35
1888	21	4	3	3	31
1889	20	6	2	7	35
1890	19	6	11	3	39
1891	19	4	2	3	28
1892	13	6	2	3	24
1893	16	2	4	4	26
1894	15	1	–	1	17

Year	(45)	(46)	(47)	(48)	(49)
1895	23	1	–	1	25
1896	18	2	2	2	24
1897	23	3	5	5	36
1898	19	4	3	3	29
1899	13	3	4	3	23
1900	15	4	3	1	23
1901	23	7	4	7	41
1902	29	2	3	5	39
1903	27	7	8	5	47
1904	25	4	6	7	42
1905	19	2	4	6	31
1906	21	1	8	1	31
1907	35	9	8	3	55
1908	32	6	5	9	52
1909	33	12	8	1	54
1910	35	3	4	9	51
1911	50	2	7	6	65
1912	39	4	5	6	54
1913	36	5	1	11	53
1914	38	6	4	7	55
1915	34	8	1	6	49
1916	41	4	5	3	53
1917	47	5	3	5	60
1918	39	3	5	–	47
1919	37	17	4	8	66
1920	55	9	4	10	78
1921	38	9	2	12	61
1922	76	9	9	9	103
1923	76	18	12	12	118
1924	48	27	12	14	101
1925	39	22	15	20	96
1926	27	14	14	18	73
1927	39	17	13	14	83
1928	37	7	18	21	83
1929	33	12	23	18	86
1930	33	12	24	21	90
1931	24	9	31	8	72
1932	26	20	24	16	86
1933	29	13	27	11	80
1934	26	15	30	23	94
1935	31	15	28	12	86
1936	20	13	37	10	80
1937	28	7	40	18	93
1938	19	11	60	12	102
1939	33	9	90	14	146
1940	16	9	72	8	105
1941	26	14	94	18	152
1942	16	5	56	15	92
1943	11	5	53	11	80
1944	10	11	63	11	95
1945	17	5	78	9	109
1946	16	3	62	14	95
1947	17	4	53	11	85
1948	14	9	68	10	101
1949	14	7	82	7	110
1950	16	5	41	4	66
1947	6	7	68	10	91
1948	6	1	39	8	54
1949	10	6	55	6	77
1950	17	4	82	15	118
1951	22	12	105	16	155
1952	21	5	60	8	94
1953	12	5	49	5	71
1954	20	4	25	8	57
1955	22	6	36	5	69
1956	37	8	70	9	124
1957	28	6	71	22	127

113

Agriculture Mixed with Other Fields

Year	Gates				Fences		
	Gate & Latch (50)	Special (51)	Misc. (52)	Total 50–52 (53)	Panel (54)	Barbed (55)	Wire exc. barbed (56)
1837	–	–	–	–	–	–	–
1838	–	–	–	–	–	–	–
1839	–	–	–	–	–	–	–
1840	–	–	–	–	–	–	–
1841	–	–	1	1	–	–	–
1842	–	–	–	–	–	–	–
1843	–	–	–	–	–	–	–
1844	–	–	–	–	–	–	–
1845	–	–	–	–	–	–	–
1846	–	–	–	–	–	–	–
1847	–	–	–	–	–	–	–
1848	–	–	1	1	1	–	1
1849	–	–	–	–	–	–	–
1850	–	–	–	–	1	–	–
1851	1	–	2	3	1	–	–
1852	2	–	3	5	–	–	–
1853	–	1	–	1	–	–	1
1854	–	1	1	2	1	–	1
1855	2	1	–	3	1	–	–
1856	2	3	3	8	8	–	–
1857	2	3	2	7	14	–	–
1858	2	6	–	8	19	–	–
1859	3	8	5	16	9	–	–
1860	–	6	3	9	3	–	–
1861	2	4	2	8	6	–	–
1862	1	2	4	7	6	–	–
1863	1	5	5	11	12	–	1
1864	–	3	3	6	7	–	–
1865	3	9	6	18	6	–	–
1866	3	31	10	44	25	–	1
1867	9	52	17	78	51	2	2
1868	12	33	13	58	28	2	–
1869	5	27	8	40	42	–	–
1870	5	15	9	29	23	–	1
1871	9	27	14	50	21	1	1
1872	9	12	11	32	16	–	3
1873	5	14	13	32	15	1	–
1874	6	16	7	29	10	6	–
1875	6	9	15	30	18	19	2
1876	5	12	8	25	28	38	7
1874	4	14	10	28	11	7	1
1875	5	11	10	26	23	19	2
1876	6	13	11	30	26	48	8
1877	12	34	11	57	26	37	28
1878	13	15	12	40	9	26	14
1879	20	18	9	47	11	24	4
1880	10	27	2	39	17	19	11
1881	13	30	3	46	20	44	10
1882	14	27	6	47	24	67	11
1883	18	45	8	71	14	39	17
1884	16	29	8	53	7	20	18
1885	24	36	10	70	13	13	22
1886	17	35	12	64	21	7	13
1887	18	39	12	69	15	11	10
1888	22	26	10	58	11	9	12
1889	27	31	16	74	11	14	16
1890	21	40	7	68	9	7	7
1891	33	30	9	72	10	19	13
1892	22	22	13	57	10	9	13
1893	14	28	11	53	9	4	11
1894	18	14	12	44	12	2	28

Year	(50)	(51)	(52)	(53)	(54)	(55)	(56)
1895	38	28	7	73	2	1	25
1896	39	28	10	77	7	5	20
1897	29	32	6	67	5	4	24
1898	32	33	9	74	7	5	19
1899	31	30	11	72	4	2	11
1900	19	20	10	49	2	4	11
1901	20	23	16	59	12	5	19
1902	21	26	18	65	5	–	24
1903	13	22	18	53	7	3	32
1904	37	19	15	71	4	3	49
1905	27	32	17	76	5	4	69
1906	27	29	14	70	1	3	61
1907	33	41	10	84	1	3	37
1908	28	33	14	75	4	1	33
1909	18	19	16	53	3	2	36
1910	18	18	25	61	2	–	15
1911	19	19	20	58	5	2	34
1912	10	15	16	41	3	2	36
1913	15	18	18	51	2	1	29
1914	17	16	17	50	7	1	32
1915	27	15	22	64	5	–	34
1916	16	17	27	60	4	1	32
1917	8	8	22	38	2	2	8
1918	6	9	8	23	4	2	7
1919	4	18	14	36	2	1	15
1920	14	10	31	55	1	1	8
1921	9	12	31	52	3	2	9
1922	11	6	16	33	8	–	13
1923	5	7	17	29	1	1	14
1924	4	9	45	58	4	–	9
1925	7	7	30	44	1	1	8
1926	2	13	30	45	2	3	12
1927	3	6	30	39	7	2	7
1928	5	7	30	42	1	5	8
1929	–	2	42	44	2	–	10
1930	3	1	43	47	2	5	9
1931	3	2	18	23	1	–	14
1932	–	2	20	22	1	1	6
1933	2	4	20	26	1	–	4
1934	–	2	31	33	1	1	3
1935	1	1	36	38	1	–	4
1936	–	2	24	26	1	1	2
1937	–	3	27	30	1	–	–
1938	2	1	33	36	1	–	–
1939	–	–	21	21	–	2	3
1940	–	–	32	32	1	–	1
1941	–	2	21	23	1	–	2
1942	–	–	3	3	2	–	3
1943	–	–	8	8	2	1	1
1944	1	–	15	16	4	–	2
1945	2	2	22	26	2	1	1
1946	5	2	12	19	3	1	1
1947	5	2	18	25	5	–	–
1948	1	–	13	14	3	–	1
1949	8	3	10	21	3	1	–
1950	2	2	11	15	3	–	2
1947	1	1	8	10	–	–	–
1948	1	1	14	16	–	1	1
1949	1	–	11	12	4	–	2
1950	3	1	19	23	7	–	1
1951	7	1	14	22	–	2	–
1952	6	2	14	22	5	–	–
1953	4	7	21	32	3	1	3
1954	5	1	11	17	3	–	–
1955	4	2	6	12	5	–	3
1956	1	–	10	11	2	–	2
1957	5	1	8	14	4	2	–

Year	Fences				Greenhouses, Nursery Equipment, Gardening	
	Wire Connections (57)	Rail (58)	Misc. (58a)	Total 54 – 58a (59)	Greenhouses, Nursery Eqpt., Gardening, Plant Receptacles (60)	Special Cutting Machines (Harvester Type) (61)
1837	–	–	–	–	–	–
1838	–	–	–	–	–	3
1839	–	–	–	–	–	1
1840	–	–	–	–	1	–
1841	–	–	–	–	–	–
1842	–	–	–	–	–	–
1843	–	1	–	1	1	–
1844	–	–	–	–	–	–
1845	–	–	–	–	–	–
1846	–	–	–	–	–	–
1847	–	2	–	2	–	1
1848	–	–	–	2	–	2
1849	1	1	–	2	–	2
1850	–	–	–	1	–	2
1851	–	2	–	3	–	7
1852	–	2	–	2	–	4
1853	1	1	–	3	–	4
1854	1	–	–	3	2	4
1855	1	–	–	2	1	11
1856	2	2	–	12	1	7
1857	1	3	–	18	–	7
1858	1	4	–	24	1	2
1859	1	5	–	15	3	4
1860	1	2	–	6	3	5
1861	–	–	–	6	5	4
1862	1	2	–	9	2	5
1863	–	1	–	14	4	2
1864	2	1	–	10	5	2
1865	2	4	–	12	4	9
1866	3	20	–	49	15	3
1867	4	23	–	82	22	6
1868	12	15	–	57	27	6
1869	6	18	–	66	13	11
1870	6	7	–	37	12	24
1871	5	10	–	38	19	15
1872	6	18	–	43	10	8
1873	6	15	–	37	4	10
1874	6	19	–	41	13	8
1875	5	13	–	57	9	8
1876	4	18	–	95	11	7
1874	5	16	4	44	15	11
1875	6	14	11	75	8	6
1876	5	23	12	122	15	11
1877	8	22	8	129	14	11
1878	7	25	17	98	9	21
1879	8	18	4	69	7	27
1880	6	19	8	80	7	15
1881	10	24	12	120	11	12
1882	11	21	18	152	15	19
1883	16	28	15	129	15	16
1884	16	33	13	107	17	22
1885	10	28	10	96	12	7
1886	24	24	17	106	16	23
1887	17	35	7	95	10	19
1888	20	28	11	91	9	14
1889	32	41	15	129	19	21
1890	30	20	15	88	11	17
1891	29	22	6	99	13	18
1892	35	19	9	95	13	25
1893	40	9	9	82	13	18
1894	56	7	4	109	15	14

Year	(57)	(58)	(58a)	(59)	(60)	(61)
1895	36	1	7	72	13	10
1896	33	5	8	78	14	16
1897	30	4	7	74	32	17
1898	30	1	4	66	14	18
1899	8	4	3	32	12	19
1900	12	2	5	34	13	11
1901	10	3	7	55	11	14
1902	14	3	4	50	21	19
1903	12	8	5	67	24	14
1904	9	1	3	69	26	23
1905	20	7	5	110	22	22
1906	14	1	2	82	27	24
1907	7	2	4	54	36	25
1908	8	4	7	57	43	32
1909	7	3	9	60	35	29
1910	7	1	3	28	27	30
1911	5	3	5	54	27	22
1912	6	—	7	54	32	28
1913	7	—	4	43	31	19
1914	6	—	5	51	29	17
1915	2	3	10	54	34	21
1916	5	2	11	55	32	26
1917	4	1	3	20	30	21
1918	—	—	8	21	24	18
1919	3	—	9	30	24	16
1920	1	—	5	16	20	16
1921	3	—	8	25	35	23
1922	1	1	6	29	35	16
1923	2	—	5	23	36	10
1924	5	—	3	21	30	20
1925	3	3	11	27	40	15
1926	1	1	5	24	52	17
1927	5	3	7	31	49	19
1928	2	5	12	33	37	30
1929	2	3	8	25	45	29
1930	4	—	3	23	41	17
1931	3	5	5	28	49	19
1932	2	1	5	16	57	19
1933	1	—	5	11	40	13
1934	3	1	4	13	48	12
1935	1	1	7	14	51	11
1936	—	—	3	7	56	10
1937	1	1	7	10	42	15
1938	—	2	8	11	27	13
1939	1	2	12	20	29	23
1940	2	—	2	6	31	15
1941	—	—	8	11	20	11
1942	—	—	7	12	14	5
1943	—	2	5	11	9	4
1944	—	—	5	11	16	6
1945	1	—	5	10	24	16
1946	1	3	12	21	15	34
1947	2	—	3	10	23	29
1948	—	1	9	14	24	23
1949	1	—	4	9	32	16
1950	2	—	11	18	26	13
1947	—	—	—	—	48	5
1948	1	—	—	3	39	5
1949	—	—	—	6	93	31
1950	2	1	—	11	100	43
1951	1	1	—	4	63	17
1952	1	2	—	8	103	16
1953	2	—	—	9	95	29
1954	2	1	—	6	108	13
1955	—	3	—	11	113	11
1956	3	2	—	9	151	20
1957	4	3	—	13	189	27

	Cotton Ginning and Compressing		Veterinary Medicine
Year	Ginning (62)	Decor- ticating (63)	Animal Medicines, Dips, Sprays, Dental & Surgical Instruments (64)
1837	4	5	–
1838	6	2	–
1839	3	–	–
1840	3	1	1
1841	4	–	–
1842	2	5	–
1843	2	4	–
1844	3	2	–
1845	4	7	–
1846	2	3	–
1847	–	2	–
1848	2	2	–
1849	4	3	–
1850	2	2	–
1851	–	3	–
1852	2	1	–
1853	1	6	–
1854	6	4	–
1855	8	3	–
1856	7	4	–
1857	7	8	–
1858	18	8	–
1859	12	9	–
1860	8	5	–
1861	3	14	1
1862	2	14	–
1863	3	12	3
1864	3	11	–
1865	5	1	3
1866	14	5	11
1867	15	8	14
1868	6	7	13
1869	17	4	15
1870	12	5	8
1871	10	7	11
1872	12	5	9
1873	12	6	2
1874	9	5	1
1875	9	–	3
1876	9	4	7
1874	10	3	1
1875	8	2	5
1876	10	3	6
1877	14	2	10
1878	17	6	19
1879	12	2	12
1880	20	12	7
1881	28	9	4
1882	27	16	5
1883	31	6	12
1884	25	9	14
1885	23	13	10
1886	16	18	18
1887	28	7	8
1888	24	11	11
1889	28	20	16
1890	28	25	6
1891	21	15	8
1892	18	18	5
1893	22	7	8
1894	15	11	7

Year	(62)	(63)	(64)
1895	42	8	4
1896	22	8	5
1897	17	5	6
1898	15	9	3
1899	24	8	5
1900	17	10	5
1901	12	9	6
1902	17	10	5
1903	18	19	4
1904	24	16	8
1905	34	29	12
1906	29	17	15
1907	26	22	8
1908	31	10	12
1909	40	16	10
1910	32	13	5
1911	34	4	7
1912	31	12	5
1913	16	11	8
1914	28	10	8
1915	37	11	8
1916	33	19	4
1917	20	16	8
1918	24	17	3
1919	32	19	8
1920	24	8	5
1921	24	3	3
1922	10	3	5
1923	9	7	7
1924	11	12	5
1925	16	10	5
1926	22	9	4
1927	32	14	8
1928	29	7	4
1929	32	5	2
1930	29	11	8
1931	26	4	1
1932	8	2	2
1933	10	3	8
1934	14	2	4
1935	12	4	5
1936	25	9	5
1937	16	7	4
1938	14	8	5
1939	14	11	4
1940	18	5	3
1941	10	10	6
1942	4	2	3
1943	4	12	5
1944	1	9	—
1945	3	4	4
1946	4	5	8
1947	3	6	9
1948	8	2	13
1949	7	5	11
1950	8	5	10
1947	2	1	3
1948	5	4	6
1949	3	5	2
1950	2	1	16
1951	6	8	14
1952	4	1	10
1953	9	8	12
1954	5	6	7
1955	3	5	8
1956	14	9	14
1957	3	2	23

Year	Traps				
	Self & Ever Set (65)	Impaling or Smiting (66)	Jaw (67)	Misc. (68)	Total 65–68 (69)
1837	–	–	–	–	–
1838	–	–	–	1	1
1839	1	–	–	–	1
1840	–	–	–	–	–
1841	–	–	–	–	–
1842	–	–	–	1	1
1843	–	–	–	1	1
1844	–	1	–	–	1
1845	–	–	–	–	–
1846	–	–	–	1	1
1847	–	–	–	–	–
1848	1	–	1	–	2
1849	–	1	–	–	1
1850	1	–	–	–	1
1851	–	–	–	–	–
1852	–	–	–	2	2
1853	–	1	–	–	1
1854	1	–	2	2	5
1855	1	2	–	–	3
1856	–	–	1	–	1
1857	1	1	1	1	4
1858	4	2	–	5	11
1859	–	–	1	4	5
1860	4	2	–	4	10
1861	3	1	1	1	6
1862	–	–	1	–	1
1863	2	1	1	2	6
1864	3	–	1	4	8
1865	6	2	2	3	13
1866	7	–	2	8	17
1867	9	1	3	25	38
1868	18	4	4	28	54
1869	9	6	6	19	40
1870	6	3	2	15	26
1871	11	6	5	14	36
1872	9	6	3	10	28
1873	7	3	3	10	23
1874	10	4	2	6	22
1875	3	1	–	7	11
1876	7	3	7	9	26
1874	4	4	2	10	20
1875	4	2	3	6	15
1876	9	1	5	9	24
1877	11	11	3	10	27
1878	14	–	1	6	29
1879	9	10	1	10	30
1880	6	6	2	6	20
1881	7	4	–	6	17
1882	9	8	3	5	25
1883	7	8	5	5	25
1884	2	4	2	10	18
1885	3	8	8	6	25
1886	4	7	17	7	35
1887	11	8	9	5	33
1888	6	4	3	9	22
1889	7	6	19	9	41
1890	11	13	7	9	40
1891	7	12	3	14	36
1892	7	7	5	9	28
1893	6	4	5	9	24
1894	10	8	4	13	35

Year	(65)	(66)	(67)	(68)	(69)
1895	9	10	4	13	36
1896	8	6	3	10	27
1897	13	13	9	13	48
1898	9	9	9	11	38
1899	9	12	6	5	32
1900	8	13	5	13	39
1901	5	7	7	12	31
1902	15	8	14	12	49
1903	10	6	7	5	28
1904	14	7	12	4	37
1905	18	5	10	11	44
1906	17	10	19	12	58
1907	29	8	16	22	75
1908	28	16	16	13	73
1909	16	15	15	15	61
1910	20	17	18	15	70
1911	17	13	20	14	64
1912	31	12	16	23	82
1913	21	15	17	13	66
1914	22	6	19	18	65
1915	18	14	14	18	64
1916	24	14	27	15	80
1917	16	6	25	7	54
1918	15	10	10	10	45
1919	16	18	22	16	72
1920	26	10	33	15	84
1921	32	17	27	23	99
1922	28	19	34	19	100
1923	20	18	21	9	68
1924	19	11	21	15	66
1925	16	21	17	14	68
1926	17	13	23	9	62
1927	13	12	10	13	48
1928	20	11	19	20	70
1929	8	8	14	9	39
1930	15	12	13	10	50
1931	7	4	13	5	29
1932	1	11	9	9	30
1933	3	15	6	4	28
1934	3	15	4	4	26
1935	4	15	6	4	29
1936	4	10	5	11	30
1937	6	12	6	13	37
1938	3	10	8	9	30
1939	9	12	9	12	42
1940	10	7	4	7	28
1941	3	9	10	5	27
1942	2	4	1	3	10
1943	4	7	3	2	16
1944	8	10	7	8	33
1945	2	12	7	6	27
1946	8	14	14	12	48
1947	9	10	10	7	36
1948	8	9	6	8	31
1949	4	15	11	3	33
1950	4	10	6	8	28
1947	1	6	4	2	13
1948	2	5	3	8	18
1949	11	9	8	8	36
1950	8	18	16	10	52
1951	11	12	11	8	42
1952	8	21	10	9	48
1953	1	8	4	5	18
1954	3	2	3	5	13
1955	1	4	7	3	15
1956	7	5	3	3	18
1957	6	4	2	4	16

121

		Excavating				
Year	Ditchers (70)	Scoops, exc. wheeled (71)	Scoops, wheeled (72)	Scrapers (73)	Misc. (74)	Total 70–74 (75)
1837	1	–	–	–	–	1
1838	3	–	–	–	–	3
1839	1	–	1	–	–	2
1840	–	–	–	–	–	–
1841	1	–	–	–	–	1
1842	4	–	–	1	–	5
1843	–	–	–	1	–	1
1844	2	1	–	1	–	4
1845	2	–	–	–	–	2
1846	4	–	–	–	–	4
1847	2	–	–	1	–	3
1848	1	–	–	–	1	2
1849	–	1	–	1	–	2
1850	–	2	–	2	1	5
1851	–	–	–	1	–	1
1852	1	–	–	–	–	1
1853	2	–	–	–	–	2
1854	3	2	2	2	–	9
1855	2	–	4	1	–	7
1856	3	–	4	1	4	12
1857	4	1	3	2	1	11
1858	2	–	1	–	4	7
1859	9	2	3	–	27	41
1860	11	1	–	1	20	33
1861	7	–	2	1	7	17
1862	6	1	–	3	1	11
1863	1	–	2	3	3	9
1864	2	–	1	2	1	6
1865	6	–	1	7	4	18
1866	15	1	1	5	1	23
1867	19	8	1	8	4	40
1868	18	9	3	8	4	42
1869	22	17	1	13	–	53
1870	26	12	2	10	2	52
1871	16	3	3	8	4	34
1872	7	5	3	8	3	26
1873	9	1	7	8	4	29
1874	12	4	8	6	11	41
1875	10	4	4	5	4	27
1876	9	7	2	9	1	28
1874	12	4	6	7	12	41
1875	7	6	3	3	3	22
1876	15	7	2	12	2	38
1877	19	3	7	10	10	49
1878	15	4	8	10	1	38
1879	18	4	6	9	3	40
1880	11	9	5	9	6	40
1881	18	15	8	11	5	57
1882	17	12	7	18	5	59
1883	30	12	6	23	11	82
1884	26	7	14	19	5	71
1885	14	4	10	19	9	56
1886	18	1	6	23	8	56
1887	12	4	13	26	6	61
1888	6	5	9	22	15	57
1889	5	4	5	24	6	44
1890	10	–	5	17	3	35
1891	10	5	7	16	3	41
1892	9	2	6	10	5	32
1893	6	3	8	12	10	39
1894	13	4	9	9	12	47

Year	(70)	(71)	(72)	(73)	(74)	(75)
1895	14	3	14	6	10	47
1896	14	7	6	13	7	47
1897	6	1	7	11	6	31
1898	4	1	5	6	4	20
1899	12	5	9	11	6	43
1900	7	5	7	7	10	36
1901	11	2	16	14	16	59
1902	24	5	12	11	17	69
1903	15	3	6	19	30	73
1904	22	8	6	14	24	74
1905	20	17	10	21	22	90
1906	30	21	9	27	19	106
1907	34	17	11	34	22	118
1908	33	19	9	53	21	135
1909	18	20	15	60	22	135
1910	21	27	4	44	13	109
1911	16	26	7	36	25	110
1912	21	13	10	43	19	106
1913	23	14	10	39	13	99
1914	24	14	5	36	11	90
1915	28	14	9	42	15	108
1916	23	11	4	55	16	109
1917	16	10	7	35	8	76
1918	22	13	7	30	13	85
1919	24	17	8	50	10	109
1920	23	19	14	41	25	122
1921	15	18	13	54	23	123
1922	13	13	13	38	8	85
1923	14	23	10	42	14	103
1924	12	17	9	45	20	103
1925	12	18	8	49	19	106
1926	13	30	9	51	13	116
1927	15	27	5	45	14	106
1928	4	22	6	54	15	101
1929	9	32	8	41	13	103
1930	9	28	10	46	18	111
1931	5	29	16	54	6	110
1932	8	22	9	46	10	95
1933	–	9	7	36	3	55
1934	3	16	7	19	5	50
1935	6	11	10	32	6	65
1936	3	8	25	29	6	71
1937	7	12	21	26	9	75
1938	8	15	25	38	10	96
1939	7	8	39	23	10	87
1940	7	13	30	36	10	96
1941	10	7	29	27	13	86
1942	5	7	11	21	5	49
1943	10	9	9	8	4	40
1944	4	6	24	20	13	67
1945	8	11	15	25	15	74
1946	8	15	19	27	14	83
1947	19	7	25	27	15	93
1948	16	14	11	29	8	78
1949	12	8	10	16	13	59
1950	16	6	6	29	16	73
1947	9	3	11	8	4	35
1948	4	4	9	11	6	34
1949	5	8	13	13	10	49
1950	5	9	15	26	16	71
1951	13	5	21	20	5	64
1952	11	11	9	19	16	66
1953	16	9	15	35	16	91
1954	18	8	8	23	9	66
1955	12	9	8	25	12	66
1956	20	9	10	36	27	102
1957	19	4	4	31	14	72

123

	Masonry and Concrete Structures					
Year	Faced Walls (76)	Block Walls (77)	Misc. Walls (78)	Arches (79)	Reinforcing Elements (80)	Misc. (81)	Total 76–81 (82)
1837	–	–	–	–	–	–	–
1838	–	–	–	–	–	–	–
1839	–	–	–	–	1	–	1
1840	–	–	–	–	–	1	1
1841	–	–	–	–	–	–	–
1842	–	–	–	–	–	–	–
1843	–	–	–	–	–	–	–
1844	–	1	–	–	1	–	2
1845	–	–	–	–	–	–	–
1846	–	–	–	–	–	1	1
1847	–	1	–	–	–	–	1
1848	–	–	1	–	–	1	2
1849	–	–	–	–	–	–	–
1850	–	–	–	–	–	1	1
1851	–	–	–	–	–	–	–
1852	–	–	–	–	–	–	–
1853	1	–	–	–	–	–	1
1854	–	–	–	–	–	3	3
1855	–	2	1	1	–	–	4
1856	–	1	1	–	1	1	4
1857	1	–	–	–	3	–	4
1858	–	–	–	1	3	–	4
1859	–	–	1	1	2	–	4
1860	–	–	–	–	–	5	5
1861	–	–	–	–	–	4	4
1862	–	–	2	–	1	2	5
1863	1	–	–	–	–	3	4
1864	–	–	1	–	1	2	4
1865	–	–	–	–	1	2	3
1866	1	2	1	1	–	5	10
1867	1	4	1	1	1	8	16
1868	–	1	2	–	2	4	9
1869	4	6	2	4	3	21	40
1870	2	2	–	4	–	21	29
1871	3	4	2	6	2	13	30
1872	5	6	2	7	3	21	44
1873	1	5	7	11	2	24	50
1874	2	4	1	4	2	17	30
1875	2	2	2	5	3	20	34
1876	1	4	1	7	4	14	31
1874	–	3	–	4	5	18	30
1875	2	2	2	4	–	22	32
1876	–	5	1	6	5	9	26
1877	3	3	1	5	1	14	27
1878	1	4	–	2	–	15	22
1879	4	6	2	5	3	24	44
1880	1	3	–	3	4	13	24
1881	2	8	1	3	4	10	28
1882	7	6	–	14	5	25	57
1883	5	7	4	11	7	19	53
1884	10	6	3	10	12	26	67
1885	8	10	1	12	8	36	75
1886	6	6	1	15	17	25	70
1887	8	3	3	6	12	27	59
1888	5	5	1	10	16	26	63
1889	9	7	7	17	17	33	90
1890	6	14	3	11	10	23	67
1891	7	3	4	25	4	26	69
1892	13	11	10	11	7	26	78
1893	4	8	10	25	17	24	88
1894	5	7	11	28	16	28	95

Year	(76)	(77)	(78)	(79)	(80)	(81)	(82)
1895	6	6	8	21	7	19	67
1896	9	6	6	36	15	30	102
1897	7	2	10	30	11	32	92
1898	10	4	9	34	11	30	98
1899	9	7	11	23	18	36	104
1900	17	14	9	31	14	43	128
1901	18	15	11	39	14	58	155
1902	41	24	18	46	17	91	237
1903	29	57	12	40	25	93	256
1904	21	55	13	33	39	98	259
1905	25	59	10	21	39	121	275
1906	18	60	11	23	66	133	311
1907	15	27	24	43	72	132	313
1908	13	28	16	47	63	137	304
1909	15	33	18	30	56	140	292
1910	11	20	19	29	41	127	247
1911	13	17	15	33	55	126	259
1912	7	19	16	24	47	125	238
1913	6	23	17	15	39	123	223
1914	9	18	15	20	47	113	222
1915	6	31	13	18	31	104	203
1916	4	41	14	18	37	134	248
1917	3	28	11	13	24	115	194
1918	5	35	17	21	42	94	214
1919	8	37	30	14	49	133	271
1920	9	51	30	14	38	142	284
1921	21	57	28	20	40	140	306
1922	20	49	25	13	70	134	311
1923	13	39	33	17	60	101	263
1924	9	32	34	19	57	136	287
1925	14	32	46	33	60	137	322
1926	19	58	59	35	67	153	391
1927	15	37	38	33	67	187	377
1928	23	35	37	35	50	172	352
1929	20	34	54	33	70	138	349
1930	34	25	42	42	70	131	344
1931	36	25	25	51	63	108	308
1932	30	20	50	27	42	99	268
1933	26	30	36	18	32	76	218
1934	20	18	27	22	16	58	161
1935	24	25	35	21	33	86	224
1936	33	40	42	32	36	83	266
1937	18	61	31	27	36	116	289
1938	25	49	29	14	51	102	270
1939	20	38	30	22	46	85	241
1940	14	32	35	8	22	66	177
1941	7	8	32	13	18	38	116
1942	3	5	9	5	7	29	58
1943	4	8	10	7	13	16	58
1944	3	6	5	7	11	33	65
1945	1	15	4	10	14	48	92
1946	4	14	10	2	7	31	68
1947	4	9	5	3	3	28	52
1948	3	16	10	3	2	30	64
1949	1	12	7	4	2	27	53
1950	5	10	10	2	1	37	65
1947	2	1	4	5	7	15	34
1948	2	5	3	3	3	20	36
1949	8	11	7	5	6	28	65
1950	4	11	3	2	3	20	43
1951	1	12	5	3	3	36	60
1952	1	8	6	6	2	40	63
1953	4	14	9	5	2	28	62
1954	3	14	14	6	1	35	73
1955	1	14	12	1	4	25	57
1956	4	10	9	3	3	24	53
1957	4	5	12	–	4	25	50

Year	Mortar Mixers, etc. (83)	Portland Type Cements (84)	Other Type Cements (85)	Total 75,82–85 General Construction (86)
1837	1	–	1	3
1838	–	–	–	3
1839	1	–	1	5
1840	–	–	–	1
1841	–	–	–	1
1842	–	–	–	5
1843	–	–	–	1
1844	1	–	1	8
1845	–	–	1	3
1846	–	–	1	6
1847	–	–	–	4
1848	–	–	–	4
1849	–	–	–	2
1850	–	–	–	6
1851	–	–	–	1
1852	–	–	1	2
1853	–	–	–	3
1854	–	–	–	12
1855	–	–	1	12
1856	–	–	1	17
1857	1	–	1	17
1858	–	–	1	12
1859	–	–	1	46
1860	–	1	1	40
1861	–	–	–	21
1862	–	–	2	18
1863	–	–	1	14
1864	–	–	2	12
1865	–	–	1	22
1866	1	3	4	41
1867	2	6	5	69
1868	–	6	3	60
1869	1	6	5	105
1870	5	6	6	98
1871	3	4	2	73
1872	4	11	6	91
1873	–	8	7	94
1874	2	9	9	91
1875	–	4	8	73
1876	2	4	4	69
1874	2	6	8	87
1875	1	4	10	69
1876	1	4	3	72
1877	–	8	2	86
1878	2	3	2	67
1879	2	5	4	95
1880	1	–	5	70
1881	3	3	9	100
1882	3	9	8	136
1883	1	10	11	157
1884	9	6	10	163
1885	4	5	9	149
1886	2	10	12	150
1887	5	6	10	141
1888	6	3	11	140
1889	8	3	13	158
1890	6	6	18	132
1891	4	6	30	150
1892	4	5	16	135
1893	4	4	19	154
1894	2	4	4	152

Year	(83)	(84)	(85)	(86)
1895	6	2	9	131
1896	3	–	7	159
1897	5	6	5	139
1898	11	1	9	139
1899	9	7	7	170
1900	9	4	5	182
1901	15	6	17	252
1902	26	8	14	354
1903	12	7	22	370
1904	24	9	11	377
1905	49	8	11	433
1906	41	15	12	485
1907	53	8	14	506
1908	55	19	17	530
1909	37	9	9	482
1910	34	8	5	403
1911	39	8	11	427
1912	34	9	6	393
1913	35	15	17	389
1914	27	3	8	350
1915	22	6	4	343
1916	36	7	13	413
1917	20	15	16	321
1918	12	17	9	337
1919	18	14	12	424
1920	25	13	19	463
1921	24	20	13	486
1922	32	9	13	450
1923	27	14	18	425
1924	31	12	23	456
1925	42	12	16	498
1926	60	11	17	595
1927	51	10	10	554
1928	72	13	10	548
1929	56	14	15	537
1930	42	12	16	525
1931	52	13	15	498
1932	21	25	25	434
1933	20	6	9	308
1934	12	17	7	247
1935	19	10	14	332
1936	21	10	9	377
1937	24	9	8	405
1938	24	21	9	420
1939	28	11	12	379
1940	25	12	8	318
1941	24	10	11	247
1942	12	7	7	133
1943	7	5	7	117
1944	17	8	2	159
1945	15	5	9	195
1946	24	13	4	192
1947	32	6	6	189
1948	35	10	7	194
1949	13	10	7	142
1950	23	6	9	176
1947	5	7	4	85
1948	16	5	8	99
1949	20	10	9	153
1950	44	12	10	180
1951	48	5	6	183
1952	19	15	9	172
1953	24	6	5	188
1954	20	4	5	168
1955	21	4	6	154
1956	24	12	6	197
1957	22	19	7	170

Metallic Building Structures

Year	Buildings (87)	Towers (88)	Metallic Poles & Posts (89)	Doors (90)	Windows (91)	Misc. (92)	Total 87–92 (93)
1837	–	–	–	–	–	–	–
1838	–	–	–	–	–	1	1
1839	–	–	–	–	–	–	–
1840	–	–	–	–	–	–	–
1841	–	–	–	–	–	–	–
1842	–	–	–	–	–	–	–
1843	–	–	–	–	–	–	–
1844	–	–	–	–	–	–	–
1845	–	–	–	–	–	1	1
1846	–	–	–	–	–	–	–
1847	–	–	–	–	–	1	1
1848	–	–	–	–	–	–	–
1849	–	1	–	–	–	1	2
1850	–	–	–	–	–	1	1
1851	–	–	–	–	–	2	2
1852	–	–	–	–	–	1	1
1853	–	–	–	–	–	2	2
1854	2	–	–	–	1	5	8
1855	–	–	–	–	–	5	5
1856	2	–	–	–	1	2	5
1857	–	1	–	–	–	–	1
1858	–	–	–	1	–	2	3
1859	6	–	–	–	–	3	9
1860	2	2	1	–	1	–	6
1861	–	2	–	–	–	2	4
1862	3	–	1	1	–	5	10
1863	–	1	–	–	–	4	5
1864	1	2	1	–	–	1	5
1865	–	2	3	–	1	–	6
1866	–	1	4	–	–	3	8
1867	1	3	7	1	–	8	20
1868	2	2	4	2	1	16	27
1869	6	–	10	1	–	20	37
1870	1	–	6	–	–	13	20
1871	1	2	4	–	2	20	29
1872	–	2	9	5	4	22	42
1873	2	–	12	8	3	17	42
1874	3	1	2	2	3	16	27
1875	6	3	8	3	2	19	41
1876	2	1	11	6	1	23	44
1874	3	3	–	3	3	19	31
1875	7	2	12	2	2	21	46
1876	–	2	12	5	2	15	36
1877	3	1	17	–	3	7	31
1878	2	2	20	2	1	6	33
1879	2	2	20	3	1	7	35
1880	1	2	5	1	2	6	17
1881	2	5	18	2	2	5	34
1882	3	14	20	2	3	9	51
1883	2	16	25	5	3	17	68
1884	2	2	16	1	1	29	51
1885	5	4	18	1	2	27	57
1886	12	8	17	6	4	23	70
1887	7	5	21	5	3	17	58
1888	4	9	17	4	–	36	70
1889	3	8	30	9	6	44	100
1890	3	11	37	6	16	32	105
1891	11	15	27	4	4	23	84
1892	9	12	27	2	1	28	79
1893	8	8	13	3	3	19	54
1894	3	12	22	11	–	26	74

Year	(87)	(88)	(89)	(90)	(91)	(92)	(93)
1895	3	8	35	7	2	11	66
1896	7	8	21	11	4	16	67
1897	9	3	20	2	19	13	66
1898	3	1	15	2	22	12	55
1899	9	8	25	4	24	12	82
1900	4	4	13	4	17	30	72
1901	4	6	17	9	19	20	75
1902	10	5	22	9	51	38	135
1903	11	13	23	13	36	52	148
1904	8	9	26	13	63	40	159
1905	4	12	19	17	61	42	155
1906	5	20	38	15	47	60	185
1907	9	10	21	20	69	58	187
1908	7	13	34	24	43	51	172
1909	18	10	28	19	61	52	188
1910	17	7	20	24	41	35	144
1911	15	11	23	28	48	42	167
1912	10	9	16	24	37	48	144
1913	17	8	22	31	38	48	164
1914	11	14	29	30	16	54	154
1915	19	8	35	33	22	67	184
1916	19	13	14	18	29	55	148
1917	13	5	18	30	25	57	148
1918	14	4	10	12	8	50	98
1919	12	7	22	20	16	68	145
1920	9	12	13	26	15	56	131
1921	14	11	15	16	25	49	130
1922	8	9	12	30	30	62	151
1923	7	16	18	12	26	65	144
1924	11	15	13	13	24	70	146
1925	18	22	20	31	31	80	202
1926	26	17	17	27	41	120	248
1927	24	22	18	35	54	138	291
1928	29	13	33	51	57	106	289
1929	21	22	25	42	66	95	271
1930	19	8	20	30	72	107	256
1931	30	10	25	21	57	92	235
1932	30	5	24	19	36	110	224
1933	19	7	14	17	31	100	188
1934	14	3	9	9	31	81	147
1935	14	5	6	7	39	93	164
1936	20	4	11	9	50	102	196
1937	22	3	10	10	37	133	215
1938	21	18	8	11	58	134	250
1939	24	4	9	7	40	107	191
1940	22	10	16	7	38	77	170
1941	16	20	10	4	17	82	149
1942	6	3	9	3	13	50	84
1943	9	5	8	2	8	47	79
1944	7	12	5	3	18	85	130
1945	15	15	8	8	19	61	126
1946	11	11	7	10	36	77	152
1947	10	5	1	5	25	51	97
1948	10	9	8	15	27	69	138
1949	8	10	10	11	21	59	119
1950	4	11	8	18	38	67	146
1947	5	5	2	3	6	37	58
1948	4	1	1	4	7	42	59
1949	7	7	5	3	11	51	84
1950	3	9	6	4	14	28	64
1951	7	8	2	11	36	49	113
1952	15	14	8	15	48	82	182
1953	9	7	7	17	38	67	145
1954	8	11	5	13	21	62	120
1955	8	10	13	20	25	54	130
1956	11	6	10	25	57	80	189
1957	6	16	8	13	46	59	148

129

Building Construction

	Wood Building Structures			
Year	Buildings (94)	Weather-board & Flooring (95)	Misc. Structures & Components (96)	Total 94–96 (97)
1837	–	–	1	1
1838	–	–	2	2
1839	–	–	–	–
1840	–	–	1	1
1841	–	–	1	1
1842	–	–	1	1
1843	–	–	1	1
1844	–	–	–	–
1845	–	–	3	3
1846	–	–	1	1
1847	–	–	1	1
1848	1	–	3	4
1849	–	–	3	3
1850	–	–	2	2
1851	–	–	3	3
1852	–	–	3	3
1853	–	–	–	–
1854	–	1	4	5
1855	–	–	9	9
1856	–	–	5	5
1857	2	–	11	13
1858	–	–	10	10
1859	1	–	5	6
1860	–	1	9	10
1861	–	–	7	7
1862	–	–	8	8
1863	–	–	7	7
1864	1	1	14	16
1865	–	2	19	21
1866	1	1	20	22
1867	1	–	41	42
1868	1	5	43	49
1869	7	3	53	63
1870	2	5	48	55
1871	–	2	29	31
1872	3	3	37	43
1873	1	4	33	38
1874	1	–	42	43
1875	2	5	47	54
1876	2	5	51	58
1874	2	2	43	47
1875	2	4	53	59
1876	1	5	52	58
1877	4	2	47	53
1878	1	1	48	50
1879	3	2	43	48
1880	6	2	44	52
1881	4	3	53	60
1882	9	3	54	66
1883	12	11	60	83
1884	5	7	99	111
1885	8	14	101	123
1886	5	2	106	113
1887	5	1	79	85
1888	7	4	76	87
1889	6	6	101	113
1890	6	7	85	98
1891	2	6	81	89
1892	19	9	78	106
1893	4	8	64	76
1894	9	4	72	85

Year	(94)	(95)	(96)	(97)
1895	4	3	102	109
1896	10	6	112	128
1897	–	5	111	116
1898	4	8	88	100
1899	4	11	115	130
1900	9	4	98	111
1901	17	16	120	153
1902	10	8	119	137
1903	16	9	135	160
1904	21	5	124	150
1905	15	7	137	159
1906	17	8	114	139
1907	14	6	127	147
1908	16	11	137	164
1909	17	9	152	178
1910	18	6	115	139
1911	30	3	117	150
1912	44	3	113	160
1913	48	9	124	181
1914	50	11	124	185
1915	35	4	122	161
1916	38	11	110	159
1917	21	5	106	132
1918	20	9	102	131
1919	38	5	117	160
1920	33	13	129	175
1921	50	12	161	223
1922	38	11	134	183
1923	30	14	159	203
1924	18	13	168	199
1925	20	21	181	222
1926	21	13	217	251
1927	22	18	222	262
1928	33	17	233	283
1929	28	23	219	270
1930	13	32	221	266
1931	16	45	220	281
1932	20	30	204	254
1933	15	17	124	156
1934	8	19	144	171
1935	8	28	202	238
1936	10	29	183	222
1937	14	32	201	247
1938	22	37	152	211
1939	9	32	154	195
1940	16	26	162	204
1941	10	24	121	155
1942	13	10	96	119
1943	6	8	92	106
1944	9	5	102	116
1945	6	10	114	130
1946	10	10	142	162
1947	9	6	144	159
1948	15	7	138	160
1949	14	11	184	209
1950	15	15	180	210
1947	2	2	51	55
1948	3	3	61	67
1949	7	5	78	90
1950	7	11	86	104
1951	14	6	230	250
1952	12	9	250	271
1953	17	17	193	227
1954	13	8	150	171
1955	19	6	152	177
1956	10	10	244	264
1957	13	16	213	242

Building Construction

Year	Scaffolds & Scaffold Supports (98)	Roofs Slat, Shingle, & Tile (99)	Roofs Other Building Roofs (100)	Total 87, 88, 90–92, 97–100 Building (101)	Filters I (102)	Filters II (103)	Filters III (104)	Total 102–104 (105)
1837	–	–	–	1	–	–	1	1
1838	–	–	1	4	–	–	–	–
1839	–	–	1	1	–	–	–	–
1840	–	1	1	3	–	–	–	–
1841	–	–	2	3	–	–	–	–
1842	–	–	2	3	–	–	1	1
1843	–	–	1	2	–	–	–	–
1844	–	–	2	2	–	–	2	2
1845	–	–	–	4	–	–	–	–
1846	–	–	–	1	–	–	5	5
1847	–	–	1	3	–	–	3	3
1848	–	–	–	4	–	–	1	1
1849	–	–	–	4	–	1	2	4
1850	–	–	–	3	–	–	2	2
1851	–	–	1	6	–	1	1	2
1852	–	–	–	4	–	–	–	–
1853	–	–	–	2	–	–	3	3
1854	1	–	2	16	–	–	1	1
1855	2	1	2	19	1	–	3	4
1856	5	–	2	17	1	–	4	5
1857	1	–	6	20	–	–	1	1
1858	1	2	6	20	–	–	2	2
1859	–	1	7	23	1	1	1	3
1860	8	1	2	24	–	2	4	6
1861	–	3	2	14	–	–	6	6
1862	1	2	8	26	–	–	3	3
1863	1	2	6	20	2	–	3	5
1864	1	1	5	25	1	1	3	5
1865	4	1	3	30	1	–	7	8
1866	8	2	17	52	4	4	19	27
1867	26	3	26	107	5	–	23	28
1868	20	1	19	110	–	–	15	15
1869	19	1	22	132	5	1	22	28
1870	19	1	27	116	5	5	22	32
1871	13	7	17	91	1	2	16	19
1872	10	4	19	107	3	–	19	22
1873	12	4	41	125	3	1	18	22
1874	20	10	33	130	3	2	17	22
1875	19	7	22	132	2	4	16	22
1876	11	7	27	135	3	5	21	29
1874	22	7	25	129	3	3	21	27
1875	18	8	26	143	3	3	16	22
1876	12	4	31	127	4	5	17	26
1877	11	6	36	119	6	4	22	32
1878	8	5	20	94	4	4	22	30
1879	14	1	23	99	4	1	25	30
1880	7	3	21	93	9	6	31	46
1881	9	9	27	116	12	3	36	51
1882	22	3	35	143	4	5	31	40
1883	21	1	42	174	8	2	36	46
1884	21	8	50	223	6	4	28	38
1885	32	7	50	247	11	3	40	54
1886	33	6	52	259	7	4	30	41
1887	27	7	39	190	10	9	34	53
1888	25	5	35	196	6	7	21	34
1889	23	13	67	278	8	7	36	51
1890	35	6	52	248	10	6	42	58
1891	29	7	44	211	6	2	32	40
1892	30	8	44	228	9	9	30	48
1893	25	7	37	178	9	6	27	42
1894	31	8	21	185	10	5	33	48

Year	(98)	(99)	(100)	(101)	(102)	(103)	(104)	(105)
1895	25	8	20	185	9	10	58	77
1896	22	3	15	206	7	5	36	48
1897	42	4	17	222	16	12	49	77
1898	20	3	28	190	9	8	50	67
1899	28	7	23	237	14	14	55	83
1900	29	3	28	226	10	9	43	62
1901	26	6	24	261	13	9	38	60
1902	39	6	46	336	13	6	58	77
1903	43	7	35	357	12	8	55	75
1904	45	8	31	358	15	17	65	97
1905	44	6	28	361	17	9	54	80
1906	37	11	42	356	17	10	58	85
1907	43	6	55	407	16	11	51	78
1908	40	11	40	380	16	15	56	87
1909	55	9	46	438	20	10	57	87
1910	54	5	34	349	16	12	50	78
1911	37	3	45	368	17	8	37	62
1912	38	13	53	383	30	8	57	95
1913	44	11	59	429	17	13	59	89
1914	44	5	60	405	15	7	58	80
1915	52	7	53	414	19	12	58	89
1916	47	10	41	378	20	6	66	92
1917	34	11	37	339	13	10	43	66
1918	36	12	44	307	17	2	32	46
1919	40	9	65	390	15	9	48	73
1920	38	20	60	399	12	5	60	77
1921	42	40	64	473	14	11	52	77
1922	52	44	63	472	13	12	49	74
1923	48	44	57	462	15	5	44	64
1924	42	49	61	469	11	8	58	77
1925	54	32	88	556	17	12	72	101
1926	60	14	86	625	26	9	83	118
1927	76	8	71	668	9	8	98	115
1928	47	15	71	659	22	10	74	106
1929	45	14	70	623	18	13	62	93
1930	27	13	88	622	19	10	61	90
1931	36	19	80	616	11	9	60	80
1932	23	11	47	530	13	9	62	84
1933	18	13	33	387	11	3	46	60
1934	39	10	42	397	5	9	75	89
1935	25	14	56	486	9	6	55	70
1936	20	21	61	505	9	11	60	80
1937	27	17	65	558	12	10	64	86
1938	30	12	55	532	7	8	70	85
1939	37	7	58	475	5	10	82	97
1940	35	6	51	440	7	7	53	67
1941	38	5	40	357	5	5	60	70
1942	29	5	34	259	8	11	46	65
1943	20	3	22	217	6	6	49	61
1944	25	6	26	286	7	10	47	64
1945	58	7	33	331	4	10	72	86
1946	70	4	39	409	13	6	68	87
1947	49	4	34	337	3	13	64	80
1948	37	1	35	354	13	13	64	90
1949	35	4	15	362	9	11	57	77
1950	34	–	31	402	7	10	60	77
1947	33	6	30	175	2	1	23	26
1948	31	3	18	176	5	9	42	56
1949	32	3	18	215	6	12	64	82
1950	24	4	18	109	4	6	59	69
1951	48	–	41	442	12	12	85	109
1952	39	2	33	505	9	14	61	84
1953	37	4	39	438	12	10	68	90
1954	30	4	26	335	10	10	60	80
1955	27	1	18	330	5	4	39	48
1956	39	1	21	498	22	19	81	122
1957	45	–	22	431	10	13	64	87

133

Highway and Street Construction

Year	Bridges (106)	Road & Pavement Structure (107)	Road Type Graders (108)	Roadway Snow Excavators (109)	Misc. Pavements (110)	Misc. Road (111)	Total 106–111 (112)
1837	1	–	–	–	–	–	1
1838	1	–	1	–	–	–	2
1839	4	–	–	–	–	–	4
1840	4	2	1	–	–	–	7
1841	4	3	1	–	–	–	8
1842	–	–	–	–	–	–	–
1843	1	1	–	–	–	–	2
1844	1	–	–	–	–	–	1
1845	2	–	–	–	1	–	3
1846	6	–	–	–	–	–	6
1847	3	–	–	–	–	–	3
1848	–	1	–	–	–	–	1
1849	3	–	–	–	–	–	3
1850	2	–	–	–	–	–	2
1851	3	2	–	–	–	–	5
1852	5	–	–	–	–	–	5
1853	2	–	–	–	–	–	2
1854	6	2	1	–	1	2	12
1855	3	3	–	–	1	4	11
1856	7	4	–	–	1	6	18
1857	10	5	–	1	4	3	23
1858	8	2	1	–	6	1	18
1859	11	5	3	–	2	–	21
1860	11	1	3	–	2	–	17
1861	16	3	1	–	1	5	26
1862	11	–	1	–	1	–	13
1863	5	–	–	–	1	2	8
1864	5	3	1	–	1	–	10
1865	9	–	–	–	1	1	11
1866	13	3	–	–	2	2	20
1867	17	20	2	–	1	4	44
1868	28	21	4	1	3	3	60
1869	32	21	4	1	11	5	74
1870	40	47	–	–	7	3	97
1871	28	40	4	–	7	6	85
1872	32	49	2	–	10	7	100
1873	36	13	1	–	34	9	93
1874	29	17	3	4	12	10	75
1875	23	19	3	2	8	5	60
1876	24	20	2	–	8	2	56
1874	28	9	3	5	15	7	67
1875	24	22	1	–	6	4	57
1876	21	15	2	–	7	1	46
1877	15	15	1	1	4	6	42
1878	18	9	1	1	8	6	43
1879	20	8	–	1	4	1	34
1880	19	4	2	1	8	1	35
1881	9	4	3	1	7	4	28
1882	15	10	1	2	12	8	48
1883	18	15	2	2	13	8	58
1884	34	18	3	4	9	12	80
1885	28	14	4	6	13	15	80
1886	23	6	2	5	12	9	57
1887	24	13	2	4	9	7	59
1888	30	15	7	4	9	15	80
1889	42	14	5	3	19	14	97
1890	42	16	4	4	10	14	90
1891	36	13	–	7	9	7	72
1892	36	11	3	3	11	17	81
1893	31	9	1	1	13	12	67
1894	19	6	6	4	8	16	59

Year	(106)	(107)	(108)	(109)	(110)	(111)	(112)
1895	30	1	1	7	4	7	50
1896	25	3	1	8	8	7	52
1897	21	5	4	5	3	5	43
1898	18	4	3	5	9	5	44
1899	25	2	7	3	11	14	62
1900	22	2	3	2	4	6	39
1901	24	8	7	–	9	20	68
1902	24	11	2	5	6	9	57
1903	24	13	6	4	11	22	80
1904	14	8	8	4	15	21	70
1905	22	8	10	7	20	15	82
1906	21	12	8	8	14	14	77
1907	29	8	8	1	9	14	69
1908	23	11	7	5	10	14	70
1909	19	13	2	7	12	16	69
1910	16	11	5	6	17	14	69
1911	24	8	5	4	20	27	88
1912	16	14	2	4	20	15	71
1913	33	16	6	5	15	27	102
1914	14	15	2	6	12	20	69
1915	19	9	4	7	16	21	76
1916	9	13	2	8	12	7	51
1917	14	11	5	5	14	10	59
1918	5	6	4	11	5	8	39
1919	11	29	5	13	14	11	83
1920	13	25	9	27	12	11	97
1921	13	32	11	20	10	10	96
1922	7	44	5	14	15	13	98
1923	9	24	4	27	9	16	89
1924	16	47	4	37	23	15	142
1925	16	52	7	33	22	32	162
1926	12	61	4	43	20	34	174
1927	22	54	11	44	24	29	184
1928	6	48	10	26	33	37	160
1929	9	50	13	29	16	34	151
1930	19	61	10	19	15	35	159
1931	9	51	14	17	16	30	137
1932	7	26	13	15	16	25	102
1933	16	31	5	8	11	14	85
1934	13	49	5	12	7	11	97
1935	10	43	4	11	7	10	85
1936	8	51	4	34	12	17	126
1937	10	48	4	23	7	25	117
1938	7	45	3	27	5	14	101
1939	7	35	1	11	5	19	78
1940	7	36	6	14	6	10	79
1941	14	26	3	12	7	14	76
1942	7	22	1	15	8	6	59
1943	7	16	1	7	9	5	45
1944	7	8	1	10	3	6	35
1945	7	26	4	9	4	5	55
1946	15	13	4	14	1	9	56
1947	5	11	6	10	2	6	40
1948	8	8	4	13	–	8	41
1949	16	5	2	14	1	6	44
1950	9	10	1	9	5	11	44
1947	5	7	1	9	1	2	25
1948	12	7	–	5	–	5	29
1949	11	6	3	4	3	5	32
1950	13	15	4	10	2	7	51
1951	17	11	2	5	2	11	48
1952	17	10	6	15	–	7	55
1953	23	17	2	12	5	8	67
1954	18	3	2	10	2	9	44
1955	10	9	1	14	–	4	38
1956	18	9	3	25	5	7	67
1957	10	7	3	22	4	6	52

Heavy Construction, except Highway and Street: Hydraulic and Earth Engineering

Year	Watergates, Dams & Levees (113)	Misc. Water Control (114)	Earth Control (115)	Stable Structures in Shifting Media (116)	Pile Drivers (117)	Other Apparatus (118)	Total 113–118 (119)
1837	–	1	–	–	–	1	2
1838	2	–	–	–	1	2	5
1839	2	2	–	–	1	–	5
1840	1	–	–	–	–	1	2
1841	3	–	–	–	1	–	4
1842	1	–	–	–	–	–	1
1843	–	–	–	–	–	2	2
1844	1	–	–	–	–	–	1
1845	–	1	–	1	–	–	2
1846	1	–	–	–	–	–	1
1847	–	1	–	–	1	–	2
1848	2	–	–	–	–	–	2
1849	3	–	–	–	–	4	7
1850	4	–	–	–	1	–	5
1851	–	–	–	–	–	–	–
1852	–	3	–	–	–	–	3
1853	–	1	1	–	–	1	3
1854	2	–	–	1	–	4	7
1855	2	–	–	2	–	1	5
1856	6	–	–	–	2	1	9
1857	1	–	–	1	–	1	3
1858	1	–	2	2	2	8	15
1859	3	3	1	2	3	3	15
1860	6	4	1	–	–	2	13
1861	1	–	–	–	–	–	1
1862	3	1	1	4	–	2	11
1863	–	4	–	–	1	2	7
1864	3	1	1	3	2	3	13
1865	5	–	–	3	–	1	9
1866	6	2	1	1	6	2	18
1867	9	6	3	1	4	4	27
1868	8	3	2	6	7	1	27
1869	6	4	–	3	7	6	26
1870	7	9	3	5	5	5	34
1871	9	3	–	–	1	5	18
1872	1	4	4	–	5	3	17
1873	2	7	1	1	5	4	20
1874	7	9	1	1	1	3	22
1875	5	5	1	1	3	2	17
1876	3	11	3	4	9	1	31
1874	8	4	–	1	1	2	16
1875	4	8	1	4	4	2	23
1876	4	10	3	1	9	1	28
1877	5	10	–	2	3	2	22
1878	4	8	–	2	4	3	21
1879	2	9	2	2	5	4	24
1880	10	9	1	5	3	5	33
1881	8	15	6	1	5	4	39
1882	6	5	1	4	5	4	25
1883	8	12	2	3	8	10	43
1884	8	11	9	1	12	4	45
1885	13	9	9	4	4	6	45
1886	7	6	10	5	5	5	38
1887	3	8	5	8	3	4	31
1888	10	14	7	5	6	9	51
1889	7	18	4	2	4	6	41
1890	11	15	6	4	13	8	57
1891	12	12	10	8	4	7	53
1892	8	9	4	2	10	12	45
1893	10	8	5	3	10	5	41
1894	8	11	3	2	4	6	34

Year	(113)	(114)	(115)	(116)	(117)	(118)	(119)
1895	10	12	2	2	4	5	35
1896	6	8	4	10	7	16	51
1897	13	11	10	5	5	15	59
1898	6	16	5	3	6	15	51
1899	9	8	9	9	3	5	43
1900	14	10	10	11	5	9	59
1901	7	14	8	10	7	11	57
1902	12	9	25	18	11	20	95
1903	13	11	20	35	17	13	109
1904	25	11	24	39	21	15	135
1905	22	21	13	43	19	30	148
1906	22	22	30	36	11	19	140
1907	25	23	23	34	14	7	126
1908	27	19	18	35	14	11	124
1909	20	33	23	44	12	12	144
1910	25	27	17	26	7	12	114
1911	27	44	19	32	17	7	146
1912	33	51	16	45	15	7	167
1913	35	35	15	20	16	11	132
1914	13	24	10	16	10	9	82
1915	15	21	21	10	10	10	87
1916	14	22	13	14	8	21	92
1917	9	13	6	11	5	11	55
1918	10	14	13	15	5	24	81
1919	11	26	17	8	8	29	99
1920	16	32	9	17	8	20	102
1921	17	32	6	12	5	8	80
1922	16	22	5	19	9	4	75
1923	9	15	5	20	9	3	61
1924	18	23	3	11	8	7	70
1925	11	34	13	23	4	8	93
1926	11	15	14	38	7	9	94
1927	18	19	17	32	8	3	97
1928	23	13	15	25	7	25	108
1929	20	14	17	29	13	12	105
1930	25	13	26	31	15	10	120
1931	21	20	27	34	14	12	128
1932	26	12	26	33	9	17	123
1933	14	18	18	16	7	15	88
1934	17	15	17	24	14	8	95
1935	14	18	16	11	2	8	69
1936	12	12	13	21	5	9	72
1937	13	25	12	17	3	8	78
1938	6	19	19	32	2	15	93
1939	10	11	23	14	4	8	70
1940	2	4	6	9	8	5	34
1941	5	6	6	3	3	5	28
1942	3	8	6	10	3	13	43
1943	2	5	4	7	3	8	29
1944	3	8	6	14	5	8	44
1945	6	16	8	19	4	5	58
1946	3	16	9	8	8	6	50
1947	7	13	8	21	3	7	59
1948	6	5	7	24	4	9	55
1949	7	7	11	17	9	6	57
1950	9	11	6	10	9	12	47
1947	2	6	3	10	3	3	27
1948	2	15	8	5	2	3	35
1949	3	5	3	8	5	2	27
1950	–	13	3	10	4	5	35
1951	6	4	7	17	7	7	48
1952	11	11	5	25	7	9	68
1953	10	20	11	13	8	11	73
1954	14	11	10	10	9	7	61
1955	7	5	4	7	3	3	29
1956	7	11	11	11	3	9	52
1957	5	11	8	7	6	9	46

137

	Heavy Construction: Sewage	Building Construction: Special Trades		Building Construction Mixed with Other Fields
Year	Treatment & Equipment (120)	Heating Systems (121)	Total 86, 105, 112, 119–121 Construction (122)	Wood Building and Other Wood Products (123)
1837	–	–	8	–
1838	–	1	15	–
1839	–	–	15	–
1840	–	–	13	–
1841	–	–	16	–
1842	–	–	10	–
1843	–	–	7	–
1844	–	1	15	–
1845	–	–	12	–
1846	–	–	19	–
1847	–	–	15	–
1848	–	4	16	–
1849	–	–	21	–
1850	–	1	19	–
1851	–	1	15	–
1852	–	–	14	–
1853	–	–	13	–
1854	–	3	51	1
1855	–	1	52	–
1856	–	2	68	–
1857	–	4	69	–
1858	1	6	76	–
1859	1	2	111	–
1860	1	2	106	
1861	1	3	74	1
1862	–	1	75	–
1863	–	2	57	–
1864	–	4	72	1
1865	–	5	90	1
1866	3	2	168	1
1867	2	1	288	4
1868	1	7	286	–
1869	5	8	388	3
1870	1	9	393	2
1871	3	5	300	4
1872	7	1	356	6
1873	8	6	380	2
1874	4	6	353	7
1875	3	6	324	6
1876	13	7	352	9
1874	3	6	338	7
1875	4	6	338	7
1876	15	6	334	7
1877	12	13	344	9
1878	25	6	308	12
1879	20	6	330	11
1880	12	12	308	18
1881	18	11	386	15
1882	19	18	463	19
1883	14	15	548	19
1884	15	17	599	13
1885	14	13	624	14
1886	22	25	607	17
1887	17	25	542	22
1888	20	8	555	27
1889	18	12	693	32
1890	22	18	673	26
1891	31	22	621	26
1892	26	24	626	13
1893	23	18	544	19
1894	29	11	552	10

	(120)	(121)	(122)	(123)
1895	23	18	562	21
1896	20	13	578	23
1897	15	5	583	17
1898	16	22	545	13
1899	17	16	661	26
1900	24	15	624	25
1901	13	20	754	39
1902	23	22	991	44
1903	27	29	1083	44
1904	27	36	1135	40
1905	29	35	1199	45
1906	26	26	1253	42
1907	19	30	1266	57
1908	28	40	1306	55
1909	31	17	1306	66
1910	30	22	1092	54
1911	25	18	1168	41
1912	30	27	1191	44
1913	24	30	1225	39
1914	26	29	1084	36
1915	25	44	1121	43
1916	22	28	1103	42
1917	14	36	913	22
1918	10	30	864	21
1919	15	21	1134	39
1920	18	28	1209	42
1921	15	25	1278	25
1922	23	25	1238	40
1923	14	27	1176	26
1924	22	31	1295	29
1925	27	27	1506	23
1926	18	27	1685	30
1927	22	43	1723	30
1928	23	40	1690	14
1929	18	37	1611	17
1930	25	39	1608	17
1931	35	45	1574	11
1932	34	32	1245	9
1933	26	24	911	21
1934	20	35	897	24
1935	26	51	1130	6
1936	52	34	1261	11
1937	21	37	1315	7
1938	20	64	1341	11
1939	25	61	1198	8
1940	21	33	1018	10
1941	14	36	858	11
1942	10	23	604	7
1943	9	17	508	4
1944	7	24	636	4
1945	21	30	799	8
1946	22	30	864	4
1947	21	27	759	11
1948	19	34	804	11
1949	15	26	743	2
1950	15	17	807	7
1947	4	10	359	1
1948	9	15	421	4
1949	18	39	578	2
1950	19	47	615	6
1951	21	32	893	15
1952	17	25	948	11
1953	22	14	906	8
1954	8	18	730	2
1955	8	16	646	7
1956	22	19	993	10
1957	18	20	850	3

Railroads: Rolling Stock

Year	Steam (124)	Electric (125)	Transmission of Electricity to Vehicles (126)	Wheel or Axle Drive (127)	Furnaces (128)	Misc. (129)	Total 124–129 (130)
1837	1	–	–	–	–	2	3
1838	–	–	–	–	–	–	–
1839	–	–	–	–	–	2	2
1840	2	–	–	–	–	1	3
1841	–	–	–	–	–	1	1
1842	–	–	–	2	–	–	2
1843	2	–	–	–	–	1	3
1844	–	–	–	1	–	–	1
1845	–	–	–	–	–	1	1
1846	2	–	–	–	–	2	4
1847	–	–	–	–	1	1	2
1848	1	–	–	–	–	–	1
1849	1	–	–	–	2	3	6
1850	–	–	–	–	1	1	2
1851	1	–	–	–	–	3	4
1852	–	–	–	–	–	–	–
1853	–	–	–	–	–	–	–
1854	1	–	–	1	1	1	4
1855	1	–	–	–	–	–	1
1856	–	–	–	–	1	–	1
1857	1	–	–	–	3	–	4
1858	–	–	–	–	2	1	3
1859	1	–	1	4	2	1	9
1860	–	–	–	1	1	6	8
1861	–	–	–	–	2	4	6
1862	1	–	–	1	1	3	6
1863	1	–	–	–	1	–	2
1864	–	–	–	3	2	3	8
1865	–	–	–	8	–	7	15
1866	3	–	–	3	–	7	14
1867	1	–	–	10	1	8	20
1868	3	–	–	6	2	7	17
1869	1	–	–	6	2	7	16
1870	–	–	–	6	3	6	15
1871	2	–	–	9	3	5	19
1872	4	–	–	10	7	11	32
1873	1	–	1	13	–	17	32
1874	2	–	–	16	–	24	42
1875	1	–	–	19	4	12	36
1876	1	–	2	12	6	22	43
1874	2	–	–	16	1	23	42
1875	2	–	–	19	4	12	37
1876	3	–	2	15	6	18	44
1877	2	–	–	18	6	11	37
1878	–	–	–	11	5	14	30
1879	2	–	3	14	7	17	43
1880	5	2	4	13	7	17	48
1881	3	–	3	14	11	8	39
1882	5	2	12	28	7	31	85
1883	3	8	16	6	8	27	68
1884	3	1	19	19	7	18	67
1885	2	9	64	23	9	17	124
1886	4	12	72	42	6	33	169
1887	–	15	74	35	5	19	148
1888	3	14	108	30	1	18	174
1889	8	27	157	34	7	21	254
1890	4	36	241	45	6	24	356
1891	3	36	169	35	9	23	275
1892	2	10	154	15	8	16	205
1893	2	9	168	7	4	16	206
1894	1	6	264	12	9	16	308

Year	(124)	(125)	(126)	(127)	(128)	(129)	(130)
1895	3	7	178	17	2	9	216
1896	–	3	201	18	2	12	236
1897	3	3	178	21	5	13	223
1898	2	4	114	18	4	5	147
1899	2	2	127	12	7	13	163
1900	11	2	154	9	5	16	197
1901	6	2	178	11	5	18	220
1902	5	10	170	11	11	30	237
1903	2	7	246	12	5	30	302
1904	4	5	223	14	10	29	285
1905	8	12	197	19	3	17	256
1906	10	11	168	17	5	20	231
1907	8	6	185	14	7	30	250
1908	8	8	185	19	17	22	259
1909	9	9	155	28	8	35	244
1910	8	8	106	12	14	33	181
1911	5	1	136	23	32	32	229
1912	8	4	105	21	21	24	183
1913	7	6	92	15	25	32	177
1914	6	4	104	19	11	35	179
1915	7	5	99	17	13	31	172
1916	3	9	67	37	18	38	172
1917	5	11	49	16	15	32	128
1918	4	8	58	15	7	22	114
1919	23	8	79	23	15	37	185
1920	17	6	85	21	17	33	179
1921	9	9	135	23	11	41	228
1922	26	5	114	30	11	43	229
1923	27	4	79	24	3	49	186
1924	32	4	62	24	6	55	183
1925	38	–	70	9	7	36	160
1926	29	6	40	22	14	44	155
1927	22	4	67	32	17	39	181
1928	15	11	46	16	25	38	151
1929	27	9	57	15	27	25	160
1930	17	10	56	10	18	36	147
1931	22	1	42	8	24	17	114
1932	16	1	32	18	16	31	114
1933	5	2	25	6	18	18	74
1934	8	1	33	8	21	28	99
1935	8	–	30	9	8	36	91
1936	3	5	33	8	12	15	76
1937	19	1	21	3	8	14	66
1938	16	3	48	5	22	20	114
1939	5	2	31	10	7	7	62
1940	5	7	31	5	9	10	67
1941	4	–	27	9	1	7	48
1942	4	2	17	8	5	4	40
1943	5	1	18	8	1	3	36
1944	4	2	27	6	1	11	51
1945	8	1	27	12	3	5	56
1946	5	1	24	6	1	9	46
1947	1	2	22	6	2	9	42
1948	2	3	14	2	–	8	29
1949	–	1	29	3	–	10	43
1950	–	1	23	3	–	9	36
1947	3	–	10	5	2	3	23
1948	2	–	18	2	–	2	24
1949	3	1	23	3	–	3	33
1950	5	–	31	8	2	7	53
1951	3	5	13	8	1	9	39
1952	3	1	24	3	1	13	45
1953	–	2	18	5	–	7	32
1954	–	2	13	2	–	5	22
1955	–	–	19	2	–	12	33
1956	–	5	8	8	–	1	22
1957	–	2	18	1	2	3	26

141

Railroads: Rolling Stock

Year	Passenger Cars					Freight Cars	
	Trains (131)	Sleeping (132)	Regular Passenger (133)	Misc. (134)	Total 131–134 (135)	Dumping (136)	Ice & Refrigerator (137)
1837	–	–	–	–	–	–	–
1838	1	–	–	–	1	–	–
1839	–	–	–	–	–	–	–
1840	–	–	–	–	–	–	–
1841	–	1	–	–	1	–	–
1842	–	–	–	–	–	–	–
1843	–	–	–	–	–	1	–
1844	–	–	–	–	–	–	–
1845	–	–	–	–	–	–	–
1846	–	–	–	–	–	–	–
1847	–	–	–	–	–	1	–
1848	–	–	–	–	–	–	–
1849	–	–	–	–	–	2	–
1850	–	–	–	1	1	–	–
1851	1	–	–	–	1	–	–
1852	1	–	–	2	3	–	–
1853	–	–	–	3	3	–	–
1854	–	–	1	4	5	3	–
1855	–	–	1	3	4	–	–
1856	–	2	1	2	5	–	–
1857	–	–	1	2	3	1	–
1958	–	16	–	5	21	–	–
1859	–	12	–	10	22	2	–
1860	1	6	2	4	13	–	–
1861	–	–	1	1	2	–	–
1862	–	–	–	–	–	–	–
1863	–	–	–	1	1	1	–
1864	–	1	1	2	4	2	–
1865	4	2	1	2	9	–	–
1866	–	3	–	1	4	1	–
1867	–	6	–	2	8	2	3
1868	–	4	1	1	6	3	2
1869	–	4	2	7	13	6	–
1870	–	5	1	2	8	8	3
1871	1	2	3	1	7	14	2
1872	–	4	4	3	11	15	1
1873	–	4	3	3	10	13	–
1874	–	4	7	6	17	13	1
1875	–	10	4	3	17	2	2
1876	–	7	4	2	13	8	3
1874	–	4	3	4	11	10	1
1875	–	8	4	4	16	3	3
1876	–	9	4	3	16	6	2
1877	–	4	1	4	9	6	6
1878	–	4	4	1	9	3	1
1879	–	2	1	3	6	4	2
1880	1	7	4	3	15	8	6
1881	–	17	2	9	28	17	7
1882	3	15	12	1	31	20	5
1883	–	8	9	3	20	18	16
1884	–	7	6	6	19	15	6
1885	–	4	9	4	17	13	6
1886	2	10	9	14	35	11	7
1887	7	6	17	7	37	17	4
1888	11	9	8	9	37	13	4
1889	12	9	8	8	37	25	4
1890	25	12	13	22	72	16	5
1891	19	7	21	7	54	18	7
1892	15	11	11	8	45	15	8
1893	12	9	13	17	51	17	14
1894	9	4	8	18	39	23	5

Year	(131)	(132)	(133)	(134)	(135)	(136)	(137)
1895	3	10	7	10	30	18	4
1896	3	5	10	5	23	17	4
1897	4	6	15	5	30	16	10
1898	2	4	12	3	21	21	2
1899	–	4	11	5	20	33	3
1900	–	3	5	3	11	47	5
1901	3	5	11	7	26	50	7
1902	6	5	17	12	40	80	2
1903	7	4	32	20	63	108	5
1904	5	6	19	16	46	68	2
1905	9	3	17	20	49	81	8
1906	12	10	26	30	78	87	2
1907	9	9	18	13	49	112	4
1908	3	8	63	21	95	107	3
1909	6	7	35	26	74	97	10
1910	6	6	31	16	59	104	4
1911	5	5	13	18	41	81	6
1912	18	6	24	37	85	72	7
1913	14	2	30	17	63	56	1
1914	20	2	10	15	47	58	4
1915	13	4	17	13	47	46	4
1916	16	3	8	6	33	36	10
1917	2	6	13	13	34	59	7
1918	1	3	10	6	20	49	4
1919	3	–	18	8	29	70	5
1920	6	–	19	6	31	39	5
1921	11	1	7	4	23	85	3
1922	6	1	12	8	27	116	5
1923	10	4	6	9	29	80	10
1924	9	7	12	2	30	65	7
1925	17	3	8	10	38	74	8
1926	20	4	7	5	36	57	27
1927	18	8	6	8	40	41	28
1928	19	5	8	9	41	59	21
1929	10	7	11	6	34	84	29
1930	16	3	7	2	28	48	30
1931	11	1	5	5	22	48	24
1932	3	5	4	6	18	22	45
1933	11	3	–	7	21	32	22
1934	21	3	1	16	41	13	36
1935	24	2	2	4	32	12	22
1936	21	2	3	2	28	14	24
1937	17	5	7	9	38	18	36
1938	6	3	9	9	27	15	47
1939	6	5	5	8	24	11	48
1940	13	4	6	7	30	6	46
1941	6	4	3	1	14	13	36
1942	3	1	–	1	5	5	10
1943	5	3	2	1	11	4	16
1944	2	2	–	5	9	7	14
1945	5	8	4	12	29	6	19
1946	2	11	4	5	22	12	22
1947	7	7	6	9	29	20	21
1948	7	13	2	9	31	13	17
1949	6	3	3	5	17	31	15
1950	1	–	–	1	2	12	22
1947	2	–	–	2	4	3	7
1948	–	–	1	1	2	2	18
1949	3	7	1	3	14	10	18
1950	2	3	5	12	22	10	32
1951	5	25	2	10	42	15	16
1952	4	8	7	7	26	18	19
1953	10	1	5	8	24	29	21
1954	3	1	5	3	12	12	22
1955	2	1	–	–	3	6	7
1956	5	5	1	6	17	28	32
1957	13	3	2	7	25	11	26

Railroads: Rolling Stock

Year	Freight Cars			General			
	General Freight (138)	Stock (139)	Total 136-139 (140)	Wheels & Axles (141)	Draft Appliances (142)	Track Sanders (143)	Brakes (144)
1837	–	–	–	1	1	–	–
1838	–	–	–	4	2	–	1
1839	–	–	–	2	–	–	–
1840	–	–	–	2	2	–	2
1841	–	–	–	2	2	2	–
1842	–	–	–	1	–	–	2
1843	–	–	1	3	–	–	–
1844	–	–	–	1	1	–	–
1845	–	–	–	1	1	–	–
1846	–	–	–	4	2	–	2
1847	–	–	1	9	2	–	1
1848	–	–	–	3	1	–	1
1849	–	–	2	13	4	–	3
1850	–	–	–	10	3	–	–
1851	1	–	1	8	4	–	1
1852	–	–	–	10	1	–	11
1853	–	–	–	6	1	–	4
1854	–	–	3	11	4	–	9
1855	–	–	–	1	5	–	6
1856	–	–	–	5	7	–	8
1857	–	–	1	7	5	–	7
1858	–	–	–	11	20	–	19
1859	1	–	3	9	23	–	9
1860	1	2	3	9	22	–	6
1861	–	1	1	5	13	–	7
1862	–	–	–	5	17	–	4
1863	2	–	3	3	23	–	4
1864	3	1	6	10	26	–	8
1865	9	–	9	8	39	1	8
1866	6	–	7	11	54	1	23
1867	5	3	13	16	101	–	17
1868	10	1	16	20	84	–	22
1869	5	6	17	34	91	–	11
1870	1	4	16	29	79	1	18
1871	3	11	30	21	91	–	15
1872	1	7	24	20	106	2	15
1873	4	4	21	20	157	1	16
1874	5	3	22	30	220	–	21
1875	5	6	15	11	157	–	24
1876	3	6	20	17	157	1	19
1874	5	3	19	20	215	–	19
1875	6	6	18	11	141	1	22
1876	2	5	15	20	150	1	17
1877	4	4	20	21	96	1	14
1878	3	4	11	21	84	1	19
1879	6	6	18	15	101	1	19
1880	8	57	79	23	136	1	28
1881	4	42	70	21	197	1	31
1882	5	34	64	27	402	2	69
1883	4	12	50	43	321	4	60
1884	14	15	50	34	291	5	40
1885	10	34	63	28	283	4	32
1886	11	14	43	46	335	6	48
1887	5	21	47	33	283	4	36
1888	12	32	61	27	241	6	51
1889	25	26	80	32	278	9	64
1890	23	26	70	28	390	7	59
1891	13	11	49	35	402	16	79
1892	17	7	47	20	419	17	48
1893	15	2	48	14	372	24	62
1894	7	5	40	11	241	21	47

144

Year	(138)	(139)	(140)	(141)	(142)	(143)	(144)
1895	13	2	37	14	226	30	56
1896	16	4	41	12	222	25	49
1897	11	5	42	8	174	19	46
1898	7	6	36	15	126	10	21
1899	23	1	60	24	143	18	36
1900	21	4	77	8	143	19	36
1901	38	1	96	22	162	16	53
1902	51	1	134	26	204	18	61
1903	38	4	155	12	187	33	74
1904	49	6	125	30	178	19	56
1905	61	5	155	30	189	23	38
1906	81	4	174	14	168	16	65
1907	66	6	188	24	156	28	64
1908	40	2	152	30	191	23	43
1909	45	5	157	26	181	27	36
1910	54	5	167	30	141	24	48
1911	39	6	132	15	160	14	42
1912	54	6	139	23	162	24	42
1913	92	3	152	16	197	21	53
1914	85	4	151	26	220	16	48
1915	83	4	137	26	212	20	42
1916	64	2	112	17	197	25	58
1917	60	2	128	10	174	16	27
1918	48	2	103	32	129	12	24
1919	74	2	151	20	124	9	27
1920	87	4	135	17	154	19	33
1921	59	6	153	14	187	12	40
1922	54	5	180	25	166	20	28
1923	45	3	138	14	214	16	22
1924	73	5	150	15	164	18	27
1925	78	3	163	16	194	13	53
1926	80	7	171	25	148	16	28
1927	67	5	141	14	148	14	34
1928	63	7	150	13	189	9	52
1929	86	1	200	28	141	21	31
1930	65	2	145	19	89	19	47
1931	94	—	166	31	116	17	47
1932	59	4	130	37	52	8	20
1933	52	2	108	37	37	3	15
1934	39	—	88	24	38	10	18
1935	48	2	84	13	38	4	28
1936	50	1	89	11	48	7	51
1937	59	—	113	9	59	18	46
1938	49	—	111	10	47	11	56
1939	29	—	88	11	54	19	52
1940	39	—	91	8	40	22	48
1941	25	—	74	4	40	10	31
1942	23	—	38	4	20	8	29
1943	16	—	36	9	39	5	18
1944	34	—	55	7	55	7	26
1945	17	1	43	9	43	7	27
1946	34	—	68	11	58	12	19
1947	32	—	73	13	34	9	16
1948	30	1	61	3	32	8	25
1949	33	—	79	3	36	7	17
1950	28	—	62	4	34	10	24
1947	17	—	27	1	29	5	18
1948	10	—	30	4	26	10	11
1949	25	—	53	9	32	10	12
1950	24	1	67	10	54	10	24
1951	43	—	74	13	45	5	14
1952	53	1	91	5	39	7	19
1953	37	2	89	12	45	9	29
1954	19	1	54	—	28	7	23
1955	19	1	33	1	27	7	10
1956	45	1	106	3	44	8	16
1957	36	—	73	3	47	5	40

145

Year	General Bogie Trucks (145)	Other Trucks (146)	Car Doors (147)	Misc. (148)	Total 141-148 (149)	Total 130, 135, 140, 149 Rolling Stock (150)
1837	1	1	–	–	4	7
1838	2	–	–	1	10	11
1839	–	1	–	–	3	5
1840	–	1	–	–	7	10
1841	1	2	–	1	10	12
1842	–	1	–	–	4	6
1843	1	1	–	–	5	9
1844	1	1	–	–	4	5
1845	2	–	–	–	4	5
1846	1	–	–	1	10	14
1847	–	–	–	–	12	15
1848	–	1	–	–	6	7
1849	2	1	–	–	23	31
1850	1	1	–	2	17	20
1851	2	1	–	2	18	24
1852	2	–	–	2	26	29
1853	–	–	–	2	13	16
1854	1	2	1	4	32	44
1855	–	–	–	12	24	29
1856	–	1	–	3	24	30
1857	–	3	–	2	24	32
1858	–	5	–	8	63	87
1859	4	3	–	9	57	91
1860	3	7	–	10	57	81
1861	1	3	–	10	39	48
1862	3	8	–	6	43	49
1863	5	4	–	13	52	58
1864	1	5	–	11	61	79
1865	6	8	–	11	81	114
1866	7	5	–	14	115	140
1867	7	14	2	23	180	221
1868	2	11	–	21	160	199
1869	7	12	3	29	187	233
1870	2	8	2	22	161	200
1871	3	16	4	21	171	227
1872	4	14	4	16	181	248
1873	3	10	3	36	246	309
1874	4	12	8	28	323	404
1875	6	11	6	27	242	310
1876	3	9	9	25	240	316
1874	9	13	8	31	315	387
1875	2	9	6	22	214	285
1876	2	7	7	36	240	315
1877	3	14	5	20	174	240
1878	4	15	10	19	173	223
1879	3	15	9	21	184	251
1880	5	17	16	26	252	394
1881	7	13	14	40	324	461
1882	3	22	17	46	588	768
1883	9	16	18	44	515	653
1884	22	21	13	39	465	601
1885	6	11	11	29	404	608
1886	9	16	19	30	509	756
1887	13	15	16	58	458	690
1888	13	27	19	60	444	716
1889	19	21	29	87	539	910
1890	11	24	31	79	629	1127
1891	11	42	25	66	676	1054
1892	13	41	13	46	617	914
1893	13	36	20	53	594	899
1894	10	45	11	50	436	823

Year	(145)	(146)	(147)	(148)	(149)	(150)
1895	27	31	22	39	445	728
1896	49	41	24	67	489	789
1897	45	27	17	56	392	687
1898	19	26	17	54	288	492
1899	25	41	34	54	375	618
1900	22	28	29	55	340	625
1901	33	49	40	48	423	765
1902	61	54	40	86	550	961
1903	51	50	43	70	520	1040
1904	41	33	41	79	477	933
1905	45	53	48	104	530	990
1906	49	48	42	87	489	972
1907	53	42	56	112	535	1022
1908	49	43	48	120	547	1053
1909	32	45	59	128	534	1009
1910	43	45	47	94	472	879
1911	53	45	47	130	506	908
1912	55	45	46	129	526	933
1913	71	46	38	114	556	948
1914	50	54	39	140	593	970
1915	58	29	45	107	539	895
1916	29	28	42	83	479	796
1917	37	36	23	64	387	677
1918	10	41	20	41	309	546
1919	22	41	37	43	323	688
1920	37	51	45	33	389	734
1921	43	48	25	42	411	815
1922	49	59	34	50	431	867
1923	53	32	27	46	424	777
1924	48	36	31	39	378	741
1925	68	60	22	64	490	851
1926	62	57	25	48	409	771
1927	73	69	42	57	451	813
1928	91	71	25	47	497	839
1929	67	74	26	70	458	852
1930	39	52	30	52	347	667
1931	73	58	23	56	421	723
1932	54	32	18	37	258	520
1933	29	35	19	25	200	403
1934	27	31	25	44	217	445
1935	32	32	13	38	198	405
1936	22	36	14	46	235	428
1937	42	21	18	43	256	473
1938	45	18	24	46	257	509
1939	45	20	14	40	255	429
1940	49	27	23	23	240	428
1941	76	23	22	24	230	366
1942	33	13	10	18	135	218
1943	55	10	4	14	154	237
1944	57	22	6	16	196	311
1945	54	19	11	20	190	318
1946	35	6	8	14	163	299
1947	33	9	18	15	147	291
1948	35	11	18	18	150	271
1949	20	2	9	12	106	245
1950	40	10	21	21	164	264
1947	22	7	1	9	92	146
1948	18	3	5	2	79	135
1949	41	13	4	15	136	236
1950	37	12	9	21	177	319
1951	40	14	25	13	169	324
1952	24	9	24	22	149	311
1953	27	10	21	20	173	318
1954	22	2	8	12	102	190
1955	34	7	18	13	117	186
1956	40	15	19	13	158	303
1957	21	14	23	18	171	295

147

Year	Ties & Tie Plates (151)	Rails, Rail seats, etc. (152)	Fastenings (153)	Misc. (154)	Total 151-154 (155)
1837	–	4	–	–	4
1838	–	–	–	1	1
1839	–	4	–	1	5
1840	–	1	–	3	4
1841	–	–	–	–	–
1842	–	–	1	–	1
1843	–	–	–	–	–
1844	–	2	–	–	2
1845	1	–	–	1	2
1846	–	–	–	–	–
1847	–	1	–	–	1
1848	–	2	–	–	2
1849	–	2	–	1	3
1850	1	2	–	–	3
1851	–	–	–	–	–
1852	–	–	–	–	–
1853	–	3	–	–	3
1854	–	1	–	1	2
1855	–	2	–	–	2
1856	–	4	–	1	5
1857	1	5	1	2	9
1858	–	28	–	6	34
1859	2	32	–	6	40
1860	–	10	–	1	11
1861	1	10	–	2	13
1862	1	10	–	2	13
1863	1	5	–	–	6
1864	–	15	–	–	15
1865	1	17	–	–	18
1866	2	19	–	4	25
1867	3	36	1	7	47
1868	3	36	–	9	48
1869	1	45	2	9	57
1870	2	34	3	9	48
1871	4	21	1	3	29
1872	9	41	–	6	56
1873	6	47	2	9	64
1874	5	23	1	12	41
1875	5	34	1	11	51
1876	11	29	–	9	49
1874	4	23	1	9	37
1875	7	32	1	9	49
1876	9	29	1	9	48
1877	3	21	1	15	40
1878	17	23	–	21	61
1879	11	30	2	17	60
1880	11	21	1	12	45
1881	14	29	2	15	60
1882	24	38	1	19	82
1883	24	47	5	21	97
1884	20	41	6	20	87
1885	29	46	6	24	105
1886	34	69	10	31	144
1887	48	67	9	34	158
1888	40	74	8	29	151
1889	45	85	10	36	176
1890	79	116	14	33	242
1891	53	101	11	27	192
1892	59	79	11	37	186
1893	40	55	6	29	130
1894	32	42	3	26	103

Year	(151)	(152)	(153)	(154)	(155)
1895	34	52	2	34	122
1896	37	44	4	26	111
1897	39	66	5	28	138
1898	40	57	8	24	129
1899	38	60	5	31	134
1900	37	61	6	29	133
1901	77	129	17	44	267
1902	85	160	8	44	297
1903	109	195	19	55	378
1904	145	175	25	57	402
1905	156	211	43	56	466
1906	195	201	40	80	516
1907	261	228	35	63	587
1908	214	195	41	64	514
1909	230	163	51	57	501
1910	173	165	48	67	453
1911	352	251	44	93	740
1912	264	222	44	69	599
1913	230	242	62	58	592
1914	205	174	58	58	495
1915	145	160	62	45	412
1916	154	165	61	53	433
1917	93	127	57	43	320
1918	62	67	38	30	197
1919	102	100	47	55	304
1920	103	88	47	46	284
1921	103	104	50	50	307
1922	74	98	47	59	278
1923	62	83	43	56	244
1924	72	72	48	61	253
1925	55	81	40	62	238
1926	67	76	65	65	273
1927	60	70	48	74	252
1928	58	61	46	58	223
1929	49	87	46	63	245
1930	46	70	34	42	192
1931	45	48	19	44	156
1932	19	25	6	27	77
1933	6	17	9	23	55
1934	11	16	10	18	55
1935	9	24	19	29	81
1936	9	21	22	21	73
1937	4	19	16	8	47
1938	8	16	23	15	62
1939	3	15	20	14	52
1940	3	9	22	19	53
1941	2	7	15	9	33
1942	3	6	9	10	28
1943	3	3	10	6	22
1944	10	6	5	11	32
1945	10	6	8	11	35
1946	7	11	17	20	55
1947	6	6	20	15	47
1948	8	7	13	18	46
1949	4	5	11	11	31
1950	7	10	6	16	39
1947	6	7	—	5	18
1948	7	5	11	7	30
1949	8	8	13	15	44
1950	8	4	18	14	44
1951	10	6	14	19	49
1952	5	8	4	16	33
1953	3	9	10	9	31
1954	6	4	6	12	28
1955	3	6	8	10	27
1956	2	11	5	14	32
1957	1	9	11	20	41

Railroads: Switches and Signals

Year	Train Dispatching (156)	Automatic Block (157)	Cab Signal or Train Control (158)	Interlocking Switch & Signal (159)	Electric Actuation, Switch & Signal (160)
1837	–	–	–	–	–
1838	–	–	–	–	–
1839	–	–	–	–	–
1840	–	–	–	–	–
1841	–	–	–	–	–
1842	–	–	–	–	–
1843	–	–	–	–	–
1844	–	–	–	–	–
1845	–	–	–	–	–
1846	–	–	–	–	–
1847	–	–	–	–	–
1848	–	–	–	–	–
1849	–	–	–	–	–
1850	–	–	–	–	–
1851	–	–	–	–	–
1852	–	–	–	–	–
1853	–	–	–	–	–
1854	–	1	–	–	–
1855	–	–	–	–	–
1856	–	–	–	–	–
1857	1	–	–	–	–
1858	–	1	1	–	–
1859	–	1	1	–	–
1860	–	–	–	–	–
1861	–	–	–	–	–
1862	–	–	–	–	–
1863	–	–	–	–	–
1864	–	–	–	–	–
1865	–	–	–	–	–
1866	–	–	1	–	–
1867	–	–	1	–	–
1868	1	–	1	1	–
1869	1	–	2	–	5
1870	2	–	2	1	6
1871	1	1	2	2	1
1872	3	10	2	2	1
1873	2	7	1	1	3
1874	–	3	2	3	2
1875	2	6	2	5	3
1876	1	6	1	6	4
1874	–	7	3	5	–
1875	2	3	2	5	3
1876	1	4	1	5	6
1877	3	3	–	6	4
1878	1	2	1	3	–
1879	2	3	7	7	1
1880	–	7	4	9	6
1881	6	11	7	9	9
1882	8	18	15	15	9
1883	7	19	9	21	9
1884	13	12	8	15	12
1885	17	10	12	22	9
1886	14	14	10	33	2
1887	6	15	8	23	2
1888	9	17	8	23	9
1889	15	30	5	24	9
1890	11	33	18	13	13
1891	10	35	19	20	16
1892	7	47	12	25	13
1893	6	48	15	24	27
1894	4	47	15	22	21

Year	(156)	(157)	(158)	(159)	(160)
1895	5	24	11	19	20
1896	8	18	15	17	20
1897	9	19	12	13	22
1898	1	16	12	16	15
1899	11	28	10	11	21
1900	5	32	16	9	11
1901	13	50	13	13	26
1902	14	106	32	22	22
1903	9	88	36	23	46
1904	12	96	39	28	34
1905	24	118	31	37	53
1906	19	117	29	29	29
1907	19	116	78	19	35
1908	15	124	60	29	48
1909	2	59	52	15	33
1910	2	48	49	20	42
1911	5	55	48	15	38
1912	6	64	59	22	17
1913	2	83	196	17	21
1914	4	69	148	20	16
1915	8	74	114	20	20
1916	3	64	80	18	18
1917	7	51	53	17	15
1918	4	42	42	11	10
1919	1	60	47	15	9
1920	4	51	43	13	11
1921	3	63	50	15	13
1922	8	87	53	11	16
1923	9	105	43	13	31
1924	6	118	35	11	18
1925	2	93	26	10	11
1926	4	135	35	11	19
1927	21	101	12	15	12
1928	26	72	18	8	24
1929	55	76	5	34	24
1930	42	71	10	29	27
1931	52	62	11	14	10
1932	27	57	6	7	20
1933	23	38	1	6	7
1934	27	50	3	10	6
1935	28	46	1	9	22
1936	25	60	5	11	3
1937	17	23	4	16	10
1938	9	48	2	20	13
1939	7	44	2	15	18
1940	6	58	3	16	13
1941	19	54	1	6	13
1942	20	29	1	6	6
1943	9	23	1	7	5
1944	8	14	7	6	6
1945	6	11	13	2	6
1946	19	25	8	7	7
1947	11	23	3	5	10
1948	6	13	6	8	10
1949	3	13	2	4	7
1950	1	12	3	3	11
1947	6	2	6	3	2
1948	–	4	4	3	2
1949	7	11	6	1	3
1950	10	15	5	4	5
1951	10	20	11	10	8
1952	10	22	4	3	14
1953	7	12	4	5	11
1954	1	6	1	3	4
1955	1	10	4	1	4
1956	5	21	3	3	5
1957	6	15	4	4	5

151

Railroads: Switches and Signals

Year	Automatic Signals & Gates (161)	Automatic Switches (162)	Switches (163)	Misc. (164)	Total 156–164 (165)
1837	–	–	–	1	1
1838	1	–	–	–	1
1839	–	1	–	–	1
1840	–	3	–	–	3
1841	–	–	–	1	1
1842	–	–	–	–	–
1843	–	–	–	–	–
1844	–	–	1	–	1
1845	–	–	–	–	–
1846	–	–	1	–	1
1847	–	1	–	–	1
1848	–	1	–	–	1
1849	2	3	–	3	8
1850	–	–	–	1	1
1851	–	3	1	–	4
1852	2	2	–	3	7
1853	–	1	–	1	2
1854	–	2	–	1	4
1855	2	–	–	1	3
1856	–	–	–	2	2
1857	–	–	1	1	3
1858	–	1	1	8	12
1859	4	1	7	6	20
1860	3	5	9	5	22
1861	–	1	6	4	11
1862	–	1	1	2	4
1863	–	–	5	5	10
1864	2	1	3	3	9
1865	1	–	6	10	17
1866	2	5	7	18	33
1867	5	10	11	24	51
1868	6	4	13	20	46
1869	6	6	11	16	47
1870	6	5	4	16	42
1871	6	5	5	22	45
1872	7	10	4	28	67
1873	6	12	8	40	80
1874	10	21	4	31	76
1875	8	11	5	36	78
1876	13	11	10	47	99
1874	8	18	6	27	74
1875	8	10	2	39	74
1876	10	8	11	39	85
1877	9	8	7	22	62
1878	5	11	12	23	58
1879	8	14	6	30	78
1880	9	7	9	54	105
1881	9	11	12	43	117
1882	19	11	13	76	184
1883	17	13	9	105	209
1884	13	8	13	82	176
1885	20	17	17	90	214
1886	24	16	12	88	213
1887	19	19	15	105	212
1888	14	26	21	122	249
1889	24	21	12	108	248
1890	16	25	11	98	238
1891	17	34	18	113	282
1892	26	41	8	97	276
1893	16	36	14	104	290
1894	24	62	11	127	333

Year	(161)	(162)	(163)	(164)	(165)
1895	15	29	20	96	239
1896	13	50	18	83	242
1897	26	49	7	80	237
1898	18	18	4	63	163
1899	16	30	15	80	222
1900	12	41	23	69	218
1901	13	51	16	94	289
1902	20	47	15	125	403
1903	20	61	28	135	446
1904	20	54	21	151	455
1905	19	75	44	158	559
1906	28	60	32	143	486
1907	20	51	25	181	544
1908	18	66	15	165	540
1909	15	61	19	152	408
1910	8	57	12	113	351
1911	9	41	18	123	352
1912	10	34	16	104	332
1913	15	26	14	106	480
1914	11	27	29	82	406
1915	20	20	12	93	381
1916	16	24	13	101	337
1917	25	13	11	88	280
1918	14	14	9	61	207
1919	24	22	18	76	272
1920	15	14	12	79	242
1921	25	19	19	93	300
1922	30	9	19	67	300
1923	28	11	19	77	336
1924	44	5	15	76	328
1925	33	6	21	57	259
1926	16	5	27	63	315
1927	17	9	18	65	270
1928	18	5	16	49	236
1929	9	6	21	68	298
1930	4	4	17	68	272
1931	3	4	10	38	204
1932	2	–	3	28	150
1933	2	2	4	20	103
1934	3	1	6	16	122
1935	1	–	4	35	146
1936	–	–	6	44	154
1937	–	–	4	30	104
1938	1	–	6	38	137
1939	–	1	5	23	115
1940	2	–	3	27	128
1941	–	2	1	21	116
1942	–	–	2	27	91
1943	–	2	1	14	62
1944	1	–	3	20	65
1945	1	–	6	9	54
1946	–	–	4	12	82
1947	–	1	2	12	67
1948	–	–	–	18	61
1949	–	–	5	9	43
1950	–	1	2	11	44
1947	–	–	–	3	22
1948	–	–	1	12	26
1949	1	–	2	10	41
1950	–	–	6	14	59
1951	–	2	2	12	75
1952	–	–	3	14	70
1953	–	–	2	11	52
1954	–	–	2	9	26
1955	–	–	3	10	33
1956	–	1	3	9	50
1957	–	–	5	12	51

Year	Railway Mail Delivery (166)	Vehicle Loading & Unloading (167)	Railway Snow Excavators (168)	Misc. (169)	Total 150, 155, 165–169 Railways (170)	Sugar Refining (171)
1837	–	–	–	3	15	
1838	–	–	–	1	14	2
1839	–	–	1	1	13	–
1840	–	–	2	6	25	–
1841	–	2	–	2	17	–
1842	–	–	–	1	8	–
1843	–	3	–	1	13	–
1844	–	–	–	–	8	1
1845	–	–	–	4	11	2
1846	–	–	2	1	18	1
1847	–	–	1	1	19	2
1848	–	–	–	2	12	1
1849	–	–	–	8	50	3
1850	–	–	–	6	30	3
1851	–	–	–	5	33	1
1852	–	–	–	5	41	2
1853	–	–	–	6	27	1
1854	–	2	2	5	59	1
1855	–	3	–	5	42	1
1856	–	–	2	5	44	1
1857	–	1	3	2	50	2
1858	–	1	5	8	147	7
1859	–	1	3	5	160	19
1860	–	1	–	3	118	10
1861	–	–	2	8	82	11
1862	–	–	2	4	72	7
1863	–	–	7	7	88	6
1864	–	2	2	8	115	14
1865	5	–	3	8	165	21
1866	3	4	6	16	227	35
1867	1	2	12	29	363	33
1868	2	2	13	32	342	14
1869	–	4	12	32	385	22
1870	1	7	12	16	326	11
1871	1	–	4	27	333	15
1872	–	5	11	23	410	15
1873	1	5	10	28	497	18
1874	3	5	15	22	566	21
1875	7	2	8	26	482	26
1876	5	2	18	30	519	8
1874	2	3	10	24	537	26
1875	6	3	11	24	452	20
1876	9	2	14	25	498	13
1877	5	2	8	15	372	10
1878	3	3	8	18	374	18
1879	1	2	10	22	424	25
1880	2	3	5	22	576	25
1881	3	14	13	29	697	30
1882	2	11	14	40	1101	50
1883	3	10	18	53	1043	36
1884	8	11	18	54	955	18
1885	6	9	28	49	1019	26
1886	2	9	15	70	1209	9
1887	3	8	22	89	1182	20
1888	5	13	29	76	1239	7
1889	1	12	19	91	1457	19
1890	15	11	19	116	1768	17
1891	21	9	12	87	1657	17
1892	12	11	8	85	1492	10
1893	9	15	14	69	1426	9
1894	12	13	12	49	1345	12

Year	(166)	(167)	(168)	(169)	(170)	(171)
1895	19	14	18	73	1213	13
1896	17	9	9	76	1253	18
1897	18	10	14	68	1172	15
1898	14	13	5	46	862	23
1899	23	9	13	58	1077	22
1900	22	13	21	55	1087	25
1901	26	21	13	76	1457	31
1902	37	17	8	87	1810	33
1903	27	23	17	86	2017	28
1904	31	25	9	97	1952	26
1905	49	30	17	102	2213	19
1906	44	32	17	112	2179	8
1907	118	32	20	94	2417	23
1908	187	29	12	123	2458	11
1909	112	36	18	110	2194	31
1910	75	28	15	90	1891	24
1911	55	30	7	92	2184	25
1912	66	20	10	97	2057	40
1913	53	21	5	92	2191	29
1914	49	21	10	105	2056	25
1915	43	22	13	72	1838	37
1916	63	20	9	68	1726	24
1917	34	25	8	80	1424	23
1918	15	24	7	69	1065	14
1919	32	23	11	106	1436	24
1920	21	36	16	98	1431	29
1921	12	32	10	112	1588	28
1922	8	23	10	79	1565	25
1923	9	34	9	71	1480	25
1924	10	21	11	83	1447	36
1925	7	34	12	102	1503	44
1926	8	28	19	80	1494	33
1927	5	31	8	101	1480	47
1928	4	20	6	75	1403	21
1929	8	13	10	68	1494	23
1930	11	14	4	71	1231	25
1931	5	7	8	70	1173	16
1932	1	5	1	45	799	19
1933	3	2	3	20	589	15
1934	2	7	–	22	653	18
1935	1	6	2	20	661	19
1936	6	4	3	21	689	31
1937	4	7	1	21	657	30
1938	4	4	2	33	751	32
1939	5	8	3	19	631	26
1940	5	11	6	24	655	36
1941	6	9	5	18	553	30
1942	4	9	3	12	365	27
1943	4	9	1	18	353	11
1944	2	16	3	23	452	19
1945	2	18	3	26	456	24
1946	2	20	8	28	494	23
1947	5	13	3	28	454	23
1948	1	10	4	24	417	20
1949	2	13	2	24	360	25
1950	2	8	4	41	402	22
1947	3	9	2	9	209	17
1948	–	8	1	13	213	12
1949	1	16	2	15	355	23
1950	3	11	2	38	476	33
1951	5	11	5	25	494	30
1952	3	17	5	36	475	28
1953	1	20	3	34	459	15
1954	–	6	5	27	282	13
1955	1	8	1	20	276	12
1956	2	9	5	24	425	34
1957	2	14	7	45	455	23

Textiles: Preparatory Spinning

Year	Cleaning & Treating Fibers (172)	Picking, Carding, & Combing (173)	Drawing (174)	Sliver Related (175)	Total 172–175 (176)	Spinning (177)	Winding (178)
1837	–	5	–	–	5	4	–
1838	–	5	–	–	5	11	–
1839	1	2	–	–	3	10	1
1840	1	5	–	–	6	6	–
1841	–	5	–	1	6	5	1
1842	3	2	–	–	5	5	1
1843	1	6	–	2	9	4	–
1844	–	5	–	–	5	4	–
1845	–	6	–	1	7	4	–
1846	1	3	–	–	4	7	–
1847	2	7	–	1	10	5	2
1848	–	3	1	–	4	5	1
1849	1	15	–	1	17	16	2
1850	1	4	1	–	6	10	2
1851	1	3	–	–	4	2	–
1852	–	3	–	1	4	13	1
1853	–	4	–	2	6	2	–
1854	1	16	–	–	17	21	1
1855	1	11	–	1	13	13	–
1856	2	11	–	2	15	10	1
1857	4	17	–	2	23	16	2
1858	5	12	2	1	20	9	2
1859	2	10	2	1	15	15	1
1860	4	11	–	1	16	11	2
1861	2	13	1	3	19	9	1
1862	–	10	1	2	13	10	1
1863	2	10	1	3	16	10	1
1864	6	8	1	2	17	25	5
1865	4	15	2	–	21	23	9
1866	7	17	4	1	29	37	6
1867	7	17	2	5	31	46	6
1868	5	26	4	5	40	48	5
1869	8	21	2	6	37	40	12
1870	13	24	4	4	45	34	11
1871	14	13	3	–	30	47	7
1872	7	26	6	4	43	39	13
1873	11	9	4	6	30	38	9
1874	9	17	2	13	41	31	10
1875	7	25	4	4	40	32	15
1876	8	22	1	4	35	40	19
1874	4	25	2	13	44	26	15
1875	10	19	4	9	42	33	17
1876	5	27	1	17	50	48	17
1877	8	21	3	24	56	39	21
1878	12	26	3	18	59	49	10
1879	5	21	2	15	43	42	11
1880	9	33	1	20	63	38	9
1881	10	29	4	14	57	67	19
1882	20	32	4	23	79	64	24
1883	14	42	12	18	86	49	21
1884	9	30	12	19	70	61	20
1885	13	40	5	11	69	49	26
1886	12	33	7	13	65	61	22
1887	13	34	3	15	65	51	28
1888	12	27	11	7	57	59	19
1889	18	34	9	10	71	78	20
1890	22	20	6	10	58	56	27
1891	15	32	3	14	64	62	19
1892	15	37	6	16	74	58	23
1893	18	19	3	24	64	72	21
1894	22	31	9	13	75	43	21

Year	(172)	(173)	(174)	(175)	(176)	(177)	(178)
1895	21	16	5	20	78	48	23
1896	17	26	6	12	61	53	28
1897	15	35	10	5	65	53	25
1898	10	22	9	6	47	55	29
1899	25	32	14	20	91	57	23
1900	21	20	4	11	56	60	39
1901	19	26	9	14	68	71	34
1902	13	26	15	14	68	74	29
1903	12	28	11	14	65	88	29
1904	7	29	19	9	64	95	59
1905	13	29	12	12	66	86	45
1906	18	24	12	11	65	70	34
1907	10	28	12	5	55	53	36
1908	9	22	5	16	52	51	50
1909	9	40	5	17	71	68	40
1910	17	24	7	8	56	79	43
1911	22	40	11	15	88	67	44
1912	14	24	12	10	60	67	48
1913	4	35	14	12	65	54	48
1914	10	19	16	10	55	50	45
1915	13	27	8	3	51	41	30
1916	8	22	5	8	43	36	40
1917	12	22	14	6	54	41	39
1918	11	19	5	9	44	30	38
1919	14	24	4	13	55	54	34
1920	16	41	9	11	77	71	27
1921	21	26	20	15	82	77	44
1922	25	32	17	10	84	87	47
1923	29	44	16	11	100	92	45
1924	34	40	20	13	107	81	51
1925	28	39	26	25	118	82	49
1926	30	47	18	16	111	101	52
1927	27	30	14	30	101	100	55
1928	33	19	19	15	86	91	61
1929	40	26	13	15	94	88	67
1930	38	28	19	18	103	115	61
1931	31	13	18	13	75	136	59
1932	33	12	17	6	68	89	49
1933	26	17	21	5	69	86	45
1934	22	15	8	7	52	114	47
1935	13	18	26	14	71	104	52
1936	22	23	15	14	74	79	57
1937	21	13	26	11	71	94	45
1938	16	12	24	19	71	71	81
1939	18	14	19	18	69	79	60
1940	17	29	22	17	85	76	50
1941	14	13	31	13	71	71	57
1942	13	13	16	12	54	62	47
1943	8	14	9	12	43	60	49
1944	11	14	13	6	44	54	48
1945	17	18	16	18	69	78	49
1946	17	21	17	13	68	74	49
1947	9	14	25	17	65	77	42
1948	15	13	25	14	67	97	45
1949	17	14	27	24	82	113	79
1950	20	23	26	16	85	74	66
1947	12	18	12	—	42	42	28
1948	8	13	8	1	30	61	27
1949	13	11	17	4	45	117	49
1950	20	11	11	2	44	64	27
1951	16	13	13	4	46	101	75
1952	9	22	36	6	73	69	69
1953	19	22	22	7	70	54	79
1954	20	19	33	6	78	44	51
1955	17	13	34	8	72	60	31
1956	29	15	46	10	100	59	58
1957	22	17	34	7	80	91	33

157

	Textiles: Spinning and Winding		Textiles: Weaving				
			Special-Type Looms	Warp			Total
Year	Misc. Spinning (179)	Total 177–179 (180)	(181)	Beaming (182)	Feeding (183)	Other (184)	182–184 (185)
1837	–	4	–	–	1	5	6
1838	–	11	2	–	–	2	2
1839	–	11	1	1	–	–	1
1840	–	6	–	–	–	2	2
1841	–	6	–	–	–	2	2
1842	–	6	–	–	2	3	5
1843	1	5	–	–	1	3	4
1844	–	4	–	–	1	–	1
1845	–	4	–	–	2	1	3
1846	–	7	1	–	–	4	4
1847	–	7	–	–	–	3	3
1848	–	6	–	–	–	2	2
1849	–	18	2	1	2	6	9
1850	–	12	1	–	2	9	11
1851	–	2	4	1	1	7	9
1852	–	14	4	–	–	10	10
1853	1	3	1	–	3	9	12
1854	–	22	2	1	–	11	12
1855	3	16	1	–	1	9	10
1856	–	11	4	2	3	3	8
1857	2	20	3	2	2	5	9
1858	1	12	1	2	3	1	6
1859	–	16	3	2	2	2	6
1860	7	20	1	1	7	3	11
1861	2	12	3	–	3	3	6
1862	1	12	1	–	4	4	8
1863	–	11	2	–	2	4	6
1864	2	32	8	2	4	5	11
1865	5	37	7	2	7	10	19
1866	4	47	16	2	4	17	23
1867	4	56	24	3	15	21	39
1868	8	61	13	5	15	26	46
1869	4	56	5	3	12	23	38
1870	2	47	5	7	7	15	29
1871	6	60	1	6	9	12	27
1872	3	55	3	8	4	15	27
1873	1	48	–	4	2	16	22
1874	3	44	5	2	4	15	21
1875	3	50	–	3	5	20	28
1876	4	63	4	4	5	16	25
1874	2	43	1	2	8	8	18
1875	6	56	6	6	5	26	37
1876	3	68	6	4	3	14	21
1877	5	65	5	3	2	17	22
1878	2	61	7	3	3	7	13
1879	3	56	5	2	4	13	19
1880	5	52	6	4	4	21	29
1881	4	90	4	8	4	12	24
1882	3	91	12	11	5	10	26
1883	8	78	3	7	8	13	28
1884	8	89	6	9	6	6	21
1885	5	80	4	11	12	10	33
1886	3	86	13	18	4	22	44
1887	7	86	12	12	13	30	55
1888	3	81	15	4	8	15	27
1889	2	100	8	8	12	28	48
1890	1	84	10	10	10	26	46
1891	6	87	5	7	7	24	38
1892	10	91	10	11	8	29	48
1893	2	95	4	9	6	17	32
1894	12	76	6	4	7	22	33

Year	(179)	(180)	(181)	(182)	(183)	(184)	(185)
1895	8	79	10	11	4	39	54
1896	9	90	8	8	11	35	54
1897	10	88	11	12	4	39	55
1898	7	91	8	10	12	24	46
1899	5	85	7	10	12	38	60
1900	7	106	2	11	13	22	46
1901	10	115	16	7	6	37	50
1902	15	118	16	11	13	43	67
1903	11	128	17	13	15	66	94
1904	15	169	12	17	17	63	97
1905	11	142	13	13	12	35	60
1906	12	116	14	18	6	26	50
1907	11	100	10	15	7	19	41
1908	19	120	8	19	6	22	47
1909	14	122	8	21	11	25	57
1910	12	134	7	23	6	19	48
1911	10	121	14	14	11	22	47
1912	13	128	7	15	5	36	56
1913	3	105	10	8	6	17	31
1914	8	103	16	15	5	21	41
1915	8	79	7	14	3	14	31
1916	4	80	12	8	7	7	22
1917	5	85	16	14	5	10	29
1918	10	78	18	14	7	2	23
1919	12	100	21	14	5	19	38
1920	10	108	16	6	8	12	26
1921	21	142	12	18	13	18	49
1922	16	150	11	17	12	23	52
1923	21	158	12	26	14	35	75
1924	23	155	22	26	18	40	84
1925	18	149	15	11	24	44	79
1926	30	183	10	17	17	22	82
1927	27	182	10	6	22	42	70
1928	34	186	18	24	19	30	73
1929	20	175	11	15	21	32	68
1930	29	205	13	12	3	33	48
1931	15	210	5	12	9	25	46
1932	22	160	18	13	4	19	36
1933	15	146	19	10	3	24	37
1934	21	182	22	19	4	23	46
1935	22	178	29	14	3	22	39
1936	27	163	18	16	6	21	43
1937	30	169	19	14	2	15	31
1938	22	174	25	9	5	17	31
1939	19	158	18	12	7	26	45
1940	9	135	9	6	6	13	25
1941	10	138	9	10	5	13	28
1942	14	123	9	9	7	11	27
1943	14	123	3	12	6	15	33
1944	12	114	9	12	8	15	35
1945	11	138	12	10	10	21	41
1946	16	139	13	23	13	20	56
1947	8	127	27	13	7	16	36
1948	14	156	14	11	6	18	35
1949	21	213	6	20	9	32	61
1950	18	158	16	16	7	36	59
1947	7	77	6	5	7	9	27
1948	9	97	9	13	13	15	50
1949	15	181	20	15	6	13	54
1950	15	106	10	9	9	14	42
1951	12	188	15	23	8	24	70
1952	12	150	13	12	10	35	70
1953	18	151	12	19	11	27	69
1954	15	110	11	30	5	33	79
1955	14	105	15	14	6	39	74
1956	17	134	11	16	7	22	56
1957	16	140	13	14	7	22	56

Textiles: Weaving
Weft (exc. narrow ware)

Year	Shuttle Motions (186)	Shuttles (187)	Replenishing (188)	Misc. (189)	Total 186-189 (190)
1837	–	1	–	1	2
1838	1	–	–	–	1
1839	–	–	–	–	–
1840	1	1	–	–	2
1841	–	–	–	–	–
1842	2	2	–	1	5
1843	2	–	–	1	3
1844	–	–	–	–	–
1845	2	–	–	1	3
1846	3	–	–	1	4
1847	–	–	–	2	2
1848	3	1	–	–	4
1849	–	–	–	4	4
1850	3	1	–	3	7
1851	2	1	–	1	4
1852	1	1	–	3	5
1853	1	1	–	4	6
1854	–	–	–	6	6
1855	8	2	–	7	17
1856	1	–	–	4	5
1857	5	1	–	3	9
1858	2	2	–	8	12
1859	1	–	–	2	3
1860	1	–	–	1	2
1861	10	–	–	4	14
1862	6	2	–	1	9
1863	3	–	–	4	7
1864	4	6	1	7	18
1865	8	3	–	3	14
1866	5	1	1	8	15
1867	11	3	–	11	25
1868	7	15	–	12	34
1869	10	8	1	22	41
1870	10	7	1	10	28
1871	13	12	–	15	40
1872	12	5	–	13	30
1873	12	9	–	20	41
1874	13	14	–	17	44
1875	7	18	–	16	41
1876	8	4	–	4	16
1874	13	9	–	14	36
1875	9	19	–	13	41
1876	9	7	1	9	26
1877	7	9	–	13	29
1878	9	6	–	9	24
1879	9	12	–	16	37
1880	5	11	–	12	28
1881	6	5	–	6	17
1882	8	6	–	17	31
1883	16	10	–	8	34
1884	12	9	–	10	31
1885	6	14	–	17	37
1886	12	17	–	26	55
1887	15	11	2	19	47
1888	20	7	2	17	46
1889	22	14	1	19	56
1890	23	14	4	25	66
1891	15	10	5	25	55
1892	7	19	–	19	45
1893	14	7	3	20	44
1894	18	16	1	21	56

Year	(186)	(187)	(188)	(189)	(190)
1895	10	9	4	19	42
1896	15	24	12	22	73
1897	15	10	17	20	62
1898	12	10	16	19	57
1899	13	23	49	19	104
1900	24	20	48	29	121
1901	27	25	54	32	138
1902	18	22	43	35	118
1903	30	28	46	48	152
1904	32	27	41	56	156
1905	19	27	48	34	128
1906	26	28	43	20	117
1907	15	17	53	29	114
1908	25	36	46	21	128
1909	18	35	41	19	113
1910	27	24	45	15	111
1911	12	32	37	14	95
1912	11	28	39	15	93
1913	12	27	30	15	84
1914	12	25	37	17	91
1915	13	28	43	15	99
1916	20	30	61	15	126
1917	17	20	50	14	101
1918	22	18	43	10	93
1919	20	23	71	13	127
1920	27	21	82	16	146
1921	31	23	52	18	124
1922	22	17	59	39	137
1923	19	31	61	32	143
1924	23	33	72	43	171
1925	28	38	83	34	183
1926	20	26	111	41	198
1927	19	35	67	31	152
1928	21	42	63	45	171
1929	18	19	77	36	150
1930	14	32	43	24	113
1931	11	20	54	38	123
1932	12	19	26	27	84
1933	10	13	42	26	91
1934	9	13	46	15	83
1935	7	18	28	18	71
1936	16	26	27	29	98
1937	9	16	32	35	92
1938	15	8	13	29	65
1939	17	13	28	19	77
1940	20	17	31	21	89
1941	15	14	24	8	61
1942	17	13	18	15	63
1943	13	8	25	6	52
1944	19	14	49	10	92
1945	20	8	26	21	75
1946	26	7	37	16	86
1947	23	6	37	25	91
1948	32	10	38	19	99
1949	29	13	29	31	102
1950	23	12	47	17	99
1947	15	5	35	10	65
1948	16	4	20	7	47
1949	33	6	44	22	105
1950	29	7	25	15	76
1951	29	19	37	24	109
1952	20	9	29	20	78
1953	20	10	32	24	86
1954	16	4	13	21	54
1955	12	9	14	22	57
1956	21	6	12	20	59
1957	18	8	25	24	75

Year	Loom Stopping (191)	Fabric Manipulation (192)	Misc. Weaving (193)	Total 181, 185, 190–193 Weaving (194)	Cloth Finishing (195)	Narrow Fabrics Weaving, etc. (196)	Misc. Prods. & Processes (197)
1837	1	1	–	10	2	–	–
1838	–	1	2	8	3	1	–
1839	–	1	–	3	–	1	–
1840	–	1	–	5	2	2	–
1841	1	2	–	5	3	–	–
1842	1	4	–	15	2	1	–
1843	–	–	–	7	1	–	–
1844	–	2	–	3	–	1	–
1845	2	1	1	10	–	1	–
1846	–	1	–	10	2	2	–
1847	–	–	1	6	–	–	–
1848	–	1	–	7	1	–	–
1849	1	2	2	20	2	1	–
1850	–	–	1	20	4	–	–
1851	–	2	1	20	2	–	–
1852	1	1	2	23	1	–	2
1853	1	2	2	24	2	1	1
1854	–	–	3	23	6	3	3
1855	–	3	4	35	3	2	1
1856	1	1	2	21	2	1	3
1857	–	2	4	27	3	1	2
1858	–	1	2	22	1	2	3
1859	1	3	2	18	2	2	8
1860	–	2	2	18	4	2	9
1861	2	2	5	32	3	4	3
1862	1	2	2	23	5	2	1
1863	1	3	–	19	4	4	3
1864	1	1	3	42	3	3	2
1865	–	–	1	41	2	3	4
1866	2	6	–	62	1	18	10
1867	2	6	2	98	11	10	17
1868	5	2	3	103	11	8	27
1869	4	8	5	101	12	7	9
1870	1	8	3	74	5	7	8
1871	3	3	5	79	6	4	6
1872	2	4	7	73	6	10	9
1873	6	10	4	83	6	4	10
1874	13	7	5	95	12	5	17
1875	12	8	5	98	9	9	16
1876	9	8	10	68	18	2	16
1874	13	6	4	78	8	4	12
1875	15	8	8	115	14	8	16
1876	4	14	9	80	15	5	15
1877	7	–	2	65	9	13	27
1878	1	6	4	55	18	6	24
1879	3	6	1	71	8	5	31
1880	5	5	7	80	11	10	26
1881	6	4	10	65	18	8	21
1882	13	6	9	97	12	8	28
1883	5	5	14	89	13	8	35
1884	4	5	10	77	13	7	27
1885	2	5	11	92	13	8	27
1886	9	4	8	133	22	16	19
1887	8	13	20	155	17	11	23
1888	8	14	19	129	14	11	27
1889	8	15	17	152	20	13	27
1890	14	12	15	163	43	27	22
1891	11	12	20	141	23	21	22
1892	10	12	23	148	25	21	20
1893	14	7	15	116	19	18	10
1894	9	8	20	132	16	14	18

Year	(191)	(192)	(193)	(194)	(195)	(196)	(197)
1895	6	10	24	146	19	25	17
1896	18	9	17	179	20	17	32
1897	22	8	18	176	33	15	24
1898	36	9	21	177	17	20	22
1899	24	15	20	230	25	20	21
1900	25	7	15	216	22	15	29
1901	42	11	26	283	9	29	35
1902	27	10	29	267	24	20	36
1903	37	18	33	351	15	18	45
1904	27	18	22	332	19	20	31
1905	54	11	36	302	24	22	41
1906	36	14	22	253	9	23	37
1907	46	10	18	239	20	34	41
1908	37	19	25	264	18	24	40
1909	22	5	25	230	30	32	37
1910	19	9	11	205	18	27	31
1911	23	6	20	205	17	43	41
1912	14	11	26	207	16	32	39
1913	21	4	35	185	27	20	35
1914	16	3	25	192	25	29	37
1915	14	3	17	171	29	20	33
1916	11	5	13	189	22	26	51
1917	15	6	31	198	23	23	56
1918	7	4	12	157	12	19	47
1919	13	9	20	228	22	22	58
1920	20	9	14	231	22	27	51
1921	21	11	20	237	18	34	75
1922	28	11	21	260	22	54	65
1923	28	14	36	308	31	32	41
1924	21	13	23	334	35	27	38
1925	21	14	28	340	41	43	40
1926	29	18	26	363	29	27	39
1927	27	11	32	302	38	27	59
1928	38	9	46	355	29	23	44
1929	29	20	39	317	33	24	34
1930	31	12	40	257	38	38	53
1931	20	13	31	238	42	20	58
1932	23	4	19	184	31	32	39
1933	22	11	35	215	29	16	31
1934	10	11	32	204	24	13	39
1935	16	8	34	197	31	26	34
1936	9	11	37	216	37	18	43
1937	5	6	42	195	21	15	35
1938	14	7	38	180	22	27	34
1939	6	10	29	185	31	10	41
1940	11	6	27	167	23	9	36
1941	17	8	38	161	21	10	27
1942	5	5	41	150	16	10	21
1943	12	4	34	138	17	7	24
1944	11	2	39	188	16	12	19
1945	11	5	40	184	15	7	33
1946	13	2	28	198	14	6	42
1947	25	10	37	226	18	21	22
1948	14	6	29	197	22	4	25
1949	22	5	50	246	39	11	25
1950	24	15	43	256	33	11	24
1947	6	4	31	139	7	8	28
1948	17	5	22	150	12	8	25
1949	19	4	32	234	32	17	24
1950	14	4	25	171	15	9	36
1951	15	4	32	245	18	10	21
1952	20	16	43	240	41	5	30
1953	22	11	51	251	25	10	28
1954	16	7	34	201	26	6	22
1955	14	5	44	209	36	11	13
1956	13	4	70	213	33	9	29
1957	7	7	59	217	15	10	28

Textiles: Knitting

Year	Feeding (198)	General Machines (199)	Products exc. hosiery (200)	Seamless Hosiery Mach. (201)	Stocking Pressing & Molding (202)	Hosiery (203)	Total 198-203 (204)
1837	–	–	–	–	–	–	–
1838	–	–	–	–	–	–	–
1839	–	1	–	–	–	–	1
1840	–	1	–	–	–	–	1
1841	–	–	–	–	–	–	–
1842	–	1	–	–	–	–	1
1843	–	1	–	–	–	–	1
1844	–	1	–	1	–	–	2
1845	–	–	–	–	–	–	–
1846	–	–	1	–	–	–	1
1847	–	–	–	1	–	–	1
1848	–	2	–	–	–	–	2
1849	–	1	–	–	–	–	1
1850	–	–	–	1	–	–	1
1851	–	3	–	1	–	–	4
1852	–	3	–	1	–	–	4
1853	–	4	1	–	–	–	5
1854	–	8	–	3	–	–	11
1855	–	8	–	2	–	–	10
1856	–	5	–	2	–	2	9
1857	–	3	1	–	–	–	4
1858	–	9	1	–	–	–	10
1859	–	6	1	5	–	–	12
1860	–	4	–	2	–	–	6
1861	–	5	–	4	–	–	9
1862	–	7	–	2	–	–	9
1863	–	8	–	1	–	–	9
1864	–	12	1	5	–	–	18
1865	1	14	–	4	–	–	19
1866	–	16	1	5	–	1	23
1867	2	18	1	4	1	2	28
1868	3	23	2	6	1	1	36
1869	–	17	2	6	–	1	26
1870	–	21	2	12	–	1	36
1871	–	13	1	4	–	1	19
1872	–	12	5	10	–	1	28
1873	1	14	5	7	1	–	28
1874	1	12	2	14	–	3	32
1875	1	8	3	10	1	–	23
1876	3	14	2	14	–	4	37
1874	1	11	4	15	–	2	33
1875	3	13	4	11	1	2	34
1876	4	17	–	6	–	3	30
1877	1	9	1	2	1	2	16
1878	8	17	5	6	–	2	38
1879	4	21	7	8	–	2	42
1880	3	18	6	7	1	6	41
1881	8	21	3	10	–	2	44
1882	9	18	4	13	–	10	54
1883	3	21	5	19	–	2	50
1884	3	24	5	10	1	3	46
1885	4	19	8	16	–	6	53
1886	2	30	10	18	–	9	69
1887	7	27	17	26	–	5	82
1888	3	39	7	23	–	8	80
1889	9	42	11	44	1	7	114
1890	9	38	5	29	–	7	88
1891	5	32	9	29	1	12	88
1892	7	34	7	23	–	7	78
1893	5	34	10	32	1	2	84
1894	10	26	10	26	2	3	77

Year	(198)	(199)	(200)	(201)	(202)	(203)	(204)
1895	8	33	5	30	–	–	76
1896	5	33	12	25	–	1	76
1897	3	30	10	21	–	1	65
1898	7	17	10	15	–	1	50
1899	6	23	6	16	–	3	54
1900	7	31	4	14	–	5	61
1901	6	28	3	20	2	14	73
1902	2	31	12	18	–	2	65
1903	7	34	7	19	3	1	71
1904	5	22	5	16	–	5	53
1905	1	20	16	13	1	5	56
1906	6	31	14	18	2	5	76
1907	5	19	12	17	1	2	56
1908	9	33	6	20	–	2	70
1909	3	28	23	17	4	2	77
1910	9	16	25	17	–	3	70
1911	14	23	9	34	7	1	88
1912	9	41	18	28	3	3	102
1913	10	32	19	25	3	6	95
1914	19	37	19	45	5	12	137
1915	15	38	17	29	5	5	109
1916	5	48	11	18	3	6	91
1917	10	40	16	16	8	1	91
1918	4	29	8	13	9	1	64
1919	9	36	17	26	10	9	107
1920	12	53	11	28	4	2	110
1921	12	39	7	27	6	8	99
1922	25	39	20	40	7	20	151
1923	18	51	13	29	5	12	128
1924	20	35	15	19	9	10	108
1925	16	33	18	29	8	8	112
1926	15	54	12	41	9	12	143
1927	29	62	24	46	14	11	186
1928	30	61	14	38	8	19	170
1929	30	91	22	49	26	9	227
1930	37	94	50	31	11	20	243
1931	26	75	59	36	12	23	231
1932	35	71	53	23	7	15	204
1933	38	67	43	22	7	21	198
1934	46	61	34	35	4	14	194
1935	39	95	37	46	8	18	243
1936	44	99	71	45	6	13	278
1937	31	103	49	34	6	11	234
1938	35	86	51	43	4	24	243
1939	33	72	65	26	5	17	218
1940	22	54	43	28	9	18	174
1941	20	54	30	13	6	14	137
1942	16	39	16	25	2	12	110
1943	12	50	10	18	2	10	102
1944	12	73	12	17	3	5	122
1945	19	60	12	18	9	15	133
1946	16	57	17	15	9	9	123
1947	14	69	16	14	9	5	127
1948	18	84	10	14	4	9	139
1949	25	77	14	14	4	12	146
1950	15	64	18	17	7	–	136
1947	19	63	8	10	5	7	112
1948	11	43	14	16	7	8	99
1949	8	58	11	10	8	4	99
1950	14	65	17	13	6	15	130
1951	25	55	15	14	6	7	122
1952	21	72	17	15	8	13	146
1953	17	63	12	16	6	14	128
1954	22	71	14	16	4	11	138
1955	18	52	14	26	2	15	127
1956	14	59	20	29	1	8	131
1957	12	45	17	22	1	9	106

165

	Textiles: Dyeing and Finishing					Textiles: Other	
Year	Azo Dyes (205)	Printing (206)	Bleaching (207)	Misc. (208)	Total 205–208 (209)	Carpet and Rug Weaving (210)	Linoleum Making (211)
1837	–	–	–	1	1	–	–
1838	–	1	–	4	5	–	–
1839	–	–	–	–	–	–	–
1840	–	–	–	1	1	–	–
1841	–	–	–	1	1	–	–
1842	–	–	–	1	1	–	–
1843	–	–	–	1	1	–	–
1844	–	–	–	–	–	–	–
1845	–	–	–	1	1	–	–
1846	–	–	1	–	1	–	–
1847	–	–	–	–	–	–	–
1848	–	–	–	1	1	–	–
1849	–	–	–	2	2	–	–
1850	–	–	–	1	1	–	–
1851	–	–	–	4	4	–	–
1852	–	–	1	1	2	–	–
1853	–	–	1	3	4	1	–
1854	–	–	1	5	6	–	–
1855	–	–	1	1	2	–	–
1856	–	1	2	1	4	1	–
1857	–	–	2	1	3	–	1
1858	–	–	–	2	2	–	–
1859	–	–	–	1	1	–	–
1860	–	–	–	2	2	3	–
1861	–	–	–	–	–	1	–
1862	–	–	–	1	1	1	–
1863	–	–	1	7	8	9	1
1864	–	–	1	3	4	6	2
1865	–	–	1	5	6	–	3
1866	–	–	6	8	14	3	6
1867	–	–	6	13	19	1	4
1868	–	–	1	12	13	4	1
1869	–	1	4	14	19	4	3
1870	–	2	2	18	22	2	3
1871	–	–	1	17	18	4	1
1872	–	–	3	13	16	8	–
1873	–	2	3	9	14	13	–
1874	–	–	1	10	11	3	2
1875	–	–	–	4	4	8	1
1876	–	–	1	11	12	7	3
1874	–	–	1	8	9	3	2
1875	–	–	–	6	6	10	4
1876	–	–	2	12	14	7	1
1877	–	2	1	8	11	4	–
1878	–	–	–	9	9	11	–
1879	–	–	–	10	10	6	2
1880	2	–	1	12	15	7	3
1881	1	1	1	9	12	19	2
1882	1	1	2	17	21	8	1
1883	–	–	2	9	11	14	3
1884	2	1	7	19	29	14	1
1885	–	2	3	21	26	16	5
1886	–	–	1	19	20	11	1
1887	–	–	1	11	12	6	1
1888	–	1	2	13	16	18	–
1889	–	4	1	10	15	27	3
1890	3	–	4	8	15	24	1
1891	2	2	–	10	14	15	5
1892	1	2	2	14	19	11	6
1893	2	11	–	14	27	11	3
1894	2	1	1	10	14	15	8

Year	(205)	(206)	(207)	(208)	(209)	(210)	(211)
1895	–	1	1	11	13	9	6
1896	1	1	–	10	12	9	2
1897	3	2	1	20	26	13	2
1898	2	1	1	14	18	13	8
1899	2	1	–	20	23	4	4
1900	1	1	1	21	24	9	5
1901	1	3	2	16	22	11	10
1902	–	5	1	17	23	13	15
1903	1	3	–	12	16	18	10
1904	–	2	1	12	15	9	5
1905	1	3	1	20	25	15	2
1906	–	–	4	15	19	13	7
1907	2	1	2	14	19	11	5
1908	1	4	1	17	23	16	8
1909	–	3	2	25	30	8	6
1910	2	2	2	24	30	19	4
1911	4	2	6	25	37	8	5
1912	3	1	5	21	30	9	2
1913	4	–	3	25	32	15	3
1914	3	3	7	24	37	12	9
1915	6	–	1	19	26	14	6
1916	–	2	5	22	29	18	3
1917	–	–	4	33	37	7	9
1918	–	–	3	16	19	6	10
1919	–	–	2	35	37	7	5
1920	–	–	4	30	34	11	7
1921	2	–	9	49	60	13	2
1922	6	–	10	50	66	26	7
1923	5	4	6	56	71	59	3
1924	11	9	11	76	107	25	13
1925	15	7	20	104	146	27	6
1926	23	3	6	117	149	27	12
1927	13	15	7	103	138	30	19
1928	22	19	20	100	161	36	17
1929	13	23	12	76	124	34	20
1930	3	22	21	86	132	42	11
1931	13	17	8	61	99	37	17
1932	24	12	16	82	134	55	21
1933	10	15	12	65	102	48	12
1934	9	12	16	95	132	18	10
1935	17	10	14	94	135	20	18
1936	16	7	16	98	137	18	2
1937	37	14	30	141	222	34	5
1938	31	19	14	100	164	26	6
1939	24	14	15	97	150	18	4
1940	9	20	10	100	139	15	8
1941	12	11	2	75	100	15	10
1942	6	3	2	54	65	9	4
1943	5	18	6	64	93	5	3
1944	2	4	4	49	59	17	4
1945	6	5	9	39	59	7	3
1946	3	2	12	58	75	16	4
1947	8	5	7	61	81	20	8
1948	3	10	4	77	94	26	8
1949	4	4	6	69	83	18	5
1950	5	5	4	42	56	21	2
1947	3	6	5	38	52	8	2
1948	2	8	3	44	57	10	3
1949	6	3	11	49	69	13	3
1950	9	4	17	111	141	20	12
1951	3	7	2	63	75	26	5
1952	2	8	4	58	72	22	5
1953	7	3	2	52	64	16	6
1954	2	3	9	51	65	16	8
1955	2	3	8	31	44	9	5
1956	10	–	7	72	89	15	10
1957	4	2	5	58	69	23	15

167

Textiles: Hats and Caps

Year	Hat Making (212)	Hats (213)	Caps (214)	Hat Fasteners (215)	Total 212–215 (216)
1837	–	1	–	–	1
1838	–	–	–	–	–
1839	1	–	–	–	1
1840	3	–	–	–	3
1841	–	1	–	–	1
1842	2	1	–	–	3
1843	1	1	–	–	2
1844	4	1	–	–	5
1845	2	2	–	–	4
1846	–	1	–	–	1
1847	2	–	–	–	2
1848	1	–	–	–	1
1849	3	1	–	–	4
1850	1	–	–	–	1
1851	1	–	–	–	1
1852	–	2	–	–	2
1853	–	–	–	–	–
1854	5	1	–	–	6
1855	1	2	–	–	3
1856	3	2	–	–	5
1857	3	1	–	–	4
1858	4	2	–	–	6
1859	6	1	–	–	7
1860	4	10	–	–	14
1861	7	3	–	–	10
1862	6	7	–	–	13
1863	7	3	–	–	10
1864	8	9	–	–	17
1865	8	12	–	–	20
1866	20	16	1	–	37
1867	22	8	–	–	30
1868	18	14	2	–	34
1869	14	10	–	–	24
1870	10	9	2	–	21
1871	12	18	–	–	30
1872	5	11	–	–	16
1873	19	6	1	–	26
1874	15	5	–	–	20
1875	22	9	1	2	34
1876	14	9	1	–	24
1874	17	2	–	–	19
1875	21	10	2	2	35
1876	17	9	–	–	26
1877	12	11	1	–	24
1878	19	26	1	1	47
1879	29	30	–	–	59
1880	28	23	3	–	54
1881	17	12	3	–	32
1882	28	20	4	–	52
1883	30	32	1	1	64
1884	28	15	–	2	45
1885	21	11	3	2	37
1886	17	24	2	2	45
1887	19	20	3	3	45
1888	19	6	–	4	29
1889	24	11	–	2	37
1890	14	9	–	5	28
1891	25	8	1	–	34
1892	23	6	–	3	32
1893	22	6	–	7	35
1894	20	4	–	6	30

Year	(212)	(213)	(214)	(215)	(216)
1895	19	7	–	14	40
1896	24	7	3	15	49
1897	11	12	1	17	41
1898	18	11	2	8	39
1899	22	7	3	12	44
1900	21	10	3	13	47
1901	20	11	–	6	37
1902	19	11	–	17	47
1903	17	13	3	11	44
1904	26	13	3	18	60
1905	21	15	4	19	59
1906	12	16	3	14	45
1907	14	16	1	6	37
1908	20	25	4	15	64
1909	25	22	3	19	69
1910	24	15	2	26	67
1911	24	10	9	23	66
1912	22	21	7	22	72
1913	21	22	6	20	69
1914	19	34	7	14	74
1915	19	24	9	10	62
1916	14	25	8	10	57
1917	7	20	5	14	55
1918	17	16	4	11	48
1919	8	28	5	11	52
1920	11	35	7	12	65
1921	9	23	18	8	58
1922	16	20	13	5	54
1923	13	22	16	7	58
1924	12	16	19	6	53
1925	13	21	14	7	55
1926	17	22	10	–	49
1927	13	30	13	2	58
1928	19	20	9	2	50
1929	18	22	17	–	57
1930	30	16	8	1	55
1931	21	12	5	–	38
1932	8	16	9	1	34
1933	12	7	4	1	24
1934	14	24	4	1	43
1935	12	28	6	–	46
1936	15	15	4	5	39
1937	15	7	9	2	33
1938	14	12	7	2	35
1939	7	13	7	1	28
1940	13	15	5	2	35
1941	4	6	5	2	17
1942	3	4	6	2	15
1943	3	5	12	3	23
1944	3	4	9	2	18
1945	4	8	5	1	18
1946	8	16	8	1	33
1947	6	16	7	1	30
1948	3	10	4	1	18
1949	5	9	8	1	23
1950	10	7	13	–	30
1947	3	7	13	–	23
1948	8	14	10	–	32
1949	5	10	4	1	20
1950	3	5	2	2	12
1951	5	8	11	1	25
1952	5	14	5	1	25
1953	8	8	8	–	24
1954	2	12	10	–	24
1955	9	4	16	3	32
1956	1	7	11	1	20
1957	6	5	13	–	24

169

	Textiles: Other			Textiles Mixed with Other Fields and Textile Related			
Year	Felting (217)	Cordage & Twine Winding & Reeling (218)	Total 176, 180, 194–197, 204, 209–211, 216–218 (219)	Coating Processes and Products: Textiles, etc. (220)	Carpet Fasteners and Stretchers (221)	Felt Roofs (222)	Fabric Winding (223)
1837	–	–	23	–	–	–	1
1838	–	–	33	–	–	–	–
1839	1	–	21	1	–	–	–
1840	1	–	27	–	–	–	–
1841	2	–	24	1	–	–	–
1842	1	–	35	–	–	–	–
1843	–	–	26	–	–	–	–
1844	–	–	20	–	–	–	–
1845	1	–	28	1	–	–	–
1846	–	1	29	–	–	–	–
1847	1	–	27	–	–	–	–
1848	1	–	23	1	–	–	–
1849	–	–	65	–	–	–	–
1850	–	–	45	–	–	–	–
1851	–	–	37	–	–	–	–
1852	3	–	55	–	–	–	–
1853	3	–	50	1	1	–	–
1854	2	–	99	1	–	–	–
1855	7	1	93	1	2	–	2
1856	15	1	88	–	1	–	–
1857	5	–	93	1	1	1	1
1858	1	1	80	1	8	2	–
1859	1	1	83	1	6	2	1
1860	3	1	98	3	1	–	1
1861	3	–	96	–	1	–	–
1862	2	1	83	–	2	1	–
1863	–	–	94	3	1	1	1
1864	1	–	147	5	3	–	2
1865	–	–	156	3	11	1	1
1866	5	2	257	2	13	–	2
1867	12	3	320	4	12	10	3
1868	6	3	347	3	9	–	2
1869	6	5	309	3	25	–	3
1870	8	7	285	3	9	–	3
1871	5	1	263	6	14	1	4
1872	1	–	265	6	13	1	4
1873	2	4	268	3	17	1	3
1874	–	3	285	6	19	1	7
1875	3	–	295	2	13	1	7
1876	1	–	286	5	23	–	1
1874	1	2	258	4	21	1	9
1875	3	–	343	3	13	–	5
1876	–	–	311	4	24	–	6
1877	5	4	299	4	7	–	13
1878	9	3	340	1	8	–	4
1879	6	–	339	3	11	–	10
1880	14	–	376	6	11	–	7
1881	18	2	388	5	18	–	6
1882	26	2	479	3	23	2	9
1883	19	–	470	8	27	2	16
1884	11	3	432	4	27	–	18
1885	15	3	444	5	21	2	30
1886	4	1	492	3	21	5	13
1887	5	5	513	2	21	–	22
1888	8	2	472	4	27	1	83
1889	2	–	581	–	26	1	59
1890	1	5	559	3	28	2	50
1891	3	2	519	2	13	–	22
1892	3	1	529	2	13	1	35
1893	–	1	483	1	11	–	35
1894	4	3	482	–	4	1	26

Year	(217)	(218)	(219)	(220)	(221)	(222)	(223)
1895	2	3	513	1	14	–	18
1896	–	2	549	2	17	–	23
1897	1	2	551	1	15	–	20
1898	1	4	507	3	13	–	16
1899	1	2	604	2	8	4	28
1900	4	3	597	3	8	–	25
1901	1	2	695	4	12	–	38
1902	5	5	706	4	13	1	46
1903	1	6	788	3	23	2	52
1904	1	6	784	5	17	4	56
1905	2	3	759	8	11	1	50
1906	1	3	667	6	14	4	55
1907	–	3	620	6	13	7	50
1908	1	5	705	6	16	3	49
1909	3	7	722	7	11	3	59
1910	3	3	667	5	5	1	78
1911	2	6	727	3	12	4	74
1912	–	2	699	3	6	5	80
1913	–	2	653	7	4	4	93
1914	1	4	715	9	8	11	94
1915	–	10	610	10	7	8	86
1916	1	12	622	7	4	3	106
1917	–	4	642	14	4	4	78
1918	–	2	506	13	3	11	53
1919	1	2	696	11	3	12	87
1920	1	7	751	11	5	10	78
1921	7	8	835	11	8	16	75
1922	3	3	945	7	2	13	77
1923	8	6	1003	12	3	9	105
1924	4	4	1010	12	6	10	83
1925	1	4	1083	19	4	36	118
1926	2	4	1138	20	2	40	104
1927	3	6	1149	27	7	24	123
1928	8	3	1168	25	3	18	95
1929	1	3	1143	37	5	18	110
1930	2	6	1185	28	3	29	126
1931	3	3	1071	46	–	36	131
1932	1	–	963	39	3	13	15
1933	–	5	895	37	2	15	91
1934	4	–	915	60	2	15	80
1935	1	2	1002	41	–	17	93
1936	4	3	1032	62	4	16	94
1937	3	6	1043	43	1	9	87
1938	4	3	989	60	3	11	94
1939	2	7	921	39	–	9	94
1940	4	6	836	43	3	12	82
1941	1	2	710	39	1	6	78
1942	1	3	581	29	1	6	61
1943	3	1	582	19	1	–	40
1944	3	1	617	23	2	8	70
1945	3	5	674	17	1	3	96
1946	4	5	727	21	3	7	99
1947	4	4	753	21	5	5	109
1948	3	5	764	24	3	5	86
1949	6	7	904	22	7	2	96
1950	8	5	825	23	5	5	109
1947	1	–	499	22	–	7	23
1948	5	2	530	10	1	5	31
1949	2	3	742	24	3	2	95
1950	5	6	707	25	6	2	92
1951	4	10	795	22	3	7	125
1952	7	5	821	16	6	5	123
1953	6	4	783	19	5	10	135
1954	3	2	699	35	4	2	91
1955	2	1	666	30	4	2	90
1956	1	2	786	49	6	–	113
1957	2	2	731	26	4	3	58

171

Textiles, Clothing and Other Finished Textile Products,
Mixed with Household and Commercial Laundry

Year	Ironing or Smoothing						Total 224–229 (230)	Forming, Pressing, Molding, & Stretching (231)
	Two-Platen Presser (224)	Roller Presser (225)	Flat Irons (226)	Ironing Tables (227)	Ironing-Table Supports (228)	Misc. (229)		
1837	–	1	–	–	–	–	1	–
1838	–	–	–	–	–	–	–	–
1839	–	–	–	–	–	–	–	–
1840	–	–	–	–	–	–	–	2
1841	–	1	–	–	–	–	1	–
1842	–	–	–	–	–	–	–	1
1843	–	–	–	–	–	–	–	–
1844	–	–	–	–	–	–	–	1
1845	–	–	–	–	–	–	–	–
1846	–	–	–	–	–	–	–	–
1847	–	–	–	–	–	–	–	–
1848	–	–	1	–	–	–	1	–
1849	–	–	–	–	–	–	–	1
1850	–	–	–	–	–	–	–	1
1851	1	–	2	–	–	–	3	1
1852	–	–	3	–	–	–	3	1
1853	–	–	–	–	–	–	–	–
1854	–	–	2	–	–	–	2	1
1855	–	–	1	–	–	–	1	–
1856	1	–	3	–	–	–	4	1
1857	–	1	2	–	–	–	3	–
1858	1	3	1	–	3	–	8	1
1859	1	3	4	–	–	1	9	1
1860	–	2	2	–	1	–	5	–
1861	–	1	3	–	–	–	4	1
1862	–	–	2	–	2	2	6	2
1863	1	1	6	1	–	–	9	–
1864	–	1	2	–	–	2	5	2
1865	–	3	4	–	–	2	9	2
1866	1	1	11	–	1	–	14	4
1867	4	6	19	2	4	3	38	7
1868	1	2	15	5	4	2	29	10
1869	2	11	7	4	7	5	36	2
1870	3	1	10	5	7	1	27	3
1871	5	4	14	3	10	1	37	–
1872	4	5	13	3	9	3	37	2
1873	5	3	16	7	9	4	44	8
1874	1	2	6	14	15	2	40	9
1875	4	8	17	16	20	3	68	14
1876	8	6	10	21	14	4	63	10
1874	2	3	12	15	17	1	50	11
1875	6	9	9	13	19	3	59	13
1876	5	5	9	21	14	7	61	8
1877	2	10	11	14	8	10	55	7
1878	2	8	14	17	9	7	57	8
1879	2	4	7	11	8	8	40	6
1880	5	4	1	8	8	6	32	13
1881	3	3	2	10	6	4	28	19
1882	1	3	9	12	7	8	40	13
1883	3	5	5	13	10	6	42	18
1884	4	9	6	7	14	6	46	11
1885	2	4	8	7	15	6	42	15
1886	2	8	14	10	10	19	63	12
1887	1	8	14	10	7	14	54	20
1888	3	11	8	3	13	13	51	22
1889	1	12	15	6	12	10	56	15
1890	2	9	6	12	17	9	55	12
1891	2	7	6	8	12	15	50	13
1892	1	6	9	12	7	9	44	16
1893	4	4	9	8	8	12	45	11
1894	1	8	7	7	9	8	40	23

Year	(224)	(225)	(226)	(227)	(228)	(229)	(230)	(231)
1895	1	7	4	9	9	11	41	17
1896	3	6	9	15	15	7	55	16
1897	4	2	5	6	15	8	40	17
1898	–	7	7	7	9	13	43	9
1899	–	7	10	7	16	14	54	18
1900	1	4	8	5	15	17	50	12
1901	1	5	17	6	24	13	66	17
1902	5	5	13	10	15	16	64	10
1903	5	5	15	7	14	27	73	28
1904	3	2	13	8	13	22	61	38
1905	9	4	11	9	21	29	83	25
1906	3	6	13	7	21	23	73	23
1907	5	6	11	7	19	16	64	26
1908	10	7	9	13	33	29	101	27
1909	6	7	14	12	36	24	99	32
1910	7	5	16	6	28	31	93	23
1911	12	4	19	8	30	20	93	41
1912	11	8	8	19	28	31	105	47
1913	12	8	9	10	16	29	84	40
1914	10	3	12	13	28	22	88	40
1915	10	2	4	20	27	47	110	41
1916	8	3	10	13	29	35	98	28
1917	9	3	12	11	25	41	101	36
1918	9	1	6	8	9	15	48	20
1919	10	12	8	15	11	30	86	29
1920	13	23	13	9	19	32	109	27
1921	8	27	5	11	31	49	131	31
1922	13	17	6	7	35	36	114	28
1923	21	9	8	11	30	29	108	18
1924	32	19	13	15	27	47	153	21
1925	25	11	11	14	25	27	113	22
1926	36	17	7	18	27	50	155	35
1927	25	13	12	10	25	33	118	51
1928	33	9	5	13	27	41	128	50
1929	41	11	9	6	17	60	144	53
1930	28	8	10	16	19	48	129	60
1931	18	4	12	8	18	30	90	54
1932	18	10	9	7	11	20	75	45
1933	19	9	16	4	14	24	86	48
1934	33	8	11	13	14	30	109	46
1935	35	1	15	7	12	27	97	46
1936	17	12	14	6	13	18	80	53
1937	18	17	14	4	3	27	83	47
1938	17	22	22	9	12	23	105	49
1939	12	7	31	12	8	26	96	36
1940	13	18	22	14	5	35	107	57
1941	14	6	29	13	9	19	90	29
1942	4	2	7	5	3	5	26	23
1943	5	3	5	2	2	6	23	19
1944	5	7	20	10	3	10	55	14
1945	5	5	22	11	14	11	68	51
1946	4	6	27	16	17	12	82	68
1947	2	7	22	16	10	20	77	59
1948	3	9	29	21	14	17	93	37
1949	7	2	17	13	8	18	65	49
1950	5	1	22	14	14	17	73	32
1947	3	2	12	5	4	7	33	27
1948	4	4	14	10	4	9	45	27
1949	7	5	13	11	8	20	64	52
1950	6	8	24	14	21	20	93	62
1951	3	6	16	24	19	11	79	48
1952	7	5	32	17	9	9	79	41
1953	8	7	33	19	12	25	104	48
1954	4	6	23	7	12	14	66	34
1955	5	2	23	9	3	11	53	30
1956	1	5	41	10	11	6	74	36
1957	1	6	34	9	4	14	68	28

Textiles, Clothing and Other Finished Textile Products, Mixed with Household and Commercial Laundry

					Laundry and Other Fluid Treatment		
		Washing Machines Combined with Other		Misc. Fluid	Wringers		Total
Year	Washboards (232)	Operations (233)	Squeezing (234)	Treatment (235)	I (236)	II (237)	232–237 (238)
1837	–	–	1	–	–	–	1
1838	–	2	1	1	–	–	4
1839	–	–	2	1	–	–	3
1840	–	1	–	1	–	–	2
1841	–	–	3	1	–	–	4
1842	1	–	1	–	–	–	2
1843	–	1	3	1	–	–	5
1844	–	3	4	3	–	–	10
1845	–	2	2	2	–	–	6
1846	–	3	4	–	–	–	7
1847	–	2	2	–	1	–	5
1848	–	1	2	2	–	–	5
1849	1	3	–	1	–	–	5
1850	–	2	–	1	–	–	3
1851	1	5	1	–	–	–	7
1852	1	1	2	2	1	–	7
1853	–	1	–	2	–	–	3
1854	–	1	–	7	–	–	8
1855	1	4	3	4	1	–	13
1856	2	4	1	8	1	–	16
1857	1	5	6	7	1	–	20
1858	5	13	8	10	2	–	38
1859	–	13	17	11	–	1	42
1860	3	15	11	18	8	–	55
1861	2	4	20	11	4	7	48
1862	–	15	10	11	9	27	72
1863	–	13	15	9	8	5	50
1864	2	14	21	18	7	5	67
1865	3	20	24	22	7	5	81
1866	1	21	30	24	14	5	95
1867	3	34	67	44	11	6	165
1868	3	29	28	64	4	7	135
1869	3	31	37	79	4	6	160
1870	4	38	46	70	5	5	168
1871	5	31	48	87	7	10	188
1872	5	42	58	102	18	11	236
1873	4	25	51	91	6	6	183
1874	4	26	29	57	13	9	138
1875	4	29	40	55	14	7	149
1876	12	36	32	54	7	7	148
1874	3	27	40	64	13	6	153
1875	5	28	27	52	14	9	135
1876	15	29	33	41	5	7	130
1877	16	24	32	54	8	7	141
1878	16	28	32	51	4	5	136
1879	11	24	29	51	3	6	124
1880	7	23	18	47	10	7	112
1881	6	24	17	44	5	1	97
1882	8	26	19	54	7	5	119
1883	3	22	10	48	4	3	90
1884	5	18	22	62	10	1	118
1885	16	25	24	68	3	2	138
1886	10	26	21	60	8	2	127
1887	7	22	14	77	–	3	123
1888	6	23	16	62	6	2	115
1889	7	26	19	62	9	3	126
1890	8	34	8	77	4	3	134
1891	8	22	18	77	9	3	137
1892	9	32	16	51	3	1	112
1893	7	17	12	44	4	5	89
1894	7	19	5	38	2	2	73

Year	(232)	(233)	(234)	(235)	(236)	(237)	(238)
1895	22	18	10	37	5	–	92
1896	5	23	8	35	3	3	77
1897	10	27	16	55	12	3	123
1898	8	16	5	50	7	1	87
1899	13	20	15	57	12	2	119
1900	5	22	10	71	9	1	118
1901	10	20	14	54	6	1	105
1902	11	16	11	57	6	2	103
1903	8	25	12	70	6	–	121
1904	7	23	11	62	4	1	108
1905	9	16	9	70	8	–	112
1906	10	17	8	73	3	1	112
1907	14	26	9	73	8	3	133
1908	7	16	13	97	9	1	143
1909	16	23	10	88	10	1	148
1910	5	18	17	69	8	–	117
1911	7	12	11	74	15	3	122
1912	6	13	12	82	13	4	130
1913	6	17	9	92	8	6	138
1914	8	29	12	74	8	5	136
1915	7	20	14	70	16	6	133
1916	18	26	12	69	15	44	184
1917	10	22	6	92	16	9	155
1918	7	22	4	59	10	5	107
1919	8	20	11	83	24	6	152
1920	4	30	23	100	28	23	208
1921	9	35	21	103	30	23	221
1922	8	17	15	113	34	14	201
1923	8	22	14	106	27	12	189
1924	3	34	11	111	17	8	184
1925	2	32	9	103	16	9	171
1926	2	28	8	109	20	3	170
1927	2	25	6	117	19	7	176
1928	3	23	9	98	16	11	160
1929	3	20	2	110	15	7	157
1930	1	33	4	98	14	1	150
1931	3	22	1	81	27	12	147
1932	2	20	3	64	21	11	121
1933	2	16	1	48	30	8	105
1934	8	14	2	51	30	4	109
1935	2	23	–	54	19	13	111
1936	1	27	1	57	20	10	116
1937	1	22	4	64	22	25	138
1938	–	32	–	53	36	14	135
1939	–	38	4	57	19	16	134
1940	2	37	1	63	16	10	129
1941	–	33	–	46	16	2	97
1942	1	16	2	29	5	–	53
1943	–	12	–	33	8	2	55
1944	2	17	2	54	7	3	85
1945	–	25	–	49	8	5	87
1946	–	37	3	67	6	3	116
1947	–	39	–	62	8	2	111
1948	–	56	–	49	8	2	115
1949	–	40	–	43	13	2	98
1950	–	26	–	52	7	3	88
1947	–	12	–	30	1	–	43
1948	1	7	–	42	5	1	56
1949	–	9	–	18	2	–	29
1950	1	39	3	74	6	2	125
1951	–	36	2	70	11	4	123
1952	–	45	–	54	19	9	127
1953	–	76	–	67	10	2	155
1954	–	32	–	45	7	2	86
1955	1	20	1	45	5	5	77
1956	–	47	–	72	7	5	131
1957	–	42	–	31	9	6	88

Woodsawing Machines

Year	Recipro-cating Saw (239)	Band Saw (240)	Circular Saw (241)	Sawmill Carriages, Setworks, & Dogs (242)	Misc. Machines (243)	Total 239–243 (244)
1837	3	–	–	–	–	3
1838	4	–	5	1	–	10
1839	–	–	–	1	1	2
1840	4	–	2	1	–	7
1841	6	–	2	3	1	12
1842	5	–	2	4	–	11
1843	3	–	2	2	1	8
1844	1	–	3	8	–	12
1845	1	–	–	3	–	4
1846	1	–	–	3	–	4
1847	7	–	–	–	–	7
1848	2	–	1	1	-	4
1849	3	1	2	–	1	7
1850	4	–	1	–	–	5
1851	1	1	–	2	1	5
1852	4	–	1	1	–	6
1853	5	–	3	–	2	10
1854	12	1	11	4	2	30
1855	15	–	10	5	2	32
1856	15	–	7	7	1	30
1857	23	1	16	6	2	48
1858	14	–	10	4	3	31
1859	15	–	12	5	–	32
1860	13	–	10	4	2	29
1861	9	2	5	2	–	18
1862	16	–	5	4	–	25
1863	15	–	7	3	–	25
1864	28	–	10	4	2	44
1865	23	–	7	6	3	39
1866	29	1	11	14	4	59
1867	20	1	10	18	4	53
1868	40	1	13	17	7	78
1869	40	2	20	20	9	91
1870	42	5	20	26	11	104
1871	33	5	22	20	8	88
1872	41	6	30	21	12	110
1873	31	5	24	17	10	87
1874	29	5	22	22	17	95
1875	27	6	18	19	7	77
1876	33	6	15	16	12	82
1874	33	6	24	29	19	111
1875	24	7	16	12	6	65
1876	28	3	17	15	11	74
1877	23	2	17	13	7	62
1878	16	1	12	13	–	42
1879	30	5	16	11	4	66
1880	48	1	21	9	3	82
1881	29	1	18	16	4	68
1882	27	3	19	25	4	78
1883	26	7	33	44	4	114
1884	23	4	33	26	6	92
1885	25	14	33	32	4	108
1886	22	20	21	41	14	118
1887	19	8	23	26	6	82
1888	22	5	26	24	8	85
1889	15	14	34	19	12	94
1890	10	12	23	24	6	75
1891	11	5	22	23	8	69
1892	8	8	16	18	7	57
1893	12	3	7	11	8	41
1894	3	8	13	19	5	48

Year	(239)	(240)	(241)	(242)	(243)	(244)
1895	14	8	15	20	11	68
1896	6	2	11	4	11	34
1897	7	4	10	10	7	38
1898	6	6	11	4	8	35
1899	7	5	12	12	13	49
1900	7	4	15	13	17	56
1901	10	8	19	13	15	65
1902	12	8	22	9	17	68
1903	17	6	19	16	32	90
1904	14	11	24	17	18	84
1905	8	3	25	10	20	66
1906	16	7	7	8	18	56
1907	15	8	24	6	10	63
1908	23	10	19	11	61	79
1909	14	4	23	10	14	65
1910	9	3	23	7	14	56
1911	14	4	13	7	21	59
1912	5	3	23	1	11	43
1913	11	1	12	2	12	38
1914	13	6	21	7	11	58
1915	6	2	20	4	11	43
1916	8	5	9	2	14	38
1917	12	4	17	5	11	49
1918	12	3	17	7	3	42
1919	12	6	18	3	7	46
1920	18	6	29	5	3	52
1921	14	4	25	11	8	62
1922	17	9	22	15	12	75
1923	7	3	28	4	13	55
1924	13	7	25	11	17	73
1925	16	2	28	7	18	71
1926	7	6	24	16	14	67
1927	10	4	24	10	10	58
1928	5	4	26	12	19	66
1929	13	2	25	7	7	54
1930	8	3	23	4	16	54
1931	9	5	14	4	6	38
1932	4	6	9	2	3	24
1933	10	2	9	1	6	28
1934	10	–	9	–	7	26
1935	8	1	7	–	4	20
1936	7	4	10	3	2	26
1937	6	–	17	1	6	30
1938	3	1	11	1	2	18
1939	–	2	10	1	7	20
1940	1	1	14	–	7	23
1941	3	2	14	2	7	28
1942	1	–	12	1	7	21
1943	–	4	11	–	4	19
1944	4	1	18	2	9	34
1945	7	3	14	3	6	33
1946	9	5	31	4	11	60
1947	10	6	17	5	4	42
1948	9	6	26	1	20	62
1949	11	3	25	9	11	59
1950	6	10	22	4	13	55
1947	2	2	4	2	4	14
1948	1	1	19	–	5	26
1949	5	4	11	–	7	27
1950	2	6	15	3	10	36
1951	17	10	44	8	21	100
1952	14	3	10	5	7	39
1953	11	8	29	9	27	84
1954	5	6	39	4	13	67
1955	11	8	23	5	17	64
1956	15	5	18	5	25	68
1957	12	7	31	3	12	65

177

Lumber and Wood Products: General Woodworking

	Hand or Machine Saws					
Year	Hand Saws and Handles (245)	Saws (246)	Saw Teeth, Teeth Fastening, Guides & Gauges (247)	Misc. (248)	Total 246–248 (249)	Total 244, 245, 249 Hand *and* Machine Saws (250)
1837	–	–	–	–	–	3
1838	–	1	–	–	1	11
1839	–	1	–	2	3	5
1840	–	–	–	1	1	8
1841	–	–	–	1	1	13
1842	–	–	–	–	–	11
1843	–	2	1	–	3	11
1844	–	–	–	–	–	12
1845	–	–	–	–	–	4
1846	–	–	–	1	1	5
1847	–	–	–	–	–	7
1848	–	–	–	–	–	4
1849	–	1	1	–	2	9
1850	–	1	–	3	4	9
1851	–	1	1	1	3	8
1852	–	–	–	–	–	6
1853	–	1	–	2	3	13
1854	–	2	2	5	9	39
1855	1	1	2	5	8	41
1856	1	2	2	9	13	44
1857	1	–	4	5	9	58
1858	–	1	–	7	8	39
1859	2	2	–	8	10	44
1860	8	5	2	–	7	44
1861	2	1	3	3	7	27
1862	1	–	1	1	2	28
1863	3	3	1	4	8	36
1864	1	–	–	4	4	49
1865	6	2	4	8	14	59
1866	5	3	9	2	14	78
1867	9	6	16	6	28	90
1868	13	14	16	14	44	135
1869	5	9	12	16	37	133
1870	14	9	13	21	43	161
1871	21	8	15	10	33	142
1872	13	2	12	7	21	144
1873	8	4	13	11	28	123
1874	15	9	13	9	31	141
1875	23	1	10	10	21	121
1876	15	5	17	10	32	129
1874	17	8	13	10	31	159
1875	21	–	13	11	24	110
1876	15	10	15	9	34	123
1877	10	6	20	5	31	103
1878	12	10	11	2	23	77
1879	6	5	12	2	19	91
1880	9	9	7	4	20	111
1881	12	9	12	11	32	112
1882	16	5	26	22	53	147
1883	29	10	27	20	57	200
1884	22	13	26	13	52	166
1885	15	14	32	11	57	180
1886	12	15	25	8	48	178
1887	14	9	22	4	35	131
1888	14	12	13	4	29	128
1889	12	14	25	10	49	155
1890	10	7	18	11	36	121
1891	14	5	12	6	23	106
1892	13	7	19	8	34	104
1893	13	4	8	5	17	71
1894	9	6	11	16	33	90

Year	(245)	(246)	(247)	(248)	(249)	(250)
1895	10	6	23	6	35	113
1896	13	5	13	4	22	69
1897	20	8	12	3	23	81
1898	13	5	5	7	17	65
1899	19	3	9	6	18	86
1900	16	2	8	10	20	92
1901	21	4	9	14	27	113
1902	15	5	7	9	21	104
1903	13	3	13	9	25	128
1904	18	6	18	18	42	144
1905	15	6	18	14	38	119
1906	18	7	8	10	25	99
1907	16	4	19	9	32	111
1908	21	2	21	5	28	128
1909	32	2	10	13	25	122
1910	11	2	9	12	23	90
1911	15	2	7	14	23	97
1912	19	5	11	17	33	95
1913	14	6	13	19	38	90
1914	15	3	6	13	22	95
1915	14	5	3	13	21	78
1916	11	1	5	14	20	69
1917	16	1	14	12	27	92
1918	11	1	8	8	17	70
1919	21	10	12	17	39	106
1920	14	5	8	12	25	91
1921	29	4	21	11	36	127
1922	23	4	11	7	22	120
1923	19	5	12	7	24	98
1924	20	5	6	19	30	123
1925	20	6	17	15	38	129
1926	8	8	6	11	25	100
1927	10	4	18	14	36	104
1928	11	1	14	10	25	102
1929	9	3	10	11	24	87
1930	10	6	10	16	32	96
1931	7	5	4	9	18	63
1932	4	1	10	6	17	45
1933	11	7	7	9	23	62
1934	9	2	5	4	11	46
1935	11	4	5	5	14	45
1936	14	4	13	5	22	62
1937	7	4	5	8	17	54
1938	6	4	7	2	13	37
1939	8	4	2	7	13	41
1940	7	6	6	8	20	50
1941	5	8	6	5	19	52
1942	7	1	1	6	8	36
1943	4	3	2	7	12	35
1944	12	1	1	10	12	58
1945	6	–	3	13	16	55
1946	10	8	5	14	27	97
1947	7	7	6	11	24	73
1948	4	9	10	18	37	103
1949	11	13	8	12	33	103
1950	12	9	7	9	25	92
1947	2	1	1	5	7	23
1948	9	2	2	8	12	47
1949	1	–	4	12	16	44
1950	11	6	8	12	26	83
1951	12	14	6	25	45	157
1952	12	6	7	8	21	72
1953	9	17	6	19	42	135
1954	8	5	16	20	41	116
1955	7	7	6	15	28	99
1956	25	21	17	33	71	154
1957	8	10	12	19	41	114

Lumber and Wood Products: General Woodworking Machines

Year	Wood Turning Circular Section (251)	Wood Turning Misc. (252)	Mortising, Tenoning, Dovetailing, & Matching (253)	Boring (254)	Planing (255)	Shaping (256)	Shaving and Slicing (257)
1837	1	–	4	–	4	–	5
1838	–	1	7	1	3	2	1
1839	–	–	3	2	2	–	7
1840	3	–	2	–	–	2	7
1841	1	–	3	–	–	–	4
1842	–	–	4	–	–	1	10
1843	–	1	2	1	–	–	5
1844	1	2	1	2	1	1	4
1845	1	2	4	2	3	1	3
1846	–	–	4	2	1	–	3
1847	1	1	2	1	1	–	1
1848	2	1	1	1	2	3	3
1849	2	4	3	5	14	3	6
1850	1	1	5	2	5	6	4
1851	1	4	1	1	6	2	5
1852	–	–	3	1	7	2	3
1853	2	3	3	1	6	2	5
1854	6	3	14	1	12	15	7
1855	7	5	17	3	6	11	7
1856	8	4	18	4	10	10	8
1857	7	1	19	6	6	4	12
1858	13	4	5	3	9	7	16
1859	5	4	11	4	5	9	15
1860	6	8	14	3	9	8	13
1861	5	2	6	6	5	11	8
1862	3	1	8	2	1	3	12
1863	5	4	10	1	6	8	8
1864	8	4	5	3	5	5	7
1865	4	3	6	4	–	8	6
1866	12	7	11	6	8	10	10
1867	8	7	12	3	5	11	7
1868	11	11	32	8	11	11	12
1869	13	4	24	11	9	11	4
1870	10	11	34	12	11	18	8
1871	13	7	31	6	13	16	4
1872	6	9	14	10	4	9	4
1873	7	7	20	8	7	17	12
1874	15	6	21	4	15	16	9
1875	11	9	18	14	23	16	13
1876	9	3	13	10	9	13	11
1874	17	7	16	9	22	17	13
1875	9	8	21	9	20	17	14
1876	7	3	12	7	4	9	5
1877	7	6	11	5	6	12	6
1878	4	7	7	7	11	13	11
1879	5	10	11	3	4	7	15
1880	11	12	6	5	11	8	11
1881	6	14	9	10	9	12	8
1882	8	12	18	9	13	6	16
1883	8	11	13	13	14	15	5
1884	10	7	13	5	13	12	4
1885	9	7	17	7	9	8	10
1886	10	5	20	11	13	23	2
1887	9	8	13	6	6	8	12
1888	8	5	15	3	17	18	4
1889	13	5	16	5	8	12	13
1890	11	11	19	10	7	20	5
1891	14	7	18	9	9	9	6
1892	10	4	22	11	3	14	9
1893	11	6	14	10	6	8	5
1894	4	4	12	7	8	12	5

Year	(251)	(252)	(253)	(254)	(255)	(256)	(257)
1895	11	4	12	7	5	17	7
1896	3	5	7	8	4	10	2
1897	6	4	8	5	5	7	2
1898	7	4	13	5	4	6	3
1899	6	8	11	7	5	7	1
1900	8	2	14	6	4	7	5
1901	9	11	10	10	7	17	2
1902	9	5	10	5	5	29	2
1903	7	5	17	9	9	11	5
1904	8	4	11	6	3	10	6
1905	9	8	13	7	5	10	8
1906	8	11	18	10	12	10	5
1907	3	15	12	8	13	10	6
1908	2	7	11	7	13	16	2
1909	6	9	12	9	7	8	–
1910	7	6	23	9	7	6	2
1911	2	4	18	6	4	12	2
1912	2	8	14	10	5	10	2
1913	3	3	12	13	9	10	1
1914	2	5	13	3	5	13	–
1915	2	7	9	4	6	7	1
1916	5	9	7	5	3	8	2
1917	2	13	6	5	10	15	3
1918	3	16	5	5	3	7	2
1919	1	11	5	1	5	13	–
1920	5	6	11	4	4	11	–
1921	2	13	13	7	2	5	2
1922	4	7	5	2	5	14	3
1923	4	9	9	4	6	20	1
1924	7	8	8	3	10	13	1
1925	6	6	12	7	7	19	2
1926	1	7	11	3	5	16	3
1927	2	10	9	4	8	16	3
1928	4	11	10	8	8	15	5
1929	3	5	14	8	5	13	7
1930	–	2	10	2	4	9	–
1931	1	4	5	5	2	8	–
1932	1	2	5	2	1	9	–
1933	5	–	5	1	–	7	1
1934	3	2	2	2	1	1	2
1935	2	3	1	2	2	7	–
1936	–	4	–	4	3	6	2
1937	1	2	–	2	2	7	2
1938	–	2	1	3	1	7	–
1939	2	–	3	1	1	3	1
1940	1	1	4	4	5	2	1
1941	–	4	1	1	1	5	1
1942	1	1	2	1	–	9	1
1943	–	6	2	4	2	4	1
1944	1	2	1	–	4	4	–
1945	2	–	1	3	6	6	1
1946	–	2	3	3	7	8	1
1947	2	6	3	3	3	4	3
1948	2	1	8	3	2	11	2
1949	1	2	1	2	1	14	1
1950	2	2	2	1	8	12	1
1947	1	–	–	–	2	1	2
1948	–	1	2	3	3	4	–
1949	1	–	–	1	3	4	–
1950	1	2	–	3	3	10	–
1951	2	5	8	5	14	26	3
1952	1	1	6	2	1	7	1
1953	3	1	3	4	7	18	2
1954	–	4	1	–	6	11	3
1955	–	2	1	4	7	6	5
1956	–	5	7	2	7	15	2
1957	–	2	4	2	3	4	6

Lumber and Wood Products: General Woodworking Machines

Year	Cutting (258)	Bending (259)	Feed and Presser Mechanism (260)	Machinery Clamps (261)	Misc. Machines (262)	Total 244, 251–262 (263)
1837	–	–	–	–	–	17
1838	2	–	–	–	–	27
1839	–	–	–	–	–	16
1840	–	–	–	–	–	22
1841	–	–	–	–	2	22
1842	1	1	–	–	–	28
1843	–	–	–	–	1	18
1844	1	–	–	–	2	27
1845	–	–	–	–	1	21
1846	–	–	–	–	1	15
1847	–	–	1	–	2	17
1848	1	–	1	–	2	21
1849	1	2	–	1	1	49
1850	1	–	–	–	2	32
1851	–	1	–	–	2	28
1852	1	–	2	–	–	25
1853	4	1	–	2	3	41
1854	5	1	1	–	5	100
1855	7	–	2	3	10	110
1856	7	5	2	2	4	112
1857	4	2	2	1	10	122
1858	6	4	–	–	7	105
1859	5	6	2	2	6	106
1860	2	8	4	3	8	115
1861	3	3	1	1	5	74
1862	–	3	–	–	5	63
1863	4	2	2	2	6	83
1864	3	3	1	1	6	95
1865	2	9	3	1	4	89
1866	4	16	5	12	12	172
1867	18	8	6	8	10	165
1868	11	14	1	6	21	227
1869	18	15	1	10	15	226
1870	18	14	5	16	17	278
1871	12	15	4	12	19	240
1872	10	4	5	8	20	213
1873	18	7	8	15	15	228
1874	7	8	12	8	23	239
1875	13	17	8	14	17	250
1876	16	8	11	6	19	210
1874	13	9	11	9	21	275
1875	15	19	7	12	18	234
1876	10	5	14	7	27	184
1877	11	6	3	6	26	167
1878	10	11	2	8	21	154
1879	6	6	3	3	19	158
1880	11	15	2	7	20	201
1881	11	8	5	9	21	190
1882	20	10	6	9	19	224
1883	31	14	7	12	35	292
1884	16	7	9	16	26	230
1885	25	9	13	9	28	259
1886	15	14	15	20	34	300
1887	12	4	9	8	22	199
1888	18	9	24	13	15	234
1889	16	7	6	18	23	236
1890	26	11	10	9	27	241
1891	12	5	8	10	28	204
1892	22	9	5	15	36	217
1893	17	5	7	7	21	158
1894	11	15	4	8	17	155

Year	(258)	(259)	(260)	(261)	(262)	(263)
1895	27	7	3	10	11	189
1896	17	5	1	10	20	126
1897	19	12	1	8	24	139
1898	12	7	3	12	18	129
1899	15	8	4	5	20	146
1900	18	7	4	8	22	161
1901	21	12	9	16	32	221
1902	16	6	5	16	32	208
1903	16	7	7	18	20	221
1904	14	11	4	12	30	203
1905	24	6	5	20	36	121
1906	23	4	8	22	32	219
1907	19	8	3	28	38	226
1908	27	10	10	18	47	249
1909	26	5	4	18	36	205
1910	18	10	4	30	33	211
1911	19	6	8	19	36	195
1912	20	5	9	22	38	188
1913	9	3	5	13	22	141
1914	14	3	5	18	29	168
1915	18	3	8	29	28	156
1916	13	2	5	23	32	152
1917	9	5	14	15	30	176
1918	12	–	4	16	32	147
1919	10	5	2	22	37	158
1920	10	6	6	27	38	180
1921	12	7	7	23	40	195
1922	13	2	3	23	33	189
1923	10	9	2	15	51	195
1924	14	6	7	28	38	216
1925	14	1	8	18	46	217
1926	13	–	3	23	42	194
1927	22	5	8	35	51	231
1928	16	7	4	21	32	207
1929	12	5	6	17	33	182
1930	16	2	5	15	31	150
1931	6	5	2	12	39	127
1932	3	1	–	6	31	85
1933	2	3	–	4	27	83
1934	4	1	1	1	18	64
1935	2	–	–	6	26	71
1936	5	–	2	5	26	83
1937	3	3	2	8	14	76
1938	3	2	2	6	14	59
1939	2	2	1	6	25	67
1940	3	3	2	11	25	85
1941	3	3	–	8	24	79
1942	2	5	–	11	17	71
1943	2	5	1	13	14	73
1944	2	3	–	16	9	76
1945	5	1	–	15	23	96
1946	4	4	1	13	30	136
1947	9	–	3	14	33	125
1948	8	2	5	16	41	163
1949	5	2	3	13	19	123
1950	6	–	5	18	28	140
1947	–	–	–	2	–	22
1948	4	–	1	15	5	64
1949	4	3	–	12	26	81
1950	4	–	–	8	17	84
1951	15	6	7	25	61	277
1952	6	1	3	17	16	101
1953	3	2	4	17	50	198
1954	7	1	6	16	31	153
1955	7	–	1	9	27	133
1956	10	4	5	23	51	199
1957	10	1	6	21	44	168

183

Lumber and Wood Products: Woodworking Tools

Year	Planes (264)	Augers (265)	Bit Frames and Stocks (266)	Handles (267)	Misc. (268)	Total 245, 264–268 (269)
1837	–	–	–	–	–	–
1838	1	1	1	–	–	3
1839	–	1	–	–	–	1
1840	–	–	–	–	–	–
1841	–	–	–	–	–	–
1842	–	–	–	–	–	–
1843	1	1	–	–	–	2
1844	1	–	–	–	–	1
1845	–	1	–	1	–	2
1846	1	–	–	–	–	1
1847	–	1	–	–	1	2
1848	2	–	–	–	–	2
1849	3	1	–	2	–	6
1850	1	1	–	3	–	5
1851	2	1	–	1	1	5
1852	3	1	1	–	1	6
1853	–	–	–	–	1	1
1854	3	2	2	2	2	11
1855	5	6	1	2	1	16
1856	5	2	1	3	1	13
1857	14	3	4	2	3	27
1858	7	6	1	3	4	21
1859	5	4	–	–	6	17
1860	3	5	1	2	4	23
1861	2	2	2	1	–	9
1862	2	1	1	1	2	8
1863	2	1	2	2	1	11
1864	8	3	2	–	2	16
1865	5	4	2	2	6	25
1866	6	6	2	2	6	27
1867	11	3	3	4	10	40
1868	9	13	6	5	15	61
1869	9	9	3	5	16	47
1870	19	9	3	2	15	62
1871	12	15	7	3	10	68
1872	17	11	1	2	12	56
1873	16	1	4	5	13	47
1874	11	10	4	6	10	56
1875	22	8	7	3	9	72
1876	16	3	1	7	15	57
1874	9	9	4	5	10	54
1875	24	6	5	5	11	72
1876	15	2	3	5	12	52
1877	10	3	2	6	12	43
1878	13	5	5	4	9	48
1879	3	3	5	2	5	24
1880	8	5	3	5	11	41
1881	5	9	6	3	7	42
1882	12	8	1	8	19	64
1883	26	13	13	11	15	107
1884	26	8	8	12	21	97
1885	17	14	7	8	17	78
1886	12	6	7	7	19	63
1887	10	5	2	11	15	57
1888	16	2	7	8	19	66
1889	13	10	10	9	25	79
1890	5	9	7	18	18	67
1891	11	8	11	9	25	78
1892	5	6	7	3	10	44
1893	14	6	7	9	12	61
1894	7	5	4	3	20	48

Year	(264)	(265)	(266)	(267)	(268)	(269)
1895	7	5	1	4	7	34
1896	3	6	7	5	15	49
1897	8	10	4	3	13	58
1898	4	3	3	7	12	42
1899	3	3	5	4	19	53
1900	7	1	2	4	15	45
1901	17	3	5	5	29	80
1902	21	5	6	7	19	73
1903	18	9	6	5	26	77
1904	22	8	10	4	22	84
1905	9	12	10	7	29	82
1906	8	7	10	12	31	86
1907	19	6	10	8	25	84
1908	7	7	10	5	17	67
1909	12	10	10	5	21	90
1910	11	7	9	3	27	68
1911	10	3	8	6	20	62
1912	20	5	9	10	19	82
1913	13	3	3	8	19	60
1914	12	6	8	5	15	61
1915	15	4	2	11	17	63
1916	3	9	–	6	21	50
1917	7	5	9	12	22	71
1918	14	6	4	8	16	59
1919	11	7	8	6	19	72
1920	13	9	18	16	22	92
1921	14	9	14	19	28	113
1922	13	9	9	19	17	90
1923	9	2	7	8	37	82
1924	18	3	11	5	22	79
1925	12	5	5	7	23	72
1926	5	4	7	5	19	48
1927	8	3	2	8	14	45
1928	6	7	–	6	24	54
1929	6	1	4	3	23	46
1930	7	6	4	4	18	49
1931	4	2	2	7	10	32
1932	5	2	2	5	15	33
1933	3	3	–	3	10	30
1934	1	3	1	2	8	24
1935	1	2	–	2	10	26
1936	–	4	1	2	9	30
1937	1	–	2	3	7	20
1938	1	3	–	3	10	23
1939	1	2	2	1	15	29
1940	1	2	1	2	11	24
1941	2	3	–	2	11	23
1942	3	2	–	1	5	18
1943	3	2	–	1	11	21
1944	1	2	1	3	12	31
1945	3	1	–	4	13	27
1946	4	6	4	8	28	60
1947	2	4	–	3	26	42
1948	10	2	2	4	16	38
1949	4	1	3	3	16	38
1950	6	–	1	3	10	32
1947	1	–	–	1	5	9
1948	1	1	–	2	8	21
1949	1	2	2	2	20	28
1950	2	1	3	3	25	45
1951	18	9	–	6	40	85
1952	2	2	1	4	4	25
1953	7	3	2	11	22	54
1954	4	3	2	3	8	28
1955	5	3	2	4	13	34
1956	9	5	3	6	32	80
1957	1	4	–	4	25	42

Lumber and Wood Products: Special Machines and Equipment

Year	Log Sawing Operations & Debarking (270)	Shingle Making & Shingle Related (271)	Coopering (272)	Veneering (273)	Misc. Machines (274)	Total 270–274 (275)
1837	–	4	2	4	–	10
1838	–	2	3	2	–	7
1839	–	–	3	–	–	3
1840	–	–	1	1	1	3
1841	–	–	1	–	–	1
1842	–	–	2	–	–	2
1843	–	2	–	2	–	4
1844	–	1	2	1	1	5
1845	–	–	2	–	–	2
1846	–	–	3	–	–	3
1847	–	1	3	2	–	6
1848	–	2	2	2	1	7
1849	–	1	9	1	–	11
1850	–	–	3	–	–	3
1851	1	–	4	–	1	6
1852	–	–	3	1	–	4
1853	–	1	6	1	–	8
1854	3	3	10	3	1	20
1855	2	5	8	5	–	20
1856	–	5	11	6	2	24
1857	–	9	12	10	1	32
1858	1	17	17	18	–	53
1859	1	16	16	19	2	54
1860	3	5	14	6	2	30
1861	2	2	6	2	–	12
1862	1	6	5	7	–	19
1863	7	8	12	8	1	36
1864	–	5	11	5	2	23
1865	–	6	13	6	2	27
1866	2	13	11	13	2	41
1867	8	6	12	9	4	39
1868	8	18	25	19	9	79
1869	8	7	12	7	9	43
1870	7	7	28	11	7	60
1871	6	11	19	11	6	53
1872	8	9	28	13	10	68
1873	10	4	21	10	11	56
1874	12	3	12	8	3	38
1875	6	3	22	5	21	57
1876	3	7	25	11	9	55
1874	8	5	11	3	6	33
1875	5	4	27	4	10	50
1876	3	6	34	3	4	50
1877	4	4	15	2	–	25
1878	6	6	19	5	3	39
1879	3	1	11	1	2	18
1880	3	6	14	1	5	29
1881	8	9	16	2	2	37
1882	7	8	23	3	3	44
1883	14	10	29	3	4	60
1884	9	11	18	4	5	47
1885	14	7	25	3	4	53
1886	8	9	22	6	2	47
1887	7	6	17	2	3	35
1888	5	11	23	7	2	48
1889	12	10	15	2	1	40
1890	10	9	27	5	5	56
1891	8	7	36	5	4	60
1892	10	5	15	4	–	34
1893	13	6	24	6	4	53
1894	7	5	19	6	5	42

Year	(270)	(271)	(272)	(273)	(274)	(275)
1895	7	2	18	–	7	34
1896	9	7	15	5	6	42
1897	10	1	15	3	11	40
1898	6	3	7	2	7	25
1899	6	2	22	6	12	48
1900	10	4	16	7	6	43
1901	10	6	18	7	7	48
1902	14	7	16	3	9	49
1903	12	8	20	3	4	47
1904	6	8	11	8	4	37
1905	9	6	11	10	5	41
1906	2	8	16	5	5	36
1907	10	9	7	3	3	32
1908	11	4	13	9	6	43
1909	7	5	18	3	6	39
1910	10	4	7	2	5	28
1911	13	6	15	10	3	47
1912	14	6	8	6	9	43
1913	8	3	6	5	6	28
1914	8	4	6	3	1	22
1915	10	5	7	2	2	26
1916	12	3	4	–	3	22
1917	8	3	6	3	6	26
1918	9	7	3	8	2	29
1919	4	3	11	–	4	22
1920	5	5	9	5	11	35
1921	6	6	10	6	15	43
1922	6	3	17	6	1	33
1923	2	4	7	3	4	20
1924	8	2	12	5	2	29
1925	4	4	2	10	4	24
1926	11	1	7	13	4	36
1927	10	7	10	10	5	42
1928	12	3	1	7	6	29
1929	9	2	5	9	4	29
1930	9	1	6	10	8	34
1931	5	4	4	15	7	35
1932	10	1	2	9	5	27
1933	3	1	4	5	1	14
1934	5	3	2	7	1	18
1935	2	4	4	7	3	20
1936	1	1	3	3	–	8
1937	5	4	1	7	1	18
1938	3	2	5	8	–	18
1939	2	–	1	9	2	14
1940	4	1	–	14	–	19
1941	4	1	–	10	1	16
1942	5	–	–	21	2	28
1943	3	–	1	25	1	30
1944	11	–	–	17	1	29
1945	9	2	1	7	–	19
1946	13	2	3	11	1	30
1947	10	2	2	12	–	26
1948	13	4	–	13	–	30
1949	14	2	–	3	3	22
1950	17	–	2	4	–	23
1947	2	–	–	–	1	3
1948	9	2	1	2	3	17
1949	10	2	3	4	10	29
1950	5	2	–	3	8	18
1951	33	4	2	6	8	53
1952	8	2	–	4	8	22
1953	23	3	–	6	19	51
1954	26	1	2	3	9	41
1955	16	4	1	5	7	33
1956	18	2	6	3	11	40
1957	21	3	–	4	15	43

187

Lumber and Wood Products: Special Products and Machines for Making Same

Year	Box Making				Baskets & Basket Making (280)
	Crates (276)	Special Cells in Boxes (277)	Misc. Boxes & Eqpt. for Mfg. Same (278)	Total 276–278 (279)	
1837	–	–	–	–	–
1838	–	–	1	1	–
1839	–	–	–	–	–
1840	–	–	1	1	–
1841	–	–	–	–	–
1842	–	–	–	–	–
1843	1	–	1	2	1
1844	–	–	–	–	–
1845	–	–	–	–	–
1846	–	–	–	–	–
1847	–	–	–	–	1
1848	–	–	–	–	–
1849	–	–	2	2	–
1850	–	–	2	2	–
1851	–	–	1	1	–
1852	–	–	1	1	–
1853	–	–	–	–	–
1854	–	–	1	1	–
1855	–	1	2	3	–
1856	1	–	1	2	1
1857	–	–	2	2	3
1858	–	–	1	1	1
1859	–	–	3	3	2
1860	–	1	3	4	1
1861	–	–	2	2	2
1862	–	2	6	8	3
1863	–	1	5	6	1
1864	1	–	4	5	5
1865	2	2	12	16	5
1866	1	–	7	8	5
1867	3	5	12	20	5
1868	7	4	11	22	6
1869	10	8	16	34	6
1870	4	10	30	44	8
1871	2	6	19	27	9
1872	4	15	27	46	21
1873	7	11	22	40	16
1874	5	15	20	40	8
1875	9	10	25	44	14
1876	7	16	30	53	7
1874	6	13	25	44	4
1875	10	9	26	45	15
1876	8	17	24	49	5
1877	6	11	28	45	7
1878	7	13	32	52	3
1879	5	23	33	61	7
1880	11	12	29	52	4
1881	15	15	34	64	8
1882	17	22	26	65	9
1883	19	17	42	78	7
1884	13	12	26	51	8
1885	12	11	36	59	6
1886	9	15	39	63	10
1887	12	10	31	53	8
1888	8	11	36	55	10
1889	24	13	45	82	10
1890	28	16	32	76	13
1891	16	13	31	60	17
1892	15	18	38	71	7
1893	21	13	39	73	11
1894	18	17	36	71	8

Year	(276)	(277)	(278)	(279)	(280)
1895	23	6	28	57	12
1896	21	6	59	86	2
1897	32	16	73	121	11
1898	24	13	28	65	12
1899	28	12	42	82	13
1900	31	15	54	100	10
1901	32	17	58	107	13
1902	56	16	55	127	14
1903	28	17	46	91	12
1904	31	20	61	112	11
1905	46	9	63	118	9
1906	33	7	60	100	8
1907	43	17	70	130	9
1908	41	18	69	128	6
1909	52	13	84	149	6
1910	36	13	74	123	7
1911	14	12	83	109	7
1912	18	18	82	118	13
1913	33	47	100	180	8
1914	34	71	94	199	12
1915	39	40	79	158	9
1916	31	28	63	122	10
1917	29	20	70	119	11
1918	15	14	52	81	7
1919	22	23	103	148	15
1920	25	14	101	140	16
1921	36	32	110	178	16
1922	25	20	93	138	18
1923	40	14	81	135	11
1924	28	18	70	116	12
1925	15	8	58	81	13
1926	22	16	42	80	19
1927	16	16	34	66	20
1928	8	16	31	55	9
1929	12	12	42	66	8
1930	23	22	42	87	23
1931	18	32	46	96	30
1932	14	21	65	100	17
1933	11	27	56	94	17
1934	16	22	52	90	20
1935	10	19	49	78	14
1936	12	10	37	59	9
1937	11	14	45	70	4
1938	6	13	39	58	2
1939	7	10	21	38	6
1940	6	4	21	31	5
1941	2	10	19	31	4
1942	3	6	16	25	3
1943	6	2	9	17	3
1944	5	3	16	24	2
1945	6	2	10	18	—
1946	5	6	12	23	1
1947	6	9	18	33	2
1948	9	7	28	44	5
1949	2	3	20	25	4
1950	3	4	18	25	—
1947	1	1	1	3	14
1948	3	1	11	15	17
1949	12	6	21	39	18
1950	6	4	16	26	14
1951	9	12	46	67	17
1952	2	2	4	8	22
1953	2	6	20	28	16
1954	3	7	12	22	21
1955	3	2	15	20	25
1956	5	4	14	23	21
1957	1	1	13	15	28

Lumber and Wood Products: Special Products

Year	Weather-boarding, Flooring, Molding (281)	Windows Sliding or Swinging Sash (282)	Other (283)	Door & Window Frames (284)	Lasts & Related Products (285)	Misc. Products (286)	Total 281–286 (287)
1837	–	–	–	–	–	–	–
1838	–	–	–	–	–	–	–
1839	–	–	–	–	–	–	–
1840	–	–	–	–	–	2	2
1841	–	–	–	–	–	2	2
1842	–	–	–	–	–	2	2
1843	–	–	–	–	–	1	1
1844	–	–	–	–	–	–	–
1845	–	1	–	–	–	1	2
1846	–	–	–	–	–	1	1
1847	–	–	–	–	–	4	4
1848	–	–	–	–	–	1	1
1849	–	–	–	–	–	1	1
1850	–	–	–	–	–	6	6
1851	–	–	1	1	1	4	7
1852	–	–	2	–	–	2	4
1853	–	–	–	–	–	3	3
1854	1	1	3	–	1	6	12
1855	–	2	1	–	–	9	12
1856	–	–	–	1	1	10	12
1857	–	–	2	1	–	17	20
1858	–	–	–	1	1	9	11
1859	–	–	–	–	2	12	14
1860	1	3	1	1	2	8	16
1861	–	1	1	–	2	8	12
1862	–	1	2	–	2	10	15
1863	1	–	–	–	2	6	9
1864	1	1	1	1	5	10	19
1865	2	3	5	–	6	13	29
1866	1	2	1	–	7	20	31
1867	1	8	3	2	6	24	44
1868	7	6	7	2	9	27	58
1869	6	8	–	–	8	22	44
1870	5	3	3	4	6	26	47
1871	3	5	3	3	–	22	36
1872	6	3	4	3	8	29	53
1873	5	6	3	1	14	24	53
1874	2	5	3	4	10	38	62
1875	8	5	4	2	3	42	64
1876	5	5	4	2	7	23	46
1874	5	2	2	2	7	33	51
1875	6	7	4	4	3	28	52
1876	5	4	3	1	9	22	44
1877	4	3	6	1	8	24	46
1878	3	6	5	2	9	18	43
1879	5	5	3	3	1	18	35
1880	3	7	4	3	3	24	44
1881	6	6	3	3	13	25	56
1882	3	9	7	1	9	29	58
1883	15	8	7	3	13	36	82
1884	11	17	8	2	12	34	84
1885	22	15	5	5	4	47	98
1886	6	15	9	5	5	50	90
1887	1	13	7	4	13	37	75
1888	4	18	1	12	19	32	86
1889	6	16	6	9	10	38	85
1890	7	16	8	4	5	40	80
1891	6	20	7	9	4	34	80
1892	9	18	4	8	12	30	81
1893	8	23	5	6	12	19	73
1894	4	19	5	7	13	23	71

Year	(281)	(282)	(283)	(284)	(285)	(286)	(287)
1895	3	45	5	9	8	26	96
1896	6	33	7	12	16	31	105
1897	5	28	12	5	17	24	91
1898	8	38	7	1	17	14	85
1899	11	26	11	8	18	16	90
1900	4	29	11	1	19	25	89
1901	16	25	12	10	21	30	114
1902	8	35	5	3	16	32	99
1903	9	24	13	8	12	41	107
1904	5	39	6	7	12	31	100
1905	7	27	18	5	12	30	99
1906	8	29	7	1	17	35	97
1907	6	27	15	6	17	31	102
1908	11	26	27	6	20	26	116
1909	9	25	30	12	24	27	127
1910	6	28	27	2	13	24	100
1911	3	28	25	6	12	28	102
1912	3	26	22	4	16	15	86
1913	9	37	20	5	24	19	114
1914	11	38	20	4	34	11	118
1915	4	22	17	6	26	18	93
1916	11	15	21	8	12	16	83
1917	5	20	13	4	9	11	62
1918	9	25	11	8	20	14	87
1919	5	24	20	2	20	25	96
1920	13	32	19	8	11	13	96
1921	12	33	32	6	20	20	123
1922	11	30	26	3	32	11	113
1923	14	24	27	8	12	20	105
1924	13	30	18	5	39	19	124
1925	21	37	36	6	27	20	147
1926	13	58	29	16	20	29	165
1927	18	43	42	13	19	29	164
1928	17	44	33	19	17	15	145
1929	23	27	57	17	10	25	159
1930	32	27	56	19	10	18	162
1931	45	24	58	9	5	24	166
1932	30	22	47	12	9	19	139
1933	17	22	26	4	9	17	95
1934	19	15	53	2	9	16	114
1935	28	29	54	3	16	14	144
1936	29	23	52	5	15	14	138
1937	32	25	45	7	9	20	138
1938	37	21	35	7	9	13	122
1939	32	18	39	9	8	5	111
1940	26	19	29	11	7	10	102
1941	24	18	21	1	3	13	80
1942	10	16	22	1	2	20	71
1943	8	16	17	1	1	7	50
1944	5	21	27	2	7	7	69
1945	10	16	31	4	9	8	78
1946	10	30	46	2	9	16	113
1947	6	20	50	4	3	13	96
1948	7	25	43	2	3	15	95
1949	11	27	64	4	2	23	131
1950	15	27	54	6	4	21	127
1947	1	7	7	—	8	9	32
1948	3	11	23	—	7	15	59
1949	9	14	22	2	4	17	68
1950	8	8	23	2	3	11	55
1951	7	60	108	11	4	58	248
1952	8	17	41	3	2	23	94
1953	16	34	61	8	9	20	148
1954	8	33	49	5	4	39	138
1955	6	26	41	11	8	28	120
1956	11	62	67	14	5	39	198
1957	15	30	34	5	4	38	126

Year	Wood Coating, Staining, Dyeing, Preserving (288)	Total 249, 263, 269, 275, 279, 280, 287, 288 Lumber & Wood Products (289)	Wood Screws (290)	Nails, Spikes, & Tacks (291)
1837	3	30	–	–
1838	3	42	–	–
1839	–	23	–	–
1840	–	29	–	–
1841	–	26	–	1
1842	–	32	–	2
1843	–	31	–	–
1844	1	34	–	–
1845	–	27	–	–
1846	–	21	1	–
1847	–	30	–	–
1848	1	32	–	–
1849	–	71	–	1
1850	1	53	–	–
1851	–	50	–	–
1852	–	40	–	–
1853	–	56	1	–
1854	–	153	–	–
1855	1	170	–	1
1856	–	177	–	–
1857	–	215	1	2
1858	–	200	1	–
1859	–	206	3	4
1860	1	197	1	1
1861	–	118	–	–
1862	–	118	–	1
1863	–	154	1	1
1864	3	170	4	5
1865	13	218	3	3
1866	6	304	5	5
1867	12	353	8	13
1868	7	504	4	7
1869	10	447	2	10
1870	13	555	1	8
1871	14	480	3	7
1872	9	487	5	4
1873	4	472	10	8
1874	4	478	1	9
1875	6	528	4	28
1876	5	465	5	7
1874	6	498	1	16
1875	5	497	5	24
1876	7	425	4	6
1877	5	369	3	9
1878	2	364	2	5
1879	3	325	1	11
1880	4	395	1	17
1881	7	436	6	13
1882	4	521	4	19
1883	6	689	10	19
1884	1	570	6	19
1885	5	615	6	43
1886	4	625	6	20
1887	5	467	11	27
1888	4	532	4	30
1889	4	585	10	25
1890	2	571	10	26
1891	2	524	5	11
1892	3	491	5	17
1893	3	449	1	15
1894	3	431	–	8

Year	(288)	(289)	(290)	(291)
1895	1	458	1	13
1896	4	436	1	15
1897	2	485	1	13
1898	8	383	2	14
1899	8	458	1	19
1900	7	475	2	11
1901	13	623	2	8
1902	14	605	3	14
1903	9	589	1	12
1904	5	594	–	11
1905	12	616	3	18
1906	11	582	4	15
1907	24	639	1	23
1908	18	655	3	15
1909	16	657	3	22
1910	19	579	3	28
1911	15	560	4	31
1912	18	581	4	30
1913	13	582	6	37
1914	11	613	9	29
1915	14	549	3	36
1916	16	475	4	26
1917	10	502	7	14
1918	2	429	–	14
1919	9	559	2	14
1920	10	594	2	29
1921	9	713	4	21
1922	7	610	3	11
1923	7	579	2	12
1924	13	619	2	21
1925	25	617	5	15
1926	18	585	5	16
1927	10	614	1	17
1928	10	534	4	8
1929	7	521	5	9
1930	6	543	5	10
1931	13	517	8	11
1932	11	429	4	10
1933	11	367	6	10
1934	8	349	6	5
1935	8	375	11	14
1936	11	360	6	12
1937	9	352	11	7
1938	4	299	10	20
1939	11	289	7	9
1940	12	298	9	19
1941	4	256	9	11
1942	10	234	7	12
1943	8	214	13	10
1944	1	244	9	10
1945	7	261	7	18
1946	3	393	3	9
1947	5	353	2	4
1948	5	417	1	10
1949	1	377	2	9
1950	3	375	1	5
1947	3	93	2	7
1948	6	211	2	2
1949	4	283	3	9
1950	5	273	4	10
1951	5	797	7	18
1952	–	293	–	7
1953	6	543	2	4
1954	4	448	2	6
1955	6	399	–	6
1956	6	638	6	11
1957	5	468	4	1

Paper and Paper Products: Basic Processes

Year	Preparing Pulp (292)	Working Stuff (293)	Web Forming, Delivering & Drying (294)	Cutting & Punching (295)	Finishing Paper (296)	Total 292-296 (297)
1837	–	–	–	–	–	–
1838	2	1	–	–	–	3
1839	–	1	1	–	–	2
1840	1	2	–	–	–	3
1841	–	–	–	–	–	–
1842	–	–	–	–	–	–
1843	2	–	–	–	–	2
1844	–	–	–	–	–	–
1845	–	1	1	–	–	2
1846	1	–	–	–	–	1
1847	–	–	–	–	–	–
1848	–	1	–	1	–	2
1849	1	1	–	–	–	2
1850	–	–	1	–	–	1
1851	1	1	1	–	–	3
1852	–	–	1	1	–	2
1853	2	–	–	–	–	2
1854	5	–	3	–	1	9
1855	1	1	–	–	–	2
1856	1	4	1	1	–	7
1857	6	–	5	–	–	11
1858	10	1	3	–	–	14
1859	7	3	2	–	1	13
1860	7	1	–	2	–	10
1861	2	1	1	–	–	4
1862	2	2	2	–	–	6
1863	15	1	5	–	3	24
1864	21	2	4	1	–	28
1865	31	4	5	1	1	42
1866	33	4	5	2	3	47
1867	23	3	3	3	3	35
1868	6	3	6	2	3	20
1869	21	5	9	3	10	48
1870	23	7	7	4	1	42
1871	22	9	5	6	2	44
1872	16	4	5	6	8	39
1873	10	4	6	1	2	23
1874	7	12	7	4	2	32
1875	5	7	7	3	7	29
1876	6	6	3	6	2	23
1874	8	13	9	4	5	39
1875	4	8	5	3	3	23
1876	6	6	3	6	5	26
1877	11	7	8	3	4	33
1878	20	7	16	6	2	51
1879	15	16	9	6	4	50
1880	26	13	7	11	5	62
1881	18	19	14	9	2	62
1882	18	12	10	3	5	48
1883	29	18	18	6	5	76
1884	31	14	15	2	10	72
1885	33	9	13	5	9	69
1886	28	18	23	6	8	83
1887	6	11	14	3	9	43
1888	24	11	12	6	5	58
1889	24	16	15	8	3	66
1890	24	6	9	12	8	59
1891	13	11	18	10	5	57
1892	13	16	15	4	5	53
1893	10	14	10	8	5	47
1894	10	18	13	7	5	53

Year	(292)	(293)	(294)	(295)	(296)	(297)
1895	7	8	12	6	3	36
1896	5	9	13	5	3	35
1897	7	13	10	9	1	40
1898	4	17	9	7	6	43
1899	13	17	17	8	4	59
1900	18	15	28	4	7	72
1901	12	30	36	14	11	103
1902	20	32	29	11	11	103
1903	18	25	31	9	12	95
1904	19	18	27	9	4	77
1905	18	24	27	9	5	83
1906	23	23	27	7	9	89
1907	21	14	31	7	4	77
1908	14	16	20	9	3	62
1909	27	27	36	11	9	110
1910	20	25	34	10	6	95
1911	28	24	29	7	7	95
1912	34	29	26	11	7	107
1913	18	23	32	10	10	93
1914	23	24	19	9	4	79
1915	21	30	60	5	8	124
1916	23	21	22	6	13	85
1917	26	26	32	2	7	93
1918	26	39	22	7	8	102
1919	35	36	51	12	12	146
1920	41	42	45	10	29	167
1921	33	46	71	4	19	173
1922	37	46	83	8	6	180
1923	28	55	68	11	10	172
1924	65	44	77	12	17	215
1925	86	46	87	7	17	243
1926	83	53	110	7	20	273
1927	73	91	83	15	26	288
1928	83	122	128	5	24	362
1929	103	94	102	11	25	335
1930	82	79	100	6	28	295
1931	79	84	98	6	24	291
1932	71	74	72	11	17	245
1933	58	52	62	9	13	194
1934	73	56	68	10	20	227
1935	52	52	48	11	8	171
1936	36	47	61	9	15	168
1937	37	27	39	14	10	127
1938	18	19	41	7	14	99
1939	16	37	37	18	14	122
1940	26	21	37	4	14	102
1941	9	23	24	9	8	73
1942	15	13	20	12	15	75
1943	13	8	15	12	7	55
1944	17	20	22	13	6	78
1945	22	24	17	11	9	83
1946	28	25	24	15	8	100
1947	32	30	21	14	11	108
1948	24	25	22	14	12	97
1949	38	23	29	7	11	108
1950	23	25	50	11	6	115
1947	10	10	14	3	5	42
1948	7	8	14	7	4	40
1949	18	13	13	8	11	63
1950	29	16	17	10	7	79
1951	17	26	22	15	16	96
1952	38	35	25	14	1	113
1953	34	52	34	9	21	150
1954	38	43	52	9	4	146
1955	42	31	43	7	11	134
1956	46	45	49	23	11	174
1957	38	23	34	15	5	115

195

Paper and Paper Products: Special Processes and Products

Year	Laminating (298)	Envelope Making (299)	Envelopes (300)	Bag Making (301)	Bags (302)	Misc. Receptacles (303)
1837	–	–	–	–	–	–
1838	–	–	–	–	–	–
1839	–	–	–	–	–	–
1840	–	–	–	–	–	–
1841	–	–	–	–	–	–
1842	–	–	–	–	–	–
1843	–	–	–	–	–	–
1844	–	–	–	–	–	–
1845	–	–	–	–	–	–
1846	–	–	–	–	–	–
1847	–	–	–	–	–	–
1848	–	–	–	–	–	–
1849	–	1	–	–	–	–
1850	–	–	–	–	–	–
1851	–	–	–	–	–	–
1852	–	–	–	1	–	–
1853	1	2	–	–	–	–
1854	–	–	–	–	–	–
1855	–	2	1	2	–	1
1856	–	2	3	–	–	–
1857	–	1	1	1	–	–
1858	–	1	2	3	–	–
1859	–	2	3	2	–	–
1860	1	–	2	3	–	1
1861	–	–	2	–	–	1
1862	–	1	5	–	–	1
1863	–	3	1	4	–	–
1864	–	2	8	2	–	1
1865	–	–	2	4	4	1
1866	1	4	2	–	–	2
1867	1	8	10	4	3	2
1868	–	3	11	4	–	2
1869	1	1	5	5	2	2
1870	1	1	5	6	–	6
1871	1	3	10	8	1	5
1872	–	1	7	8	2	3
1873	–	1	6	12	3	6
1874	2	1	3	11	5	3
1875	–	1	3	14	7	3
1876	1	4	15	8	9	2
1874	2	1	4	11	5	6
1875	2	1	9	12	9	2
1876	–	3	8	9	6	4
1877	–	1	14	11	6	12
1878	1	3	16	9	11	16
1879	3	4	6	31	6	8
1880	2	2	4	20	8	13
1881	4	5	6	27	6	9
1882	3	4	11	8	12	9
1883	4	7	7	10	10	12
1884	1	5	11	10	8	4
1885	4	9	9	14	8	9
1886	5	13	10	8	12	3
1887	2	7	7	8	7	9
1888	–	15	13	15	8	3
1889	–	8	16	29	10	4
1890	3	24	20	24	14	5
1891	3	8	18	12	6	9
1892	3	10	21	16	6	13
1893	4	8	16	8	1	11
1894	1	9	25	7	2	10

Year	(298)	(299)	(300)	(301)	(302)	(303)
1895	2	5	21	6	8	2
1896	1	4	43	14	8	5
1897	1	2	32	14	8	11
1898	3	7	16	9	4	8
1899	7	5	28	17	11	13
1900	4	5	35	27	8	16
1901	1	5	39	18	8	6
1902	8	10	39	17	5	12
1903	7	8	44	13	3	8
1904	4	5	37	15	7	10
1905	5	8	23	14	4	5
1906	2	13	46	9	13	13
1907	8	6	58	18	6	12
1908	9	6	38	13	7	14
1909	4	13	51	14	13	19
1910	15	4	37	4	8	9
1911	10	12	37	5	11	19
1912	14	13	41	10	13	23
1913	7	15	52	7	7	17
1914	15	7	70	9	20	21
1915	18	20	70	2	12	17
1916	19	15	54	8	16	16
1917	13	17	47	5	12	12
1918	11	6	47	6	7	18
1919	13	13	49	2	13	18
1920	7	14	33	5	11	20
1921	17	15	56	7	11	22
1922	3	12	41	9	17	18
1923	13	12	23	6	5	14
1924	7	13	32	7	10	14
1925	8	13	21	11	15	26
1926	10	13	25	10	13	20
1927	12	17	27	13	25	20
1928	7	11	29	17	23	12
1929	12	9	14	18	12	17
1930	26	9	16	22	29	23
1931	26	22	32	18	45	24
1932	26	14	33	32	28	29
1933	23	11	28	18	29	39
1934	21	9	23	31	28	30
1935	28	8	26	25	41	28
1936	18	11	23	20	31	22
1937	21	8	22	25	29	34
1938	15	7	21	23	34	19
1939	16	6	23	27	26	18
1940	14	7	13	27	27	15
1941	5	7	19	9	15	14
1942	4	3	17	13	15	15
1943	8	—	13	13	22	14
1944	12	1	7	6	22	4
1945	17	—	13	8	14	7
1946	15	2	8	12	22	10
1947	15	1	10	9	13	17
1948	15	4	5	10	23	7
1949	18	3	9	6	21	9
1950	21	8	8	11	18	10
1947	8	—	4	2	11	4
1948	5	—	5	7	6	4
1949	12	2	9	9	15	8
1950	25	—	6	8	15	12
1951	19	3	10	8	23	13
1952	16	2	10	8	23	10
1953	21	4	4	14	25	10
1954	22	5	9	11	16	11
1955	18	5	12	8	12	5
1956	25	5	13	25	26	36
1957	22	5	11	15	23	21

197

Paper and Paper Products: Special Processes and Products

Year	Misc. Packages (304)	Box Making (305)	Boxes, exc. Folded Blank (306)	Boxes, Folded Blank (307)	Tube Making (308)	Tubes, Conduits, Bobbins, & Spools (309)
1837	–	–	–	–	–	–
1838	–	–	–	–	–	–
1839	–	–	–	–	–	–
1840	–	–	–	–	–	–
1841	–	–	–	–	–	–
1842	–	–	–	–	–	–
1843	1	–	–	–	–	–
1844	–	–	–	–	–	–
1845	–	–	–	–	–	–
1846	–	–	–	–	–	–
1847	–	–	–	–	–	–
1848	–	–	–	–	–	–
1849	–	–	–	–	–	1
1850	–	–	–	–	–	–
1851	1	–	–	–	–	–
1852	–	–	–	–	–	–
1853	–	–	–	–	–	–
1854	–	1	–	–	–	–
1855	–	2	–	–	–	–
1856	1	–	–	2	–	–
1857	–	–	–	–	–	–
1858	–	1	–	–	–	–
1859	4	1	–	–	2	–
1860	1	–	–	–	–	–
1861	–	1	–	1	–	–
1862	3	1	–	–	–	–
1863	2	–	–	2	2	–
1864	–	1	–	1	–	2
1865	4	1	1	6	1	1
1866	4	1	4	3	–	–
1867	6	4	4	5	2	2
1868	9	2	6	5	–	6
1869	7	2	6	5	2	4
1870	8	7	10	6	2	3
1871	12	3	7	9	1	3
1872	12	5	8	15	–	6
1873	7	2	2	6	3	5
1874	5	3	8	14	8	8
1875	18	4	7	14	8	10
1876	22	1	9	20	2	8
1874	9	5	7	13	9	10
1875	19	3	10	20	6	11
1876	20	1	11	18	1	8
1877	28	1	10	14	2	5
1878	20	4	8	26	2	4
1879	21	4	5	14	2	2
1880	18	3	6	12	1	3
1881	18	7	9	15	3	2
1882	20	8	5	29	2	2
1883	28	19	13	30	1	8
1884	24	10	9	33	1	7
1885	23	12	19	27	5	4
1886	18	22	13	28	10	4
1887	26	14	16	33	8	6
1888	26	22	14	32	4	4
1889	31	23	17	36	6	6
1890	19	18	12	17	12	6
1891	24	11	11	18	9	4
1892	20	28	12	36	8	4
1893	20	23	12	18	7	1
1894	24	23	15	22	8	1

Year	(304)	(305)	(306)	(307)	(308)	(309)
1895	26	26	16	26	10	5
1896	26	34	16	28	5	5
1897	23	22	15	26	3	11
1898	19	21	16	30	8	6
1899	27	31	16	55	11	6
1900	28	26	22	52	10	8
1901	26	29	28	62	4	11
1902	43	48	26	47	14	8
1903	23	35	13	46	9	10
1904	31	31	26	44	15	15
1905	43	38	29	46	6	11
1906	41	33	15	38	13	6
1907	47	34	23	36	7	8
1908	50	47	31	61	18	20
1909	58	44	38	70	14	16
1910	48	42	21	53	24	12
1911	55	58	37	59	14	20
1912	49	61	46	69	14	22
1913	57	57	52	70	15	30
1914	58	62	78	90	11	20
1915	82	57	67	73	10	28
1916	65	43	34	55	9	21
1917	67	40	37	49	17	6
1918	38	40	40	46	13	11
1919	103	38	39	37	9	13
1920	91	72	48	40	5	18
1921	140	58	55	72	16	24
1922	127	55	49	53	5	22
1923	115	64	44	42	8	11
1924	111	68	62	43	19	8
1925	107	50	64	47	17	13
1926	130	58	47	49	7	11
1927	133	63	64	61	6	19
1928	133	49	71	58	7	17
1929	115	67	79	62	15	14
1930	147	72	60	79	13	28
1931	181	60	74	75	10	27
1932	173	54	106	102	8	37
1933	156	56	106	89	10	32
1934	149	50	94	93	14	26
1935	123	57	98	93	14	33
1936	134	70	117	103	9	40
1937	128	61	80	99	14	24
1938	126	76	84	91	8	34
1939	125	44	75	76	10	18
1940	128	73	86	72	12	19
1941	112	44	56	75	10	19
1942	72	45	68	85	6	21
1943	54	32	49	74	4	22
1944	86	40	53	61	7	17
1945	76	36	39	74	8	15
1946	109	44	39	84	8	11
1947	104	43	56	88	5	11
1948	98	49	54	86	4	7
1949	137	54	73	100	3	5
1950	124	43	55	83	7	6
1947	49	31	24	33	3	11
1948	35	29	30	57	4	7
1949	101	27	38	68	2	13
1950	133	32	45	78	7	8
1951	132	59	70	94	9	13
1952	123	69	55	85	9	10
1953	142	58	49	96	6	3
1954	94	30	57	86	10	9
1955	101	42	48	84	9	10
1956	149	57	110	108	5	12
1957	196	52	81	93	2	7

199

Paper and Paper Products: Special Processes and Products

Year	Pulp Molding (310)	Misc. (311)	Total 297–299, 301, 305, 308, 310 Processes (312)	Total 300, 302–304, 306, 307, 309 Products (313)	Total 311–313 Paper (314)
1837	–	–	–	–	–
1838	–	–	3	–	3
1839	–	–	2	–	2
1840	–	–	3	–	3
1841	–	–	–	–	–
1842	–	–	–	–	–
1843	–	–	2	1	3
1844	–	–	–	–	–
1845	–	–	2	–	2
1846	–	–	1	–	1
1847	–	–	–	–	–
1848	–	–	2	–	2
1849	–	–	3	1	4
1850	–	–	1	–	1
1851	–	–	3	1	4
1852	–	1	3	–	4
1853	–	–	5	–	5
1854	–	–	10	–	10
1855	–	–	8	2	10
1856	–	1	9	6	16
1857	1	1	14	1	16
1858	3	2	22	2	26
1859	–	4	21	7	32
1860	–	2	13	4	19
1861	–	1	5	4	10
1862	1	–	9	9	18
1863	–	8	33	5	46
1864	1	4	34	12	50
1865	–	3	48	19	70
1866	–	7	53	15	75
1867	1	3	55	32	90
1868	1	8	30	39	77
1869	–	13	59	31	103
1870	1	6	60	38	104
1871	2	4	62	47	113
1872	2	5	55	53	113
1873	–	3	41	35	79
1874	2	9	59	41	114
1875	3	6	59	62	127
1876	–	7	39	85	131
1874	2	8	69	54	131
1875	2	4	49	80	133
1876	–	8	40	75	123
1877	1	7	49	89	145
1878	3	4	73	101	178
1879	1	5	95	62	162
1880	2	9	92	64	165
1881	11	6	119	65	190
1882	7	7	80	88	175
1883	7	6	124	108	238
1884	10	7	109	96	212
1885	16	7	129	99	235
1886	14	12	155	88	255
1887	20	5	102	104	211
1888	10	9	124	100	233
1889	23	10	155	120	285
1890	20	8	160	93	261
1891	9	10	109	90	209
1892	12	4	130	112	246
1893	18	6	115	79	200
1894	14	9	115	99	223

Year	(310)	(311)	(312)	(313)	(314)
1895	14	6	99	104	209
1896	17	9	110	131	250
1897	13	8	95	126	229
1898	17	6	108	99	213
1899	18	15	148	156	319
1900	19	11	163	169	343
1901	21	22	181	180	383
1902	26	22	226	180	428
1903	17	32	184	147	363
1904	15	25	162	170	357
1905	16	22	170	161	353
1906	15	23	174	172	369
1907	13	28	163	190	381
1908	9	27	164	221	412
1909	12	23	211	265	499
1910	8	28	192	188	408
1911	17	23	211	238	472
1912	11	27	230	263	520
1913	5	29	199	285	513
1914	11	30	194	357	581
1915	19	35	250	349	634
1916	5	22	184	261	467
1917	12	32	197	230	459
1918	9	31	187	207	425
1919	20	42	241	272	555
1920	16	36	286	261	583
1921	11	52	297	380	729
1922	7	49	271	327	647
1923	7	40	282	254	576
1924	14	31	343	280	654
1925	9	42	351	293	686
1926	9	54	380	295	729
1927	10	47	409	349	805
1928	8	48	461	343	852
1929	7	30	463	313	806
1930	9	38	446	382	866
1931	11	46	438	458	942
1932	7	37	386	508	931
1933	9	37	321	479	837
1934	9	28	361	443	832
1935	20	36	323	442	801
1936	37	53	333	470	856
1937	28	45	284	416	745
1938	41	39	269	409	717
1939	18	44	243	361	648
1940	31	57	266	360	683
1941	25	36	173	310	519
1942	20	35	166	293	494
1943	15	20	127	248	395
1944	20	27	164	250	441
1945	25	36	177	238	451
1946	22	49	203	283	535
1947	29	39	210	299	548
1948	20	50	199	280	529
1949	16	46	208	354	608
1950	11	42	216	304	562
1947	12	13	98	136	247
1948	16	26	101	144	271
1949	17	23	132	252	407
1950	37	47	188	286	521
1951	18	68	212	355	635
1952	11	36	228	316	580
1953	10	51	263	329	643
1954	10	48	234	282	564
1955	9	30	225	272	527
1956	6	60	297	454	811
1957	10	39	221	432	692

201

	Synthetic Fibers					Fertilizer	
Year	Carbon Chemistry: Cellulose & Derivatives (315)	Carbohydrate or Deriv. Containing Cellulose or Derivative (316)	Making & Treating Fibers & Filaments (317)	Stapilizing (318)	Total 315–318 (319)	Plant Growth Regulators (320)	Organic Fertilizers (321)
1837	–	–	–	–	–	–	–
1838	–	–	–	–	–	–	–
1839	–	–	–	–	–	–	–
1840	–	–	–	3	3	–	–
1841	–	–	–	–	–	–	–
1842	–	–	–	1	1	–	–
1843	–	–	–	–	–	–	–
1844	–	–	–	1	1	–	–
1845	–	–	–	–	–	–	–
1846	–	–	–	–	–	–	–
1847	–	–	–	1	1	–	–
1848	–	–	–	2	2	–	–
1849	–	–	–	2	2	–	1
1850	–	–	–	1	1	–	–
1851	–	–	–	–	–	–	–
1852	–	–	–	–	–	–	–
1853	–	–	–	2	2	–	–
1854	–	–	–	1	1	–	–
1855	–	1	–	1	2	–	1
1856	–	–	–	–	–	–	–
1857	–	1	–	–	1	–	2
1858	–	–	–	3	3	–	–
1859	–	–	–	2	2	–	5
1860	–	–	–	–	–	–	–
1861	–	1	–	3	4	–	2
1862	–	1	–	4	5	–	3
1863	–	–	–	1	1	–	2
1864	1	1	–	4	6	–	4
1865	3	–	–	3	6	–	8
1866	1	4	–	–	5	1	1
1867	–	2	–	3	5	1	9
1868	–	3	–	1	4	1	9
1869	–	6	–	1	7	1	8
1870	–	2	–	2	4	1	20
1871	–	2	–	3	5	–	9
1872	1	3	–	4	8	–	10
1873	2	2	–	3	7	1	6
1874	–	7	–	1	8	–	9
1875	–	1	–	1	2	–	3
1876	1	2	–	2	5	–	2
1874	–	7	–	1	8	–	8
1875	1	3	–	2	6	–	4
1876	–	2	–	2	4	–	2
1877	–	2	–	7	9	–	2
1878	1	4	–	8	13	–	6
1879	–	6	–	5	11	1	2
1880	1	7	–	5	13	–	5
1881	–	10	–	10	20	1	8
1882	1	14	–	13	28	–	10
1883	–	10	–	3	13	1	5
1884	–	6	1	10	17	–	6
1885	1	7	–	10	18	–	1
1886	3	7	–	12	22	–	3
1887	–	4	–	7	11	–	2
1888	2	10	–	9	21	–	8
1889	3	1	1	11	16	1	5
1890	2	10	1	4	17	1	11
1891	2	5	–	9	16	2	9
1892	–	5	–	7	12	–	5
1893	3	22	1	2	28	1	6
1894	1	2	1	3	7	2	6

Year	(315)	(316)	(317)	(318)	(319)	(320)	(321)
1895	–	18	1	2	21	3	1
1896	–	11	–	4	15	1	2
1897	2	8	3	4	17	2	3
1898	2	18	2	2	24	1	2
1899	3	16	3	8	30	4	2
1900	3	13	3	10	29	1	–
1901	6	12	3	7	28	3	1
1902	4	11	8	5	28	–	6
1903	2	9	5	9	25	–	2
1904	5	8	3	8	24	–	–
1905	4	10	20	18	52	1	2
1906	5	15	12	11	43	–	3
1907	5	11	7	14	37	1	4
1908	3	9	5	5	22	1	3
1909	2	25	3	6	36	–	1
1910	5	18	5	8	36	4	5
1911	13	35	7	5	60	1	6
1912	5	31	6	9	51	1	8
1913	7	18	7	5	37	1	6
1914	6	17	8	7	38	–	10
1915	9	9	4	4	26	5	7
1916	3	11	3	10	27	1	12
1917	1	15	7	10	33	1	6
1918	5	27	3	7	42	2	12
1919	15	36	15	4	70	1	9
1920	11	47	27	3	88	2	12
1921	22	78	19	6	125	2	6
1922	34	71	23	3	131	2	13
1923	18	52	27	11	108	3	8
1924	23	41	33	6	103	5	6
1925	42	55	55	5	157	4	7
1926	51	42	32	6	131	6	7
1927	67	38	55	12	172	–	9
1928	64	52	83	3	202	6	3
1929	100	70	95	8	273	8	7
1930	88	54	89	8	239	7	6
1931	46	83	104	10	243	6	8
1932	58	87	98	9	252	9	13
1933	56	69	87	11	223	5	15
1934	48	107	131	4	290	4	8
1935	57	49	98	7	211	7	6
1936	57	63	101	19	240	7	2
1937	89	50	119	16	274	23	8
1938	49	53	90	18	210	13	9
1939	45	50	97	18	210	12	4
1940	39	50	99	8	196	20	3
1941	29	51	76	10	166	11	1
1942	47	60	48	5	160	11	1
1943	28	29	56	11	124	15	1
1944	27	40	51	11	129	10	2
1945	29	38	36	4	107	12	1
1946	39	43	49	13	144	8	–
1947	30	32	38	13	113	19	1
1948	25	27	54	5	111	13	2
1949	36	39	38	6	119	27	3
1950	33	42	32	8	115	54	6
1947	22	25	25	4	76	6	2
1948	9	34	45	4	92	9	–
1949	38	40	53	5	136	4	–
1950	46	32	72	2	152	19	2
1951	35	41	64	13	153	32	3
1952	42	36	50	8	136	40	5
1953	25	31	14	14	84	70	4
1954	29	36	16	8	89	36	3
1955	9	31	21	5	66	54	1
1956	27	34	39	10	110	56	8
1957	37	37	34	7	115	31	6

203

	Fertilizer			Petroleum	Refining		
Year	Inorganic Fertilizers (322)	Misc. (323)	Total 320–323 (324)	Bubble Towers (325)	Fractionation, etc. (326)	Refining with Chemicals (327)	Distillation Vaporizing Apparatus (328)
1837	–	–	–	–	–	–	–
1838	–	–	–	–	–	–	–
1839	–	–	–	–	–	–	–
1840	–	–	–	–	–	–	–
1841	–	–	–	–	–	–	–
1842	–	–	–	–	–	–	–
1843	–	1	1	–	–	–	–
1844	–	–	–	–	–	–	–
1845	–	–	–	–	–	–	–
1846	–	–	–	–	–	–	–
1847	–	–	–	–	–	–	–
1848	–	–	–	–	–	–	–
1849	–	–	1	–	–	–	–
1850	–	2	2	–	–	–	–
1851	–	–	–	–	–	–	–
1852	–	–	–	–	–	–	–
1853	–	–	–	1	–	–	1
1854	–	–	–	–	–	1	–
1855	–	–	1	–	–	–	–
1856	–	1	1	–	–	–	–
1857	1	–	3	–	–	–	–
1858	1	–	1	2	–	–	–
1859	–	3	8	2	–	1	1
1860	–	3	3	–	–	–	4
1861	–	–	2	1	–	2	6
1862	–	1	4	–	–	–	4
1863	–	3	5	–	–	1	4
1864	–	3	7	3	–	5	4
1865	2	1	11	1	–	–	15
1866	–	1	3	2	2	9	17
1867	1	4	15	3	2	5	17
1868	3	3	16	4	2	1	5
1869	3	4	16	4	–	2	9
1870	5	5	31	2	–	4	9
1871	–	3	12	–	–	2	7
1872	1	13	24	3	1	3	3
1873	1	4	12	2	–	1	3
1874	1	2	12	3	–	1	9
1875	1	11	15	5	1	–	4
1876	4	6	12	3	1	1	4
1874	2	6	16	3	–	–	10
1875	2	9	15	6	1	–	3
1876	2	4	8	3	3	1	3
1877	3	3	8	3	–	–	3
1878	–	1	7	4	–	1	4
1879	–	8	11	–	–	–	6
1880	2	3	10	1	–	1	4
1881	2	4	12	6	–	1	4
1882	2	2	17	–	1	–	4
1883	4	3	13	2	–	3	10
1884	1	2	9	1	–	2	4
1885	2	3	6	5	–	3	3
1886	–	6	9	–	–	2	3
1887	2	2	6	9	–	4	1
1888	–	3	11	–	–	13	4
1889	7	4	17	6	–	6	–
1890	2	1	15	5	–	4	4
1891	1	–	12	6	–	6	4
1892	1	–	6	8	1	4	1
1893	–	1	8	4	1	4	2
1894	2	6	16	5	–	6	–

Year	(322)	(323)	(324)	(325)	(326)	(327)	(328)
1895	3	3	10	9	3	4	4
1896	1	5	9	9	1	4	–
1897	2	7	14	7	4	4	1
1898	–	2	5	3	–	1	1
1899	1	2	9	7	–	4	2
1900	–	3	4	8	1	2	–
1901	2	5	11	5	1	1	1
1902	4	1	11	7	–	7	10
1903	1	1	4	14	–	6	6
1904	2	3	5	5	–	5	1
1905	1	3	7	10	–	–	–
1906	2	1	6	13	1	3	–
1907	2	8	15	11	1	1	2
1908	9	4	17	5	2	1	2
1909	7	8	16	8	2	1	2
1910	13	6	28	15	–	4	3
1911	17	4	28	12	3	2	2
1912	16	4	29	6	–	3	6
1913	13	7	27	10	–	5	12
1914	9	6	25	7	1	3	7
1915	5	6	23	11	3	6	17
1916	9	3	25	7	–	2	36
1917	16	11	34	10	–	6	57
1918	14	1	29	10	3	9	22
1919	9	6	25	9	2	11	26
1920	11	6	31	12	8	12	52
1921	12	12	32	9	6	10	56
1922	5	6	26	14	7	15	48
1923	9	5	25	6	9	32	44
1924	5	–	16	16	4	25	38
1925	11	6	28	24	10	45	55
1926	17	4	34	21	6	53	51
1927	20	4	33	38	28	47	39
1928	22	4	35	24	17	46	47
1929	27	9	51	20	8	66	43
1930	30	2	45	22	18	74	46
1931	15	4	33	17	36	108	39
1932	15	4	41	22	65	68	20
1933	7	4	31	20	96	47	27
1934	13	6	31	13	84	37	22
1935	15	5	33	11	67	32	15
1936	8	2	19	20	47	55	12
1937	4	4	39	14	58	57	18
1938	6	4	32	13	47	47	23
1939	3	4	23	14	30	90	10
1940	2	5	30	12	23	75	14
1941	5	4	21	16	21	71	3
1942	5	4	21	15	13	37	7
1943	1	2	19	9	14	44	4
1944	3	–	15	12	12	30	3
1945	1	1	15	9	11	29	4
1946	8	3	19	12	15	37	2
1947	8	1	29	23	22	33	2
1948	6	2	23	20	21	44	3
1949	5	4	39	16	23	60	1
1950	6	5	71	11	26	57	3
1947	3	–	11	2	6	9	3
1948	3	1	13	8	11	25	4
1949	3	1	8	9	13	33	4
1950	12	2	35	20	21	39	–
1951	4	–	39	20	16	67	2
1952	8	4	57	16	21	53	1
1953	4	8	86	18	20	48	3
1954	5	7	51	15	29	36	5
1955	6	9	70	15	20	52	1
1956	21	13	98	18	30	144	2
1957	16	12	65	16	10	55	–

Year	Distillation with Cracking (329)	Paraffin Wax—Treatment or Recovery (330)	Distillation without Cracking (330a)	Other Distillation (331)	Misc. (332)	Total 325–332 (333)
1837	–	–	–	–	–	–
1838	–	–	–	–	–	–
1839	–	–	–	–	–	–
1840	–	–	–	–	–	–
1841	–	–	–	–	–	–
1842	–	–	–	–	–	–
1843	–	–	–	–	–	–
1844	–	–	–	–	–	–
1845	–	–	–	–	–	–
1846	–	–	–	–	–	–
1847	–	–	–	–	–	–
1848	–	–	–	–	–	–
1849	–	–	–	–	–	–
1850	–	–	–	–	–	–
1851	–	–	–	–	–	–
1852	–	1	–	–	–	1
1853	–	–	1	–	–	3
1854	–	–	–	–	1	2
1855	–	–	1	–	–	1
1856	–	–	2	–	–	2
1857	–	–	–	–	–	–
1858	1	–	–	–	–	3
1859	–	–	–	2	–	6
1860	1	–	2	3	–	10
1861	–	–	2	4	–	15
1862	–	–	3	2	–	9
1863	–	–	1	1	2	9
1864	–	–	3	1	3	19
1865	–	1	7	6	4	34
1866	–	–	11	7	2	50
1867	–	2	6	2	5	42
1868	–	–	1	1	2	16
1869	–	1	7	3	2	28
1870	–	1	2	1	5	24
1871	1	3	4	4	–	21
1872	–	4	3	2	2	21
1873	–	–	2	2	3	13
1874	–	–	1	1	1	16
1875	–	1	2	–	2	15
1876	–	2	3	1	5	20
1874	–	1	2	1	3	20
1875	–	1	2	–	3	16
1876	–	3	3	1	5	22
1877	–	–	1	1	–	8
1878	–	1	3	2	1	16
1879	–	1	6	4	1	18
1880	1	1	3	2	1	13
1881	–	3	2	–	–	16
1882	–	5	3	2	2	17
1883	–	1	6	2	7	31
1884	1	–	1	–	4	12
1885	1	–	3	3	1	19
1886	2	3	5	1	–	14
1887	–	2	2	–	3	21
1888	–	–	1	–	–	18
1889	–	–	2	3	–	18
1890	1	–	3	2	1	20
1891	–	–	1	1	1	21
1892	–	1	2	1	1	19
1893	1	–	6	–	1	18
1894	–	–	2	–	2	15

Year	(329)	(330)	(330a)	(331)	(332)	(333)
1895	–	1	1	–	1	24
1896	1	1	1	2	2	20
1897	–	–	–	–	3	19
1898	–	–	1	–	2	9
1899	–	–	4	–	1	18
1900	1	1	5	1	–	18
1901	–	–	4	1	–	14
1902	2	–	4	2	4	34
1903	4	–	5	1	3	35
1904	5	–	–	–	–	11
1905	1	–	1	–	2	14
1906	2	1	2	2	1	23
1907	7	–	–	–	–	17
1908	24	1	2	–	2	19
1909	25	3	5	2	2	30
1910	33	–	10	1	4	38
1911	57	3	4	1	4	33
1912	85	3	8	2	3	38
1913	42	1	12	3	7	74
1914	46	1	7	8	4	63
1915	111	1	9	6	5	91
1916	77	2	7	12	4	127
1917	99	2	12	8	4	184
1918	88	–	18	9	3	116
1919	72	3	22	11	16	146
1920	101	3	17	21	12	248
1921	114	9	14	17	21	219
1922	136	6	14	28	29	260
1923	130	8	23	30	14	254
1924	126	6	18	18	29	226
1925	–	5	21	20	27	308
1926	–	7	24	38	46	360
1927	–	15	23	28	37	391
1928	–	12	44	40	47	407
1929	–	12	32	25	36	368
1930	169	22	53	28	34	466
1931	134	44	24	13	24	439
1932	121	40	29	17	40	422
1933	98	41	22	18	30	399
1934	98	62	24	9	21	370
1935	90	51	26	11	18	321
1936	72	27	19	3	31	286
1937	85	22	21	6	26	307
1938	114	26	21	8	25	324
1939	205	13	8	3	26	399
1940	250	31	14	8	24	451
1941	207	17	9	8	35	387
1942	133	10	14	3	19	251
1943	129	7	4	2	16	229
1944	132	8	13	1	11	222
1945	67	8	10	2	14	154
1946	116	5	4	1	13	205
1947	139	25	2	–	20	266
1948	56	21	3	1	25	194
1949	84	19	9	1	19	232
1950	100	18	7	–	15	237
1947	94	5	7	1	3	130
1948	114	6	9	2	14	193
1949	117	8	9	1	20	214
1950	103	3	2	–	15	203
1951	79	24	6	–	23	237
1952	60	26	5	1	11	194
1953	82	29	8	1	24	233
1954	71	12	8	–	21	197
1955	70	15	5	1	20	199
1956	185	22	18	–	47	466
1957	79	12	10	4	28	214

Boot and Shoe Making — Products

Year	Boots & Shoes (334)	Sole-Attaching Means (335)	Soles (336)	Heels (337)	Uppers (338)	Misc. (339)	Total 334–339 (340)
1837	–	–	–	–	–	–	–
1838	–	–	–	–	–	–	–
1839	1	–	–	1	–	–	2
1840	–	–	–	–	1	–	1
1841	–	–	–	–	–	–	–
1842	–	–	–	1	–	1	2
1843	–	–	1	–	–	1	2
1844	–	–	1	–	–	–	1
1845	–	–	–	–	–	–	–
1846	–	–	–	–	–	–	–
1847	–	1	–	–	–	–	1
1848	–	–	–	–	–	–	–
1849	–	–	–	1	–	–	1
1850	–	–	–	–	–	–	–
1851	–	–	–	–	–	–	–
1852	–	–	–	1	1	–	2
1853	–	1	1	–	1	–	3
1854	–	1	–	–	–	–	1
1855	–	1	–	–	2	1	4
1856	–	2	–	–	–	3	5
1857	–	–	1	1	1	–	3
1858	–	1	–	2	1	3	7
1859	–	2	1	3	4	2	12
1860	–	5	2	6	2	4	19
1861	1	–	1	4	3	6	15
1862	1	3	3	2	1	9	19
1863	1	2	2	2	5	10	22
1864	–	6	3	1	4	2	16
1865	1	9	3	3	9	12	37
1866	1	4	4	6	15	7	37
1867	2	9	2	11	8	15	47
1868	2	10	6	11	13	23	65
1869	4	5	3	10	14	12	48
1870	5	5	4	9	12	13	48
1871	1	7	6	18	18	8	58
1872	8	8	3	13	29	21	82
1873	3	5	2	3	23	11	47
1874	7	12	3	6	14	21	63
1875	1	6	4	6	22	15	54
1876	3	9	1	6	22	21	62
1874	3	11	2	3	16	15	50
1875	2	6	4	6	21	19	58
1876	2	9	2	5	21	19	58
1877	2	3	2	4	32	22	65
1878	3	10	5	7	38	22	85
1879	1	4	1	10	33	24	73
1880	1	5	2	13	20	25	66
1881	6	16	3	9	24	39	97
1882	9	19	3	7	25	45	108
1883	9	17	10	4	24	42	106
1884	4	15	7	10	32	49	117
1885	12	23	6	4	26	29	100
1886	13	5	6	15	29	50	118
1887	14	14	3	10	29	37	107
1888	3	11	3	6	25	22	70
1889	3	8	2	11	8	21	53
1890	2	6	2	3	19	30	62
1891	2	12	5	6	11	34	70
1892	3	6	1	11	9	23	53
1893	–	10	5	8	13	16	52
1894	6	10	9	5	6	20	56

Year	(334)	(335)	(336)	(337)	(338)	(339)	(340)
1895	1	11	5	10	10	16	53
1896	1	8	4	4	15	24	56
1897	2	10	3	14	13	24	66
1898	3	5	3	9	7	18	45
1899	2	12	3	17	7	24	65
1900	1	13	1	18	2	18	53
1901	–	7	2	15	3	17	44
1902	3	6	3	16	12	32	72
1903	4	5	3	11	10	33	66
1904	5	11	3	12	9	31	71
1905	4	9	3	22	9	39	86
1906	6	12	5	19	8	44	94
1907	7	8	4	22	11	68	120
1908	11	11	2	20	10	60	114
1909	6	10	3	24	9	42	94
1910	9	12	2	24	13	56	116
1911	11	22	4	22	9	81	149
1912	9	24	13	29	7	73	155
1913	7	22	12	30	13	74	158
1914	7	21	16	39	17	82	182
1915	20	36	17	27	17	90	207
1916	10	36	19	33	15	88	201
1917	11	33	18	49	17	87	215
1918	14	29	14	40	8	81	186
1919	12	29	10	83	8	74	216
1920	11	18	5	90	13	67	204
1921	19	18	3	60	10	71	181
1922	13	14	8	54	16	77	182
1923	19	25	12	40	15	67	178
1924	20	28	8	42	21	73	192
1925	11	25	9	38	11	71	165
1926	14	22	11	35	19	76	177
1927	27	30	16	32	13	107	225
1928	20	26	3	41	15	71	176
1929	16	28	7	43	13	99	206
1930	22	26	6	28	15	66	163
1931	24	32	5	26	18	69	174
1932	12	28	–	26	16	62	144
1933	17	38	6	25	12	53	151
1934	19	38	11	18	16	56	158
1935	28	35	4	24	20	82	193
1936	24	45	8	21	24	84	206
1937	21	24	2	34	15	51	147
1938	24	23	5	27	14	59	152
1939	35	19	9	27	11	59	160
1940	21	20	10	23	18	52	144
1941	20	28	11	15	14	46	134
1942	16	26	23	4	6	25	100
1943	24	38	21	12	3	27	125
1944	17	33	18	19	4	22	113
1945	26	25	10	11	4	44	120
1946	16	21	6	12	3	53	111
1947	18	17	5	10	8	45	103
1948	19	17	5	8	6	30	85
1949	20	9	5	8	1	26	69
1950	25	11	4	5	3	26	74
1947	11	26	7	13	6	33	96
1948	16	15	9	13	2	42	97
1949	14	20	9	8	4	41	96
1950	24	17	5	8	9	35	98
1951	24	15	8	12	4	30	93
1952	23	11	3	5	2	32	76
1953	21	7	3	5	3	30	69
1954	19	7	4	2	2	18	52
1955	14	10	1	6	2	34	67
1956	31	4	2	12	3	39	91
1957	11	4	–	11	2	31	59

209

Stone and Clay Products:
Blocks, Bricks, and Earthenware Manufacturing Apparatus

Year	Block Molding (341)	Block Presses (342)	Die Expressing (343)	Cutters (344)	Kilns Continuous (345)	Other (346)	Pipe Machines (347)	Pipe Molds (348)
1837	–	3	–	–	–	–	–	–
1838	–	8	–	–	–	–	–	–
1839	–	1	–	–	–	–	–	–
1840	1	3	–	–	–	1	–	–
1841	–	6	–	–	–	–	–	–
1842	–	3	–	–	–	–	–	–
1843	–	3	–	–	–	1	1	–
1844	–	5	1	–	–	–	–	–
1845	–	3	–	–	–	–	–	–
1846	–	4	–	–	–	–	–	–
1847	–	3	–	–	–	–	–	–
1848	–	7	–	–	–	2	–	–
1849	–	7	–	–	–	–	–	–
1850	–	7	–	–	–	1	–	–
1851	–	10	–	–	–	–	1	–
1852	–	5	–	–	1	2	–	–
1853	–	3	–	1	–	–	–	1
1854	–	13	–	–	1	1	1	1
1855	1	8	2	2	–	2	–	–
1856	–	22	1	1	–	–	1	–
1857	–	21	2	–	–	–	–	–
1858	–	14	3	1	–	2	1	1
1859	–	9	5	1	–	–	4	–
1860	–	8	4	1	–	–	3	–
1861	–	5	3	–	–	1	–	3
1862	–	6	1	–	–	–	1	2
1863	–	10	4	1	–	2	2	–
1864	–	7	4	2	–	1	5	2
1865	–	17	1	1	1	2	2	1
1866	1	50	8	1	2	3	–	2
1867	–	84	15	3	2	8	4	–
1868	1	81	9	8	6	7	2	2
1869	1	34	7	2	4	12	8	–
1870	2	32	6	7	5	10	5	1
1871	2	23	5	2	7	4	11	5
1872	2	27	3	1	5	10	7	5
1873	1	25	7	3	2	4	–	5
1874	1	19	8	1	2	14	5	6
1875	2	43	5	4	4	13	6	3
1876	1	27	6	2	3	18	3	1
1874	1	21	9	1	3	16	7	6
1875	2	43	2	5	3	14	6	3
1876	3	27	8	2	4	20	2	1
1877	2	22	5	1	2	14	2	1
1878	–	19	7	–	–	10	1	1
1879	3	10	6	2	2	9	2	–
1880	–	16	6	2	3	11	1	1
1881	1	12	3	5	2	9	2	4
1882	2	31	5	7	6	17	9	4
1883	–	33	23	5	5	21	7	2
1884	2	39	8	5	4	19	1	3
1885	5	34	5	3	1	20	5	–
1886	4	35	4	7	4	20	5	1
1887	3	17	7	5	2	17	11	6
1888	3	24	13	6	5	17	5	2
1889	2	32	9	6	6	21	5	3
1890	3	32	3	11	–	19	6	1
1891	7	34	15	9	12	14	6	–
1892	4	20	3	12	18	25	5	–
1893	2	21	9	9	19	16	4	8
1894	4	17	4	8	8	18	2	2

Year	(341)	(342)	(343)	(344)	(345)	(346)	(347)	(348)
1895	3	18	4	6	4	8	3	5
1896	2	12	6	8	4	3	1	–
1897	7	15	6	4	2	4	2	–
1898	8	10	10	7	5	7	4	–
1899	6	15	7	3	6	21	4	1
1900	3	11	14	13	7	5	2	4
1901	11	22	10	5	9	19	5	1
1902	14	35	11	10	5	9	13	4
1903	28	46	9	6	3	16	9	7
1904	76	66	5	10	2	16	4	12
1905	106	66	5	12	2	24	9	17
1906	84	47	9	6	4	17	18	19
1907	53	39	9	13	4	13	24	29
1908	41	44	9	12	–	15	20	27
1909	35	29	10	3	1	22	12	23
1910	26	24	7	5	1	6	20	23
1911	30	26	2	5	5	14	15	16
1912	20	18	3	12	2	15	13	8
1913	10	17	5	8	5	14	12	16
1914	8	26	3	5	4	9	13	8
1915	14	23	9	4	1	9	4	9
1916	28	20	3	2	4	20	9	14
1917	15	20	6	4	7	19	6	12
1918	10	23	6	3	6	17	5	4
1919	19	26	7	2	7	40	16	9
1920	29	28	10	2	5	49	17	18
1921	37	35	9	6	5	29	12	12
1922	38	47	9	4	3	23	12	13
1923	26	26	12	4	4	17	16	18
1924	36	32	16	5	1	26	14	11
1925	30	12	7	5	4	34	19	14
1926	36	35	7	3	3	34	21	5
1927	31	25	10	5	2	31	8	6
1928	16	22	8	7	–	35	25	11
1929	11	19	7	4	1	25	10	3
1930	15	14	3	1	1	27	14	2
1931	15	15	7	3	–	23	18	3
1932	12	7	8	2	2	9	12	5
1933	8	4	4	4	4	5	11	1
1934	2	7	3	4	–	8	5	3
1935	4	6	3	3	1	4	–	4
1936	13	10	4	2	2	12	12	4
1937	7	8	2	4	–	9	8	8
1938	13	7	2	7	–	3	16	1
1939	13	2	3	3	1	1	10	2
1940	8	6	4	3	–	6	14	7
1941	9	6	2	5	–	6	8	3
1942	9	3	7	2	–	1	6	1
1943	9	7	4	3	–	1	6	5
1944	2	4	2	5	–	–	3	5
1945	20	7	–	2	–	1	5	3
1946	28	10	2	3	–	5	9	4
1947	22	11	6	1	–	5	10	4
1948	27	7	2	3	–	10	10	5
1949	15	7	6	2	–	5	9	5
1950	12	3	3	4	–	5	12	5
1947	5	–	–	1	–	1	–	1
1948	11	5	–	1	–	1	1	2
1949	20	9	2	5	–	1	10	3
1950	30	8	5	2	–	11	12	5
1951	16	11	2	2	–	12	12	6
1952	21	10	7	3	–	5	11	7
1953	13	1	3	4	–	2	6	3
1954	8	5	1	3	–	2	6	13
1955	4	7	1	2	–	2	12	3
1956	7	5	3	1	–	5	14	8
1957	9	5	2	2	–	–	8	2

211

Stone and Clay Products: Blocks, Bricks, etc. Stone and Clay Products: Miscellaneous Materials and Products

Year	Pottery Machines, Dies, & Molds (349)	Misc. (350)	Total 341–350 (351)	Glass Ceramic Composition (352)	Ceramic Composition (353)	Refractory Clay Products (354)	Clay, Concrete, or Masonry Conduits (355)
1837	–	1	4	–	–	1	–
1838	–	–	8	–	–	–	–
1839	–	–	1	–	–	–	1
1840	–	–	5	–	–	–	–
1841	–	–	6	–	–	–	–
1842	1	–	4	–	–	–	–
1843	–	–	5	–	–	–	–
1844	–	1	7	1	1	–	–
1845	–	1	4	–	–	–	–
1846	–	–	4	–	1	–	–
1847	1	–	4	–	–	–	–
1848	–	1	10	1	–	–	–
1849	–	1	8	–	–	–	–
1850	–	1	9	1	–	–	–
1851	–	2	13	–	–	1	–
1852	2	1	11	1	–	–	–
1853	1	–	6	–	1	–	–
1854	–	2	19	–	–	–	–
1855	–	–	15	–	–	–	–
1856	1	–	26	1	–	–	–
1857	1	–	24	–	–	–	–
1858	–	1	23	–	–	1	–
1859	–	4	23	1	1	1	–
1860	1	3	20	2	–	–	1
1861	2	–	14	–	–	–	1
1862	–	1	11	–	–	–	–
1863	3	2	24	–	–	–	1
1864	1	1	23	–	–	–	2
1865	3	6	34	2	1	1	–
1866	3	9	79	4	–	–	–
1867	1	9	126	6	2	6	–
1868	3	6	125	1	4	–	1
1869	4	6	78	2	2	1	1
1870	3	7	78	2	3	1	1
1871	1	11	71	4	1	–	1
1872	3	8	71	1	3	3	1
1873	2	4	53	–	1	2	2
1874	4	11	71	2	1	9	–
1875	2	5	87	–	3	2	1
1876	3	4	68	–	2	4	1
1874	4	8	76	1	2	7	2
1875	2	4	84	–	3	2	–
1876	2	8	77	–	2	4	1
1877	9	4	62	–	1	2	–
1878	3	10	51	3	4	6	–
1879	3	5	42	–	3	5	2
1880	4	3	47	–	–	3	1
1881	11	9	58	–	3	3	5
1882	6	18	105	2	3	14	5
1883	2	7	105	2	5	2	2
1884	4	12	97	2	5	5	1
1885	9	11	93	2	5	4	1
1886	3	6	89	3	5	4	7
1887	5	7	80	–	12	5	3
1888	5	11	91	1	10	4	1
1889	5	13	102	3	1	5	11
1890	5	16	96	3	6	4	4
1891	4	11	112	2	6	4	6
1892	2	12	101	2	4	4	1
1893	3	13	104	3	–	3	2
1894	6	7	76	5	1	1	1

Year	(349)	(350)	(351)	(352)	(353)	(354)	(355)
1895	2	11	64	6	3	1	2
1896	4	3	43	2	–	2	2
1897	3	7	50	3	5	3	3
1898	4	6	61	3	1	1	1
1899	7	8	78	1	1	1	1
1900	3	18	80	–	4	4	2
1901	3	22	107	2	–	6	7
1902	4	31	136	1	4	7	3
1903	4	47	175	1	6	3	5
1904	6	58	255	1	6	5	3
1905	2	95	338	1	7	13	10
1906	4	93	301	2	5	7	10
1907	7	50	241	1	2	2	11
1908	1	61	230	1	2	8	6
1909	8	57	200	8	1	9	8
1910	8	71	191	1	3	7	10
1911	7	55	175	1	6	9	5
1912	3	62	156	6	8	6	9
1913	3	55	145	8	4	15	8
1914	6	37	119	10	6	8	15
1915	1	58	132	6	2	14	14
1916	7	56	163	11	8	6	11
1917	5	40	134	7	11	11	13
1918	4	42	120	8	13	11	6
1919	10	62	198	4	13	18	6
1920	16	67	241	12	8	14	6
1921	5	54	204	7	11	15	7
1922	11	62	222	9	7	20	9
1923	9	66	198	9	8	26	2
1924	10	79	230	3	11	30	1
1925	8	100	233	13	9	26	11
1926	18	79	241	11	4	43	8
1927	19	70	207	14	11	20	9
1928	15	71	210	9	7	39	11
1929	17	71	168	5	13	31	3
1930	5	67	149	16	11	47	6
1931	11	58	153	15	5	33	11
1932	5	59	121	15	14	36	3
1933	3	45	89	9	13	34	1
1934	6	26	64	15	11	10	3
1935	11	36	72	20	12	19	4
1936	5	44	108	23	14	22	3
1937	7	42	95	16	20	22	2
1938	9	37	95	18	19	16	2
1939	7	47	89	27	13	17	1
1940	8	58	114	18	13	16	5
1941	8	50	97	25	16	20	2
1942	7	34	70	12	3	13	2
1943	10	33	78	18	22	14	2
1944	11	28	60	28	5	15	1
1945	9	33	80	20	8	20	–
1946	4	56	121	42	6	16	2
1947	6	53	118	21	17	19	1
1948	12	45	121	20	11	16	1
1949	11	75	135	11	6	28	5
1950	6	59	109	26	10	26	1
1947	2	9	19	21	8	10	–
1948	5	18	44	20	6	9	–
1949	17	49	116	39	9	25	1
1950	4	69	146	26	14	31	2
1951	14	64	139	30	15	21	2
1952	15	70	149	13	17	16	1
1953	9	64	105	11	11	27	4
1954	4	35	77	24	13	15	–
1955	3	40	74	11	4	15	3
1956	8	43	94	15	13	12	1
1957	4	43	75	10	19	18	–

213

Stone and Clay Products: Miscellaneous Materials and Products

Year	Concrete Products (356)	Gypsum Related Products (357)	Mineral Wood Related Products (358)	Blackboards, etc. (359)	Misc. Packing & Insulating Material (360)	Rod or Shaft Packing (361)	Fixed Flange Type Packing (362)
1837	–	1	–	–	–	–	–
1838	–	–	–	–	–	–	–
1839	–	1	–	–	–	–	–
1840	–	–	–	–	–	–	–
1841	–	–	–	–	–	–	–
1842	–	–	–	–	–	–	–
1843	–	–	–	–	–	–	–
1844	–	2	–	–	–	–	–
1845	–	1	–	–	–	–	–
1846	1	1	–	–	–	–	–
1847	–	–	–	–	–	–	–
1848	–	–	–	–	–	–	–
1849	–	1	1	–	–	–	–
1850	–	–	–	–	–	–	–
1851	–	–	–	–	–	–	–
1852	1	–	1	–	1	–	–
1853	–	–	–	–	1	–	–
1854	1	1	1	1	–	–	–
1855	1	1	–	–	–	1	–
1856	–	–	1	1	–	–	–
1857	1	1	–	1	–	2	–
1858	1	1	2	1	–	–	–
1859	1	1	–	1	–	1	2
1860	3	3	–	1	1	–	–
1861	2	1	–	1	–	1	–
1862	1	–	–	–	1	3	–
1863	–	1	–	1	3	–	–
1864	–	1	1	–	–	1	–
1865	1	–	–	1	1	4	–
1866	2	1	2	5	3	4	2
1867	3	1	1	5	3	5	1
1868	6	2	1	9	2	4	1
1869	11	3	3	9	4	2	2
1870	5	5	4	9	5	3	1
1871	5	4	1	6	4	6	2
1872	8	2	–	5	4	7	2
1873	7	5	–	7	2	4	–
1874	1	3	–	5	3	4	–
1875	7	6	1	10	8	4	–
1876	14	5	2	17	3	5	–
1874	4	2	1	7	5	5	–
1875	6	8	–	10	5	2	–
1876	12	5	2	25	3	7	–
1877	2	1	1	11	8	1	4
1878	7	2	–	11	12	8	–
1879	9	5	2	13	4	6	1
1880	9	1	–	6	15	6	2
1881	10	2	3	7	8	3	–
1882	10	5	3	12	6	7	1
1883	9	9	5	19	17	6	2
1884	12	7	1	6	14	5	1
1885	12	8	1	12	12	5	3
1886	17	8	3	9	12	3	–
1887	7	7	–	8	8	4	2
1888	8	10	3	6	11	8	1
1889	12	9	2	13	10	4	2
1890	15	10	6	9	8	1	3
1891	15	19	2	10	9	9	–
1892	12	10	–	7	9	5	4
1893	21	12	1	5	9	5	4
1894	20	4	1	5	6	6	1

Year	(356)	(357)	(358)	(359)	(360)	(361)	(362)
1895	18	9	–	4	9	3	1
1896	31	5	1	8	2	2	1
1897	24	4	2	4	2	8	4
1898	28	5	1	4	6	3	1
1899	28	6	1	6	10	7	2
1900	37	3	1	4	14	12	4
1901	44	7	9	4	9	9	2
1902	77	8	5	2	11	16	5
1903	86	11	5	4	4	15	4
1904	79	7	5	2	9	12	7
1905	92	2	4	3	10	12	7
1906	98	3	2	2	9	14	9
1907	104	7	2	5	11	12	6
1908	122	8	2	3	11	9	11
1909	105	9	5	–	9	11	8
1910	70	3	5	3	8	9	8
1911	112	4	6	6	6	12	4
1912	82	4	7	1	8	3	3
1913	81	4	3	3	21	12	5
1914	81	8	4	3	16	14	4
1915	78	11	3	4	14	9	7
1916	82	14	4	2	23	7	7
1917	68	15	13	6	12	12	–
1918	80	14	5	2	10	10	3
1919	91	25	13	3	27	8	7
1920	91	20	10	4	17	15	2
1921	81	16	6	1	19	10	8
1922	82	23	6	4	16	20	7
1923	69	17	4	3	12	18	6
1924	77	33	9	2	21	18	1
1925	95	21	7	4	23	17	23
1926	96	33	6	3	25	13	18
1927	94	25	9	1	41	15	11
1928	79	31	8	2	36	15	13
1929	82	27	13	5	32	16	21
1930	61	32	9	3	55	30	25
1931	72	15	13	4	65	19	19
1932	64	28	13	4	50	32	20
1933	39	22	13	2	33	27	7
1934	49	23	9	–	25	14	16
1935	44	27	7	2	54	20	14
1936	44	18	19	1	38	26	11
1937	43	24	13	1	51	27	7
1938	46	16	21	3	36	21	7
1939	30	13	19	2	27	34	6
1940	28	21	9	1	30	21	6
1941	30	21	13	–	22	24	8
1942	24	10	11	2	26	20	8
1943	17	11	14	1	14	25	5
1944	29	16	22	2	14	10	8
1945	37	11	12	1	16	33	5
1946	27	26	26	3	13	26	7
1947	40	22	18	–	12	12	4
1948	42	18	20	1	19	16	–
1949	28	20	21	2	13	15	3
1950	30	28	23	4	9	14	7
1947	9	8	6	1	7	9	3
1948	21	13	16	1	12	15	11
1949	37	27	22	4	23	24	5
1950	42	27	14	1	18	13	–
1951	40	16	36	1	17	19	3
1952	31	23	25	1	19	19	1
1953	31	28	31	2	14	14	3
1954	19	25	25	2	8	17	5
1955	36	12	30	1	17	16	7
1956	26	24	34	2	19	20	11
1957	26	25	15	1	22	17	5

Stone and Clay Products: Miscellaneous Materials and Products

Stone and Clay Products: Stone Working

Year	Ground Minerals & Earths, etc. (363)	Nonclay Refractory Ceramics (364)	Misc. Materials & Products (365)	Total 352-365 (366)	Sawing (367)	Misc. Tools (368)	Stone Monuments, Markers, Guards (369)
1837	–	–	–	2	–	4	–
1838	–	–	–	–	–	4	–
1839	–	–	–	2	–	1	–
1840	–	–	–	–	1	1	–
1841	–	–	–	–	1	–	–
1842	–	–	–	–	–	1	–
1843	–	–	–	–	–	–	–
1844	–	–	–	4	–	2	–
1845	–	–	–	1	1	2	–
1846	–	–	–	3	–	–	–
1847	–	1	–	1	–	2	–
1848	–	–	–	1	–	1	–
1849	–	–	–	2	1	3	–
1850	–	–	–	1	1	2	–
1851	–	–	–	1	–	4	–
1852	–	–	–	4	1	6	–
1853	–	–	–	2	2	2	–
1854	–	–	2	6	4	10	–
1855	–	–	1	4	15	6	–
1856	–	–	–	3	32	5	–
1857	–	–	–	5	–	2	–
1858	–	3	1	10	2	6	–
1859	–	1	–	10	2	8	–
1860	–	–	1	12	1	14	1
1861	–	–	2	8	1	6	–
1862	–	1	2	8	–	11	1
1863	–	–	1	7	–	4	–
1864	–	3	–	8	–	5	–
1865	–	1	–	12	1	3	–
1866	–	–	–	23	2	9	–
1867	1	1	3	38	1	15	–
1868	–	1	1	33	3	16	1
1869	–	1	4	45	5	27	1
1870	1	3	2	45	12	13	–
1871	–	4	3	41	4	18	1
1872	1	2	7	46	6	28	2
1873	–	5	4	39	3	32	3
1874	–	9	12	49	8	22	2
1875	–	4	6	52	3	17	3
1876	–	5	4	62	7	28	2
1874	–	10	7	53	5	22	2
1875	–	3	7	46	2	22	4
1876	–	4	3	68	6	27	1
1877	–	4	6	41	6	20	2
1878	–	3	3	59	1	22	2
1879	–	3	2	55	2	26	4
1880	–	4	6	53	3	17	7
1881	–	7	13	64	5	18	2
1882	1	22	4	95	5	22	2
1883	1	5	3	87	6	20	–
1884	1	3	7	70	6	25	1
1885	–	5	5	75	24	18	2
1886	–	2	7	80	15	15	1
1887	1	1	7	65	20	6	2
1888	–	2	1	66	6	11	2
1889	–	1	15	88	6	17	1
1890	1	2	7	79	5	11	–
1891	1	1	8	92	9	20	3
1892	–	3	10	71	2	19	1
1893	1	1	7	74	6	14	4
1894	1	1	9	62	2	13	1

Year	(363)	(364)	(365)	(366)	(367)	(368)	(369)
1895	4	3	10	73	9	17	–
1896	1	5	6	68	12	14	2
1897	4	1	6	73	5	7	4
1898	2	2	3	61	5	3	2
1899	1	4	7	76	10	9	2
1900	5	4	4	98	6	9	2
1901	4	3	7	113	2	17	2
1902	1	6	9	155	11	4	4
1903	3	9	8	164	7	8	2
1904	1	8	9	154	8	11	1
1905	4	5	10	180	14	23	4
1906	2	5	13	181	8	15	2
1907	6	4	4	177	6	20	5
1908	5	7	11	206	15	21	1
1909	–	9	12	194	8	16	2
1910	2	7	9	145	7	13	3
1911	3	6	3	183	6	12	–
1912	2	3	9	151	4	21	2
1913	8	3	6	181	5	11	2
1914	8	5	3	185	2	10	–
1915	3	11	9	185	5	21	1
1916	2	8	7	192	7	10	–
1917	6	18	10	202	5	19	2
1918	5	15	14	196	3	14	1
1919	4	11	7	237	3	26	2
1920	9	13	16	237	3	35	1
1921	11	10	13	215	8	26	–
1922	11	16	14	244	15	25	1
1923	8	6	7	195	12	24	2
1924	13	8	11	238	9	32	–
1925	11	10	18	288	6	15	2
1926	13	12	11	296	11	30	–
1927	9	11	13	283	25	24	2
1928	11	10	8	279	19	25	1
1929	7	4	7	266	9	30	–
1930	15	7	14	331	7	16	1
1931	14	13	14	312	5	17	1
1932	19	14	11	323	4	14	–
1933	4	14	19	237	4	7	–
1934	8	17	15	215	7	9	–
1935	10	21	9	263	4	21	1
1936	10	12	8	249	8	14	–
1937	11	23	8	268	1	18	–
1938	11	25	7	248	6	35	1
1939	12	29	4	234	5	20	–
1940	15	14	7	204	6	31	1
1941	12	14	4	211	2	38	–
1942	13	14	6	164	4	22	–
1943	18	13	6	181	5	31	–
1944	22	12	5	189	8	38	–
1945	11	10	4	188	10	35	1
1946	33	13	3	243	14	29	–
1947	28	10	4	208	10	23	–
1948	17	10	7	198	9	26	–
1949	19	17	4	192	11	18	–
1950	17	13	3	211	8	27	–
1947	10	14	4	110	5	18	–
1948	24	10	2	160	8	26	–
1949	51	11	6	284	16	38	–
1950	15	12	4	219	5	8	–
1951	20	20	7	247	10	19	–
1952	18	13	3	200	12	41	1
1953	14	14	6	210	3	37	–
1954	14	17	3	187	6	10	–
1955	8	5	3	168	12	21	–
1956	19	21	3	220	10	36	–
1957	10	17	7	192	15	33	–

Year	Tanks (370)	Outlet Siphons & Valves (371)	Urinals (372)	Ventilation (373)	Disinfection (374)	Misc. (375)	Total 370–375 (376)
1837	–	–	–	–	–	–	–
1838	–	–	–	–	–	–	–
1839	–	–	–	–	–	–	–
1840	–	–	–	–	–	–	–
1841	–	–	–	–	–	–	–
1842	–	–	–	–	–	–	–
1843	–	–	–	–	–	–	–
1844	–	–	–	–	–	–	–
1845	–	–	–	–	–	–	–
1846	–	–	–	–	–	–	–
1847	–	–	–	–	–	1	1
1848	–	–	–	–	–	–	–
1849	–	–	–	–	–	1	1
1850	–	–	–	–	–	–	–
1851	–	–	–	–	–	–	–
1852	–	–	–	–	–	1	1
1853	–	–	–	–	–	1	1
1854	1	–	–	–	–	1	2
1855	–	–	–	–	–	–	–
1856	–	–	–	–	–	1	1
1857	–	–	–	–	–	1	1
1858	–	–	–	1	–	4	5
1859	–	–	–	–	–	5	5
1860	1	–	–	–	–	1	2
1861	–	–	–	1	–	3	4
1862	–	–	–	–	–	2	2
1863	–	–	–	–	–	1	1
1864	–	–	1	–	–	1	2
1865	–	–	–	–	–	–	–
1866	–	–	1	–	–	3	4
1867	1	1	–	–	–	–	2
1868	–	–	2	1	–	10	13
1869	1	1	1	1	–	10	14
1870	1	–	4	–	–	6	11
1871	–	–	1	–	1	2	4
1872	–	–	2	1	1	6	10
1873	–	–	2	–	1	10	13
1874	2	–	1	2	2	6	13
1875	–	3	–	2	2	8	15
1876	1	–	2	6	2	16	27
1874	2	1	1	1	4	10	19
1875	–	2	1	4	2	9	18
1876	1	1	3	6	–	18	29
1877	1	1	1	3	1	23	30
1878	4	1	2	4	2	22	35
1879	1	1	1	11	1	15	30
1880	4	–	1	5	2	13	25
1881	5	6	2	6	6	30	55
1882	10	7	8	12	8	41	86
1883	4	6	2	6	7	35	60
1884	12	4	4	3	4	22	49
1885	10	13	1	7	8	26	65
1886	18	16	3	4	2	18	61
1887	11	22	2	4	–	25	64
1888	11	22	–	6	2	14	55
1889	12	26	13	1	2	27	81
1890	5	20	6	4	3	22	60
1891	6	17	6	3	2	20	54
1892	4	14	3	3	5	20	49
1893	7	13	3	1	3	23	50
1894	8	17	2	3	1	18	49

Year	(370)	(371)	(372)	(373)	(374)	(375)	(376)
1895	10	16	4	6	5	8	49
1896	7	13	3	2	1	12	38
1897	6	15	1	1	6	16	45
1898	10	9	4	1	8	8	40
1899	10	13	5	4	5	10	47
1900	17	14	6	5	2	14	58
1901	8	10	6	8	9	6	47
1902	9	8	2	11	5	14	49
1903	18	14	3	5	1	8	49
1904	18	10	4	3	1	15	51
1905	24	22	5	4	5	14	74
1906	22	17	2	4	2	10	57
1907	19	8	1	8	3	16	55
1908	38	20	9	9	8	19	103
1909	19	37	7	6	9	8	86
1910	16	32	3	9	6	16	82
1911	21	18	1	4	7	10	61
1912	20	19	1	3	12	10	65
1913	12	32	6	4	7	22	83
1914	16	25	3	3	13	10	70
1915	18	35	2	3	10	18	86
1916	11	31	8	8	8	14	80
1917	13	30	2	8	8	10	71
1918	10	21	5	2	5	5	48
1919	13	27	2	1	5	8	56
1920	2	17	3	4	6	10	42
1921	9	20	3	4	–	3	39
1922	12	38	2	11	5	7	75
1923	8	16	2	4	1	6	37
1924	8	15	1	8	2	9	43
1925	5	32	4	2	2	8	53
1926	4	27	6	6	4	8	55
1927	8	21	2	4	3	12	50
1928	8	12	4	6	5	7	42
1929	7	14	4	5	3	19	52
1930	5	17	1	3	6	14	46
1931	3	15	2	9	4	11	44
1932	4	12	3	6	1	17	43
1933	7	9	1	4	1	7	29
1934	5	18	5	9	4	15	56
1935	2	11	2	3	3	17	38
1936	9	14	1	8	5	15	52
1937	3	11	–	11	2	19	46
1938	8	14	3	12	4	14	55
1939	3	14	2	9	3	9	40
1940	4	8	2	3	5	2	24
1941	3	9	–	15	3	3	33
1942	4	8	2	1	1	3	19
1943	2	5	–	2	7	1	17
1944	1	7	2	4	6	5	25
1945	5	14	1	6	3	3	32
1946	3	12	4	6	3	6	34
1947	4	12	1	3	6	12	38
1948	6	18	2	2	4	8	40
1949	3	22	5	2	3	2	37
1950	7	22	6	3	6	4	48
1947	–	3	1	1	1	2	8
1948	5	6	1	5	4	8	29
1949	2	17	2	2	3	6	32
1950	8	24	2	6	3	9	52
1951	2	17	3	2	5	7	36
1952	6	23	5	3	9	5	51
1953	8	25	2	2	3	2	42
1954	–	22	4	3	5	4	38
1955	9	17	2	5	3	4	40
1956	9	44	4	4	4	4	69
1957	7	22	2	4	3	13	51

Stone and Clay Products: Bathtubs, Sinks, etc.

Year	Tubs (377)	Showers (378)	Basins & Sinks (379)	Bath & Basin Receptacle Fittings (380)	Strainers & Stoppers (381)	Misc. (382)	Total 377–382 (383)
1837	–	–	–	–	–	–	–
1838	–	–	–	–	–	–	–
1839	–	–	–	–	–	–	–
1840	–	1	–	1	–	–	2
1841	–	–	–	–	–	–	–
1842	–	–	–	–	–	1	1
1843	–	2	–	–	–	1	3
1844	–	–	–	–	–	–	–
1845	1	2	–	–	–	2	5
1846	–	1	–	–	–	–	1
1847	–	2	–	–	–	–	2
1848	–	1	–	–	–	–	1
1849	–	3	–	–	–	–	3
1850	–	–	–	–	–	–	–
1851	–	1	–	–	–	–	1
1852	–	1	–	–	–	–	1
1853	–	1	–	1	–	–	2
1854	–	1	1	–	–	–	2
1855	–	–	–	–	–	2	2
1856	–	–	–	–	–	–	–
1857	–	4	–	–	–	1	5
1858	1	1	1	–	–	–	3
1859	–	–	1	–	–	1	2
1860	1	–	2	–	–	–	3
1861	–	1	1	–	–	1	3
1862	–	1	1	–	–	2	4
1863	–	–	–	–	–	–	–
1864	–	1	2	–	–	–	3
1865	1	–	2	–	–	–	3
1866	1	–	6	–	–	1	8
1867	2	1	5	–	1	1	10
1868	3	1	2	1	–	–	7
1869	4	1	3	2	1	1	12
1870	1	1	4	–	–	4	10
1871	–	5	2	1	3	2	13
1872	4	1	4	2	1	1	13
1873	2	–	4	–	1	3	10
1874	1	–	1	2	2	7	13
1875	4	2	7	2	3	4	22
1876	2	1	6	7	3	4	23
1874	3	–	2	2	3	8	18
1875	1	2	5	3	2	5	18
1876	2	1	8	7	4	1	23
1877	2	6	7	3	3	8	29
1878	2	3	3	13	2	7	30
1879	1	6	1	5	7	–	20
1880	10	2	5	6	1	5	29
1881	6	5	7	7	7	1	33
1882	2	6	12	7	–	6	33
1883	4	3	5	12	4	2	30
1884	5	2	–	16	7	3	33
1885	4	6	3	19	7	3	42
1886	5	7	6	12	1	2	33
1887	5	3	2	12	2	1	25
1888	7	2	7	9	6	1	32
1889	5	9	8	19	5	1	47
1890	12	4	9	18	3	4	50
1891	6	4	15	11	1	4	41
1892	8	1	8	13	1	4	35
1893	8	2	13	10	7	6	46
1894	7	8	9	10	–	8	42

Year	(377)	(378)	(379)	(380)	(381)	(382)	(383)
1895	14	9	6	11	4	6	50
1896	11	3	3	5	4	11	37
1897	8	8	10	8	8	6	48
1898	7	2	2	7	1	7	26
1899	9	5	6	8	5	13	46
1900	10	4	5	6	4	12	41
1901	8	5	7	10	4	7	41
1902	8	6	6	5	7	5	37
1903	10	7	10	18	2	4	51
1904	10	10	11	7	4	1	43
1905	8	5	6	8	8	5	40
1906	11	7	11	15	5	6	55
1907	14	4	13	26	6	4	67
1908	8	11	13	19	11	5	67
1909	10	7	13	23	18	7	78
1910	11	9	6	14	8	5	53
1911	19	7	13	13	5	5	62
1912	13	8	4	7	2	6	40
1913	10	9	14	9	8	10	60
1914	11	14	10	15	5	7	62
1915	19	18	5	4	10	8	64
1916	3	10	6	9	7	7	42
1917	6	12	12	9	1	2	42
1918	11	3	8	9	6	2	39
1919	11	13	9	6	8	4	51
1920	9	8	10	2	3	7	39
1921	10	9	10	14	4	3	50
1922	10	9	13	12	7	10	61
1923	12	8	8	14	8	8	58
1924	9	8	7	15	2	8	49
1925	17	13	8	21	12	11	82
1926	15	11	12	14	11	7	70
1927	19	9	10	9	7	6	60
1928	21	9	14	13	11	4	72
1929	19	10	15	13	4	10	71
1930	14	16	9	11	4	8	62
1931	23	14	3	10	5	8	63
1932	11	5	14	8	8	7	53
1933	11	9	7	8	10	5	50
1934	26	14	13	6	8	7	74
1935	13	12	12	3	12	10	62
1936	29	7	10	8	5	7	66
1937	20	6	12	6	4	2	50
1938	21	12	11	6	13	3	66
1939	12	9	4	9	5	1	40
1940	16	5	15	5	7	3	51
1941	14	3	11	4	6	4	42
1942	5	8	4	1	3	1	22
1943	7	3	3	4	3	–	20
1944	11	5	8	4	3	2	33
1945	9	10	14	3	8	3	47
1946	29	13	12	2	7	3	66
1947	28	12	11	3	6	4	64
1948	24	10	7	3	5	1	50
1949	16	6	19	1	2	2	46
1950	13	3	8	3	5	3	35
1947	12	2	4	–	3	–	21
1948	5	9	8	1	5	–	28
1949	20	17	12	5	8	4	66
1950	37	10	21	2	4	3	77
1951	24	10	7	4	4	7	56
1952	21	8	15	1	5	3	53
1953	16	4	9	7	3	3	42
1954	8	4	9	2	5	1	29
1955	18	3	9	1	3	3	37
1956	17	12	13	4	4	2	52
1957	24	10	14	2	2	3	55

Stone and Clay Products: Mixed

Year	Spittoons (384)	Misc. Toilet Fixtures (385)	Total 376, 383–385 WCs, Bathtubs, Sinks, etc. (386)	Making Portland Cement (387)	Total 351, 367, 368, 387 Processes & Apparatus (388)	Total 366, 369, 386 Products (389)	Total 388, 389 Stone & Clay (390)
1837	–	–	–	1	9	2	11
1838	–	–	–	–	12	–	12
1839	–	–	–	–	2	2	4
1840	–	–	2	–	7	2	9
1841	–	–	–	–	7	–	7
1842	–	–	1	–	5	1	6
1843	–	–	3	–	5	3	8
1844	–	–	–	–	9	4	13
1845	–	–	5	–	7	6	13
1846	–	–	1	–	4	4	8
1847	–	–	3	–	6	4	10
1848	–	–	1	–	11	2	13
1849	–	–	4	–	12	6	18
1850	–	–	–	–	12	1	13
1851	–	–	1	–	17	2	19
1852	–	–	2	–	18	6	24
1853	–	–	3	–	10	5	15
1854	–	–	4	–	33	10	43
1855	–	–	2	–	36	6	42
1856	–	–	1	–	63	4	67
1857	–	–	6	1	27	11	38
1858	1	–	9	–	31	19	50
1859	–	–	7	–	33	17	50
1860	–	1	6	–	35	19	54
1861	–	–	7	–	21	15	36
1862	–	–	6	–	22	15	37
1863	–	2	3	–	28	10	38
1864	–	–	5	–	28	13	41
1865	2	2	7	–	38	19	57
1866	7	3	22	–	90	45	135
1867	5	1	18	–	142	56	198
1868	4	–	24	–	144	58	202
1869	5	2	33	–	110	79	189
1870	2	2	25	2	105	70	175
1871	4	5	26	1	94	68	162
1872	3	2	28	–	105	76	181
1873	6	–	29	2	90	71	161
1874	1	3	30	1	102	81	183
1875	3	5	45	1	108	100	208
1876	5	4	59	4	107	123	230
1874	–	4	41	2	105	96	201
1875	4	3	43	2	110	93	203
1876	5	7	64	3	113	133	246
1877	9	2	70	1	89	113	202
1878	8	2	75	6	80	136	216
1879	2	6	58	2	72	117	189
1880	4	2	60	3	70	120	190
1881	5	5	98	3	84	164	248
1882	17	2	138	4	136	235	371
1883	8	5	103	7	138	190	328
1884	12	6	100	9	137	171	308
1885	4	4	115	9	144	192	336
1886	6	5	105	4	123	186	309
1887	11	6	106	3	109	173	282
1888	5	4	96	4	112	164	276
1889	8	6	142	3	128	231	359
1890	5	8	123	5	117	202	319
1891	8	8	111	4	145	206	351
1892	5	12	101	1	123	173	296
1893	4	13	113	5	129	191	320
1894	5	20	116	1	92	179	271

Year	(384)	(385)	(386)	(387)	(388)	(389)	(390)
1895	5	20	124	1	91	197	288
1896	14	12	101	–	69	171	240
1897	23	8	124	2	64	201	265
1898	11	13	90	1	70	153	223
1899	9	14	116	2	99	194	293
1900	19	11	129	7	102	229	331
1901	17	7	112	7	133	227	360
1902	16	16	118	4	155	277	432
1903	26	16	142	7	197	308	505
1904	22	20	136	3	277	291	568
1905	19	18	151	7	382	335	717
1906	24	20	156	6	330	339	669
1907	12	23	157	9	276	339	615
1908	22	31	223	8	274	430	704
1909	28	36	228	6	230	424	654
1910	39	29	203	–	211	351	562
1911	30	25	178	5	198	361	559
1912	27	31	163	5	186	316	502
1913	25	40	208	3	164	391	555
1914	27	35	194	6	137	379	516
1915	15	40	205	2	160	391	551
1916	25	25	172	1	181	364	545
1917	11	31	155	1	159	359	518
1918	8	18	113	–	137	310	447
1919	11	35	153	2	229	392	621
1920	8	18	107	3	282	345	627
1921	11	27	127	2	240	342	582
1922	6	18	160	5	267	405	672
1923	10	27	132	3	237	329	566
1924	7	24	123	10	281	361	642
1925	6	29	170	10	264	460	724
1926	9	27	161	8	290	457	747
1927	3	38	151	13	269	436	705
1928	8	36	158	9	263	438	701
1929	5	30	158	7	214	424	638
1930	5	29	142	6	178	474	652
1931	3	34	144	11	186	457	643
1932	4	18	118	7	146	441	587
1933	4	27	110	12	112	347	459
1934	6	28	164	10	90	379	469
1935	3	35	138	4	101	402	503
1936	6	18	142	10	140	391	531
1937	5	24	125	9	123	393	516
1938	4	35	160	9	145	409	554
1939	3	22	105	5	119	339	458
1940	–	27	102	7	158	307	465
1941	–	19	94	1	138	305	443
1942	5	5	51	–	96	215	311
1943	–	7	44	2	116	225	341
1944	–	12	70	1	107	259	366
1945	–	11	90	2	127	279	406
1946	1	26	127	2	166	370	536
1947	1	22	125	3	154	333	487
1948	2	25	117	5	161	315	476
1949	–	23	106	5	169	298	467
1950	1	19	103	2	146	314	460
1947	–	5	34	2	44	144	188
1948	–	17	74	–	78	234	312
1949	1	15	114	3	173	398	571
1950	1	13	143	2	161	362	523
1951	1	28	121	3	171	368	539
1952	–	20	124	5	207	325	532
1953	2	22	108	5	150	318	468
1954	–	22	89	3	96	276	372
1955	1	16	94	2	109	262	371
1956	–	24	145	4	144	365	509
1957	–	18	124	5	128	316	444

Year	Tile Structures (391)	Solid Block Walls (392)	Metallic Monuments, Markers, Guards, Memorial Tablets (393)	Tennis (394)	Table Tennis (395)	Golf Course & Bags (396)	Balls (397)	Clubs (398)
1837	–	1	–	–	–	–	–	–
1838	–	–	–	–	–	–	–	–
1839	–	–	–	–	–	–	–	–
1840	–	–	–	–	–	–	–	–
1841	–	–	–	–	–	–	–	–
1842	–	–	–	–	–	–	–	–
1843	–	–	–	–	–	–	–	–
1844	1	–	–	–	–	–	–	–
1845	–	–	–	–	–	–	–	–
1846	–	–	–	–	–	–	–	–
1847	–	1	–	–	–	–	–	–
1848	–	–	–	–	–	–	–	–
1849	–	–	–	–	–	–	–	–
1850	–	–	–	–	–	–	–	–
1851	–	–	1	–	–	–	–	–
1852	–	–	–	–	–	–	–	–
1853	1	–	–	–	–	–	–	–
1854	–	1	1	–	–	–	–	–
1855	2	2	–	–	–	–	–	–
1856	–	1	–	–	–	–	–	–
1857	1	–	–	–	–	–	–	–
1858	–	–	–	–	–	–	–	–
1859	–	–	2	–	–	–	–	–
1860	–	–	–	–	–	–	–	–
1861	–	–	1	–	–	–	–	–
1862	–	–	1	–	–	–	–	–
1863	1	–	–	–	–	–	–	–
1864	–	–	–	–	–	–	–	–
1865	–	–	–	–	–	–	–	–
1866	1	1	–	–	–	–	–	–
1867	2	3	1	–	–	–	–	–
1868	–	2	–	–	–	–	–	–
1869	6	5	–	–	–	–	–	–
1870	4	1	1	–	–	–	–	–
1871	8	–	–	–	1	–	–	–
1872	8	4	1	–	–	–	–	–
1873	10	2	1	–	–	–	–	–
1874	4	2	1	1	–	–	–	–
1875	7	2	3	–	–	–	–	–
1876	5	2	1	–	–	–	–	–
1874	3	2	1	1	–	–	–	–
1875	6	2	2	–	–	–	–	–
1876	5	2	2	–	–	–	–	–
1877	9	2	4	–	–	–	–	–
1878	5	2	–	–	–	–	–	–
1879	9	3	1	2	–	–	–	–
1880	6	1	2	1	–	–	–	–
1881	6	1	3	1	–	–	–	–
1882	19	7	2	1	–	–	–	–
1883	16	6	5	3	–	–	–	–
1884	20	2	2	3	–	–	–	–
1885	19	7	4	9	–	–	–	–
1886	10	3	2	5	–	–	–	–
1887	15	1	2	2	–	–	–	–
1888	14	2	1	4	–	–	–	–
1889	14	6	1	3	–	–	–	–
1890	16	7	2	–	–	–	–	–
1891	23	3	4	–	1	–	–	–
1892	27	6	2	3	–	–	–	–
1893	19	2	3	–	–	–	–	1
1894	20	4	5	1	–	–	–	1

Year	(391)	(392)	(393)	(394)	(395)	(396)	(397)	(398)
1895	17	3	2	–	–	–	–	3
1896	26	3	–	–	–	–	–	3
1897	22	2	1	–	–	1	–	1
1898	21	3	–	–	–	1	1	3
1899	25	7	1	1	–	1	1	5
1900	31	9	1	–	–	2	2	7
1901	40	9	3	1	–	3	18	8
1902	67	11	–	2	13	2	142	11
1903	61	32	2	3	1	1	18	11
1904	54	24	1	2	–	1	3	7
1905	52	29	1	2	–	2	2	4
1906	43	34	4	6	–	–	2	7
1907	38	15	2	2	–	3	6	3
1908	52	10	2	3	–	1	2	3
1909	38	14	2	1	–	6	1	3
1910	34	11	1	2	–	3	1	3
1911	40	9	1	2	–	1	3	2
1912	27	9	–	3	–	6	–	6
1913	24	11	–	2	–	8	–	13
1914	21	12	2	11	–	9	2	19
1915	24	21	4	11	–	10	3	10
1916	36	22	–	9	–	7	9	11
1917	21	16	1	2	1	2	2	6
1918	37	15	2	3	–	7	1	6
1919	27	24	3	4	–	5	3	16
1920	42	22	2	3	–	3	3	16
1921	58	29	2	12	–	18	4	30
1922	43	30	2	27	1	34	4	29
1923	40	25	2	14	–	23	3	40
1924	31	23	4	20	–	18	3	37
1925	41	14	6	16	1	26	6	33
1926	60	23	–	14	1	26	2	52
1927	44	23	4	12	–	36	5	55
1928	59	18	4	8	–	35	6	37
1929	48	26	3	12	–	18	1	24
1930	62	6	3	9	–	44	5	27
1931	60	10	8	11	–	28	3	37
1932	47	6	1	12	3	15	2	29
1933	44	12	7	16	5	6	1	15
1934	33	8	3	20	2	11	–	18
1935	43	7	2	10	2	8	2	17
1936	64	13	6	12	2	10	3	11
1937	54	23	3	10	4	9	7	9
1938	52	22	3	10	3	6	5	16
1939	48	11	2	7	4	7	3	14
1940	28	12	1	17	4	7	6	7
1941	13	6	–	7	2	6	3	13
1942	5	2	2	1	1	5	1	4
1943	9	4	2	1	–	5	1	3
1944	5	6	–	1	–	7	–	10
1945	10	2	–	–	2	9	–	10
1946	11	3	1	3	2	11	–	9
1947	8	3	2	3	1	21	2	13
1948	10	7	1	6	–	12	1	11
1949	12	2	2	2	–	6	–	5
1950	8	3	1	1	1	15	–	6
1947	4	–	–	–	–	4	–	5
1948	4	2	–	2	1	14	–	9
1949	8	8	–	1	1	18	–	25
1950	11	2	2	2	2	11	–	8
1951	6	6	1	4	–	12	1	4
1952	12	2	3	4	1	13	1	2
1953	11	4	–	4	2	4	2	8
1954	6	4	2	2	2	10	–	8
1955	8	4	–	2	3	14	1	6
1956	11	1	1	5	2	19	1	5
1957	3	2	–	4	2	10	3	8

Year	Golf Tees (399)	Practice Devices (400)	Total 396–400 (401)	Simulated Golf Game (402)	Baseball (403)	Boxing, Football, Basketball, Scoreboards (404)	Ice Skates (405)	Roller Skates (406)
1837	–	–	–	–	–	–	–	–
1838	–	–	–	–	–	–	–	–
1839	–	–	–	–	–	–	–	–
1840	–	–	–	–	–	–	–	–
1841	–	–	–	–	–	–	–	–
1842	–	–	–	–	–	–	–	–
1843	–	–	–	–	–	–	–	–
1844	–	–	–	–	–	–	–	–
1845	–	–	–	–	–	–	–	–
1846	–	–	–	–	–	–	–	–
1847	–	–	–	–	–	–	1	–
1848	–	–	–	–	–	–	–	–
1849	–	–	–	–	–	–	1	–
1850	–	–	–	–	–	–	–	–
1851	–	–	–	–	–	–	–	–
1852	–	–	–	–	–	–	1	–
1853	–	–	–	–	–	–	–	–
1854	–	–	–	–	–	–	–	–
1855	–	–	–	–	–	–	2	–
1856	–	–	–	–	–	–	2	–
1857	–	–	–	–	–	–	2	–
1858	–	–	–	–	–	–	1	–
1859	–	–	–	–	–	–	3	–
1860	–	–	–	–	–	–	12	1
1861	–	–	–	–	–	–	14	3
1862	–	–	–	–	–	–	9	–
1863	–	–	–	–	–	–	9	–
1864	–	–	–	–	–	–	7	–
1865	–	–	–	–	–	–	7	1
1866	–	–	–	–	1	–	9	–
1867	–	–	–	–	–	1	7	1
1868	–	–	–	–	1	–	10	1
1869	–	–	–	–	–	–	4	6
1870	–	–	–	–	–	–	2	6
1871	–	–	–	–	–	–	1	11
1872	–	–	–	–	–	1	–	2
1873	–	–	–	–	–	–	–	2
1874	–	–	–	–	–	–	2	6
1875	–	–	–	–	2	–	3	–
1876	–	–	–	–	3	–	1	7
1874	–	–	–	–	–	–	3	6
1875	–	–	–	–	4	–	3	–
1876	–	–	–	–	1	–	5	9
1877	–	–	–	–	1	–	–	9
1878	–	–	–	–	–	2	–	6
1879	–	–	–	–	–	1	2	6
1880	–	–	–	–	1	–	4	6
1881	–	–	–	–	–	–	1	22
1882	–	–	–	–	1	1	–	13
1883	–	–	–	–	5	2	2	32
1884	–	–	–	–	4	2	1	73
1885	–	–	–	–	1	2	2	122
1886	–	–	–	–	2	1	–	5
1887	–	–	–	–	6	1	4	2
1888	–	–	–	–	5	3	4	–
1889	–	–	–	1	5	4	5	–
1890	–	–	–	–	7	4	2	1
1891	–	–	–	–	4	4	6	2
1892	–	–	–	–	2	3	9	3
1893	–	–	1	–	2	6	–	4
1894	–	–	1	–	4	9	6	4

Year	(399)	(400)	(401)	(402)	(403)	(404)	(405)	(406)
1895	2	–	5	–	4	13	5	3
1896	–	–	3	–	2	10	1	10
1897	–	–	2	–	–	12	8	4
1898	–	–	5	–	3	–	1	10
1899	2	1	10	1	1	5	3	3
1900	3	1	15	3	3	9	4	3
1901	2	1	32	2	1	10	3	1
1902	–	1	156	4	6	14	6	2
1903	–	–	30	1	5	16	4	1
1904	–	–	11	–	8	12	4	1
1905	–	1	9	–	7	9	1	9
1906	–	–	9	–	7	10	1	8
1907	–	2	14	–	5	4	1	21
1908	–	–	6	–	8	8	4	20
1909	–	1	11	–	14	13	1	19
1910	–	2	9	–	9	8	8	12
1911	–	1	7	1	10	12	4	10
1912	–	1	13	2	11	15	7	4
1913	–	1	22	–	6	8	2	6
1914	1	1	32	1	3	8	4	6
1915	5	1	29	3	4	9	13	10
1916	1	5	33	1	1	11	8	5
1917	2	1	13	1	2	10	8	4
1918	1	3	18	–	1	1	3	4
1919	–	4	28	1	4	4	7	8
1920	1	6	29	3	3	3	8	11
1921	4	9	65	3	8	13	11	13
1922	2	7	76	4	8	20	8	13
1923	3	9	78	1	11	33	8	11
1924	17	16	91	4	9	29	7	13
1925	24	8	97	2	9	37	9	12
1926	24	12	115	6	10	36	8	10
1927	19	15	130	5	4	29	12	11
1928	18	8	104	8	6	30	10	13
1929	12	11	66	–	4	17	7	9
1930	16	6	98	6	4	26	7	11
1931	13	7	88	–	6	20	11	9
1932	8	11	65	–	4	19	5	7
1933	2	13	37	2	6	19	5	19
1934	1	12	42	2	1	9	7	18
1935	6	7	40	–	8	23	7	20
1936	7	2	33	–	6	18	9	9
1937	3	5	33	–	7	19	12	14
1938	6	10	43	–	7	15	24	13
1939	5	10	39	–	4	18	20	7
1940	5	4	29	1	7	25	6	14
1941	1	4	27	–	9	7	10	5
1942	1	1	12	–	1	7	9	2
1943	–	3	12	–	3	4	10	2
1944	2	1	20	1	2	4	6	7
1945	3	5	27	–	2	9	3	7
1946	7	3	30	2	13	15	9	27
1947	5	10	51	1	3	19	5	21
1948	8	11	43	1	6	16	6	17
1949	9	6	26	2	4	16	4	10
1950	3	2	26	1	5	14	4	11
1947	–	1	10	–	2	3	2	9
1948	5	5	33	–	6	9	5	3
1949	8	14	65	4	8	16	6	12
1950	7	8	34	2	6	12	6	19
1951	2	2	21	–	3	17	10	22
1952	5	6	27	1	3	13	4	14
1953	4	5	23	1	11	13	5	16
1954	6	4	28	1	4	9	3	10
1955	3	11	35	–	3	6	–	11
1956	1	12	38	1	8	11	2	5
1957	6	16	43	2	6	12	2	1

227

Sporting and Athletic Goods

Year	Misc. Skates (407)	Billiard & Pool Tables (408)	Misc. Billiard & Pool Equipment (409)	Bowling Alleys & Equipment (410)	Bowling Pins & Balls (411)	Exercising Devices (412)	Total 394, 395, 401, 402–412 (413)
1837	–	–	–	–	–	–	–
1838	–	–	–	–	–	–	–
1839	–	–	–	–	–	–	–
1840	–	–	–	–	–	–	–
1841	–	–	–	–	–	–	–
1842	–	–	–	–	–	–	–
1843	–	–	–	–	–	–	–
1844	–	–	–	–	–	–	–
1845	–	–	–	–	–	1	1
1846	–	–	–	–	–	–	–
1847	–	–	–	–	–	–	1
1848	–	1	–	–	–	–	1
1849	–	–	–	–	–	–	1
1850	–	–	–	–	–	–	–
1851	–	–	–	2	–	–	2
1852	–	–	–	–	–	–	1
1853	–	–	–	1	–	1	2
1854	–	–	–	–	1	–	1
1855	–	–	–	–	–	–	2
1856	–	2	1	–	–	–	5
1857	2	3	–	–	–	–	7
1858	–	10	1	–	–	1	13
1859	16	6	3	–	1	1	30
1860	8	2	2	–	–	1	26
1861	10	–	–	1	–	3	31
1862	8	1	–	–	–	–	18
1863	14	1	–	–	–	–	24
1864	11	1	–	–	–	1	20
1865	7	1	2	–	–	6	24
1866	9	2	2	–	–	1	24
1867	16	3	7	3	1	5	44
1868	18	1	9	1	4	3	48
1869	13	6	3	3	1	12	48
1870	11	5	2	2	1	3	32
1871	4	9	3	–	4	13	46
1872	7	13	5	–	–	5	33
1873	7	14	5	1	2	10	41
1874	4	9	5	4	4	3	38
1875	5	7	2	1	1	11	32
1876	12	5	3	2	3	8	44
1874	5	10	4	4	3	5	41
1875	3	8	2	2	1	14	37
1876	14	4	3	1	5	11	53
1877	4	6	7	1	3	12	43
1878	5	5	5	3	–	13	39
1879	5	5	3	2	2	12	40
1880	8	7	7	4	–	10	48
1881	11	12	11	3	1	16	78
1882	4	13	8	3	3	6	53
1883	8	8	11	3	7	6	87
1884	14	10	11	2	1	7	128
1885	28	–	10	–	1	21	196
1886	2	6	6	2	5	12	46
1887	5	8	4	1	5	12	50
1888	6	5	3	–	2	17	49
1889	3	2	4	6	3	20	56
1890	6	3	9	2	3	25	62
1891	2	7	7	9	4	15	61
1892	7	9	7	7	3	14	67
1893	7	7	14	3	3	13	60
1894	6	6	7	4	8	8	64

Year	(407)	(408)	(409)	(410)	(411)	(412)	(413)
1895	2	8	9	5	5	13	72
1896	18	12	12	2	6	18	94
1897	9	4	15	5	5	11	75
1898	6	5	4	9	3	15	61
1899	3	12	7	8	5	14	73
1900	6	3	17	13	6	18	100
1901	2	17	9	10	10	13	111
1902	1	10	14	28	9	16	281
1903	4	4	10	12	6	15	112
1904	5	8	10	17	9	36	123
1905	7	8	8	18	5	29	112
1906	5	9	10	19	11	19	114
1907	10	8	12	11	8	19	115
1908	6	7	16	15	6	15	114
1909	5	7	20	20	10	21	142
1910	2	8	11	10	10	19	108
1911	4	6	13	6	10	33	118
1912	4	9	17	18	9	18	130
1913	5	8	16	19	18	15	127
1914	5	24	24	18	12	23	171
1915	6	16	24	17	20	25	187
1916	6	15	24	14	11	17	155
1917	6	7	16	20	6	13	109
1918	6	5	8	13	6	10	78
1919	3	6	13	22	13	23	136
1920	6	13	16	7	8	23	133
1921	4	12	15	9	10	34	209
1922	6	3	18	10	22	27	243
1923	3	13	8	10	17	28	235
1924	7	8	10	15	15	23	251
1925	8	10	16	21	16	32	286
1926	8	10	8	11	13	24	274
1927	3	10	13	17	16	32	294
1928	9	4	1	16	13	25	247
1929	3	5	2	9	12	18	164
1930	9	10	1	11	10	20	222
1931	5	5	2	16	16	21	210
1932	11	1	3	4	17	26	177
1933	8	7	1	9	17	19	170
1934	11	2	–	7	4	20	145
1935	14	7	1	6	5	13	156
1936	19	1	1	6	–	15	131
1937	15	2	–	10	–	13	139
1938	24	2	2	18	–	16	177
1939	25	2	2	30	–	26	184
1940	17	5	2	29	–	19	175
1941	12	1	–	23	–	10	113
1942	11	3	–	14	–	5	66
1943	4	2	1	10	–	3	52
1944	6	2	2	15	–	8	74
1945	10	–	2	17	–	20	99
1946	11	6	2	27	–	22	169
1947	12	–	–	36	–	6	158
1948	21	–	2	19	–	19	156
1949	11	3	–	29	–	13	120
1950	12	1	2	26	–	15	119
1947	3	–	2	5	18	6	60
1948	13	–	1	5	15	11	104
1949	11	3	3	16	38	29	213
1950	14	3	–	16	38	15	169
1951	14	3	1	18	41	7	161
1952	17	–	1	31	33	11	160
1953	10	2	2	29	39	17	174
1954	11	–	–	31	31	16	148
1955	8	–	1	19	39	19	146
1956	11	3	–	20	41	11	158
1957	9	–	2	22	42	25	172

Year	Fish Butchering (414)	Fishing Rods (415)	Artificial Bait (416)	Line-Attached Bodies exc. hooks (417)	Hooks (418)	Misc. (419)	Total 414–419 (420)
1837	–	–	–	–	–	–	–
1838	–	–	–	–	–	3	3
1839	–	–	–	–	–	–	–
1840	–	–	–	–	–	–	–
1841	–	–	–	–	–	1	1
1842	–	–	–	–	–	1	1
1843	–	–	–	–	–	1	1
1844	–	–	–	–	–	1	1
1845	–	–	–	–	–	1	1
1846	–	–	–	–	–	4	4
1847	–	–	–	–	–	–	–
1848	–	–	–	–	–	–	–
1849	–	–	–	–	–	–	–
1850	–	–	–	–	–	2	2
1851	–	–	–	–	–	–	–
1852	–	–	1	–	–	2	3
1853	–	–	–	–	–	–	–
1854	–	1	1	1	–	1	4
1855	–	–	1	–	–	1	2
1856	1	–	–	–	1	1	3
1857	–	–	–	–	–	1	1
1858	1	1	–	–	–	4	6
1859	–	1	1	–	–	3	5
1860	–	–	–	–	–	–	–
1861	–	–	–	–	–	–	–
1862	–	1	–	–	–	3	4
1863	–	–	–	–	–	3	3
1864	–	1	–	–	–	–	1
1865	–	1	1	1	–	1	4
1866	–	1	–	1	4	6	12
1867	1	1	–	1	1	5	9
1868	–	–	1	1	2	11	15
1869	–	1	–	2	3	2	8
1870	–	–	1	1	–	2	4
1871	–	1	2	–	1	6	10
1872	–	–	1	2	–	6	9
1873	1	2	2	–	1	1	7
1874	–	1	3	–	1	7	12
1875	–	3	1	1	1	3	9
1876	1	–	3	1	1	6	12
1874	–	1	1	–	1	5	8
1875	1	3	2	1	2	5	14
1876	–	1	3	3	–	6	13
1877	–	1	–	–	1	8	10
1878	–	2	3	–	–	6	11
1879	1	–	–	–	1	5	7
1880	1	7	1	3	2	6	20
1881	1	6	2	3	2	11	25
1882	1	6	5	2	–	17	31
1883	–	2	6	3	1	14	26
1884	2	4	3	–	2	14	25
1885	1	7	1	5	1	15	30
1886	1	5	5	1	1	11	24
1887	–	6	4	1	1	18	30
1888	–	10	3	3	2	17	35
1889	–	8	3	1	–	16	28
1890	1	4	5	4	1	24	39
1891	2	9	3	1	8	21	44
1892	2	8	2	–	–	10	22
1893	–	3	4	3	5	20	35
1894	1	4	6	2	4	15	32

Year	(414)	(415)	(416)	(417)	(418)	(419)	(420)
1895	2	4	3	4	2	14	29
1896	4	3	7	3	4	15	36
1897	5	3	2	1	5	11	27
1898	–	1	5	1	4	9	20
1899	2	6	7	2	4	14	35
1900	6	9	9	3	5	15	47
1901	6	6	4	4	6	22	48
1902	7	5	11	9	6	28	66
1903	7	10	8	7	9	16	57
1904	3	8	12	10	9	22	64
1905	2	11	13	4	12	20	62
1906	6	14	16	8	6	20	70
1907	3	14	12	5	12	22	68
1908	2	11	12	4	7	28	64
1909	2	8	12	4	6	38	70
1910	9	6	6	5	10	12	48
1911	9	14	11	–	2	18	54
1912	1	3	9	4	3	27	47
1913	7	5	16	5	3	17	53
1914	8	7	19	6	9	25	74
1915	8	2	16	10	7	18	61
1916	13	3	24	7	4	23	74
1917	12	8	25	2	4	15	66
1918	11	4	17	5	3	15	55
1919	14	13	33	4	7	29	100
1920	9	9	23	3	4	24	72
1921	11	9	26	6	7	35	94
1922	14	7	32	8	7	43	111
1923	9	11	34	5	5	37	101
1924	11	6	37	6	3	33	96
1925	17	7	31	4	2	34	95
1926	16	12	36	4	7	24	99
1927	24	11	38	4	3	29	109
1928	10	4	31	1	8	35	89
1929	13	13	45	9	4	27	111
1930	15	12	42	9	2	44	124
1931	6	7	65	3	8	24	113
1932	5	14	37	3	7	23	89
1933	3	14	32	8	2	22	81
1934	9	13	33	7	7	30	99
1935	14	10	31	11	6	31	103
1936	8	12	30	12	8	26	96
1937	17	21	33	9	10	51	141
1938	7	22	55	20	8	49	161
1939	9	29	53	18	20	41	170
1940	11	21	48	18	1	36	135
1941	9	21	43	13	7	28	121
1942	7	7	13	4	3	15	49
1943	6	5	18	5	4	16	54
1944	19	10	22	11	6	32	100
1945	9	20	48	9	6	43	135
1946	25	30	77	22	10	73	237
1947	19	26	86	25	17	100	273
1948	9	27	78	32	10	98	254
1949	21	27	91	35	18	86	278
1950	18	18	63	35	14	98	246
1947	9	6	13	4	3	13	48
1948	4	7	18	4	3	31	67
1949	15	25	67	26	11	80	224
1950	26	24	73	23	18	72	236
1951	28	35	116	34	15	108	336
1952	19	31	128	46	23	106	353
1953	21	18	49	15	7	92	202
1954	16	13	31	14	6	65	145
1955	13	24	39	26	9	79	190
1956	13	28	84	50	18	138	331
1957	21	33	69	45	22	125	315

231

Year	Leather Sewing		Leather Nailing		Lasting Operations (425)	Lasts (426)
	Soles (421)	Other (422)	Heels (423)	Other (424)		
1837	–	–	–	–	–	–
1838	–	–	–	–	–	–
1839	–	–	–	–	–	–
1840	–	–	–	–	–	–
1841	–	–	–	–	–	–
1842	–	–	–	–	–	–
1843	–	–	–	–	–	–
1844	–	–	–	–	–	–
1845	–	–	–	–	2	–
1846	–	–	–	–	1	–
1847	–	–	–	–	1	–
1848	–	–	–	1	–	–
1849	–	–	–	–	–	–
1850	–	–	–	–	1	–
1851	–	–	–	1	1	1
1852	–	–	–	–	2	–
1853	–	–	–	2	–	–
1854	–	3	–	5	2	1
1855	–	1	–	1	–	–
1856	–	2	–	2	2	1
1857	–	–	–	4	2	–
1858	1	–	–	3	1	1
1859	–	–	–	3	5	2
1860	–	2	–	4	1	2
1861	1	1	1	–	1	2
1862	3	1	–	7	1	2
1863	–	2	–	2	4	1
1864	1	4	–	5	4	5
1865	3	7	–	1	2	5
1866	3	5	–	2	5	5
1867	2	2	–	6	4	6
1868	1	3	–	7	6	8
1869	14	8	1	6	8	8
1870	2	3	4	4	9	5
1871	8	6	1	4	9	–
1872	9	10	2	12	6	8
1873	6	9	4	11	15	14
1874	5	3	8	18	12	7
1875	6	7	2	27	6	3
1876	5	1	1	14	16	7
1877	7	3	1	14	10	8
1878	6	7	2	1	10	8
1879	1	5	1	15	18	3
1880	6	7	1	9	11	3
1881	6	10	3	16	23	11
1882	4	8	7	21	14	4
1883	5	8	12	15	16	12
1884	2	4	7	8	16	13
1885	9	10	29	10	15	6
1886	2	6	16	21	13	5
1887	5	6	8	8	17	7
1888	6	7	25	18	28	13
1889	8	18	21	18	9	13
1890	8	13	4	20	25	5
1891	12	12	8	10	22	3
1892	14	12	10	14	16	6
1893	8	16	10	16	21	12
1894	17	11	3	6	17	7

232

Year	(421)	(422)	(423)	(424)	(425)	(426)
1895	12	22	11	9	14	8
1896	17	18	21	24	32	10
1897	17	10	14	20	34	5
1898	9	6	7	14	20	19
1899	8	10	7	8	16	20
1900	8	8	5	10	16	19
1901	14	16	2	13	12	18
1902	7	15	13	8	17	14
1903	9	11	6	6	16	13
1904	8	8	4	5	8	9
1905	6	6	5	3	14	6
1906	8	18	1	7	14	11
1907	5	6	4	10	7	24
1908	8	22	7	17	12	19
1909	9	17	6	17	28	28
1910	4	21	17	20	25	13
1911	6	18	21	18	46	14
1912	13	37	9	48	76	13
1913	8	18	9	15	45	9
1914	19	23	14	27	52	24
1915	23	36	15	14	66	32
1916	25	34	12	11	42	24
1917	16	31	1	12	16	18
1918	8	20	10	19	31	14
1919	4	12	6	14	26	13
1920	13	17	7	10	29	7
1921	11	15	15	24	35	9
1922	9	15	11	11	31	8
1923	7	16	6	13	22	22
1924	7	9	4	8	29	26
1925	7	8	14	3	29	34
1926	9	13	7	14	13	26
1927	8	7	6	8	12	24
1928	3	14	9	8	25	16
1929	2	21	13	12	30	19
1930	2	15	14	10	21	18
1931	7	13	7	15	14	11
1932	6	11	11	14	32	8
1933	14	21	6	11	21	8
1934	5	21	14	11	32	6
1935	6	20	4	7	34	13
1936	11	14	11	9	40	16
1937	5	8	8	8	36	13
1938	3	5	8	3	31	12
1939	7	16	16	4	42	12
1940	4	24	11	5	29	6
1941	8	15	7	5	42	5
1942	4	9	13	4	30	6
1943	4	17	8	5	29	2
1944	6	21	2	4	18	2
1945	1	8	2	2	18	2
1946	1	10	3	1	14	7
1947	7	6	–	4	14	7
1948	5	6	2	3	10	7
1949 (6 mos.)	–	1	2	–	6	–

*All data in this table are for patents granted counted as of the year of the grant.

233

Special Series: Shoe Making*

Year	Toe & Heel Stiffener Machines (427)	Sole & Heel Edge Trimmers (428)	Sole Machines		Heel Machines (431)	Upper Machines	
			Laying & Leveling (429)	Other (430)		Assembling, Folding, Turning, etc. (432)	Crimping, Stretching, Creasing (433)
1837	–	–	–	–	–	–	2
1838	–	–	–	–	–	–	5
1839	–	–	–	–	–	–	2
1840	–	–	–	–	–	–	–
1841	–	–	–	–	–	–	1
1842	–	–	–	–	–	1	1
1843	–	–	–	–	–	–	1
1844	–	–	–	–	–	–	2
1845	–	–	–	–	–	–	3
1846	–	–	–	–	–	–	3
1847	–	–	–	–	–	–	–
1848	–	–	–	–	–	–	2
1849	–	–	–	–	–	–	5
1850	–	–	–	–	–	–	–
1851	–	–	–	–	–	–	2
1852	–	–	–	–	–	–	1
1853	1	1	–	–	–	–	–
1854	1	–	–	–	–	–	1
1855	1	–	1	2	–	–	4
1856	–	–	1	1	–	1	1
1857	–	–	1	1	–	–	3
1858	–	–	3	2	1	1	–
1859	–	5	–	1	1	–	1
1860	1	2	–	–	1	–	5
1861	–	1	1	–	–	2	2
1862	–	–	–	1	2	–	2
1863	–	–	1	2	2	–	2
1864	1	3	1	7	3	–	2
1865	1	3	–	1	1	–	4
1866	2	2	–	2	2	–	4
1867	–	3	1	4	1	–	6
1868	1	3	1	5	1	2	18
1869	–	3	–	6	1	2	11
1870	–	8	–	6	2	–	4
1871	7	3	1	8	2	–	4
1872	4	9	2	7	4	5	7
1873	5	9	2	13	13	4	8
1874	11	6	5	6	5	3	5
1875	15	9	3	9	7	1	8
1876	10	4	1	11	3	1	7
1877	7	6	4	6	–	3	8
1878	9	11	1	1	2	4	5
1879	13	10	4	6	2	1	5
1880	6	8	2	7	4	2	6
1881	2	16	5	9	4	3	10
1882	5	10	3	11	5	2	6
1883	5	11	1	13	6	4	3
1884	18	10	6	2	8	4	8
1885	7	21	5	13	12	5	6
1886	6	9	4	15	3	4	11
1887	10	14	7	7	10	2	9
1888	10	19	7	10	17	8	4
1889	2	30	4	9	13	1	2
1890	8	12	5	13	9	7	–
1891	8	14	4	20	6	8	8
1892	8	4	3	9	6	7	4
1893	8	5	3	13	3	9	4
1894	5	8	6	21	5	5	3

Year	(427)	(428)	(429)	(430)	(431)	(432)	(433)
1895	8	15	12	20	3	9	1
1896	5	11	13	17	4	2	–
1897	6	7	10	22	9	6	1
1898	5	15	5	27	2	2	–
1899	5	7	4	29	8	3	–
1900	2	5	6	19	5	5	1
1901	10	13	4	14	4	5	–
1902	2	4	5	12	3	5	–
1903	5	6	5	8	8	6	2
1904	8	1	–	6	11	5	–
1905	2	5	1	4	6	2	2
1906	2	4	3	11	3	–	–
1907	6	6	6	22	3	7	1
1908	10	4	7	19	4	10	2
1909	7	8	12	27	13	7	1
1910	13	13	4	25	13	6	2
1911	8	12	5	30	6	11	3
1912	20	15	6	59	12	33	5
1913	8	8	7	26	9	4	1
1914	14	15	11	33	21	17	5
1915	13	12	14	45	27	10	6
1916	14	3	13	42	19	15	8
1917	9	9	7	50	29	6	2
1918	13	7	12	28	32	19	1
1919	13	5	7	21	11	14	1
1920	8	3	4	20	22	8	3
1921	9	5	5	22	19	4	1
1922	6	5	3	22	15	12	5
1923	6	7	5	19	27	10	–
1924	4	5	6	34	33	3	4
1925	7	4	4	20	14	16	–
1926	4	12	2	22	16	14	1
1927	7	8	13	30	11	7	1
1928	5	13	18	42	19	15	4
1929	8	11	32	37	25	24	4
1930	11	14	15	29	14	17	–
1931	6	10	11	19	16	11	1
1932	9	2	12	42	23	23	4
1933	4	4	21	23	18	9	1
1934	3	6	22	29	12	12	–
1935	3	4	31	30	17	18	–
1936	4	7	26	33	15	16	4
1937	9	4	29	39	13	16	–
1938	5	1	26	39	7	5	2
1939	7	2	21	24	11	29	2
1940	10	6	14	37	7	18	1
1941	4	4	20	28	12	23	3
1942	1	5	15	24	4	21	6
1943	8	1	17	17	14	12	1
1944	–	–	9	16	3	5	2
1945	2	2	6	12	7	4	2
1946	1	1	5	7	1	3	1
1947	3	1	9	9	2	1	1
1948	–	3	15	6	3	4	1
1949 (6 mos.)	2	3	4	11	2	4	–

*All data in this table are for patents granted counted as of the year of the grant.

235

Special Series: Shoe Making*

Year	Formers (434)	Burnishing (435)	Boot Trees (436)	Misc. (437)	Total 421–437 (438)
1837	—	—	1	1	4
1838	—	—	—	—	5
1839	—	—	—	—	2
1840	—	—	—	2	2
1841	—	—	—	1	2
1842	—	—	—	—	2
1843	—	—	—	—	1
1844	—	—	—	—	2
1845	—	—	—	—	5
1846	—	—	1	—	5
1847	—	—	—	—	1
1848	—	—	—	2	4
1849	1	—	—	—	7
1850	—	—	2	—	3
1851	—	—	1	—	6
1852	—	—	2	1	6
1853	—	—	—	1	5
1854	1	—	—	—	14
1855	1	2	2	—	15
1856	—	—	2	2	15
1857	1	—	5	1	18
1858	1	—	5	1	20
1859	1	—	3	2	24
1860	—	1	4	4	27
1861	—	1	—	1	14
1862	1	—	1	1	22
1863	—	1	4	1	22
1864	—	3	1	1	41
1865	1	2	5	4	40
1866	2	3	8	4	49
1867	2	2	6	3	48
1868	6	3	6	3	74
1869	3	1	7	4	83
1870	4	1	6	3	61
1871	3	10	5	4	75
1872	1	18	10	8	122
1873	2	18	8	13	154
1874	5	15	7	11	132
1875	3	8	6	8	128
1876	—	11	5	16	113
1877	1	8	6	10	102
1878	1	1	6	14	89
1879	4	9	6	17	120
1880	4	9	10	17	112
1881	3	11	13	7	152
1882	3	13	11	18	145
1883	3	12	14	13	153
1884	7	15	11	13	152
1885	9	11	20	15	203
1886	7	8	19	19	168
1887	7	18	16	15	166
1888	4	11	10	25	222
1889	4	7	11	13	183
1890	2	10	21	12	174
1891	3	9	10	13	170
1892	6	7	12	13	151
1893	9	2	7	14	160
1894	11	1	7	3	136

Year	(439)	(434)	(435)	(436)	(437)	(438)
1895		7	4	16	15	186
1896	3	12	3	7	10	206
1897	5	10	5	14	4	194
1898	8	11	1	13	6	162
1899	6	18	4	11	2	160
1900	6	19	2	5	4	139
1901	8	17	2	6	6	156
1902		9	4	5	6	129
1903		15	10	7	12	145
1904		21	3	5	13	115
1905		17	5	3	12	99
1906		22	1	2	11	118
1907		17	6	5	12	147
1908		21	1	4	15	182
1909		26	4	12	17	239
1910		22	11	23	32	264
1911		16	5	10	28	257
1912		13	6	17	49	431
1913		13	4	9	41	234
1914		31	17	20	57	400
1915		16	6	23	74	432
1916		6	12	15	56	351
1917		9	6	11	53	285
1918		15	5	12	52	298
1919		7	6	12	35	207
1920		12	6	10	47	226
1921		8	5	24	48	259
1922		12	3	15	42	225
1923		16	3	15	25	219
1924		15	4	13	29	233
1925		16	5	11	52	244
1926		8	2	6	44	213
1927		18	6	5	37	208
1928		13	6	11	60	281
1929		24	4	13	67	346
1930		27	9	8	59	283
1931		16	3	8	64	232
1932		28	1	9	61	296
1933		16	8	11	62	258
1934		9	7	13	72	274
1935		22	5	9	87	310
1936		19	4	13	94	336
1937		19	2	9	80	298
1938		12	2	7	79	247
1939		14	3	11	76	285
1940		12	3	7	91	285
1941		14	1	5	70	266
1942		8	5	11	70	236
1943		10	5	3	64	217
1944		13	1	3	40	145
1945		11	—	3	28	110
1946		8	—	3	42	108
1947		5	1	1	45	116
1948		14	1	4	38	122
1949 (6 mos.)		13	3	1	29	81

*All data in this table are for patents granted counted as of the year of the grant.

Special Series: Glass*

Year	Glass Making			Molding (448)	Light Bulbs (449)	Misc. Processes (450)	Total 445–450 (451)
	Annealing & Heating (445)	Flat Glass (446)	Laminated Glass (447)				
1837	—	—	—	—	—	—	1
1838	—	—	—	—	—	—	1
1839	—	—	—	1	—	—	2
1840	—	—	—	—	—	—	2
1841	—	2	—	—	—	—	3
1842	—	2	—	—	—	—	2
1843	—	—	—	2	—	—	2
1844	—	—	—	2	—	—	2
1845	2	1	—	2	—	—	1
1846	—	—	—	1	—	—	—
1847	—	—	—	—	—	—	4
1848	—	—	—	—	—	1	4
1849	—	—	—	2	—	3	7
1850	—	—	—	—	—	2	4
1851	—	1	—	2	—	3	5
1852	—	1	—	1	—	3	1
1853	2	—	—	—	—	1	5
1854	—	—	—	—	—	1	5
1855	2	—	—	—	4	4	12
1856	—	—	—	—	1	5	3
1857	—	—	—	—	6	2	8
1858	—	—	—	—	—	5	3
1859	1	—	—	—	2	1	8
1860	1	—	1	—	1	4	12
1861	—	—	—	—	2	4	15
1862	1	—	—	—	5	6	19
1863	2	—	—	—	7	5	25
1864	3	—	—	—	7	9	22
1865	1	—	1	—	13	7	22
1866	5	—	2	—	11	9	15
1867	2	—	2	—	9	5	38
1868	2	—	1	—	9	9	24
1869	3	—	1	—	22	7	22
1870	—	—	1	—	12	6	40
1871	6	—	1	—	8	17	48
1872	3	—	2	—	18	23	33
1873	6	—	2	—	13	18	37
1874	5	—	—	—	7	16	41
1875	10	—	2	—	9	24	40
1876	6	—	1	1	10	16	44
1877	10	—	1	2	12	24	46
1878	4	—	1	—	12	15	54
1879	11	—	1	1	17	19	51
1880	7	—	3	—	23	17	42
1881	10	—	1	—	21	13	53
1882	9	—	3	—	11	34	40
1883	9	—	4	—	10	22	18
1884	13	—	4	—	7	12	62
1885	4	—	7	—	2	35	66
1886	3	—	—	—	13	31	42
1887	4	—	3	—	15	22	47
1888	10	—	—	—	7	21	72
1889	12	—	7	—	8	36	58
1890	8	—	5	2	15	28	
1891	10	—	5	3	8		
1892	8	—	10	5			
1893	10	—	6				
1894							

Year	(445)	(446)	(447)	(448)	(449)	(450)	(451)
1895	3	7	5	11	1	24	51
1896	8	1	2	4	2	27	44
1897	10	1	1	15	–	29	56
1898	3	4	4	21	–	42	74
1899	15	4	–	18	–	67	104
1900	5	4	5	14	–	60	88
1901	7	11	2	16	1	59	96
1902	14	12	–	12	1	55	94
1903	12	15	4	11	3	64	109
1904	20	10	6	14	6	80	136
1905	21	16	15	19	4	82	157
1906	23	17	16	29	7	92	184
1907	24	5	18	26	12	61	146
1908	15	7	9	14	6	40	91
1909	8	8	19	13	4	67	119
1910	17	13	15	13	3	56	117
1911	8	3	1	8	4	58	82
1912	20	2	–	4	1	66	93
1913	12	1	2	4	–	34	53
1914	17	6	2	7	4	50	86
1915	40	3	8	17	2	109	179
1916	34	10	5	5	2	86	142
1917	28	5	3	9	–	61	106
1918	31	10	3	11	–	53	108
1919	26	9	2	11	3	79	130
1920	26	11	3	8	4	82	134
1921	23	13	2	5	1	47	91
1922	19	5	2	9	7	60	102
1923	21	9	1	14	5	78	128
1924	34	17	–	13	6	86	156
1925	57	32	7	20	12	146	274
1926	85	35	8	19	12	150	309
1927	64	22	6	15	14	128	249
1928	55	22	18	11	11	108	225
1929	47	19	11	9	12	91	189
1930	57	30	24	7	1	109	228
1931	95	62	32	15	5	155	364
1932	88	60	43	25	9	192	417
1933	87	29	52	14	9	134	325
1934	67	12	38	15	9	120	261
1935	66	12	25	20	8	123	254
1936	69	6	28	13	10	87	213
1937	50	2	23	7	5	59	146
1938	45	4	11	6	4	87	157
1939	46	4	13	8	4	93	168
1940	47	1	18	19	7	104	196
1941	57	6	12	13	8	133	229
1942	48	3	15	13	8	111	198
1943	25	6	8	20	13	75	147
1944	19	2	5	14	9	47	96
1945	25	4	7	6	4	51	97
1946	11	3	2	10	4	38	68
1947	10	2	2	4	7	21	46
1948	6	3	1	5	5	32	52
1949	20	4	3	7	7	73	114
1950	18	1	4	10	11	115	159
1951	20	1	2	17	10	76	126
1952	25	2	–	4	9	65	105
1953	20	6	5	7	6	64	108
1954	21	2	9	7	12	62	113
1955	16	4	8	5	4	51	88
1956	11	6	6	11	3	54	91

*All data in this table are for patents granted counted as of the year of the grant.

241

Year	Bottles & Jars, General (452)	Non-refillable Bottles (453)	Globes, Lamp Chimneys, Refractors (454)	Glass Coating Compositions (455)	Total 452–455 Glass Products (456)	Total 451, 456 Glass (457)	Glass Container Related: Bottle & Jar Caps & Other Closures (458)
1837	–	–	–	–	–	–	–
1838	–	–	1	–	1	1	–
1839	–	–	–	–	–	1	–
1840	–	–	–	–	–	–	–
1841	1	–	–	–	1	2	–
1842	–	–	–	–	–	2	1
1843	–	–	–	–	–	2	–
1844	1	–	–	1	2	2	–
1845	1	–	–	–	1	3	–
1846	–	–	–	–	–	3	1
1847	–	–	–	–	–	2	–
1848	–	–	–	1	1	3	–
1849	–	–	–	–	–	1	2
1850	–	–	–	1	1	1	–
1851	–	–	–	–	–	–	–
1852	–	–	–	1	1	5	1
1853	–	–	–	–	–	4	2
1854	3	–	–	–	3	10	2
1855	1	–	–	–	1	5	4
1856	–	–	–	1	1	6	3
1857	–	–	1	–	1	2	4
1858	1	–	1	–	2	7	6
1859	2	–	3	1	6	11	7
1860	1	–	5	3	9	21	6
1861	–	–	6	–	6	9	11
1862	1	–	24	–	25	33	15
1863	1	–	16	–	17	20	29
1864	2	–	7	–	9	17	32
1865	4	–	2	3	9	21	28
1866	4	–	8	4	16	31	32
1867	6	–	12	6	24	43	36
1868	4	–	19	1	24	49	44
1869	12	–	21	2	35	57	38
1870	6	–	13	2	21	43	45
1871	7	–	8	4	19	34	21
1872	11	–	17	2	30	68	21
1873	10	–	6	1	17	41	38
1874	9	–	8	2	19	41	30
1875	18	–	11	–	29	69	36
1876	19	–	12	–	31	79	54
1877	15	–	14	–	29	62	66
1878	6	–	9	2	17	54	81
1879	16	–	7	3	26	67	57
1880	8	–	2	–	10	50	59
1881	14	–	5	–	19	63	46
1882	21	–	13	–	34	80	64
1883	15	1	7	3	26	80	81
1884	15	3	5	2	25	76	75
1885	16	1	7	1	25	67	106
1886	14	–	5	2	21	74	81
1887	21	2	7	2	32	72	62
1888	13	1	4	1	19	37	64
1889	13	–	7	–	20	82	66
1890	18	2	1	3	24	90	57
1891	17	–	8	4	29	71	37
1892	16	9	9	3	37	84	60
1893	9	9	4	1	23	95	55
1894	25	35	6	5	71	129	63

Year	(452)	(453)	(454)	(455)	(456)	(457)	(458)
1895	21	46	7	6	80	131	56
1896	88	83	15	2	188	232	76
1897	117	119	19	3	258	314	101
1898	68	73	19	2	162	236	103
1899	40	53	13	5	111	215	88
1900	39	52	9	1	101	189	87
1901	39	72	11	–	122	218	92
1902	50	72	7	2	131	225	126
1903	56	100	15	1	172	281	159
1904	46	125	19	2	192	328	133
1905	52	111	15	–	178	335	182
1906	66	140	25	1	232	416	164
1907	53	104	11	2	170	316	144
1908	54	68	3	–	125	216	145
1909	56	66	21	1	144	263	97
1910	44	58	16	2	120	237	90
1911	49	63	16	3	131	213	44
1912	40	99	25	1	165	258	102
1913	49	95	16	1	161	214	79
1914	35	93	16	9	153	239	104
1915	54	87	17	10	168	347	142
1916	51	60	17	6	134	276	117
1917	26	33	11	11	81	187	80
1918	26	33	10	6	75	183	69
1919	24	20	13	12	69	199	86
1920	27	14	8	6	55	189	99
1921	11	1	3	6	21	112	67
1922	44	11	6	9	70	172	124
1923	46	1	2	3	52	180	112
1924	25	1	10	9	45	201	78
1925	20	1	10	12	43	317	61
1926	32	3	14	6	55	364	106
1927	43	2	7	11	63	312	127
1928	44	1	7	9	61	286	122
1929	40	6	9	9	64	253	127
1930	34	3	9	14	60	288	64
1931	20	–	6	9	35	399	62
1932	29	2	2	5	38	455	95
1933	20	3	5	12	40	365	70
1934	26	4	3	20	53	314	70
1935	39	23	2	15	79	333	77
1936	42	28	1	20	91	304	87
1937	55	30	3	20	108	254	80
1938	26	22	3	13	64	221	86
1939	23	16	1	16	56	224	87
1940	18	6	3	28	55	251	67
1941	9	11	5	28	53	282	56
1942	17	6	5	18	46	244	51
1943	18	11	4	22	55	202	37
1944	12	3	2	17	34	130	41
1945	16	5	1	14	36	133	39
1946	3	4	–	21	28	96	34
1947	9	5	–	23	37	83	30
1948	13	4	1	23	41	93	45
1949	17	4	3	35	59	173	33
1950	26	5	3	32	66	225	15
1951	21	3	2	31	57	183	32
1952	18	2	2	13	35	140	31
1953	17	2	3	12	34	142	22
1954	8	3	1	26	38	151	31
1955	15	2	3	13	33	121	23
1956	32	2	4	13	51	142	56

*All data in this table are for patents granted counted as of the year of the grant.

243

Industrial Classification of

Patent Office Subclasses

NOTE: Headings and numbers at the left margin correspond to column headings and numbers in the time series. The remainder of the compilation below indicates the Patent Office classes included in each time series, by number and title, with a description of these classes and the numbers of the subclasses included therein.

AGRICULTURE

EARTH PREPARATION AND PLANTING

1. Harrows and Diggers
   55. Harrows and diggers: various harrows and diggers including clod crushers, diverse harrows, land rollers, stalk choppers and pullers, stone gatherers. Component parts including harrow teeth, pivoted teeth, pivoted tooth bars, etc. Potato diggers excluded. (1, 3, 6-8, 11-13, 17, 19, 21-24, 29-37, 46-49, 60-64, 73-78, 80-96, 102-105, 118, 122, 124-131, 149, 150, 152-154)

2. Plows
   22. Metal founding: plow chills and plow vent chills (175, 176)
   29. Metal working: making plow and cultivator irons. (14)
   78. Metal forging and welding: plow and cultivator iron dies. (68.5)
   97. Plows: plows, cultivators, harrows, rollers, and scrapers in various combinations. Soil elevators and treaters. Alternating and hillside plows, driven implement plows, plows with motor or ground wheel-operated implement control. Diverse control and adjustment devices. Implements with self-propelled vehicles, hand cultivating tools, foot-operated lift plows, cultivators of many types. Guide wheels, runners, connections, implement frames and elements, sharpeners, etc. Excluded are cotton chopper type plows and orchard cultivators. (1-10, 24-47, 91, 52-71.1, 76-136, 138-231, 233-245)
   104. Railways: reciprocating farm tool traction. (169)
   192. Clutches and powerstop control: plow lifting type clutches. (62)
   308. Machine elements, bearings, and guides: rotary bearing supports for plow or colter disk. Radial antifriction plain disk plow bearings. (19, 181)

3. Planting
   47. Plant husbandry: miscellaneous, mushroom and water culture, frost preventing, mulching, tree surgery, etc. (1-4, 8-12)
   111. Planting: various drilling devices and elements of same. Dibbling and liquid or gas planting machines. (6-7, .4, 14-99)

4. Manure Spreaders
    275. Scattering-unloaders: manure spreader type traversing machines. (3-6)

5. Total Earth Preparation and Planting (includes time series 1-4)

6. Fruit Harvesters and Orchard Plows
    56. Harvesters: fruit gatherers including catchers, berry strippers or clippers, and pole-supported devices. (328-340)
    97. Plows: orchard cultivators. (137)

HARVESTING

7. Harvesters–Cutting
    56. Harvesters: cutting, windrowing, raking, and catching devices in various combinations. Reciprocating side cutters of many kinds and including components of same. (192-206, 264-320)

8. Cutting, Conveying, and Binding
    56. Harvesters: cutting, conveying, and binding machines including different types of binding. Various cutting and conveying devices. (131-193)

9. Harvester Motors (except corn and cotton)
    56. Harvesters: harvester motors for seed gatherers or strippers, cutting, conveying, threshing, and binding machines in various combinations. Motors for cotton and cornstalk type harvesters excluded. (10, 19-27)

10. Shockers
    56. Harvesters: shockers including automatic feed, vertical position, self binding, etc. (401-431)

11. Tedders and Rakes
    56. Harvesters: combined rakes and tedders, other tedders. (365-374)

12. Corn Harvesting, Threshing, Cutting
    56. Harvesters: cornstalk type motor harvesters. Other cornstalk type harvesters including stalk breakers, cutters, pickers or huskers, gatherers or guides, sheaf loaders or carriers. (15-18, 51-121)
    130. Threshing: corncribs, corn-husking implements and machines, corn shellers. (3-10)
    139. Textiles, weaving: vertical shed special type looms for seed-corn stringers. (19)
    146. Vegetable and meat cutters and comminutors: green corn shellers, haystack cutters. (4, 70)
    192. Clutches and power-stop control: corn planter type latch-operated devices. (23)
    296. Land vehicles, bodies and tops: grain tank bodies. (15)

13. Hay Handling
    99. Foods and beverages: processes and products for curing and preserving hay and fodder. (8)
    146. Vegetable and meat cutters and comminutors: haystack cutters. (70)
    188. Brakes: hayrack type brakes. (14)
    214. Material or article handling: hay distributers. Self-loading or unloading

vehicles with laterally movable rigid platform type conveyor. Shovel or
fork type hay retaining load support. (5, 83. 24, 144)

280. Land vehicles: wheeled vehicles with hay load binding attachments.
     (180)
294. Handling, hand and hoistline implements: various hay fork type grapples
     and other hay fork type handling devices. (98, 105, 107-109, 120-130)
296. Land vehicles, bodies and tops: hay rack bodies, convertible hay and
     box bodies. (6-9, 11-14)

14. Cotton Harvesting, Picking, and Chopping Plows
    56. Harvesters: cotton motor harvesters. Other cotton harvesters including
        flail or whip, pneumatic, strippers, pickers, endless belt, spindles. (11-14,
        28-50)
    97. Plows: cotton chopper type plows. (11-23)

15. Grain Harvesting, Threshing, Cutting
    56. Harvesters: shelled grain catchers, standing grain gatherers, grain wheels
        and casters, grain cradles, grain adjusters. (207, 219-227, 322, 324, 324.5,
        466-473)
    130. Threshing: band cutters and feeders, clover hullers, flax threshers, grain
         separators, threshing machines. (1, 2, 13, 21-26, 27-29)

16. Miscellaneous Harvesting
    29. Metal working: processes of mechanical manufacture for agricultural
        devices. (148.3)
    47. Plant husbandry: cotton treating. (5)
    56. Harvesters: miscellaneous, gang, and convertible harvesters. Cutting,
        conveying, and threshing motor harvesters. Other cutting, conveying,
        and threshing harvesters. Platform and tongue adjustments, transporting
        attachments, anti-side draft devices, seats. Raking, bundling, or loading
        harvesters, horse rakes, and rotary or endless hand rakes. Several other
        types of hand rakes. Compressing and binding devices. Sheaf or bundle
        discharging carriers and other carriers. (1-7, 20, 21, 122-125, 208-218,
        228, 321, 323, 341-364, 375-400.03, 400.16-400.21, 432-465, 473.5-
        480)
    150. Cloth, leather, and rubber receptacles: bags for harvesting. (2)
    189. Metallic building structures: arrangement of skeleton tower windmills.
         (18)
    193. Conveyers, chutes, skids, guides, and ways: grain drill chutes. (9)
    214. Material or article handling: tobacco stringers or unstringers. (5.5)
    222. Dispensing: dispenser with totalizer for successive dispenser cycles,
         pivoted ejector, pivoted ejector with striker. (36, 222, 223)
    294. Handling, hand and hoistline implements: hand forks and shovels
         excluding snow shovels. (49-53.5, 55-60)

17. Unearthing Plants
    171. Unearthing plants or buried objects: various unearthing machines
         including many kinds of attachments such as separators or sorters, rakes,
         pilers, cleaners, markers, etc. Diggers with plant cutters, extractors,
         plow or blade with vibrating separator, separating digger with collecting
         tines. Digger, conveyor, or drive parts or details. Earth removal and
         separation, miscellaneous. (1-15, 17-144)

18. Total Harvesting (includes time series 7-17)

19. Bins and Granaries
    20. Wooden buildings: bins and silos. (1.2, 1.4-1.42)
    72. Masonry and concrete structures: elevators and bins. (6)
    98. Ventilation: ventilation of grain storage bins. (55)
    130. Threshing: granaries and bins. (14)
    189. Metallic building structures: bins. (3)

LIVESTOCK AND MISCELLANEOUS AGRICULTURE

20. Bee Culture
    6. Bee culture: beehives and bee culture appliances. (1-12)

21. Milkers
    119. Animal husbandry: various kinds of machines for milking, parts of same, milking methods and apparatus. (14.01-14.55)

22. Miscellaneous Dairy Farm Equipment
    31. Dairy: milk-treating apparatus, separators and cooling devices, churns and butter workers. (2-4, 33-41)
    155. Chairs and seats: milk stools. (35.1-35.7)
    220. Metallic receptacles: leg or lap supported pails. (17.1-17.3)

23. Poultry Husbandry Equipment
    119. Animal husbandry: brooders and incubators, nests and nest appliances. (30-50)
    237. Heating systems: brooder and incubator controls and systems. (3, 4, 14, 15)

24. Animal Housing and Confining
    119. Animal husbandry: perches, cages, barns and sheds, pens, stalls. (15-28)

25. Animal Feeding
    119. Animal husbandry: hoppers, troughs, racks, feed bags. (51-69)

26. Animal Watering
    119. Animal husbandry: watering devices including automatic, animal controlled, temperature regulating, etc. (72-81)

27. Animal Grooming
    119. Animal husbandry: currycombs and similar devices. (83-94)

28. Animal Controlling
    119. Animal husbandry: restraining devices including stocks, blinders, collars, drags, hitching means, hopples, mouth guards and nose rings, pokes, shields, stanchions, catching tools. (96-154)
    160. Closures, partitions and panels, flexible and portable: animal blocking and repelling. (18)

28a. Miscellaneous Animal Husbandry
    119. Animal husbandry: miscellaneous, training and exercising devices, stock sorters, gangways, manure pouches, antivermin treatment. (1, 29-29.5, 82, 95, 155-160)

29. Total Livestock (includes time series 21-28a, excluding bee culture)

30. Total "Pure" Agriculture (includes time series 5, 6, 18-20, and 29)

AGRICULTURE MIXED WITH OTHER FIELDS

ANIMAL POWER

31. Animal Draft Appliances I
    278. Land vehicles, animal draft appliances: draft equalizers where more than one animal is used, horse detachers, trace and pole connectors, neck yokes, hold-backs, miscellaneous. (1-32, 118-130)

32. Animal Draft Appliances II
    278. Land vehicles, animal draft appliances: poles and thills, thill couplings, thill and pole supports, whiffletrees and connecting devices. (33-117)

33. Animal-Powered Motors
    185. Motors, spring, weight and animal powered: animal-powered motors including belt, drum, sweep type, pivoted disk tread, etc. (15-25)

34. Harness: Bridles and Harness
    54. Harness: bridles and bits, hames, hame and trace connectors, hame and tug connectors. (6-15, 25-33)

35. Harness: Buckles
    24. Buckles, buttons, clasps, etc.: harness and strap buckles of various kinds. (164-183)

36. Harness: Miscellaneous
    54. Harness: various harness and harness parts excluding contents of time series 34 and excluding saddles. Including breaking and training devices, yokes, halters, various kinds of reins and attachments, hitching straps, collars, breast straps. Including harness straps, tugs, traces, girths, pads, loops, trimmings, blankets, fly nets, spurs, etc. (1-5, 16-24, 34-36, 48-59, 61-87)

37. Total Harness (includes time series 34-36)

38. Farriery: Shoes
    168. Farriery: animal shoes and treads, devices for attaching same. (4-25)

39. Farriery: Calks
    168. Farriery: various kinds of antiskid devices for animal shoes, mainly removable attachments. (29-43)

40. Farriery: Making Shoes
    59. Chain, staple, and horseshoe making: machines which combine cutting, bending, shaping, punching, and creasing operations in making animal shoes. Other devices and machines including calk makers, tools and dies, ox shoe making, etc. (36-70)

41. Farriery: Miscellaneous
    168. Farriery: overshoes, sole pads, shoeing stands and tools. (1-3, 26-28, 44-48)

42. Total Farriery (includes time series 38-41)

43. Whips and Whip Apparatus
    231. Whips and whip apparatus: whip machines, whips and lashes, fastenings. (1-6)

44. Total Animal Power Related (includes time series 31-33, 37, 42, and 43)

ANIMAL TRAPPING AND DESTROYING

45. Insect and Vermin Destroying
     43. Fishing, trapping, and vermin destroying: insect traps including operator controlled, mechanically operated, electrocuting, illuminated. Fly vases, crawling insect traps, fumigators, poison holders for destroying vermin, insect-catching machines, burners, powder dusters or sprayers. (107, 110-113, 121-131, 138-148)

46. Insecticides, Fungicides, Germicides, and Disinfectants: Inorganic
     167. Medicines, poisons, and cosmetics: inorganic poisons such as arsenic, copper, sulfur, etc. (14-21)

47. Insecticides, Fungicides, Germicides, and Disinfectants: Organic
     167. Medicines, poisons, and cosmetics: organic poisons such as carbon disulphide, plant extracts, formaldehyde, tars, nicotines, etc. (22-34)

48. Miscellaneous Poisons
     167. Medicines, poisons, and cosmetics: miscellaneous poisons, animal dips and sprays, seed disinfectants. Saturants for wood, paper, hides, textiles. Fumigants, suspending agents, oil emulsions, animal poisons, baits, limes. (13, 36, 38-46, 48, 49)

49. Total Pest Destroying, Etc. (includes time series 45-48)

FENCES AND GATES

50. Gate and Latch
     39. Gates: various kinds of mechanically operated gate and latch. (26-48)

51. Special Gates
     39. Gates: mechanically operated gates which are vertically pivoted or have a translational movement. Multiple movement gates. (51-59, 63-73, 76-83)

52. Miscellaneous Gates
     39. Gates: mechanically operated gates with multiple movement, automatic return, horizontally pivoted. Tension or compound gates, other gates and gate parts. (9-18, 22-25, 60-62, 74, 75, 84-96)

53. Total Gates (includes time series 50-52)

54. Fences: Panel
     256. Fences: panel fences. (24-31)

55. Fences: Barbed
     256. Fences: barbed fences. (2-9)

56. Fences: Wire Excluding Barbed
     256. Fences: wire connections including cross connections which are plastic, multiple, clamp, tie, etc. (47-58)

57. Fences: Wire Connections
     256. Fences: wire fences including picket, braced, stretcher, fabrics, strands. Barbed wire fences excluded (32-46)

58. Fences: Rail
     256. Fences: rail fences and various connecting devices for same. (59-72)

58a. Fences: Miscellaneous
> 256. Fences: miscellaneous, top-guarded, electric, driftage control fences. Earth, stone, wooden fences. Hedges, fence panels, etc. (1, 10-12.5, 19-23, 73)

59. Total Fences (includes time series 54-58a)

GREENHOUSES, NURSERY EQUIPMENT, GARDENING

60. Greenhouses, Nursery Equipment, Gardening, Plant Receptacles
> 47. Plant husbandry: mushroom culture, seed testers, greenhouses, hotbeds, plant covers and shades. Plant stands, supports, irrigators, and fertilizers. Other processes and equipment, flowers. (1.1, 14-19, 26-41, 44-47, 48.5, 55-61)
> 189. Metallic building structures: greenhouses. (4)

61. Special Cutting Machines (Harvester Type)
> 56. Harvesters: various cutting devices including hedge trimmers, hand-operated cutters, rotary, oscillating, and reciprocating cutters, etc. (229, 233-263)
> 30. Cutlery: sickle or scythe. (309)
> 306. Tool handle fastenings: scythe type handle fastenings. (1.1-1.3)

COTTON GINNING AND COMPRESSING

62. Ginning
> 19. Textiles, fiber preparation: boll hulling and ginning devices including delinters, gins, various gin components. Mechanisms for liberating fibers. (35-64)
> 76. Metal tools and implements, making: miscellaneous, gin saw sharpeners. (1-4, 32)

63. Decorticating
> 19. Textiles, fiber preparation: decorticating and depulping devices. (5-34)

VETERINARY MEDICINE

64. Animal Medicines, Dips, Sprays, Dental and Surgical Instruments
> 32. Dentistry: veterinary dental instruments. (47)
> 128. Surgery: veterinary surgical instruments. (14, 19, 324, 223, 336)
> 167. Medicines, poisons, and cosmetics: dips and sprays, animal poisons, veterinary medicines, hog cholera sera. (36, 46, 53-53.2, 80)

HUNTING AND TRAPPING

65. Traps: Self and Ever Set
> 43. Fishing, trapping, and vermin destroying: self- and ever-set traps including nonreturn entrance, sinking compartment, tilting or rotating platform (64-72)

66. Traps: Impaling or Smiting
    43. Fishing, trapping, and vermin destroying: traps with a striker movement. (77-83.5)

67. Traps: Jaw
    43. Fishing, trapping, and vermin destroying: traps with a jaw movement, triggering mechanisms, setting attachments. (88-97)

68. Traps: Miscellaneous
    43. Fishing, trapping, and vermin destroying: other traps including self reset, explosive, choking or squeezing. (73-76, 84-87)

69. Total Traps (includes time series 65-68)

CONSTRUCTION – GENERAL

70. Excavating: Ditchers
    37. Excavating: ditchers including screw, endless bucket, wheel excavator, plow, shovel or scoop. (80-103)

71. Excavating: Scoops Excluding Wheeled
    37. Excavating: scoops including fork or rake type, sledded, cable operated, handled, digging edge. (118, 120-123, 135-142)

72. Excavating: Scoops Wheeled
    37. Excavating: two- and four-wheeled scoops, plural rear gate, and other types. (124-134)

73. Excavating: Scrapers
    37. Excavating: scrapers including ditch fillers, scrapers with harrow or roller, four and two wheeled. Scrapers with V shaped, parallel, diagonal, or transverse blades. (143-181)

74. Excavating: Miscellaneous
    37. Excavating: stump and stone removers, scraper combined with scoop or shovel, orange peel and clamshell buckets, rotary and endless diggers, mole plows, miscellaneous. (1, 2, 117.5, 182-193, 195)

75. Total Excavating (includes time series 70-74)

MASONRY AND CONCRETE STRUCTURES

76. Faced Walls
    72. Masonry and concrete structures: tile and monolithic faced walls. (17-28)

77. Block Walls
    72. Masonry and concrete structures: block walls including faced, solid, hollow, parallel spaced, fiber. (35-45)

78. Miscellaneous Walls
    72. Masonry and concrete structures: miscellaneous walls including block and plastic, wood and plastic, monolithic. (16, 29-33, 46-50)

79. Arches
>72. Masonry and concrete structures: arches including fireplace, plastic filled or metal reinforced girders, tile and/or concrete floor arches. Bridge arches excluded. (55, 58-63, 65-71)

80. Reinforcing Elements
>72. Masonry and concrete structures: reinforcing elements including studding, lathing, bars, joints, spacers, compounds for reinforcing. (109-122)

81. Miscellaneous Masonry and Concrete Structures
>25. Plastic block and earthenware apparatus: temporary means for casting concrete at site. (131.5, 131.6)
>72. Masonry and concrete structures: buildings, monuments, markers and guards, cellars, wells, tanks, poles and posts, smoke flues, stairs. Integral building elements and supports, columns, doors, sills and jambs, windows. Manholes, bonding and tying, plastering, waterproofing. Implements such as bricklaying and plastering machines, trowels and floats, miscellaneous. (.5-7.3, 10-15, 72-77, 82-85, 90-108, 123-138)

82. Total Masonry and Concrete Structures (includes time series 76-81)

CONSTRUCTION – GENERAL

83. Mortar Mixers, etc.
>125. Stone working: brick cleaning. (26)
>259. Agitating: mortar mixing processes, gravity and other types. Mixers combined with other devices such as driers, elevators, feeders, dischargers. Mixers with movable receptacle or stirrer. (145-179)
>263. Heating: processes for heating cement, lime, or gypsum. (53)

84. Portland Type Cements
>106. Compositions, coating or plastic: portland type cement including additives such as proteins, resins, wax, or filler. (89-99)

85. Other Type Cements
>106. Compositions, coating or plastic: aluminous, oxy salt type, calcium sulfate, slag, lime, and magnesia cements. (104-121)

86. Total General Construction (includes time series 75, 82-85)

BUILDING CONSTRUCTION

METALLIC BUILDING STRUCTURES

87. Buildings
>189. Metallic building structures: metallic buildings including aircraft type, bins, greenhouses, jails, portable buildings. (1-10)

88. Towers
>189. Metallic building structures: portable towers, skeleton towers including

tanks, windmills, derricks, etc. Brace adjustments, caps, and bases for skeleton towers. (11-21)

89. Poles and Posts
> 189. Metallic building structures: poles and posts including compound, supported, sectional, insulated, braced poles and posts, bases, and cross arms. (23-33)

90. Doors
> 189. Metallic building structures: sliding or swinging thermal control doors, sectional or panel doors. (46-53)

91. Windows
> 189. Metallic building structures: windows including weather proofing, windows with various movements, frames and sashes, removable windows. (64-78)

92. Miscellaneous
> 189. Metallic building structures: land anchors, grills, girders, columns, sheathing, metal stairs, shutters of various kinds, miscellaneous. (34-45, 54, 59-63, 82-92)

93. Total Metallic Building Structures (includes time series 87-92)

WOOD BUILDING STRUCTURES

94. Buildings
> 20. Wooden buildings: various types of wooden buildings including apartments, auditoriums, bleachers and grandstands, bins and silos, stores, storage. Building plans. (1-1.7)

95. Weatherboard and Flooring
> 20. Wooden buildings: weatherboarding, floors, slatted floor covering, moldings. (5-9, 74, 78-78.6)

96. Miscellaneous Structures and Components
> 20. Wooden buildings: service station type buildings, stair covers, wall construction, weather stripping. Detachable splices and joints, hollow wall filling, mosaics and inlaying, veneering. Sliding and swinging sash windows, windows of other types, sash construction, pane fastenings. Window cranes, shutters, door and window frames, doors, wooden columns, floors, miscellaneous. (.5, .8, 4, 6, 10-12, 15, 16, 18, 19, 35, 36, 38-40.5, 42-73, 75-77, 79, 89, 92.4-95, 97, 98, 101)

97. Total Wood Building Construction (includes time series 94-96)

98. Scaffolds and Scaffold Supports
> 248. Supports: scaffold supports. (235-238)
> 304. Scaffolds: scaffolds including self sustaining, building propped, suspended, platforms, scaffold parts, miscellaneous. (1-41)

99. Roofs: Slat, Shingle, and Tile
> 108. Roofs: slat and shingle roofs including laying same, tile roofs. (8-10)

100. Roofs: Other Building Roofs
> 108. Roofs: observatory domes, skylights. Composite, fabric, or metallic

roofs. Trusses, eaves and troughs, cleats and fasteners, etc. Miscellaneous. (1-4, 6-7, 11-33)

101. Total Building Construction (includes time series 87, 88, 90-92, and 97-100)

102. Filters I
   210. Liquid purification and separation: diverse distinct separators including filtering means of various kinds such as moving filters, liquid as a separating medium, trapping features, spaced filters. (295-318)

103. Filters II
   210. Liquid purification and separation: plural distinct separators including filters which are movable, have liquid agitation, are in series or in parallel, and other types. (323-347)

104. Filters III
   210. Liquid purification and separation: one hundred sixty-two subclasses of filters as distinct from separators. (348-510)

105. Total Filters (includes time series 102-104)

HIGHWAY AND STREET CONSTRUCTION

106. Bridges
   14. Bridges: various kinds of bridges including combination truss and arch, truss, girder, suspension, arch, floating, draw bridges. Gangways, bridge floors and coverings, piers, miscellaneous. (1-77)
   72. Masonry and concrete structures: bridges, bridge arches, bridge floors. (8, 56, 57, 64)

107. Road and Pavement Structure
   94. Roads and pavements: pavement structures of bituminous and hydraulic cement material, antislip surfaces, block or other preformed element pavements, pavement joints. (4-18, 47)

108. Road Type Graders
   37. Excavating: excavators of the road-grader type including transverse endless scraper or bucket, road-grader type plows. (108-114)

109. Roadway Snow Excavators
   37. Excavating: self-loading vehicles for snow. Snow excavators including rotary, automobile, conveyor, V-plow, diagonal blade, hand operated. (5, 41-53)

110. Miscellaneous Pavements
   94. Roads and pavements: composition pavements, pavement processes. Side or cross walks including light transmitting with lenses, lens mounts, concrete frames. Miscellaneous pavements and floors. (2, 3, 19-30)

111. Miscellaneous Roads
   25. Plastic block and earthenware apparatus: clay type road ballast processes. (158)
   72. Masonry and concrete structures: manholes and covers. (100)

94. Roads and pavements: traffic guides and street markers, curbs or gutters, drains, vault covers, miscellaneous roads. (1, 1.5, 31-38)
210. Liquid purification or separation: structural installation of grated inlet surface drain. (163-166)

112. Total Highway and Street Construction (includes time series 106-111)

HEAVY CONSTRUCTION EXCEPT HIGHWAY AND STREET

HYDRAULIC AND EARTH ENGINEERING

113. Watergates, Dams, and Levees
   61. Hydraulic and earth engineering: watergates of several types including collapsible, removable. Dams and levees, cofferdams. (22-34)

114. Miscellaneous Water Control
   61. Hydraulic and earth engineering: underground fluid storage, water control channels including methods of forming and preserving same. Canals, drainage, irrigation, flumes and culverts, intakes and spillways, power channels, fish ways. (.5-21)

115. Earth Control
   61. Hydraulic and earth engineering: solidifying or thawing earth; revetments, retaining walls, shafts, tunnels. (35-45)

116. Stable Structures in Shifting Media
   61. Hydraulic and earth engineering: floatable or marine floor supported structures such as drilling platforms, cribbing, wharves, foundations or piers, piles of different types. (46-62)

117. Pile Drivers
   61. Hydraulic and earth engineering: pile drivers of the swinging hammer, piston, or water-jet type. Caps, bands and followers, preparatory piles, monkeys. (73-80)

118. Other Apparatus
   61. Hydraulic and earth engineering: drydocks, marine ways, ship caissons, diving apparatus, pipe and cable laying, caissons, tunnels. (63-72, 81-85)

119. Total Hydraulic and Earth Engineering (includes time series 113-118)

SEWAGE

120. Sewage Treatment and Equipment
   4. Baths, closets, sinks, and spittoons: sewer ventilation. (219-221)
   15. Brushing, scrubbing, and general cleaning: sewer pipe and tube cleaning implements. (104.3)
   110. Furnaces: garbage and sewage furnaces of various types. (8-16)
   137. Fluid handling: fluid handling with liquid trap seals where the seal is in the liquid flow line. (247.11-247.51)
   204. Chemistry, electrical and wave energy: electrolysis processes for water sewage and other waste waters. (149-152)
   210. Liquid purification or separation: chemical treatment processes for liquids. (59-64)

BUILDING CONSTRUCTION

SPECIAL TRADES

121. Heating Systems
237. Heating systems: heating systems with automatic control. Ventilation of stoves, furnaces, and radiators. Heating with air, water, or steam. Heat radiators, miscellaneous. (1, 2, 7-12, 16-19, 47-79, 81)

122. Total Construction (includes time series 86, 105, 112, and 119-121)

BUILDING CONSTRUCTION MIXED WITH OTHER FIELDS

123. Wood Buildings and Other Wood Products
20. Wooden buildings: poles and posts, grain car doors, sliding car doors, car door construction. (21-34, 37, 99, 100)

RAILROADS

ROLLING STOCK

124. Locomotives: Steam
105. Railway rolling stock: steam locomotives including turbines, articulated boilers, boilers, superheaters, fireboxes, controls, etc. (37-48)

125. Locomotives: Electric
105. Railway rolling stock: electric locomotives including batteries, rotors, motor coolers, insulation, controls. (49-61)

126. Locomotives: Transmission of Electricity to Vehicles
191. Electricity, transmission to vehicles: transmission of electricity to vehicles including systems of distribution, drawbridge and transfer table, magnetic induction, vehicle in series, flexible extensions. Conductors including plate and sectional, conduit, third rail, trolley. Collectors of various kinds including many types of trolley, trolley retrievers, miscellaneous. (1-95)

127. Locomotives: Wheel or Axle Drive
105. Railway rolling stock: wheel or axle drive of the following kinds: axle box mounted transmission, fluid transmission, planetary, tandem, articulated radial drive, epicyclic drive wheels, belt gears, worm gears, belt gears and tighteners, pitman drives, pawl and ratchet, rack and pinion, clutches, torque arms, etc. (96-132.1)

128. Locomotives: Furnaces
110. Furances: chain progressive-fed furnace structure for locomotive, feeding air and steam to locomotive firebox and under grate, locomotive firebox, locomotive stoker type fuel feeders, locomotive smoke and gas return. (42, 50, 57, 61, 70, 76, 87, 105.5)

129. Locomotives: Miscellaneous
103. Pumps: scoop pumps. (82)

105. Railway rolling stock: auxiliary functions, turntables, rack rails, gripping drivers. Track pushers, driver pickup, bogie on car, generating electric locomotives. Explosive engines, pneumatic, pump motor and storage. Springs, traction regulators, inside drive boxes, equalizers, etc. (26-36, 62-85)
158. Liquid and gaseous fuel burners: locomotive type furnaces. (3)
198. Conveyors, power driven: locomotive stoker type conveyors. (15)
240. Illumination: locomotive headlight, number plate, and signal illuminators. Automatic locomotive light supports. (7.12, 7.15, 62.1)
299. Fluid sprinkling, spraying, and diffusing: railroad sprinklers, locomotive-cab squirts. (31-33, 82)
308. Machine elements, bearings, and guides: locomotive car journals. (43)

130. Total Locomotives (includes time series 124-129)

131. Passenger Cars: Trains
105. Railway rolling stock: streamline, articulated, nontelescoping, and one-track passage trains. Vestibule connections of various kinds. (1-25)

132. Passenger Cars: Sleeping
105. Railway rolling stock: special car bodies for sleeping, berths of several kinds, partitions, curtains and rods, ladders and steps, etc. (314-326)

133. Passenger Cars: Regular Passenger
105. Railway rolling stock: passenger car bodies of diverse types including rolling, combined or convertible open and closed, double deck. Entrance and exit controls, motorman's compartment, door and passenger placement, emergency exits, dust guards, storm fronts, hand straps, etc. (329-354)

134. Passenger Cars: Miscellaneous
4. Baths, closets, sinks, and spittoons: railway-train closets. (8)
29. Metal working: railway chair making. (16)
105. Railway rolling stock: special car bodies, dining cars, merchandizing cars, expansible car bodies, armored and protected cars. Shock-absorbing devices, automatic door locks, passenger car framing and structure. (238, 327, 328, 392.5-395, 397-403)
155. Chairs and seats: convertible seats and berths, reclining seats. (6, 8)

135. Total Passenger Cars (includes time series 131-134)

136. Freight Cars: Dumping
105. Railway rolling stock: dump car bodies including gondolas, hoppers, inclined bottoms, tilting bodies, etc. Doors and door actuators of various kinds, door locks, dump controls. (239-313)

137. Freight Cars: Ice and Refrigerator
62. Refrigeration: ice-cooled cars, cars cooled by liquefied gas, cars cooled by compressor-condenser-expander circuits. (15-24, 25, 117-117.45)

138. Freight Cars: General Freight
105. Railway rolling stock: freight car bodies of many kinds including vacuum walls, tank cars, knockdown bodies, mine bodies, automobile bodies, removable units, etc. Load braces, convertible decks, buffers, partitions, removable wall sections, etc. Freight car framing and structure. (355-392, 404-412)

139. Freight Cars: Stock
    119. Animal husbandry: railway cars for livestock. (7-14)

140. Total Freight Cars (includes time series 136-139)

141. General: Wheels and Axles
    295. Railway wheels and axles: various railway wheels, axles excluding mine
    car axles. Wheel attaching devices, loose wheels. (1-40, 43-50)

142. General: Draft Appliances
    213. Railway draft appliances: combined coupler and electric connector,
    locomotive and tender draft appliances. Draft appliances which are
    cushioned by various means, continuous or radially movable draft
    appliances. Couplings of many kinds (one hundred thirty-nine sub-
    classes), bumpers or buffers, side track push rods, miscellaneous.
    (1-224)

143. General: Track Sanders
    291. Track sanders: track sanding devices including wheel slip control, fluid
    delivery, control systems and alarms. Jet-in hopper, heaters, power-
    actuated sanders, sand feeders and hoppers, sand delivery pipe, sand
    screens, miscellaneous. (1-48)

144. General: Brakes
    188. Brakes: train, wheel and rail, track, and rail brakes for railway vehicles.
    Connected trucks, maximum-traction type, four-wheel opposing or
    spreading brakes, clasp, top shoes, disk on axle, positive lock, one way,
    and on track brakes. Brake operators for railway vehicles including
    speed responsive, drawbar, train, strain release, and fluid pressure.
    Position adjusters for railway vehicle-body movement and railway car
    slack. Locomotive type shoe fasteners. (33-41, 46-54, 56-63, 124-127,
    153, 193, 197-203, 235)
    303. Fluid-pressure brake and analogous systems: multiple fluid-receiving
    points with sectional train and/or multiple brake valves. Automatic
    systems with train rear end first, motorman's valves, engine and train
    multiple motors. (7, 8, 47, 50, 53)

145. General: Bogie Trucks
    105. Railway rolling stock: bogie trucks including eight wheel, maximum
    traction, bolsters and bolster connections, equalizers, six wheel, body
    connections, transoms, etc. (182-208.2)

146. General: Other Trucks
    105. Railway rolling stock: all railway trucks except bogie trucks. (157-181,
    209-230)

147. General: Car Doors
    20. Wooden buildings: wooden car doors and car door construction. (21-37)

148. General: Miscellaneous
    78. Metal forging and welding: forged dies for railway-car irons, axles and
    axle boxes, drawbars and couplings, railway-track irons. (73-76)
    98. Ventilation: locomotive-cab dust guards and ventilation. Ventilation
    of railway cars, railway tunnels, subways. Windows for locomotive and
    railway car. (3-28, 49, 91-93)

105. Railway rolling stock: trackman's-car drive including hand levers and cranks, pedals, treadles, etc. Motor placement. Tenders including tanks, coal feeders. Underframes, draft still framing, end sills for cars, floors, linings, antileak joints, platforms, steps, guards, other devices and accessories. (86-95, 133-140, 231-237, 396, 413-462)

224. Package and article carriers: vehicle attached package carrier for railway car. (29.5)

228. Ladders: ladders attached to railway cars. (49)

267. Spring devices: springs for railway cars including coil springs. (3, 4)

268. Closure operation: railway car doors, gates, freight car doors. (17, 29, 43-45)

149. Total General Rolling Stock (includes time series 141-148)

150. Total Rolling Stock (includes time series 130, 135, 140, and 149)

TRACK

151. Ties and Tie Plates

238. Railways, surface track: tie arrangements, ties, tie forms, rods, cross section, corrugated, nonmetallic ties, spacers, anchor lugs and ribs, insulation, end closures. Tie plates of various kinds. (27-108, 287-309)

152. Rails, Rail Seats, etc.

238. Railways, surface track: rails, rail joints, and rail seats. (122-286)

153. Fastenings

238. Railways, surface track: rail fastenings of various kinds including anchors, braces, clamps, spikes, etc. (310-378)

154. Miscellaneous

51. Abrading: rail grinders. (178)

104. Railways: track layers including distributers, track raisers, tie replacers, tampers, spike drivers, etc. (2-17)

238. Railways, surface track: roadbed, portable track, electrical connections, track curves, guard rails, stringers, laterally assembled longitudinal lock scarf, foot guards, noise deadening, miscellaneous. (1, 2, 6-12, 14.05-28, 238, 379-382)

254. Pushing and pulling implements: car-pusher type implements, rail or tie shifters. (35-38, 43, 44)

155. Total Track (includes time series 151-154)

SWITCHES AND SIGNALS

156. Train Dispatching

246. Railway switches and signals: train dispatching by means of central signal control, train-order cab signal or train control, train telegraphy or telephony, station block or train-order signals. (2-18)

157. Automatic Block

246. Railway switches and signals: automatic block signals which are electric, fluid pressure, electromechanical, mechanical, or some combination. (27-103)

158. Cab Signal or Train Control
    246. Railway switches and signals: controls and signals for train parting, train defect, derailment, switch signals, speed control systems, recording devices, train mechanism, track trips, etc. (167-207)

159. Interlocking Switch and Signal
    246. Railway switches and signals: interlocking switch and signal which is electrically, fluid-pressure, or manually actuated. Approach locks, derails, indicators, etc. (131-163)

160. Electric Actuation, Switch and Signal
    246. Railway switches and signals: control circuits, motor systems, switch signals, car-actuated generators and circuit controllers. Switch- or signal-actuated controllers, trolley-completed circuits, car-wheel-completed circuits, relays. (218-256)

161. Automatic Signals and Gates
    246. Railway switches and signals: vehicle-energy-actuated automatic signals and gates for highway crossing, track mechanism. (292-313)

162. Automatic Switches
    246. Railway switches and signals: vehicle-energy-actuated automatic switches of various kinds. (314-357)

163. Switches
    246. Railway switches and signals: many kinds of railway switches and switch parts. (415-453)

164. Miscellaneous
    246. Railway switches and signals: staff and tablet systems, semiautomatic and manual block-signal systems, automatic time indication, protection for grade crossing, drawbridge and roadway defect signals. Train-position indication, electric automatic highway signals, mine doors and gates signals. Slotting and control, pilot or signal cars, car-displayed crossing signals, passenger station signals, torpedo mechanisms. Fluid and mechanical motor actuation for signals, switches, and gates. Point throwers, vehicle-energy-actuated devices of several kinds including automatic switch stands, switch locks, and train trips. Safety sidings, continuous-rail crossings, switch-connected frogs, switch stands, crossings, frogs and mates, signals, manual actuation devices, miscellaneous. (1, 19-26, 104-130, 164-166, 208-217, 257-291, 358-414, 454-489)

165. Total Switches and Signals (includes time series 156-164)

OTHER

166. Railway Mail Delivery
    258. Railway mail delivery: various devices for transmitting and receiving mail, particularly from or to trains in motion. (1, 2-26)

167. Vehicle Loading and Unloading
    214. Material or article handling: railway vehicle loading or unloading with external cooperating means (not all types). (39-44, 46.22, 46.24, 46.28, 46.3, 46.32, 52-64.2)

168. Railway Snow Excavators
    37. Excavating: snow excavators specialized to railroad use including explosive, rotary, scoop, or plow types. Also railway graders. (17-40, 104-107)
    171. Unearthing plants or buried objects: railroad ballast removal and assorting or separating. (16)

169. Miscellaneous
    10. Bolt, nail, nut, rivet, and screw making: devices, processes, and dies for making spikes. (56-63)
    15. Brushing, scrubbing, and general cleaning: railway car cleaners and rail sweepers. (53-55)
    39. Gates: mechanically operated automatic return track guard gates. (19-21)
    56. Harvesters: cutting devices to be used along roadbeds. (230-232)
    104. Railways: safety ladder and passenger transfer with moving train. Car yards, terminals, and stations. Truck changers, vehicle battery replacer, turntables, transfer tables, locomotive-shed fixtures, selective delivery. Cable and rigid railways, suspended railways, trolley transfer and trolley rails, elevators, posts and towers. Electric, hydraulic, pneumatic, pusher, and tilting track car-propulsion systems. Derailment guards, car stops, car-attached derailer, car replacer, hose bridges, track cleaners, miscellaneous. (1, 18-21, 26-52, 87-111, 122-132, 147-164, 242-280)
    116. Signals and indicators: station indicators, car and train markers, pneumatic train pipe. (29, 30, 55)
    256. Fences: track guard fences. (14-18)

170. Total Railways (includes time series 150, 155, and 165-169)

SUGAR REFINING

171. Sugar Refining
    100. Presses: concurrent pressing and conveying devices which are roll type with plural stage or pass and roll adjustment. (161-171)
    127. Sugar, starch, and carbohydrates: apparatus for hydrolyzing and treating sacchariferous material. Sugar products. Processes for hydrolysis of carbohydrates and for sugar manufacture and refining. (1-22, 30, 34-64)
    130. Threshing: cane strippers. (31)
    195. Chemistry, fermentation: fermentative liberation or purification of sugar. (11)
    204. Chemistry, electrical and wave energy: treatment of sugar by electrolysis. (138)
    210. Liquid purification or separation: separation processes with destruction of cake or separation of solid component. (67)
    257. Heat exchange: horizontal rotary tube tank agitators, conveyers with heat exchange. (79, 80)

TEXTILES

172. Cleaning and Treating Fibers
     8. Bleaching and dyeing; fluid treatment and chemical modification of textiles and fibers: cleaning or laundering including removing formation impurities from artificial fibers, degumming or desizing, scouring, degreasing or debowking, carbonizing, reclaiming waste. Manipulative fluid treatment of pulp or fibers in bulk. (137-141, 156)
    19. Textiles, fiber preparation: working fibers by fluid or special treatment, feeding and cleaning. (65-79)
   204. Chemistry, electrical and wave energy: electrolysis of organic fibrous materials. (132, 133)

173. Picking, Carding, and Combing
    19. Textiles, fiber preparation: picking devices which are nonrotary, disintegrating, but removing, or have beaters, gripping feed, or rotors. Carding and combing devices of several types. (80-129)

174. Drawing
    19. Textiles, fiber preparation: drawing devices for fibers. (130-143.5)

175. Silver Related
    19. Textiles, fiber preparation: assembling in fiber preparation including sliver or web forming, etc. Stopping including electrical and sliver. (144-153, 155-161, 163-169)

176. Total Preparatory Spinning (includes time series 172-175)

177. Spinning
    57. Textiles, spinning, twisting, and twining: many kinds of spinning apparatus including covering or wrapping devices, drawing mule type spinning, unitary multiple twist devices, receiving and false twist type. Stopping, starting, and driving spinning apparatus. Apparatus elements including drag, nippers, fliers, rings and travelers, caps, delivering and receiving elements, rails and rail guides, dies and mandrels. Strand guiding or guarding apparatus. Strand structure and spinning processes. Spinning for nontextile uses excluded. (1-3.5, 6-19, 24-30, 34-139, 143, 149-156, 163-165, 167)

178. Winding
   242. Winding and reeling: spoolers, bobbin and cop winding excluding sewing-machine shuttles and wire devices. Reeling and unreeling including slivers and rovings. Bobbins and spools of various kinds, skein holders. Bobbin supporters and holders, spool holders. Take-ups, cone wind special packages and bobbins, cops and spools special packages. (16-19, 26-46.8, 54, 54.4, 119-127, 130-140, 161, 160)

179. Miscellaneous Spinning
    8. Bleaching and dyeing; fluid treatment and chemical modification of textiles and fibers: manipulative fluid treatment of yarn in wound packages, kier treatment. (154-155.2, 157)
    28. Textiles: strand packaging and thread finishing apparatus. Processes for dyeing or coating strands, filaments, or fibers. Strand structures, filaments, or fibers as textile products. (21, 57-71.4, 75, 81, 82)
    73. Measuring and testing: filament testing. (160)
    101. Printing: multicolor printing of yarn. (172)
    206. Special receptacles and packages: thread packages. (64)

180. Total Spinning and Winding (includes time series 177-179)

WEAVING

181. Special Type Looms
    139. Textiles, weaving: special type looms including progressive shedding, open-back and supplemental open-back shed, multiple shed (excluding narrow ware), irregular warp feed, pushed shed pocket, hand looms. (11-21, 24-34)

182. Warp: Beaming
    28. Textiles: warp preparing apparatus including chain manipulation, dressing, pattern setting, reeling, beaming, leasing, loom replenishing, stopping, combs and guides, singeing, clearing. Processes for preparing warps including those with coating, dyeing, or fluid treatment. (22-55.3, 72.5, 72.6)

183. Warp: Feeding
    139. Textiles, weaving: warp manipulation devices for feeding. (97-115)

184. Warp: Other
    139. Textiles, weaving: warp manipulation including fluid treatment, pile, traversing, shedding. Vibrating griff and rotating actuator dobby warp manipulation. (35-65, 67-96)

185. Total Warp (includes time series 182-184)

186. Weft: Shuttle Motions (excluding narrow ware)
    139. Textiles, weaving: shuttle motions including magnetic motions, positive end engagement, fly motions. (133, 134, 141-170)

187. Weft: Shuttles
    139. Textiles, weaving: shuttles of various types including supported cop, roller bearing, detecting, thread-carrier supports. Excluded are bow type shuttles. (196-198, 202-223)

188. Weft: Replenishing
    139. Textiles, weaving: many types of replenishing devices including bobbin changing, thread control, feeler mechanisms, etc. (224-289)

189. Weft: Miscellaneous
    139. Textiles, weaving: weft manipulation including pile, special length, stationary supply, separate wefts, inactive-weft restrainers, box change motions, shuttle boxes, lays or beat-ups, tensions, selvage-loop retainers. (116-132, 170.3-195)

190. Total Weft (excluding narrow ware) (includes time series 186-189)

191. Loom Stopping
    139. Textiles, weaving: loom stopping devices of various kinds including shuttle position and thin-place detectors. Warp stopping excluding nonarrestable vibrator but including arrestable vibrator and weft stopping. (336-358, 360-379)

192. Fabric Manipulation
    139. Textiles, weaving: fabric manipulation devices including temples, selvage trimmers, take-ups. (291-316)

193. Miscellaneous Weaving
    28. Textiles: tuft or tassel making, heddle making, needling apparatus. Thread frames, fabric ravelers, bobbin strippers. Processes including needling and those with incorporation of plasticizable material, with coating and dyeing, with fluid treatment, and with stitching. Needled or felted and coated products, impregnated or dyed products. (1-4, 15, 17-20, 72, 72.2, 73, 74, 76-80)

194. Total Weaving (includes time series 181, 185, 190-193)

195. Cloth Finishing
    26. Textiles, cloth finishing: cloth finishing methods and devices including singeing, cutting, shrinking, beating, rubbing, napping, stretching or spreading and/or working, ornamental finishing, inspecting, pile fabrics, miscellaneous. (1-37, 51-70)
    73. Measuring and testing: testing sheet or woven fabric or fiber. (159)
    223. Apparel apparatus: fabric spotting devices. (45)

196. Narrow Fabrics: Weaving, etc.
    87. Textiles, braiding, netting, and lace making: processes and products including elastic goods, intertwisted strands, material incorporated in diverse ways (excluding tubular fabric with core), braided lace and braided variable form, knotted mesh. Apparatus with pattern mechanism, apparatus controls. Other types of apparatus including twisted strand type, incorporation of diverse material, braiding, tatting, knotted mesh, shuttles, miscellaneous. (2-5, 7, 10-22, 24-62)
    139. Textiles, weaving: narrow ware looms, bow shuttles, narrow ware shuttle motions, separable fabrics, elastic materials. (22, 23, 135-140, 199, 407, 421-423)

197. Narrow Fabrics: Miscellaneous Products and Processes
    1. Nailing, stapling, and clip clenching: belt-hook inserters. (49.4)
    2. Apparel: hat bands, torso or limb encircling garment supports and retainers. Belt, strap or strip constructions. (179, 311-322, 338-340)
    24. Buckles, buttons, clasps, etc.: belt fasteners. (31-39)
    26. Textiles, cloth finishing: venetian blind tapes. (11.4)
    57. Textiles, spinning, twisting, and twining: endless band strand structure, elastic strand making processes. (141, 168)
    154. Laminated fabric and analogous manufactures: belt making, belt type fabrics, ribbon, strip, or strand type fabrics. (3, 4, 52.1-52.4, 53.6)
    206. Special receptacles and packages: packages for ribbons, braids, and trimmings. (51-55)

KNITTING

198. Feeding
  66. Textiles, knitting: various feeding devices. (125-146)

199. General Machines
  66. Textiles, knitting: reknitting, darning, looper pin and hook. United-needle knitting and independent needles. Straight independent-needle machines, straight united-needle machines. Needle incorporating elements, needle beds, needles, fabric manipulation devices. Pattern mechanisms, stopping devices, cleaning attachments. (1-6, 60-78, 82-124, 147-168)

200. Products, excluding hosiery
  2. Apparel: bathing suits, sweaters. (67, 90)
  66. Textiles, knitting: all knitted fabrics or articles except hosiery. (169-176, 189-202)

201. Seamless Hosiery Machines
  66. Textiles, knitting: circular independent-needle machines, circular united-needle machines. (7-59, 79-81)

202. Stocking Pressing and Molding
  223. Apparel apparatus: stocking pressing or molding, stocking forms. (60, 75-77)

203. Hosiery
  66. Textiles, knitting: hosiery fabrics or articles. (178-188)

204. Total Knitting (includes time series 198-203)

DYEING AND FINISHING

205. Azo Dyes
  8. Bleaching and dyeing; fluid treatment and chemical modification of textiles and fibers: azo dyeing processes and compositions. (41-51)

206. Printing
  8. Bleaching and dyeing; fluid treatment and chemical modification of textiles and fibers: textile printing processes and compositions. (62-72)

207. Bleaching
  8. Bleaching and Dyeing; fluid treatment and chemical modification of textiles and fibers: bleaching including color stripping or subduing, wave energy, pulp bleaching, chemical. (101-111)

208. Miscellaneous
  8. Bleaching and dyeing; fluid treatment and chemical modification of textiles and fibers: dyeing processes and compositions including wave energy, transfer dyeing, effect coloring, combined processes, mixed textile materials, mordant dyeing, oxidation dyes, vat or sulfur dyes, anthraquinone dyes, metallic azo dyes, inorganic and natural dyes, cellulose and artificial fibers, improving fastness, miscellaneous compositions and methods of preparing same. Weighting or mordanting, improving felting, ornamental effects, chemical modification of textiles and

fibers, manipulative fluid treatment of textiles, etc. (1-2.5, 14-42, 52, 53, 54.2-61, 73-94, 95-100, 112-134, 147-150, 151, 151.1, 152, 158, 159)

154. Laminated fabric and analogous manufactures: fabric uniting and parchmentizing or coating. (34-37)

252. Compositions: organic or ether group textile treating compositions. (8.6-8.9)

209. Total Dyeing and Finishing (includes time series 205-208)

OTHER

210. Carpet and Rug Weaving
  2. Apparel: miscellaneous trimming stock. (278)
  28. Textiles: needling apparatus, carpet-rag loopers, needling processes. (4, 16, 72.2)
  112. Sewing machines: carpet and rug sewing machines, machines for preparing looped fabrics, embroidering machines for turfing. (7-9, 26, 79, 79.5)
  139. Textiles, weaving: tuft piling around warp and with portable supply, tufted fabrics. (2-10, 399-401)

211. Linoleum Making
  117. Coating; processes and miscellaneous products: felted or loose fibrous material base coated. (140)
  154. Laminated fabric and analogous manufactures: linoleum making including inlaid and inlaid processes, floor fabrics. (20-26, 49)

HATS AND CAPS

212. Hat Making
  112. Sewing machines: hat sewing machines, hat sewing methods and seams. (12-15, 263)
  223. Apparel apparatus: hat making apparatus. (7-26)

213. Hats
  2. Apparel: hats including shade, brim bindings, bands, frames, attachments, materials and processes. (175-194)

214. Caps
  2. Apparel: caps including women's wear, adjustable size, attachments, materials. (195-201)

215. Hat Fasteners
  132. Toilet: hat fasteners of various kinds (attachments to head or body). (57-72)
  140. Wireworking: making hat wires. (77)

216. Total Hats and Caps (includes time series 212-215)

OTHER

217. Felting
  28. Textiles: apparatus for felting and felting processes. (5-14, 72.3)

218. Cordage and Twine Winding and Reeling
    242. Winding and reeling: cordage winding and reeling, twine holders. (47-53, 141-146)

219. Total Textiles (includes time series 176, 180, 194-197, 204, 209-211, and 216-218)

TEXTILES MIXED WITH OTHER FIELDS, AND TEXTILE RELATED

220. Coating Processes and Products: Textiles, etc.
    117. Coating; processes and miscellaneous products: coating textile, leather, or paper-like base with surface deformations, or removing portions of coating. Coating textiles with printing. Coating textiles with fibers or particular material. Stripping, bordering, or edging textiles. Superposed different coatings on textiles. Particular base or coating including preserving textiles (including mothproofing), textile lubrication, cellulose or derivative base where base is regenerated cellulose, cellulose ether or ester. (11, 15, 28, 44, 76, 80, 83, 86, 90, 138.5, 139.5, 140, 143-146)

221. Carpet Fasteners and Stretchers
    16. Miscellaneous hardware: carpet fasteners. (4-17)
    45. Furniture: carpet stretchers. (89)
    254. Pushing and pulling implements: carpet stretcher type implements. (57-63)

222. Felt Roofs
    108. Roofs: fabric type (felt) roofs. (7)

223. Fabric Winding
    242. Winding and reeling: various devices and associated elements for reeling and unreeling fabrics. (55-76)

TEXTILES, CLOTHING, AND OTHER FINISHED TEXTILE PRODUCTS, MIXED WITH HOUSEHOLD AND COMMERCIAL LAUNDRY

224. Ironing or Smoothing: Two-Platen Presser
    38. Textiles, ironing or smoothing: platen presser or smoothing machine having two platens. (25-43)

225. Ironing or Smoothing: Roller Presser
    38. Textiles, ironing or smoothing: roller type presser or smoothing machine. (44-62)

226. Ironing or Smoothing: Flatirons
    38. Textiles, ironing or smoothing: flatirons of various kinds including combinations with other types of pressers and presser attachments. Flatiron elements and attachments. (74-98)

227. Ironing or Smoothing: Ironing Tables
    38. Textiles, ironing or smoothing: ironing tables combined with table,

with rack, with iron support, with clamp or stretcher, with shaper, or with fabric support. Plural or single pressing surfaces, covers or cover securing means. (103-113, 135-140)

228. Ironing or Smoothing: Ironing Table Supports
    38. Textiles, ironing or smoothing: various kinds of supports or legs for ironing tables. (114-134)

229. Ironing or Smoothing: Miscellaneous
    38. Textiles, ironing or smoothing: miscellaneous smoothing machines and elements. Smoothing and stretching devices, platen presses, wrapping devices. Stationary nonplanar pressing surface, pressing rollers, stretchers. Ironing accessories, pressing or smoothing processes. (1-16, 63-73, 99-102, 141-144)

230. Total Ironing or Smoothing (includes time series 224-229)

231. Forming, Pressing, Molding, and Stretching
    45. Furniture: fabric-stretching frames including curtain dryers, quilting frames, etc. (24)
    223. Apparel apparatus: ironing devices for hat making. Apparatus for forming, pressing, stretchings, and molding collars, cuffs, neckbands, corsets, dress shields, stocking, pants, ties, etc. Forms used in above apparatus. (21, 52-84)

232. Laundry and Other Fluid Treatment: Washboards
    68. Textiles, fluid treating apparatus: washboards including brandboards, soap holders, soap supply. Splash guards and breast boards, rubbing surfaces of various kinds. (223-231)

233. Laundry and Other Fluid Treatment: Washing Machines Combined with Other Operations
    68. Textiles, fluid treating apparatus: washing machines combined with scrub board, tank heater, soap supply, solvent recovery, or fluid extractor such as squeezer or centrifugal extractor. Washing machines with combined operations such as tumbling, scrubbing, squeezing, impulsing, dragging, liquid flowing, liquid applying. (13-26, 28-62)

234. Laundry and Other Fluid Treatment: Squeezing
    68. Textiles, fluid treating apparatus: squeezing apparatus including squeezer and textile cover, deformable receptacle, roll type, chasers, movable squeezer and bed, nonrotary squeezers. Squeezer mountings and roll strippers. (94-130)

235. Laundry and Other Fluid Treatment: Miscellaneous Fluid Treatment
    68. Textiles, fluid treating apparatus: waste reclaiming and carbonizing apparatus, miscellaneous fluid treatment machines. Rotary scrubbing machines, tumbling and liquid flowing machines. Movable carrier in vat, fixed liquid receptacle with liquid pump, liquid applying. Steamers, scrubbers, pounders, miscellaneous. (1-12, 27-30, 84-93, 131-222, 232, 233)

236. Wringers I
    68. Textiles, fluid treating apparatus: wringer and wringer supports combined with wash bench, wash tub, or wash boiler. Flexible diaphragm

squeezers, twisters. Rollers interconnected as functional units. Guards, guides, feeds, gears, mountings, etc. for roller type wringers. (235-243, 249-255, 264-276)

237. Wringers II
68. Textiles, fluid treating apparatus: pressure applying or release mechanisms for roller type wringers. (256-263)

238. Total Laundry and Fluid Treatment (includes time series 232-237)

LUMBER AND WOOD PRODUCTS

GENERAL WOODWORKING

239. Woodsawing Machines: Reciprocating Saw
143. Woodsawing: reciprocating saw machines including drag, scroll, special cut, piston connected, vibrated saw. Adjustable arm and roller feed for reciprocating saw. (60-84)

240. Woodsawing Machines: Band Saw
143. Woodsawing: band saw machines excluding centered log machines but including horizontal or inclined saw, multiple or retarded idlers, multiple saw, frames, carriages, feeders, tension regulators, pulleys, adjustments, etc. (17, 19-31)

241. Woodsawing Machines: Circular Saw
143. Woodsawing: circular saw machines excluding angular centered log machines but including pile cutting, adjustable saw, drop saw, portable or rim-driven saw, swinging or traveling saw. Various feeds, carriages, and work supports. (33-38, 40-59)

242. Woodsawing Machines: Sawmill Carriages, Setworks, and Dogs
143. Woodsawing: friction- or motor-fed carriages, offsetting carriages. Automatic, power-operated, wedge, or other kind of sawmill setworks. Lever and cam, gear, rack, and/or pawl sawmill dogs. Screw type sawmill dogs. (105-131)

243. Woodsawing Machines: Miscellaneous Machines
143. Woodsawing: combination, mitering, or arc-saw machines. Chain-saw machines, miter boxes. (1, 6, 7, 16, 32, 86-90)

244. Total Woodsawing Machines (includes time series 239-243)

245. Hand Saws and Handles
145. Woodworking tools: handsaws including truss frame, U frame, attachments for hand saws. Various handles for hand saws. (31-35, 108-113)

246. Hand or Machine Saws; Saws
143. Woodsawing: saws including bent, chain, dished, expansion, gumming aperture, sectional, smoothing. (133-140)

247. Hand or Machine Saws: Saw Teeth, Teeth Fastenings, Guides, and Gauges
143. Woodsawing: crosscut, planer, reversible, and other types of saw teeth. Diverse types of saw teeth fastenings. Saw guides and saw table gauges. (141-154, 160-176)

248. Hand or Machine Saws: Miscellaneous
     37. Excavating: sawmill-carriage wheel guards. (194)
   143. Woodsawing: resawing and chain-saw machines. Saw bucks and saw tables. Saw hanging, sawing-machine appliances, saw guards, saw cleaners and oilers. (4, 5, 32, 91, 132, 155-159)

249. Total Hand *or* Machine Saws (includes time series 246-248)

250. Total Hand *and* Machine Saws (includes time series 244, 245, and 249)

GENERAL WOODWORKING MACHINES

251. Wood Turning: Circular Section
   142. Wood turning: circular section wood turning including many spindle lathes, spiral grooving, automatic spindle lathes, clamped work, cutters and cutter heads of various kinds. (4, 5, 17-46, 51)

252. Wood turning: Miscellaneous
   142. Wood turning: wood turning including miscellaneous, polygonal section, attachments and elements of wood turning machines. (1-3, 6-16, 47-50, 52-57)

253. Mortising, Tenoning, Dovetailing, and Matching
   144. Woodworking: tools and devices for mortising, dovetailing, matching, tenoning, and tenon turning. (67-91, 198-206)

254. Boring
   144. Woodworking: boring devices excluding brush, wheel hub, and wheel felly. Included are devices for special work and long work, swinging, portable, and multiple boring devices, hollow auger. (92, 93, 103-113)

255. Planing
   144. Woodworking: planing devices and machines including scrapers and bevelers, planers with rotary, stationary, or reciprocating cutter, endless cutters, etc. (114-132)

256. Shaping
   144. Woodworking: shaping devices excluding box trimming but including grooving, patterns, knives and cutters of diverse types, etc. (134, 136-154)

257. Shaving and Slicing
   144. Woodworking: shaving devices. Slicers including reslicers, strip cutting, arc cut, beveling, cylinder, fixed knife, rotary disk, stay log, feeding. (155-181)

258. Cutting
   144. Woodworking: rotary cutters of various kinds including elements of cutting devices. Cutter guards, cutter hoods and dust covers. Punching cutters. (196, 197, 218-241, 251, 252)

259. Bending
   144. Woodworking: wood bending including bending rollers and presses, hoop gauging, bending formers of diverse kinds, clamps, etc. (254-271)

260. Feed and Presser Mechanism
   144. Woodworking: feed and presser mechanisms including presser bars and chip breakers, blank feeders, rolls, miscellaneous. (242-250)

261. Machinery Clamps
   144. Woodworking: clamps for wood working including door supporting, rectangular framework, box joint, miter, bench, portable, etc. (289-293, 295-305)

262. Miscellaneous Machines
   144. Woodworking: some special work machines, combined machines for boring and sawing or turning and sawing. Miscellaneous single-operation machines. Gaining devices, riving devices, miter cutters, work guides, machine work clamps, workbenches and tool chests, bench dogs, woodworking processes. (1-4, 20-24, 32, 35, 48, 49, 182-184, 216, 217, 253, 278, 285-288, 306, 309)

263. Total General Woodworking Machines (includes time series 244 and 251-262)

WOODWORKING TOOLS

264. Planes
   145. Woodworking tools: hand-manipulated power planers. Bench planners including plane elements. (4-20)

265. Augers
   145. Woodworking tools: augers of diverse kinds including square hole cutters and countersinks among others. (116-124, 126-128)

266. Bit Frames and Stocks
   145. Woodworking tools: bit frames and bit stocks including straight, U-crank arm, ratchet, miscellaneous. (60.5, 66-74)

267. Handles
   145. Woodworking tools: handles for woodworking tools including magazine, hollow, cross bar, ratchet and pawl, ratchet clutch, shield attachments. (61-65, 75-78)

268. Miscellaneous
   145. Woodworking tools: axes, chisels, hammers, mallets, nail sets, screw drivers, spiral tool drivers, reamers, cutter in series with piercer, guides, miscellaneous. (1-3, 24-26, 29-30.5, 36, 46, 50-54, 114, 114.5, 125, 129, 130)

269. Total Woodworking Tools (includes time series 245 and 264-268)

SPECIAL MACHINES AND EQUIPMENT

270. Log Sawing Operations and Debarking
   143. Wood sawing: centered log band and circular saw. Log transfers, log turners and/or deck blocks. (18, 39, 92-104)
   144. Woodworking: osier peelers, rossing bark, lath holders. (207, 208, 288.5)

271. Shingle Making and Shingle Related
   33. Geometrical instruments: gauges for making shingles. (188)

143. Wood sawing: shingle making machines of several types. (8-15)
144. Woodworking: special work machines for shingles. Splitting and/or bundling devices. (13, 192-195)

272. Coopering
   1. Nailing, stapling, and clip clenching: nailing and stapling machines for baskets and barrels. (13.5, 13.6)
143. Wood sawing: hoop-pole machines, tubular saw machines. (2, 3, 85)
144. Woodworking: cork and bung presses. (284)
147. Coopering: machines for barrel making, for setting up, and for barrel compressing. Hoops, hoop drivers, and hoop machines. Crozing and chamfering tools and barrels. Jointing and shaping staves. Barrelhead making and heading machines. (1-46, 49)

273. Veneering
144. Woodworking: veneer lathes, glue applying and pressing apparatus, veneer presses. (209-215, 279, 281-283)
154. Laminated fabric and analogous manufactures: plywood making processes. (133)

274. Miscellaneous Machines
   1. Nailing, stapling, and clip clenching: nailing and stapling machines for baskets and barrels. (13.5, 13.6)
144. Woodworking: special work machines for chair-round tenoning and sawing, for conveyor flight, for spool, for comb-teeth cutting, for pin pointing and setting. Combined machines for riving and shaving. (8, 10, 14, 26, 30, 31, 40)
147. Coopering: basket nailing and/or forming. (47, 48)
217. Wooden receptacles: baskets including bottoms, closures, and handles. (122-125)

275. Total Special Machines (includes time series 270-274)

SPECIAL PRODUCTS AND MACHINES FOR MAKING SAME

276. Box Making: Crates
217. Wooden receptacles: crates including bicycle and fruit box crates. Other crates including ventilating, knockdown, cylindrical, wired slat, cushioned. (36-55)

277. Box Making: Special Cells in Boxes
217. Wooden receptacles: cells in boxes including bottle cells, pockets, strip cells, cushioned cells, etc. (18-35)

278. Box Making: Miscellaneous Boxes and Equipment for Manufacturing Same
   1. Nailing, stapling, and clip clenching: nailing and stapling machines for box making. (8.1-13)
144. Woodworking: special work machines for box blanks and for box hooping. Shaping devices for grooving. Box joint clamps. (7, 25, 135, 294)
145. Woodworking tools: box openers. (21)
217. Wooden receptacles: miscellaneous boxes, box parts, and box structures. (1-3, 5-17, 56-71, 127)

279. Total Box Making (includes time series 276-278)

280. Baskets and Basket Making
    1. Nailing, stapling, and clip clenching: nailing and stapling machines for baskets and barrels. (13.5, 13.6)
    47. Plant husbandry: fruit plants. (62)
    147. Coopering: basket nailing and/or forming. (47, 48)
    217. Wooden receptacles: fruit box crates; baskets including bottoms, closures, and handles. (40, 122-125)

281. Special Products: Weatherboarding, Flooring, Molding
    20. Wooden buildings: floors including composite, interlocking, joist bridging. Slatted floor coverings, moldings, weatherboarding. (5-9, 74, 78-78.6)

282. Special Products: Windows, Sliding or Swinging Sash
    20. Wooden buildings: diverse sliding and/or swinging sash windows. (42-53)

283. Special Products: Windows, Other
    20. Wooden buildings: other windows including show windows, condensation preventing windows, parallel pane windows. Window sashes and sash construction. Corner posts, mullions, window cranes, awnings. (40, 40.4, 40.5, 54-56.5, 57, 57.5)

284. Special Products: Door and Window Frames
    20. Wooden buildings: door and window frames and jambs. Doors including wickets, rotating and sliding doors. Door construction and door braces. (11, 12, 16, 18, 19, 35, 36, 38, 39)

285. Special Products: Lasts and Related Products
    12. Boot and shoe making: last structures and elements used for making boots and shoes. (133-141)
    223. Apparel apparatus: darning lasts. (100)

286. Special Products: Miscellaneous Products
    20. Wooden buildings: many kinds of building elements including stairs, panels and wainscoting, diverse shutters, thresholds, mantels, corner shields, compound lumber, splices and joints, wooden columns, poles and posts. (10, 15, 58-64, 73, 76, 91-92.7, 97-100)
    88. Optics: mirror and reflector frames and holders with support, including bureau and door type. (96, 97, 99, 100)
    138. Pipes and tubular conduits: wooden structure for pipes and tubular conduit. (79)
    144. Woodworking: combined special work machines for blind and sash cutting, for clothespins, for handles and pins, for various operations in wheel construction, and for window-stile-pocket cutting. Special work machines for hinge-seat making and for tray making. Boring devices for brushes and for wheel making. Slivering, splitting, and bundling devices. Cork and bung presses. (5, 6, 9, 11, 12, 15-19, 27, 33, 94-102, 185-192, 284)
    145. Woodworking tools: cue trimmers. (27)
    217. Wooden receptacles: tanks. (4)

287. Total Special Products (includes time series 281-286)

288. Wood Coating, Staining, Dyeing, Preserving
    8. Bleaching and dyeing; fluid treatment and chemical modification of textiles and fibers: dyeing compositions and processes for wood including stains. (6.5)
    21. Preserving, disinfecting, and sterilizing: wood treatment methods, wood treatment apparatus. (7, 62-73)
    117. Coating; processes and miscellaneous products: coatings for wood with preparatory treatment of base. Coating of wood by vapor, gas, mist, or smoke. Immersion of wood. Coating wood base with synthetic or natural resin, or with heavy metal or aluminum. (57-59, 108, 116, 117, 147-151)

289. Total Lumber and Wood Products (includes time series 249, 263, 269, 275, 279, 280, 287, and 288)

LUMBER AND WOOD PRODUCTS – RELATED

290. Wood Screws
    85. Driven, headed, and screw-threaded fastenings: diverse screws for use in fastening. (41-48)

291. Nails, Spikes, and Tacks
    85. Driven, headed, and screw-threaded fastenings: diverse nails, spikes, and tacks including among others horseshoe nails, glaziers' points, locking devices such as for rail flange and tread, sheet-metal fastenings, string nails, barbed, ribbed or spiral nails, nail heads and points, etc. (10-31)

PAPER AND PAPER PRODUCTS

BASIC PROCESSES

292. Preparing Pulp
    8. Bleaching and dyeing; fluid treatment and chemical modification of textiles and fibers: bleaching pulp, manipulative fluid treatment of pulp. (104-106, 156)
    92. Paper making and fiber liberation: stock treatment including purifying and defibering waste paper, by-product recovery, combined digestive and grinding processes, diverse digestive devices, etc. (1-19)
    241. Solid material comminution or disintegration: disintegrative processes for wood and similar natural fibrous vegetable material. (28)

293. Working Stuff
    92. Paper making and fiber liberation: stuff working including processes incorporating special materials, beating and refining engines, sand separators, strainers, stuff chests. (20-37)

294. Web Forming, Delivering, and Drying
    34. Drying and gas or vapor contact with solids: rotary drum or receptacle drying apparatus with external belt or felt dryer, with plural external gas or vapor circulation for contact with treated material, with plural

external belts or felts, with plural external heat-exchange fluid supply and/or removal, with treading, stripping, or guiding devices, with mounting and/or driving means, etc. (111, 114, 116-121, 124)

92. Paper making and fiber liberation: web forming including special work, cylinder and Fourdrinier machines, feed regulators. Couch, dandy, and press rolls and water-marking devices. Press felts, felt and wire cleaners, suction boxes. (38-53)

271. Sheet or web feeding or delivering: special article web feeding or delivering. (1)

295. Cutting and Punching
164. Cutting and punching sheets and bars: cutting machines with reciprocating cutter including those with automatic clamp, with separately operated clamp, with draw cut. Punching and/or pricking machines with punch selector. (51-54, 111, 115)

296. Finishing Paper
92. Paper making and fiber liberation: paper finishing including wrinkling, flexibility imparting, various calenders. (68-76)
117. Coating, processes and miscellaneous products: coating of paper base including parchmentized coating, coating with organic material. (152-158)

297. Total Basic Processes (includes time series 292-296)

SPECIAL PROCESSES AND PRODUCTS

298. Laminating
154. Laminated fabric and analogous manufactures: strand or filament laminating apparatus, also with means to apply intersecting or zigzag strands to web. Corrugating and indenting devices, structures, and processes. Fabric parchmentizing and uniting. Corrugated and indented fabrics. Paper lamina processes. (1.7, 1.76, 30-32, 33.05, 34, 55, 138)

299. Envelope Making
93. Paper manufactures: various types of envelope machines. (61-76)
271. Sheet or web feeding or delivering: web feeding for envelopes. (2)

300. Envelopes
229. Paper receptacles: diverse types of envelopes, envelope closures, envelope openers. (68-86)

301. Bag Making
93. Paper manufactures: various kinds of paper bag making machines, elements of such machines, printing attachments, bag making methods. (8-35)

302. Bags
229. Paper receptacles: paper bags including reinforced bags, bag closures, etc. (53-66)

303. Miscellaneous Receptacles
229. Paper receptacles: pressed, liquid proofed, and other miscellaneous paper receptacles. Paper wrappers including coin type, pocketed, bag, bottle, mailing sheets. (1.5, 2.5, 3.1, 3.5, 87-92)

304. Miscellaneous Packages
    206. Special receptacles and packages: display receptacles, excluding those with terraced or stepped shelves and sectional or multiple movable compartments. Special packages for various products including combination type packages, tobacco products, sewing supplies, surgical supplies, stationery, etc. (44-44.12, 45.12-45.34, 46-71)

305. Box Making
    93. Paper manufactures: machines for making many kinds of boxes, elements of such machines, mandrels and dies, etc. (36-60)

306. Boxes, excluding folded blank
    229. Paper receptacles: paper boxes including savings, slide boxes, collapsible boxes, box closures, handles, etc., but excluding folded blank boxes. (6-11, 14, 15, 41-52)

307. Boxes, Folded Blank
    229. Paper receptacles: various types of folded blank boxes including buckets, trays, tubes, wrappers, multiples, etc. (16-40)

308. Tube Making
    93. Paper manufactures: machines for making paper tubes including fuses, spiral or convolute wind tubes, etc. Tube making methods. (77-83, 94)

309. Tubes, Conduits, Bobbins, and Spools
    138. Pipes and tubular conduits: paper structure tubes and conduits. (78)
    229. Paper receptacles: cylindrical or conical, body or wall structure paper receptacle. End structure including crimped seam, separate fastener, pressed bottoms and tops. Barrels and cylindrical tubes. (4.5-5.8, 67, 93)
    242. Winding or reeling: paper, pulp, or leather bobbins and spools including cross-referenced patents for these subclasses. (119, 122)

310. Pulp Molding
    92. Paper making and fiber liberation: pulp molding including compressors, winders, centrifugal action, etc. (54-67)

311. Miscellaneous
    8. Bleaching and dyeing; fluid treatment and chemical modification of textiles and fibers: dyeing processes and compositions for paper. Chemical modification of paper. (7, 119)
    22. Metal founding: matrices for sterotype-casting apparatus. (5.5)
    40. Card, picture, and sign exhibiting: picture frames which are extensible, folding, or knockdown. Card or picture retainers and cover retainers for picture frames. Mats, mounts, and backs for picture frames. (155-159)
    93. Paper manufactures: paper fastenings, disk closures, machines for making paper tags, miscellaneous paper manufactures. (1-1.3, 87-92)
    154. Laminated fabric and analogous manufactures: matrix stock, transfers, paper lamina processes. (46, 46.5, 138)
    164. Cutting and punching sheets and bars: tearing devices. (84.5)
    215. Bottles and jars: disk stopper type closures. (51)
    229. Paper receptacles: postal cards or packets, coin cards. (92.8, 92.9)

312. Total Processes (includes time series 297-299, 301, 305, 308, and 310)

313. Total Products (includes time series 300, 302-304, 306, 307, and 309)

314. Total Paper (includes time series 311-313)

SYNTHETIC FIBERS

315. Carbon Chemistry: Cellulose and Derivatives
   260. Chemistry, carbon compounds: cellulose and derivatives including hetero-N-atom, esters, ethers, and alkali cellulose. (212-233)

316. Carbohydrate or Derivative Containing Cellulose or Derivative
   106. Compositions, coating or plastic: coating or plastic compositions containing carbohydrate or derivative; all cellulose or derivative subclasses including viscose, cuprammonium cellulose, regenerated cellulose, cellulose ether or ester, etc. (163-204)

317. Making and Treating Fibers and Filaments
   8. Bleaching and dyeing; fluid treatment and chemical modification of textiles and fibers: chemical modification of cellulose ether or ester fibers, saponifying. Swelling or plasticizing artificial fibers. (129-132)
   18. Plastics: molding devices for forming filaments. Processes for forming filaments, including cross-referenced patents. (8, 54)
   57. Textiles, spinning, twisting, and twining: strand structure of synthetic filaments and/or fibers. Processes for synthetic filaments and/or fibers. (140, 157)
   117. Coating, processes and miscellaneous products: coating regenerated cellulose, cellulose ether, or ester base. (144-146)

318. Stapilizing
   19. Textiles, fiber preparation: stapilizing fibers by various means. (.3-.64)

319. Total Synthetic Fibers (includes time series 315-318)

FERTILIZER

320. Plant Growth Regulators
   71. Chemistry, fertilizers: processes and compositions for regulation of plant growth with chemicals, including inorganic compounds and heterocyclic, carbocyclic, or acyclic organic compounds. (2.1-2.7)

321. Organic Fertilizers
   71. Chemistry, fertilizers: chemical fertilizer processes and products containing organic material from sewage, from garbage, from animal matter, from vegetation, from industrial waste, or from synthetic material. (11-30)

322. Inorganic Fertilizers
   71. Chemistry, fertilizers: chemical fertilizer processes and products using inorganic materials, including phosphorus and nitrogen containing compounds. (32-63)

323. Miscellaneous
    23. Chemistry: apparatus for manufacturing chemical fertilizer. (259.1-259.3)
    47. Plant husbandry: plant irrigators and/or fertilizers. (48.5)
    71. Chemistry, fertilizers: miscellaneous fertilizer processes and products including bacterial processes. (1, 3-10, 31, 64)

324. Total Fertilizer (includes time series 320-323)

PETROLEUM REFINING

325. Bubble Towers
    261. Gas and liquid contact apparatus: wet baffle contact devices including gas-flow and liquid-flow control, perforated and overflow baffles. (108-114)

326. Fractionation, etc.
    196. Mineral oils: extracting mineral oils with solvents including organic solvents, liquid sulfur dioxide, manipulative processes, apparatus, etc. (13-14.52)

327. Refining with Chemicals
    196. Mineral oils: refining mineral oils with chemicals including processes for removing sulfur, distillation or treatment of vapors with chemicals, thinning with solvents, acid and/or alkaline treatment, oxidizing or reducing agents, contacting processes, refining apparatus, etc. (23-46)

328. Distillation Vaporizing Apparatus
    196. Mineral oils: diverse distillation vaporizing apparatus, elements, special parts, attachments. (104-137)

329. Distillation with Cracking
    196. Mineral oils: various distillation vaporizing processes with cracking. (47-70)

330. Paraffin Wax — Treatment or Recovery
    196. Mineral oils: paraffin processes including those with chilling, with separation of paraffin from oil; separation of residual oil from paraffin, chemical treatment. (17-21)

330a. Distillation without Cracking
    196. Mineral oils: various distillation vaporizing processes without cracking. (71-92)

331. Other Distillation
    196. Mineral oils: vapor treatment processes, combined vaporizing and condensing apparatus, condensing apparatus. (93-103, 138-141)

332. Miscellaneous
    196. Mineral oils: miscellaneous processes and apparatus, dehydrating oil, asphalt treatment, compositions and products, oxidation, washing, sludge treatment, etc. (1-5, 22, 142-152)

260. Chemistry, carbon compounds: partial oxidation of nonaromatic hydrocarbons, alkylation or condensation of acyclic hydrocarbons. (451, 452, 683.4)

333. Total Petroleum Refining (includes time series 325-332)

BOOT AND SHOE MAKING – PRODUCTS

334. Boots and Shoes
   36. Boots, shoes, and leggings: boots and shoes including heated or ventilated shoes, snowshoes, overshoes, bathing, burial, or dancing shoes. Shoe fitting, orthopedic shoes, moccasins, sandals, rubber or felt and fabric shoes. (2.5-11.5)

335. Sole-Attaching Means
   36. Boots, shoes, and leggings: sole-attaching means for rubber, wood, and other types of soles. Various attachment methods and elements including welt, seams, cement, pegs, etc. (12-24)

336. Soles
   36. Boots, shoes, and leggings: diverse types of soles including cushion, laminated, sectional, rubber, wooden, etc. (25-33)

337. Heels
   36. Boots, shoes, and leggings: heels including cushion, rotary, metallic shell, detachable. (34-42)

338. Uppers
   36. Boots, shoes, and leggings: uppers including preparation for lasting, blanks, closures, linings, pulls, seams, stays and pipings, etc. (45-58)

339. Miscellaneous
   36. Boots, shoes, and leggings: boots or shoes and detachable leg covers, leggings and gaiters, interfitted sole and heel, insoles, counter stiffening and support, shanks, toe caps and tips, antislipping devices, wear-correcting attachments, protectors, miscellaneous, etc. (1, 1.5, 2, 24.5, 43, 44, 58.5-75)

340. Total Products (includes time series 334-339)

STONE AND CLAY PRODUCTS

BLOCKS, BRICKS, AND EARTHENWARE MANUFACTURING APPARATUS

341. Block Molding
   25. Plastic block and earthenware apparatus: block molding machines including flat tile, roofing tile, undercutting. (41-44)

342. Block Presses
   25. Plastic block and earthenware apparatus: block presses including portable mold, reciprocating mold, rotary mold, stationary mold, endless chain of molds, etc. (45-104)

343. Die Expressing
    25. Plastic block and earthenware apparatus: die expressing including pottery devices, detached blocks, screw or plunger ejector, dies, (11-20)

344. Cutters
    25. Plastic block and earthenware apparatus: plastic block and earthenware cutters excluding soap cutters. (105, 107-114)

345. Continuous Kilns
    25. Plastic block and earthenware apparatus: various types of continuous kilns. (134-139)

346. Other Kilns
    25. Plastic block and earthenware apparatus: diverse kilns and kiln elements not classified as continuous. (132, 133, 140-153)

347. Pipe Machines
    25. Plastic block and earthenware apparatus: machines and elements of machines for making earthenware pipe. (30-40)

348. Pipe Molds
    25. Plastic block and earthenware apparatus: earthenware pipe molds including expanding separable molds and mold cores. (126-128)

349. Pottery Machines, Dies, and Molds
    25. Plastic block and earthenware apparatus: pottery die expressing diverse pottery machines and presses, pottery molds. (13, 22-29, 129)

350. Miscellaneous
    25. Plastic block and earthenware apparatus: knob machines, playing-marble machines, roller forming machines. Molds including one part molds, block molds. Reinforcing and finishing processes, clay type processes including firing. (4, 5, 21, 118.5, 118, 119-123, 154, 156, 157)
    106. Compositions, coating or plastic: enamel and ways of applying same to stone, clay, glass, and metals. Silica-line lime mixtures. (48, 49, 120)
    117. Coating, processes and miscellaneous products: vitreous coating of siliceous or calcareous base (including cross-referenced patents). (125)
    138. Pipes and tubular conduits: excluding 66-67, 78, and 80-86.
    294. Handling, hand and hoist-line implements: brick carriers, including hoist-line frames. (62, 63)

351. Total Block, Brick, and Earthenware Manufacturing Apparatus (includes time series 341-350)

MISCELLANEOUS MATERIALS AND PRODUCTS

352. Glass Ceramic Composition
    106. Compositions, coating or plastic: ceramic glass coating or plastic composition including enamel, fibrous, slag, silica containing. (47-54)

353. Ceramic Composition
    106. Compositions, coating or plastic: ceramic coating or plastic composition including pore forming, carbide and silicon carbide containing, sulfur or clay containing. Ceramic fluxes. (39-41, 43, 44, 70-73, 313)

354. Refractory Clay Products
  25. Plastic block and earthenware apparatus: furnace wall or lining type processes, clay type processes. (155.5-157)
  75. Metallurgy: reactive furnace linings. (95)
  106. Compositions, coating or plastic: clay refractory compositions. (67, 68)
  263. Heating: checker bricks. (51)

355. Clay, Concrete, or Masonry Pipes and Conduits
  138. Pipes and tubular conduits: clay, concrete, or masonry pipe and tubular conduit structure including sectional blocks, plural duct, metal reinforced, composite. (80-86)

356. Concrete Products
  25. Plastic block and earthenware apparatus: molds for cistern, fence, tank and sarcophagi, wall. Processes for conditioning or handling material while forming concrete blocks. (124, 125, 130, 131, 155)
  61. Hydraulic and earth engineering: concrete piles and concrete sheet piling. (56, 57, 59)
  72. Masonry and concrete structures: vaults, cisterns, tanks, concrete arches, manholes and covers. (7, 9, 13, 14, 69-71, 100)
  238. Railways, surface track: concrete railway roadbeds, concrete stringers, concrete block pedestals. (5, 7, 25, 115-117)

357. Gypsum Related Products
  23. Chemistry: alkali earth metal sulfate compounds. (122)
  106. Compositions, coating or plastic: coating or plastic compositions containing alkali metal silicate with calcium sulfate, containing calcium sulfate as an inorganic settable ingredient including plaster of paris. (77, 109-116)
  154. Laminated fabric and analogous manufactures: apparatus and processes for making plaster board. (1.2, 1.25, 86-88)

358. Mineral Wood Related Products
  18. Plastics: liquid comminuting and solidifying apparatus with fluid blast or stream, with rotary projection means, processes for same. (2.5, 2.6, 47.2, 47.3)
  49. Glass: slag processes. (77.5)
  106. Compositions, coating or plastic: fibrous glass ceramic coating or plastic composition. (50)
  117. Coating, processes and miscellaneous products: coating of asbestos or mineral wool. (126)
  154. Laminated fabric and analogous manufactures: processes for formation of lamina in bat or loose fibrous base. (101)

359. Blackboards, etc.
  35. Education: erasable surfaces. Included are frames and special mounts, folding surfaces, chalk and eraser rails, etc. (61-65, 67)
  312. Supports, cabinet structures: structures with erasable surface, eg. blackboards. (230)

360. Miscellaneous Packing and Insulating Material
  106. Compositions, coating or plastic: pore-forming ceramic coating or plastic composition containing alkali metal silicate, pore-forming coat-

ing or plastic composition containing inorganic settable ingredient. (75, 86-88, 122)

122. Liquid heaters and vaporizers: vertical insulated outlet flue. (164)
154. Laminated fabric and analogous manufactures: closure cushion or liner applying apparatus, making heat insulating covering, making joint packing. Heat insulating coverings. (1.5, 27, 28, 33.1, 44, 45)
217. Wooden receptacles: gaskets for barrels. (109)
252. Compositions: heat or sound insulating compositions. (62)

361. Rod or Shaft Packing
288. Joint packings: rod or shaft type joint packings, jointing structure, miscellaneous. (1-19, 35)

362. Fixed Flange Type Packing
288. Joint packings: opposed fixed flange type joint packings. (20-34)

363. Ground Minerals and Earths, etc.
106. Compositions, coating or plastic: slag compositions. (117)
125. Stone working: mica splitting. (24)
241. Solid material comminution or disintegration: processes for disintegrating laminated or fibrous mineral material. (4)
252. Compositions: catalysts or solid absorbents containing silica or silicate. Exfoliated or intumesced compositions. (378, 449-460)

364. Nonclay Refractory Ceramics
106. Compositions, coating or plastic: refractory ceramic compositions including those containing elemental carbon, zirconium or magnesium compound, alkali earth, a trivalent metal compound such as chromium or silica. (55-66, 69)

365. Miscellaneous Materials and Products
18. Plastics: processes for imitating marble, processes for making electrode for electric device. (48.8, 54.7)
106. Compositions, coating or plastic: electrical insulating type ceramic porcelain or earthenware composition. (46)
108. Roofs: tile roofs. (10)
138. Pipes and tubular conduits: clay, concrete, or masonry pipes and tubular structure with metal. (66, 67)

366. Total Miscellaneous Materials and Products (includes time series 352-365)

STONE WORKING

367. Sawing
125. Stone working: sawing methods and devices including rotary, reciprocating, oscillating, endless cutting, saw teeth, etc. (12-22)

368. Miscellaneous Tools
51. Abrading: stone and glass grinding. (283)
125. Stone working: miscellaneous tools and stone working devices including dressing, planing, or turning devices; splitting, shearing, punching, slate surfacing, or millstone dressing devices; work supports. Other tools excluding surface traversing diamond tools, miners' picks. (1-11, 23-25, 27-29, 35-38, 40-42)

369. Stone Monuments, Markers, Guards
    72. Masonry and concrete structures: monuments, markers, and guards. (7.1-7.3)

WATER CLOSETS, ETC.

370. Tanks
    4. Baths, closets, sinks, and spittoons: tanks for water closets including pressure or dumping tank, plural flushers, alternate or in-series compartments, conjoined supply and outlet valves, tanks which are normally empty or controlled by weight of liquid. Structure and supports for water closet tanks. (18-41, 68)

371. Outlet Siphons and Valves
    4. Baths, closets, sinks, and spittoons: various types of outlet siphons and outlet valves for water closet tanks. (42-67)

372. Urinals
    4. Baths, closets, sinks, and spittoons: diverse water closet urinals and operating devices. (99-110)

373. Ventilation
    4. Baths, closets, sinks, and spittoons: ventilation for railway car, house plumbing, sewer. Different kinds of pumps for ventilation. Bowl structure or vent valve, seat structure, roof outlet. (209-221)

374. Disinfection
    4. Baths, closets, sinks, and spittoons: dispensing and chemical holder devices for disinfecting water closets. (222-233)

375. Miscellaneous
    4. Baths, closets, sinks, and spittoons: miscellaneous water closets and water closet parts including combined tank and bowl, siphon or bowl, siphon or valved bowls, plunger or washout bowl, etc. (9-17, 69-98)

376. Total Water Closets, etc. (includes time series 370-375)

BATHTUBS, SINKS, ETC.

377. Tubs
    4. Baths, closets, sinks, and spittoons: diverse bathtubs. Excluded are tank baths, sea baths, and shower baths. (173-186)

378. Showers
    4. Baths, closets, sinks, and spittoons: shower baths, elements of shower baths, head washers and supports. (145-159)

379. Basins and Sinks
    4. Baths, closets, sinks, and spittoons: washbasins, washstands, sinks, and elements thereof. (166-170, 187-190)

380. Bath and Basin Receptacle Fittings
    4. Baths, closets, sinks, and spittoons: receptacle fittings including hot and

cold supply, supply and outlet, outlet valve and trap or overflow, airbound trap, etc. (191-208)

381. Strainers and Stoppers
    4. Baths, closets, sinks and spittoons: strainers and stoppers including combinations, receptacles, covers, plugs, etc. (286-295)

382. Miscellaneous
    4. Baths, closets, sinks, and spittoons: miscellaneous bathing apparatus including head washers and supports, vapor or hot-air baths, sea baths, tank baths. (159-165, 171, 172)

383. Total Bathtubs, Sinks, etc. (includes time series 377-382)

MIXED

384. Spittoons
    4. Baths, closets, sinks, and spittoons: various types of spittoons, spittoon elements, spittoon controls and valves. Dental spittoons. (258-285)

385. Miscellaneous Toilet Fixtures
    4. Baths, closets, sinks, and spittoons: mixed toilet fixtures and parts including basin and closet and/or tub, seats and/or covers, buffers and dashpots, flush valve or seat and cover operators, closet bowl closures or supports, couplings, drip catchers, obstruction removers, closures, miscellaneous. (1-5, 234-257)

386. Total Water Closets, Bathtubs, Sinks, etc. (includes time series 376 and 383-385)

387. Making Portland Cement
    106. Compositions, coating or plastic: portland type cement making including color modification, subsequent treatment, making from calcium sulfate, slag, cinders, or residue. (100-103)
    263. Heating: lime gypsum, and cement heating processes. (53)

388. Total Processes and Manufacturing Apparatus (includes time series 351, 367, 368, and 387)

389. Total Products (includes time series 366, 369, and 386)

390. Total Stone and Clay (includes time series 388 and 389)

391. Tile Structures (patents already included in a variety of construction series)
    72. Masonry and concrete structures: tile faced walls, hollow block walls, tile and tile and concrete floors for arches, tile covered columns. (18-26, 41, 42, 65-68, 73)

392. Solid Block Walls
    25. Plastic block and earthenware apparatus: brickmaking plants. (2)
    72. Masonry and concrete structures: solid block walls. (37-40)

393. Metallic Monuments, Markers, Guards, and Memorial Tablets
    40. Card, picture, and sign exhibiting: memorial tablets. (124.5)
    189. Metallic building structures: metal markers, monuments, and guards. (21.1-21.3)

SPORTING AND ATHLETIC GOODS

394. Tennis
   273. Amusement devices, games: tennis games including court marking strips, tennis balls, tennis rackets, presses, cases, and handle grips. (29, 31, 61, 73-75)

395. Table Tennis
   273. Amusement devices, games: table tennis games and rackets. (30, 76)

396. Golf: Course and Bags
   150. Cloth, leather, and rubber receptacles: golf type bags. (1.5)
   273. Amusement devices, games: golf games, including condensed, minature or restricted courses, putting holes, hole markers. (32, 34, 176-182)

397. Golf: Balls
   273. Amusement devices, games: golf balls, including alarm or identification means, ball structure, centers, surface configurations, covers. (62, 213-235)

398. Golf: Clubs
   273. Amusement devices, games: various types of golf clubs and golf club elements including combined golf clubs, handles and hand grips of special type (general subclass "handles and hand grips" omitted by error), adjustable ball engaging face, shafts and shaft fastenings, etc. (77-80.9, 81.2-81.6, 162-175)

399. Golf: Tees
   273. Amusement devices, games: various golf tees of diverse materials. Included are tethers and restraints, tees with ball feeding means. (33, 201-212)

400. Golf: Practice Devices
   273. Amusement devices, games: devices for practicing golf including devices with recorder or indicator, body guides or restraints, club guides, practice clubs and mats, practice tees and projectiles, tethered projectiles. (35, 183-200)

401. Total Golf (includes time series 396-400)

402. Simulated Golf Game
   273. Amusement devices, games: simulated golf games including projector and manikin type projector. (87-87.4)

403. Baseball
   2. Apparel: baseball gloves. (19)
   273. Amusement devices, games: baseball games including practice devices, field covers, ball curvers. Bats and balls for baseball. (25-28, 60, 72)

404. Boxing, Football, Basketball, Scoreboards
   2. Apparel: boxing gloves. (18)
   116. Signals and indicators: game indicators (scoreboards). (120)
   272. Amusement and Exercising devices: excercising devices for striking, striking bags, bag supports (punching bags). (76-78)

273. Amusement devices, games: basketball equipment, football equipment, balls for basketball and football, simulated football games. (1.5, 55, 65, 94)
340. Communications, electrical: game reporting communications systems (electric scoreboard). (323)

405. Ice Skates
   51. Abrading: clamps for holding ice skates while being sharpened by abrading. (228)
   76. Metal tools and implements, making: making skate sharpeners. (83)
   280. Land vehicles: runner type skates and skate elements, including snow skates and skis. Scabbards for skates. (11.12-11.18, 11.38)

406. Roller Skates
   280. Land vehicles: various types of roller skates and roller skate elements. (11.19-11.28)
   301. Land vehicles, wheels and axles: wheels for roller skates. (5.3, 5.7)

407. Miscellaneous Skate
   280. Land vehicles: shoe attaching means including toe and/or heel clamps, ski fasteners, ankle braces. Miscellaneous skates including skates with propulsion means. Skaters' appliances and attachments, riding sticks. (11.1, 11.11, 11.3-11.37, 11.39)

408. Billiard and Pool Tables
   273. Amusement devices, games: tables for playing billiards and pool including elements, special game attachments, accessories. (3-14)

409. Miscellaneous Billiard and Pool Equipment
   273. Amusement devices, games: billiards and pool games including cue chalkers, ball spotting racks, cue rests. Billiard and pool balls, billiard cues. (2, 17-24, 59, 68-71)

410. Bowling Alleys and Equipment
   273. Amusement devices, games: bowling games and equipment including mechanical pin setters, pin spotters, ball return, foul indicators, beds and gutters, accessories, etc. (37-54)

411. Bowling Pins and Balls
   33. Geometrical instruments: gauges. (174)
   273. Amusement devices, games: bowling balls including hand grips. Bowling pins. (63, 64, 82)

412. Exercising Devices
   272. Amusement and exercising devices: devices for gymnastic exercise including trapeze and ring, horizontal and parallel bars, vaulting horses, projectors and springboards. Seesaws, slides, exercising chairs and sofas. Other exercising devices including hand and wrist devices, treadmill, walking devices such as stilts, rowing and bicycle exerciser, push and pull devices, dumbbells and clubs. (54-56.5, 58-73, 79-84)

413. Total Athletic and Sporting Goods (includes time series 394, 395, 401, and 402-412)

FISHING – SPORT AND COMMERCIAL

414. Fish Butchering
    17. Butchering: fish butchering including cutters, scaling machines, washers, etc. (2-8)

415. Fishing Rods
    43. Fishing, trapping, and vermin destroying: various kinds of fishing rods, reel sections and mounts, line guides, cases, etc. (18-26)

416. Artificial Bait
    43. Fishing, trapping, and vermin destroying: many kinds of artificial baits, lures, spinners, spoons, etc. for fishing. Included are methods of making same. (42-42.53)

417. Line-Attached Bodies excluding hooks
    43. Fishing, trapping, and vermin destroying: line-attached bodies and rigs such as casting weights, trolling vanes, sinkers, etc. (43.1-43.15, 44.87-44.97)

418. Hooks
    43. Fishing, trapping, and vermin destroying: fishing hooks including hook guards, bait holders and retainers, multiple-point hooks, hooks with leaders and/or line connection feature, etc. (43.16-44.86)

419. Miscellaneous
    29. Metal working: fish hook making (including cross-referenced patents). (9)
    43. Fishing, trapping, and vermin destroying: fishing including fishing methods, landing devices, harpoons and spears, gathering or catching device with conveyor to boat, nets of many sorts, automatic hookers or catchers, signaling devices, releasing devices, luminous bait, electric current or sonic wave energy. Snagging and shellfish rigs for fishing, spreaders for plural lines and/or hooks, lines and/or leaders, chumming devices, disgorgers and gags, holders such as bait buckets or catch baskets. Several kinds of fish traps. (4-17.6, 42.7-42.74, 44.98-57.5, 100-106)
    61. Hydraulic and earth engineering: water control of fish ways (channels constructed to enable fish to pass an obstruction in a stream). (21)
    87. Textiles, braiding, netting, and lace making: knotted mesh processes and products (fish nets), apparatus for making knotted mesh fabric. (12, 53)
    224. Package and article carriers: body and belt attached game bags. (7)

420. Total Fishing (includes time series 414-419)

SPECIAL SERIES

SHOE MAKING

421. Leather Sewing: Soles
    112. Sewing machines: sewing of leather shoe soles including fair, chain, and lock stitch. Tack pulling, loop lock, back gauges and rests, guards, etc. (28-40)

422. Leather Sewing: Other
   112. Sewing machines: leather sewing including welt slitting and beveling, welt handling, channeling, edge guides, crease and channel guides, feeding, thread handling, presser devices, work supports, etc. (41-62)

423. Leather Nailing: Heels
   1. Nailing, stapling, and clip clenching: machines for attaching or fastening heel plates or heels to shoes, loose heel fastener-inserter. (32-39.1)

424. Leather Nailing: Other
   1. Nailing, stapling, and clip clenching: wire nail forming and driving machines, strip nailing machines and strips, staple forming and setting machines, nail driving or staple setting machines, work supports. (18-31, 41)

425. Lasting Operations
   12. Boot and shoe making: all types of lasting machines for making boots and shoes. Boot and shoe making tools including sole and heel burnishing, lasting tools, fly holder. (7-14.5, 103-113)

426. Lasts
   12. Boot and shoe making: lasts for forming boots and shoes (133-141)

427. Toe and Heel Stiffener Machines
   12. Boot and shoe making: machines for heel and toe stiffening including skiving and molding. Welt and rand machines and formers, welt beaters. (60-67.2)

428. Sole and Heel Edge Trimmers
   12. Boot and shoe making: edge trimming machines for sole and/or heel including combined machines, shank trimming machines, rotary cutters and cutter heads, clamped work devices. (85-95)

429. Sole Machines: Laying and Leveling
   12. Boot and shoe making: machines for laying and/or leveling soles including combined operations, machines with fastener, heating, or welt pressing means. Work supports, pads or formers, etc. (33-38)

430. Sole Machines: Other
   12. Boot and shoe making: various kinds of sole machines including those with diverse operations, separate rib machines, blank molding channeling, channel-flap layers and turners, heel seat forming, imitation stitch devices, slitting, grooving, pliabilizing soles, etc. (17, 18-32, 39-41.3)

431. Heel Machines
   12. Boot and shoe making: heel machines including assembling machines, seat cutting, breasting, molding, beading, machines with diverse operations, etc. (42-50.5)

432. Upper Machines: Assembling, Folding, Turning, etc.
   12. Boot and shoe making: upper machines including assembling, assembled shoe shaping, folding, turning, trimming, strap covering, tape appliers. (51-59.5)

433. Upper Machines: Crimping, Stretching, Creasing
   12. Boot and shoe making: upper creasing, upper crimping and stretching including shank stretchers, former and wiper, formers and clamps. (96-102)

434. Formers
    12. Boot and shoe making: stretchers and shapers, forms, heated forms. (81, 128-129.4)

435. Burnishing
    12. Boot and shoe making: machines for burnishing sole and/or heel, sole and/or heel wax polishing machines, shoe filling machines. (70-79.6)

436. Boot Trees
    12. Boot and shoe making: longitudinal and/or lateral lock variable expander tools for interior stretching of assembled shoes. Tools for upper crimping, stretching, and sole straightening. Shoemakers' benches. Diverse work supports. (116-127)

437. Miscellaneous
    12. Boot and shoe making: assorted boot and shoe making machines and devices including combined lasting with laying and/or leveling machines, last inserting and delasting machines, lasting-fastener removing machines, sole-flap heel-breast covering machines, buttoning or unbuttoning and lacing or unlacing machines, inseam trimmers, peg cutters, smoothers and finishers. Boot and shoe making processes. (1, 1.5, 15-16.7, 68-69.5, 82-84, 142-148)

438. Total Shoe Making (includes time series 421-437)

TOBACCO PRODUCTS

439. Tobacco Products
    131. Tobacco: tobacco products including tobacco substitutes, pipe cartridges, combined products such as plug tobacco or products with ignition facilitating means. Cigars and cigarettes including those with filters or traps, wrappers or binders, shapes, tobacco compositions. (1-17)

440. Cigar and Cigarette Making: Cooperating Rolling Surfaces
    131. Tobacco: cigar and cigarette making devices using cooperating rolling surfaces. Included are apron type, belt type, roller type machines, and rollers. Also included are machines combining operations with rolling, such as tip and mouthpiece applying, tobacco treatment, wrapper cutting, adhesive supplying, filler tobacco or bunch feeding, end trimming, etc. (27-57)

441. Cigar and Cigarette Making: Other
    131. Tobacco: cigar and cigarette making devices excluding those with cooperating rollers. Included are automatic controlled devices, combined operations with printing, coating, collecting, or with packaging. Wrapping devices, molding or forming devices some combined with other operations, tip or mouthpiece applying or forming devices, tobacco recovery devices, tobacco feeding devices, etc. (20-26, 58-110)

442. Plug or Compressed Shape Making
    131. Tobacco: devices for making plug or compressed shape tobacco products including packing or bundling, turret or continuous sheet type devices, molds. (111-119)

443. Tobacco Stemming and Treatment
    131. Tobacco: tobacco treatment methods and devices including those with electrical or radiant energy, various stemming devices, treatment with fluids or fluent material, fluid treatment processes, leaf disintegrating, etc. (120-149)

444. Total Tobacco Products (includes time series 439-443)

GLASS

445. Glass Making: Annealing and Heating
    13. Electric furnaces: glass furnaces. (6)
    49. Glass: annealing, annealing furnaces. Heating apparatus including tank and reheating furnaces, pot furnaces, melting pots, floats. Heat-developed coloring and annealing processes. (45-47, 53-61, 88, 89)

446. Glass Making: Flat Glass
    49. Glass: combined machines for sheet and plate making, devices for molding by rolling. Glass flattening, processes for molding sheets and plates. (3, 4, 33, 34, 44, 87)
    51. Abrading: glass grinding. (283)

447. Glass Making: Laminated Glass
    49. Glass: wire glass molding devices and processes. (32, 86)
    154. Laminated fabric and analogous manufactures: laminated glass making including edge sealing or treating, platen presses. Various processes and products. (2.7-2.81)

448. Glass Making: Molding
    49. Glass: molding devices including presses and casting devices. Mold coolers, supports, carriers, and mold separating devices. Various bending, blowing, pressing, and other kinds of molds. Molding processes. (29, 35-43, 65-76, 85)

449. Glass Making: Light Bulbs
    49. Glass: processes and combined machines for making electric lamp or electric space discharge device. (2, 78)

450. Glass Making: Miscellaneous Processes
    23. Chemistry: laboratory apparatus elements. (292)
    41. Ornamentation: relief and intagli surface type ornamentation. (23)
    49. Glass: machines combining one or more of the following processes, charging, cutting, molding, shaping, reheating and reshaping, pressing blowing, casting. Molding curved or vertical pipes or tubes, pinheading, drawing, blowing devices. Cutting, perforating, gathering, and ladling devices. Batch mixers, tools, snaps and sockets. Processes including quartz glass, combined processes, slag, processes for uniting parts such as bifocal lenses. Blowing, drawing, and reshaping processes. Glass structure. (5-28, 30, 31, 48, 50, 52, 62-64, 77, 77.5, 78.1-84, 92, 92.5)
    214. Material or article handling: glass cylinders. (3.1)
    241. Solid material comminution or disintegration: bottle breaker apparatus. (99)

451. Total Glass Making (includes time series 445-450)

452. Glass Products: Bottles and Jars, General
    215. Bottles and jars: miscellaneous bottles and jars including bottom filled, ejecting, compartment, indicating, nesting, nursing, spaced wall type bottles. Bottle necks including breakable stoppers and stopper fasteners. Bottle and jar attachments. (1-13, 31-36, 100-101)

453. Glass Products: Nonrefillable Bottles
    215. Bottles and jars: Nonrefillable bottles including air trap, ejecting, guard or valve type bottles. (14-30)

454. Glass Products: Globes, Lamp Chimneys, Refractors
    240. Illumination: chimneys, globes, and refractors used in illumination devices. (94-100, 106, 106.1)

455. Glass Products: Glass Coating Compositions
    106. Compositions, coating or plastic: glass ceramic coating compositions including enamel, fibrous, slag, or silica containing compositions. (47-54)
    117. Coating, processes and miscellaneous products: glass base coating. (124)

456. Total Glass Products (includes time series 452-455)

457. Total Glass (includes time series 451 and 456)

458. Glass Container Related: Bottle and Jar Caps and Other Closures
    215. Bottles and jars: many types of closures including diverse caps, stopper type closures, vented, internal, or pivoted closures. Tube type closures, liquid or plastic seal, fruit depressing closures, closure retainers. Cap, expanding, clamp, and ring fasteners. (37-99)